KARMA AND REBIRTH IN CLASSICAL INDIAN TRADITIONS

Sponsored by the
JOINT COMMITTEE ON SOUTH ASIA
of the
SOCIAL SCIENCE RESEARCH COUNCIL
and the
AMERICAN COUNCIL OF LEARNED SOCIETIES

KARMA AND REBIRTH IN CLASSICAL INDIAN TRADITIONS

WENDY DONIGER O'FLAHERTY
Editor

UNIVERSITY OF CALIFORNIA PRESS
Berkeley Los Angeles London

for MIRCEA ELIADE *and* JOSEPH M. KITAGAWA

University of California Press
Berkeley and Los Angeles, California
University of California Press, Ltd.
London, England

Printed in the United States of America
1 2 3 4 5 6 7 8 9

Library of Congress Cataloging in Publication Data
Main entry under title:
Karma and rebirth in classical Indian traditions.

Bibliography: p.
Includes index.
1. Karma—Addresses, essays, lectures. 2. Reincarnation—Addresses, essays, lectures. I. O'Flaherty, Wendy Doniger.
BL2015.K3K37 294 79-64475
ISBN 0-520-03923-8

Contents

Contributors

WILHELM HALBFASS is Associate Professor of Indian Philosophy at the University of Pennsylvania. He is the author of *Descartes' Frage nach der Existenz der Welt* (1968), *Zur Theorie der Kastenordnung in der indischen Philosophie* (1975), and of numerous articles.

GEORGE L. HART, III, is Associate Professor of Tamil at the University of California, Berkeley. His book *The Poems of Ancient Tamil: Their Milieu and their Sanskrit Counterparts* was published by the University of California Press in 1975.

PADMANABH S. JAINI is Professor of Buddhist Studies at the University of California, Berkeley, and author of *The Jaina Path of Purification*, University of California Press, 1978.

GERALD JAMES LARSON is Professor of the History of Religions in the Department of Religious Studies, University of California, Santa Barbara. He is the author of *Classical Sāṃkhya: An Interpretation of Its History and Meaning* (Delhi, 1969) and editor of *Myth in Indo-European Antiquity* (Los Angeles, 1974), and is currently working on the Sāṅkhya and Yoga volumes for the *Encyclopedia of Indian Philosophies*.

J. BRUCE LONG is Director of the Blaisdell Institute in Claremont, California. Among his most recent publications are "Life Out of Death: A Structural Analysis of the Myth of the 'Churning of the Ocean of Milk,' " in *Hinduism: New Essays in the History of Religions*, edited by Bardwell L. Smith (Leiden, 1976), pp. 171–207, and *The Mahābhārata. An Annotated Bibliography* (South Asia Occasional Papers and Theses, Cornell, 1974).

JAMES MCDERMOTT is Assistant Professor of Religious Studies at Canisius College, Buffalo, New York. His previous articles on karma include "Undetermined and Indeterminate Kamma," in the *Indo-Iranian Journal;* "Is There Group Karma in Theravāda Buddhism?" in *Numen;* and "The Kathāvatthu Kamma Debates" and "Kamma in the Milindapañha," both in the *Journal of the American Oriental Society.*

GANANATH OBEYESEKERE is Professor of Anthropology at the University of California, San Diego. He is the author of *Land Tenure in Village Ceylon* (Cambridge, 1966), "Theodicy, Sin and Salvation in a Sociology of Buddhism" (in Edmund R. Leach, ed., *Dialectic in Practical Religion,* Cambridge, 1968, pp. 7–40), and many articles on religion and social structure in Sri Lanka. He has just completed a monograph, "The Goddess Pattini: Virgin, Wife and Mother: An Interpretation of a Mother Goddess Cult in Sri Lanka and South India in Its Historical and Institutional Setting."

WENDY DONIGER O'FLAHERTY is Professor of the History of Religions and Indian Studies at the University of Chicago and author of *Asceticism and Eroticism in the Mythology of Śiva* (Oxford, 1973); *Hindu Myths* (Penguin, 1975); *The Origins of Evil in Hindu Mythology* (University of California Press, 1976); and *Women, Androgynes, and Other Mythical Beasts* (University of Chicago Press, 1980).

KARL H. POTTER is Professor of Philosophy at the University of Washington. He is the author of *Presuppositions of India's Philosophies* and the General Editor of the *Encyclopedia of Indian Philosophies.*

LUDO ROCHER is Professor of Sanskrit and Chairman of the Department of South Asia Regional Studies at the University of Pennsylvania. He is the editor and translator of Sanskrit legal texts, and the author of a bibliography of classical Hindu law, of a manual of Hindi, and of over one hundred articles.

WILLIAM STABLEIN has taught in the Department of Religion at Columbia University and the University of California at Santa Cruz. He has published a number of articles on the healing traditions in Tibetan Buddhism.

MITCHELL G. WEISS is a Sanskritist specializing in Āyurveda, and is currently in training at the University of Pennsylvania School of Medicine. He is the author of a cross-cultural study of mental disorders based on early Indian texts.

Introduction

WENDY DONIGER O'FLAHERTY

These twelve essays are the first fruit (*phala*) of two conferences that took place as part of a project sponsored by the Joint Committee on South Asia of the American Council of Learned Societies–Social Science Research Council. At the first meeting, on the serene shores of Lake Wilderness near Seattle, on October 22–23, 1976, preliminary problems were discussed and plans made to develop a series of publications and to hold further meetings. At the Association for Asian Studies meeting on March 25–27, 1977, early drafts of six of the papers in this volume were presented and subjected to spirited and enthusiastic discussion. At the second karma conference, in Pasadena on January 26–29, 1978, further questions arising out of the revised papers were argued and new plans made for further conferences—and on and on, world without end, until we exhaust the patience and the pocketbook of the ACLS-SSRC.

There was a very special mood at all of these encounters, inspired in part by the great pains taken by Karl Potter, the organizer of the project (together with David Szanton of the SSRC), to make sure that everything ran smoothly, and in part by the openness and relaxed intelligence of the participating scholars. Instead of wasting time and energy on the uneasy one-upmanship that so often plagues such meetings, everyone seemed genuinely interested in learning something from colleagues, in trying to find out what we wanted to know and how we might go about finding it out. Although we left each meeting with the feeling that we had raised more questions than we could answer, and perhaps had not even asked all the right questions, I think we found out a lot; the reader will judge for himself. (A list of the participants at the two conferences appears at the end of this volume.) I was also fortunate in finding a particularly sympathetic and intelligent student, William K. Mahony, to prepare the index for this volume.

In reading over the papers for the final editing, I was struck by the degree to which they draw upon one another and by the harmony, if not uniformity, of their approaches. To some extent this is the result of two scholars arriving at the same idea about a problem because it was a reasonable idea (one hesitates to say "the right idea"). But this harmony was further enhanced by the circulation of many of the papers (including some not included in this volume) before and after each conference; one by-product of this cross-fertilization is a kind of leapfrog cross-referencing in the essays, paper A referring to an earlier draft of paper B, which, in turn, cites an earlier draft of A.

Karl Potter and McKim Marriott are the two central and unifying forces in this volume, the hubs from which all the other papers devolve like spokes: Karl an immanent presence, organizing and suggesting and asking provocative questions, while Kim was more transcendent, an éminence grise whose revolutionary perceptions of Indian social interaction cropped up again and again in our discussions. Though he wrote no essay for this volume, several of the essays refer to a concept central to his published work, a concept that will be summarized in the following pages.

In preparing this introduction, I have tried to reconstruct something of the spirit of those exciting interactions, to point out the links and conflicts that came to light as we talked, to help the reader put the papers together and derive his own insights from them as we did in Seattle and Pasadena. I have drawn heavily upon notes made during the final meetings and am indebted to my colleagues for their ideas and for allowing me to make my own (often very different) sense of them. I have arranged the papers in three categories, each in a roughly chronological sequence: Hinduism (beginning with the Vedas, through the *Mahābhārata*, Dharmaśāstras, medical texts, and early Tamil texts), Buddhism and Jainism (beginning with the postulated sources of Buddhism, through Theravāda to Tantric Buddhism and Jainism), and philosophical texts (Potter's article in response to Marriott, then Halbfass on the development of the theory, and Larson in response to Potter). For readers unfamiliar with the karma theory, it might be easiest to begin with the philosophical section, setting forth the basic ideas in their various abstract permutations; another logical starting point might be Gananath Obeyesekere's article, which is here used as the anchor piece for the section on Buddhism but which also provides a useful theoretical framework in which to view both the historical and the logical development of the karma theory.

The Definition of Karma

Much of our time at the first conference at Lake Wilderness was devoted to a lively but ultimately vain attempt to define what we meant by karma and rebirth. The unspoken conclusion was that we had a sufficiently strong idea of the parameters of the topic to go ahead and study it, in the hope that perhaps *then* we would be able to see more clearly precisely what we had studied (rather like the woman who said to Abraham Lincoln, "How do I know what I think 'til I hear what I say?"). After all the papers were written and had been discussed at Pasadena, we mustered our courage to attempt the definition again, and came up with several possible formulations. The general consensus that we were dealing with a theory of rebirth based on the moral quality of previous lives was further refined by A. K. Ramanujan (A) and Charles Keyes (B): The three essential constituents of a karma theory are A: (1) causality (ethical or non-ethical, involving one life or several lives); (2) ethicization (the belief that good and bad acts lead to certain results in one life or several lives); (3) rebirth. B: (1) explanation of present circumstances with reference to previous actions, including (possibly) actions prior to birth; (2) orientation of present actions toward future ends, including (possibly) those occurring after death; (3) moral basis on which action past and present is predicated.

Though there remain certain ambiguities and exceptions even in these careful summaries, it seemed a sufficiently solid basis on which to proceed to other problems. We had, at one point, hoped to be able to construct a typology of karma theories: "A differs from B in the following ways." This is still a desideratum and a task that might well be undertaken by making intelligent use of the data assembled in this volume, but it is a task that we found impossible to begin until we had surveyed the vast native literature, and one which even then presents major organizational and theoretical problems. Someday, perhaps, it will be possible to present family trees of karma theories, grids of karma theories, a kind of police Identikit for all theoretically possible as well as actually occurring karma theories. For the moment, however, it seemed wise to pause at this point and publish the fruits of our preliminary treasure-hunting: all you wanted to know about karma and never dared (bothered?) to ask.

Abstract Theory versus Historical Explanation

As a result of an unresolved argument as to whether karma was a theory, a model, a paradigm, a metaphor, or a metaphysical stance, the question of our own approach to the subject was scrutinized: do we seek to construct a purely theoretical model or to explain a historical process? In defense of the first view it was suggested that a historical approach is too narrow, depending on esoteric texts, while a typology would at least allow us to see the patterns that may underlie not only the extant texts but a broader Indian concept of karma; that although models as analogies do not generate further knowledge, models as ideal types enable one to define terms. In favor of the second view it was argued that models cannot be arbitrary but must be predictive, that they must attempt to explain what actually happened. Fully aware of the pitfalls inherent not only in each of the theoretical positions but, even more, in the attempt to apply either one to the karma material, we threw caution to the wind and tackled both. I should like to devote the rest of this introduction to a summary of a few of the insights in these two areas derived from the conferences and from the papers in this volume.

The Historical Origins of the Karma Theory

Gananath Obeyesekere's essay suggests that we look for the origins of the idea of karma in ancient Indian tribal religions in the Gangetic region where Buddhism and Jainism, as well as the religion of the Ājīvakas, flourished. He argues that it is reasonable to suppose that a simple theory of rebirth, not unlike those which occur in other parts of the world, underwent certain changes in order to develop into the specifically Indian theory of karma; that ethicization transformed rebirth into the Buddhist and Jaina theories of karma. (Similarly, the transactions implicit in the Vedic ritual of *śrāddha*, when applied to the equally amoral Vedic concept of entry into heaven, resulted in the Hindu theory of karma.) Obeyesekere shows the way that Buddhism approached the potential conflict between layman-oriented and *bhikku*-oriented religion (which has clear parallels in the Hindu conflict between householder and *sannyāsin*, *dharma* and *mokṣa*). In fact, the overwhelming acceptance of merit transfer in Buddhism despite its doctrinal inappropriateness may be seen as a solution to this conflict: the *bhikku*'s merit is transferred to the layman, as the layman transfers food to the *bhikku* (a process that is seen not only in the *śrāddha* transaction but in the *svadharma* basis of the caste system, whereby one group achieves merit for another group restricted to a less auspicious profession).

It is clear from Obeyesekere's presentation that the karma theory of rebirth is not a linear development from Vedic and Upaniṣadic religion, but a composite structure. At this point one might ask if it would be possible to separate these strands and to determine the chronological order in which they developed. It seems implicit in Obeyesekere's argument that the "tribal" substratum came first, and indeed many scholars have long supported a theory that all three of the great ancient religions of India originated with non-Āryan tribal teachers in the Ganges valley. But since we know virtually nothing about these hypothetical sages other than our own defining assumption that they were *not* Vedic, it might be argued that "tribal" is merely a scholarly way of saying "we do not know who they were."

The remaining candidates for historical primacy are the Vedic thinkers, the heterodox thinkers (Jaina, Buddhist, and Ājīvaka), and the Dravidians (ancestors of the Tamil speakers, or, hypothetically, inhabitants of the Indus Valley Civilization). Let us examine each of these witnesses in turn. The Vedic sacrifice was called "karma" and the word retains that meaning in the Upaniṣads (and even later), but with additional, superseding connotations. The *Bṛhadāraṇyaka Upaniṣad* (4.4.5–6) says that karma is what determines one's good or evil rebirth, karma surely designating action including but not limited to sacrifice. The *Śvetāśvatara Upaniṣad* begins with a discussion of the various causes for man's birth—time, inherent nature, necessity, chance, and so forth—*not* including the word "karma," which may be implicit in the others.

One aspect of the karma theory, at least, seems firmly rooted in the Vedic tradition, and that is the concept of transfer of merit. Karl

Potter has formulated a possibly historical contrast between theories of karma that assume a possibility of transfer of karma and those that do not. The first of these assumptions may be understood in terms of McKim Marriott's transactional model of Hindu society:

> By Indian modes of thought, what goes on *between* actors are the same connected processes of mixing and separation that go on within actors. Actors' particular natures are thought to be results as well as causes of their particular actions (*karma*). Varied codes of action or codes of conduct (*dharma*) are thought to be naturally embodied in actors and otherwise substantialized in the flow of things that pass among actors. Thus the assumption of the easy, proper separability of action from actor, of code from substance (similar to the assumption of the separability of law from nature, norm from behavior, mind from body, spirit or energy from matter), that pervades both Western philosophy and Western common sense . . . is generally absent.[1]

Marriott describes the manner in which various groups are defined in relationship to one another by the degree to which they do or do not accept from one another what Marriott calls "code-substance" or "substance-code," though all transactions take place on a spectrum in which actor and action, substance and code, are one. These transactions are classified as optimal, pessimal, maximal, and minimal. He distinguishes paradigmatic approaches involving minimal transactions, with the emphasis on the actor (such as Jainism), from syntagmatic approaches involving maximal transactions, with the emphasis on the action (Buddhism).

The second assumption, that karma may *not* be transferred, underlies the Yoga and Advaita Vedāntic philosophical models, in Potter's view. Gerald Larson, however, challenges this dichotomy and redefines the apparent conflict in terms provided by Sāṅkhya philosophy. A very different attempt to resolve the views of Marriott and Potter occurs in Ashok K. Gangadean's essay on karma.[2] I am grateful to Dr. Gangadean for allowing me to present some of his

1. McKim Marriott, "Hindu Transactions: Diversity without Dualism," in *Transaction and Meaning,* ed. Bruce Kapferer, Institute for the Study of Human Issues (Philadelphia, 1976), pp. 109–110. See also Marriott and Ronald Inden, "Caste Systems," *Encyclopedia Britannica* (1973), vol. C, pp. 983 ff.

2. Ashok K. Gangadean, "Comparative Ontology and the Interpretation of 'Karma,'" paper presented at the Society for Asian and Comparative Philosophy session on karma, Chicago, March 30, 1978, in conjunction with the meeting of the Association for Asian Studies; and at the International Society for the Comparative Study of Civilizations, University of Wisconsin, Milwaukee, April 15, 1978. Revised and published in the *Indian Philosophical Quarterly,* n.s. 6:2 (January, 1979).

conclusions—outside the context of his long and carefully reasoned argument—to illuminate this particular point for us:

> Potter and Marriott are speaking on different levels. Marriott is developing a *general* conceptual model which applies to all existent entities in a *saṃsāric* world. And in this world of qualificational monism, where all existents are "dividual," existential transformations or transactions are *possible* or *conceivable* on all levels. But it is clear that dividual entities retain their identity through such transformations. Which *specific* constituent qualities (substance-code) of an individual are *in fact* transferred or transacted is open to differing interpretations. It is perfectly plausible for Yoga and Advaita to be ontologically committed to the generic paradigm and nevertheless *deny* that karmic residues are *in fact* transferred between different persons. But this does not mean that qualificational transference (transaction of substance-code) in general must be rejected, much less the rejection of the generic paradigm as a whole. On the contrary, both Yoga and Advaita are committed to the ontological features of the *karma* paradigm: to *saṃsāra,* to transmigration, and to qualificational monism. . . .
>
> Again, if Yoga and Advaita are simply *denying* the specific case of karmic transference between persons, then the disagreement between Potter and Marriott is accommodated, indeed made possible, by the generic paradigm. For this paradigm in principle (and formally) allows for qualitative transference at *all* levels of existence. This makes it possible for a particular theory to *deny* that there is transfer of karma, while another contrary theory *affirms* this. . . . Such diversity at the level of specifics is to be expected and celebrated, rather than found problematic or to be explained away.[3]

We have, therefore, two different aspects of a consistent ontology. The first element, the concept of transfer, seems very old in India, and very persistent. James McDermott demonstrates that the idea of transferred karma continued to plague the Buddhists, with whose canonical formulations it is demonstrably inconsistent, and he supports B. C. Law's suggestion that this idea was taken over from the Brāhmaṇic *śrāddha* rites. P. S. Jaini points out that the idea of transfer is even more repugnant to the Jainas, who therefore adamantly refuse to allow it to influence their doctrine; the Jaina cosmology does not even allot any place for the world of the ancestors (*pitṛs*) to whom *śrāddha* would be offered. Wilhelm Halbfass offers evidence that the *śrāddha* was a central target of ridicule even among Hindus, an archaism, perhaps, that remained stubbornly in the way of certain later developments. Further support for the *śrāddha* as the basis of

3. Gangadean, pp. 30–31. Further citations from Marriott's article appear in Karl Potter's and Gerald Larson's articles in this volume.

the transactional karma model may be seen in some of the arguments presented in my essay in this volume. Finally, it is clear from material presented by Potter and Mitchell Weiss that food is the basic medium by which parental karma is transferred; the *piṇḍa* offered to the ancestors is a primary form of karma; might it not be *the* primary karmic transaction? If the transactional karma theory is indeed primary, and linked intimately with parental karma, it is surely significant that parental karma looms largest in non-philosophical, transaction-oriented contexts: in popular Buddhism (as reflected in certain theories described by McDermott and Stablein), in Purāṇic Hinduism, and in the medical texts cited by Weiss and Stablein.

Another reflection of the *śrāddha* ritual in karma theory appears in the persistence of rice (the basic element of the *śrāddha* offering of *piṇḍa*) in the so-called non-transactional karma model: the grain of rice as the seed of causation (the heart of the karma problem), the Upaniṣadic suggestion that a man may be born as a grain of rice, the rice crop in the agricultural metaphor for karma cited by Potter, the likening of embryonic development to the separation of rice into sediment and water, and so forth. In contemporary Tamil thought, too, sexual union is likened to the hand of a mother feeding rice into a child's mouth, the woman opening as the child naturally opens his mouth, the man feeding seed as the mother feeds rice.[4] The metaphor works in the other direction, as well: the Tamils speak of ploughing as "mixing," a reference to the mixing of male and female to make a child; the paddy is an embryo that sprouts just as the human embryo "sprouts" fingers and toes. The word *piṇḍa,* which in Tamil as well as in Sanskrit (as we shall see) designates an embryo, is also used to refer to the paddy seed. The paddy plants are likened to children, cared for by women (after the men have ploughed and sown the seed); the harvest therefore produces considerable guilt.[5]

The rice imagery raises several possible historical questions. If this is the earlier form of the theory of rebirth, why was rice chosen as the symbolic grain, rather than some other form of grain, such as wheat or barley? The prevalence of the rice imagery seems to exclude the

4. Margaret Trawick Egnor, "The Sacred Spell and Other Conceptions of Life in Tamil Culture," a dissertation submitted . . . for the degree of doctor of philosophy, Department of Anthropology, University of Chicago, March, 1978, p. 142.

5. Margaret Trawick Egnor, "The Symbolism of Paddy in Tamilnadu," paper presented at the Conference on Religion in South India at Martha's Vineyard, May 13, 1979.

Indus Valley as a source of the karma theory, for this was a wheat-growing civilization. Rice was developed on the other side of the Gangetic plain, among tribal peoples dwelling on the borderlands of South and Southeast Asia—tribes among whom an aboriginal idea of merit for the dead also occurs.[6] This would lend support to Obeyesekere's theory of the primary role of tribal people in the karma theory, and it is easy to see why the rice imagery would be so persistent and, perhaps, even why the karma theory would arise among rice-growers rather than wheat-growers: rice is planted twice, first the seed and then the seedling that is replanted; rice is also harvested over and over in a year, rather than at a single harvest season; hence it is a natural symbol for rebirth. The rice evidence supports a tribal rather than an Indus Valley origin for the karma theory, and this is further substantiated by George Hart's argument that the Tamils did not believe in reincarnation at all until the Āryans came and that the karma theory reflects Buddhist and Jaina influence when it does appear in Tamil texts.

This brings us, finally, to the heterodox sources of the karma theory. Though Jaini and McDermott have shown that the idea of merit transfer is foreign (and repugnant) to these traditions, other elements of the karma theory may well have originated here. By the third century A.D., the Jainas had by far the most copious karma literature, which may imply that they were the ones who first devoted their attention to certain aspects of that theory. Yet Jaini argues that the linear theory of *saṃsāra* which is one component of the Jaina view comes from the Ājīvakas with their finite *saṃsāra;* it is, moreover, a non-ethical theory, like that postulated for the ancient "tribals." Once again problems arise from the largely unknown nature of Ājīvaka thought, despite A. L. Basham's thorough study of it; yet perhaps there is sufficient evidence to show that at least this one strand of the karma theory may be traced back to the Ājīvakas. To postulate an "Ājīvaka origin" or "Dravidian origin" or "tribal origin" is to some extent a way of passing the buck away from the major religions which must be explained; it is a scholarly way of saying "somewhere else." Indeed, the scholars who have examined each of the major traditions seek the source of the karma theory elsewhere.

There was such constant interaction between Vedism and Bud-

6. Personal communication from Charles Keyes.

dhism in the early period that it is fruitless to attempt to sort out the earlier source of many doctrines; they lived in one another's pockets, like Picasso and Braque (who were, in later years, unable to say which of them had painted certain paintings from their earlier, shared period). To postulate *śrāddha* as the "source" of transfer of merit in Buddhism is to ignore the stark chronological fact that the *śrāddha* first appears in *Gṛhya Sūtras* roughly contemporaneous with Buddhism, and that many Vedic doctrines continued to develop under Buddhist influence. One can, of course, find earlier traces of merit transfer in Vedic texts, but it is impossible to isolate them and fix them in time. Rather than looking for one central "source" which was then embroidered by "secondary influences" like a river fed by tributary streams, it would be better to picture the intellectual fountainhead of ancient India as a watershed consisting of many streams—each one an incalculably archaic source of contributing doctrines—Vedic, Ājīvaka, Jaina, Dravidian, and tribal.

Logical Oppositions in Theories of Karma

This leads us back again to the logical or abstract approach to karma, in contrast with the historical approach. If we are forced to ignore chronology, the attempt to distinguish various ancient influences is reduced to a logical problem: how many distinct factors can we differentiate in the karma theory? Looked at in this way, the various karma theories seem to be remarkably amenable to a dialectic analysis—perhaps because all of the scholars looking at karma are, after all, Indo-Europeans, who tend naturally to lapse into dialectic whenever faced with contradictions, but perhaps because there really *are* dialectic forces at work in the material itself, as well as in the minds of the scholars dealing with the material; the ancient Indians, after all, were Indo-Europeans par excellence. To what extent these oppositions may be said to represent "indigenous conceptual schemes" and to what extent they are merely convenient fictions, ways for us to explain karma to ourselves, it is difficult to say. Is nature mirroring art, or are we imposing a false logical model on a real historical system?

Despite this caveat, it appears that none of us has been able to resist some sort of dialectic swipe at karma. A summary of the major dialectic oppositions discussed in this volume appears in the accompanying chart. McKim Marriott has distinguished paradigmatic approaches involving minimal transactions from syntagmatic approaches involving maximal transactions. Similarly, *bhakti* and the doctrines of the classical philosophical *darśanas* depart somewhat from Marriott's model—but in a consistent way, *bhakti* emphasizing willing subordination and pessimal transactions, the *darśanas* emphasizing optimal transactions; and both of them exalt *mokṣa,* which is difficult to fit into a conceptual graph of karma doctrine in any way. (Indeed, as Obeyesekere has shown, *mokṣa,* or *nirvāṇa,* is not an integral part of a karmic eschatology at all.) Similarly, McDermott sees a conflict between karma doctrine based on the existence of the soul (transactional) and Buddhist doctrine which is based on the non-existence of the soul. Another formulation of this doctrine appears when one realizes that karmic transfer in Hinduism is very materialistic, visualized as a thing—money or food—in a system of limited good: if one goes up, another must come down, on the karmic seesaw. In Buddhism, however, the transfer is spiritualized: somehow, the more you give, the more you have, as with love or cell division.

Some Basic Oppositions in Karma Theories

O'Flaherty	*śrāddha*	reincarnation of the soul
	parental karma	individual karma
	heaven	*mokṣa*
Long	*bhakti*	Vedānta
	god	man
	karmic causation	time, fate
Weiss	practical, empirical	fatalistic
	human action	fate
	material present	non-material past
Hart	rebirth in stones	reincarnation
	standpoint of living	standpoint of dead
	crossing boundaries	keeping boundaries
Obeyesekere	amoral rebirth	ethicized karma
	Vedic or tribal	Buddhist or Jaina
McDermott	eternalist	annihilationist
	existence of soul	denial of soul
	patent	latent
	will	deed
	karmic causation	repentance/expiation

Some Basic Oppositions in Karma Theories *(continued)*

Stablein	positive value of womb	negative value of womb
	flesh body	thought body
	suffering	awareness
	contamination	*śūnyatā*
	duality	non-duality
	dull light	clear light
	entering the womb	Buddhahood
Jaini	linear	evolutionary
Potter	transactional	philosophical
	Vedic	Vedāntic (Advaita, Yogic)
	pravṛtti	*nivṛtti*
	dharma	*mokṣa*
Halbfass	physical	ethical
	cosmic	soteriological
	empirical	theoretical
	karmic causation	non-karmic causation
Larson	*puruṣa*	*prakṛti*
	consciousness	awareness
	freedom (*kaivalya*)	release and bondage
	liṅga	*bhāva*
	diachronic transactions	synchronic transactions
	antecedent non-existence	consequent non-existence
Marriott*	maximal transactions	minimal transactions
	syntagmatic	paradigmatic
	Buddhist	Jaina

*From the articles cited in fn. 1 of this Introduction.

Karl Potter distinguishes basically between transactional and philosophical approaches to karma, while noting other related dyads that can be built upon this opposition, dyads that recur in other essays in this volume: *pravṛtti* and *nivṛtti* (which J. Bruce Long sees as the underlying opposition of the diverse *Mahābhārata* attitudes to karma), *dharma* and *mokṣa* (central to almost all of our essays), and the contrast between Vedic and Vedāntic goals. Wilhelm Halbfass then demonstrates the way in which other philosophical theories were able to incorporate the transactional model into the "philosophical" model through the concept of omnipresent souls (useful also to Buddhist and Jaina thinkers). In this way, the physical and ethical levels of karma, as well as the cosmological and soteriological levels, are reconciled through the concepts of *apūrva* and *adṛṣṭa*, though Halbfass still sees a conflict between karmic and "non-karmic" or "natural" ideas of causation (a valid observation which cannot really be represented on a graph of karmic oppositions at all, since it is off the chart).

This conflict may also be seen as an opposition between empirical and theoretical approaches to causation, and raises again the point first illuminated by Karl Potter regarding the relevance of empirical evidence for the validation of a theory. Halbfass states that reversals of expectations require that the theory be adjusted to fit the facts; indeed, the karma theory itself is inspired (or at least invoked) precisely as a response to reversals of expectations on numerous occasions in the *Mahābhārata*, as Bruce Long makes clear. Is the theory of karma purely formal, and therefore not subject to empirical verification? Or, to put it another way, is the theory of karma a scientific theory or a metaphysical theory? Western scientific paradigms remain constant, despite experimentation and growing counterevidence, until finally overthrown by overwhelming refutation, as Thomas Kuhn has demonstrated; this is all the more true of metaphysical theories, such as the Western attempts to prove the existence of God, which seem emotionally irrefutable. Scientific and metaphysical paradigms never die; their scope of application merely changes. Whether the karma theory is metaphysical or scientific or both (as one could well argue), it ought to be subject to certain standards of verification and falsification—though it is likely to remain a viable theory even if faced with irrefutable counterevidence. Indeed, texts such as the *Yoga Vaśiṣṭha* narrate tales involving material witnesses and physical proof of multiple lives, and Nyāya texts argue about memory of previous lives, answering a Hindu need to establish a scientific basis of rebirth.[7]

The widening gap between theory and empirical evidence is highly relevant to the way in which many post-Vedāntic or non-Vedāntic thinkers dealt with the dialectics of karma. Halbfass sees *apūrva* as an escape clause, a built-in foil against empirical evidence; a far more elaborate example of this confrontation (perhaps because of a far more pervasive commitment to empiricism) appears in the medical

7. I am indebted to Allen Thrasher for this reference, from a paper on the *Yoga Vaśiṣṭha* narratives that he presented at the December 1977 meeting of the American Academy of Religion, in San Francisco.

textbooks, as Mitchell Weiss's essay makes abundantly clear. The conflict between inherited karma and fortuitous ingestion of poison, for example, is expressed in a travesty of common sense reminiscent of Lewis Carroll ("if you drink much from a bottle marked 'poison,' it is almost certain to disagree with you sooner or later," the "sooner or later" perhaps corresponding to the karmic escape clause). Weiss demonstrates how the medical textbooks attempt to reconcile the fatalism of the indigenous concept of karma with a more practical, empirical attitude toward human enterprise. He sees an implicit conflict between the view of the *ātman* (and hence of karma) as physical/materialist or as non-physical/non-materialist, and he shows how a shift from an emphasis on past karma to an emphasis on present karma leads to a shift from abstract philosophy to practical empiricism. Here again, karma is used not to invalidate a medical theory (with which it is clearly incompatible in some very basic ways) but rather to shore it up, to account for those occasions on which it does not work. Thus, as Karl Potter points out, empirical evidence is really not relevant after all; for all its scars and patches, the theory survives healthily in the face of all the facts. As Leon Festinger suggests, a psychologically useful theory is *not* discarded when its predictions fail to actualize; it merely results in cognitive dissonance.[8] In Tibetan medical texts too, as William Stablein demonstrates, the problem of *anātman* leads to elaborations of the karma theory; here, even more than in the Hindu medical texts, Tibetan Buddhist soteriology emphasizes the ways in which karma may be altered by ritual. Stablein points out another, related conflict which is relevant to many problems tackled by other essays in this volume: the conflict between karma as the womb in the negative sense (in soteriology and philosophy, where it is contrasted with Buddhahood) and karma as the womb in the positive sense (in myth and ritual). The former may be derived from Vedāntic, non-transactional Indian thought, the latter from Vedic and transactional levels.

Moving from philosophy and medicine to the realms of Dharmaśāstra, Epic, and Purāṇa, we encounter still more varied oppositions. Ludo Rocher isolates at least five different, discrete systems of karma in one Dharmaśāstra alone; though he is unwilling to say which is chronologically first, there is a fairly clear logical development. J. Bruce Long then points out that the *Mahābhārata* intro-

8. Leon Festinger, *A Theory of Cognitive Dissonance* (Stanford, 1957).

duces *bhakti* as yet another alternative to the Vedāntic view of karma, surely a transactional alternative, and one to be placed on the side of heaven-oriented Vedic views despite the theoretical emphasis on *mokṣa* that pervades the *bhakti* texts. Perhaps *bhakti* could best be viewed as itself a mediation: Vedāntic or philosophical in its belief that karma exists and that *mokṣa* is the highest desideratum, but Vedic or transactional in its belief that karma may be removed and that heaven is the reward for the devotee.

Like *bhakti,* the forces of time and fate appear in the *Mahābhārata* as "non-karmic" elements (like the factors cited by Halbfass). As is apparent from the Purāṇic materials, too, karma and fate (*vidhi, niyati,* or *daivam*) are sometimes equated and sometimes explicitly contrasted. The conflict may be viewed in terms of free will: according to karma, the individual is responsible for what happens to him; with fate, he is not responsible. In other expressions of the theory, karma appears to mediate between responsibility and non-responsibility: since the act regarded as the cause of present circumstances was committed by me, but by me in a previous life (i.e., by a "me" that I cannot know and for whom I cannot truly repent), it is my fault and not my fault, like a crime committed by someone temporarily insane or by someone who has subsequently developed amnesia. This shift of emphasis from active to passive responsibility is also manifest in the shift from sin to evil: the karma theory may explain either why the actor acts as he does (why the thief steals, why one sins) or why certain things are done to the actor (why the thief is caught, why evil befalls the innocent); the former is emphasized in Buddhist texts with their concern for the psychological genesis of sin, and the latter occurs more often in Hindu texts, where previous sin (such as killing a Brahmin in a former life) is used as the starting point by which present evil (why the former Brahmin-killer now has leprosy) may be explained. The contrast between active and passive karma appears in the medical texts, when karma is equated with either passively received fate *(daivam)* or actively pursued human action *(puruṣakāra).* Here again, karma may appear on one side of a dialectic or may function as a mediation between two sides.

When we turn to Buddhism and Jainism, we encounter further fascinating complications. McDermott describes a compromise between an eternalist and an annihilationist approach to the problem of human existence, achieved by means of the postulation of the further dichotomies between patent and latent action, will and deed; this serves also to reconcile transmigration (a non-Buddhist theory based on the existence of the soul) with the Buddhist need to deny the existence of the soul. He further points out how repentance serves to negate karma; as Ludo Rocher made clear, and I seconded, expiation serves a similar function for Hindus. Jaini describes the manner in which several complexities of the Jaina philosophy of karma (and complex it surely is) arise from the need to deny karmic transfer as well as to account for the presence of life in several of the elements used by other systems (Hindu and Buddhist) as inanimate vehicles for the karma of others. Jaini sees the Jaina system as a reconciliation of yet another set of historical oppositions: a linear view of the life process and an evolutionary view.

Among the Tamils, one sees other syntheses taking place, the most basic being that between an ancient Tamil view that the souls of the dead inhabit stones and a superimposed Āryan view that the souls transmigrate. George Hart points out an opposition that may well be present in other Indian systems, though no one else seems to discuss it: a conflict between theories of afterlife composed from the standpoint of the living and those composed from the standpoint of the dead. His emphasis on the powerful tension in Tamils between the need to build boundaries (as reflected in traditional caste ethics) and the need to cross them (emphasized in the native system) is also strongly reminiscent of the interaction between transactional and non-transactional models that interact in Sanskrit texts (and in the theories of Marriott and Potter). Here, as in so many of the systems under discussion, lip service is paid to karma, but the emotional thrust of devotionalism negates the power of karma.

Clearly, one could not possibly reduce all of these concepts to "the" Indian theory of karma, though, equally clearly, certain patterns of thought do emerge. Is there some way to construct a hierarchy of these various karma theories? Is there an indigenous measure to determine which text is more important? And important in what way—known by more people, or used by those of higher status? When two theories conflict, which one is really *believed*? Perhaps the most basic opposition of all is that between the assumptions held by philosophers and those held by hoi polloi, between scholastic or *śāstraic* ideas that are games and experiential folk attitudes that people use in their lives; the "inner logic" of one system may well be nonsense to the other. The Indians themselves have developed highly sophisticated ways of dealing with such differences of strata, for they do not hold assumptions in the same way on different levels; they treat karma sometimes as a concept, sometimes as a theory, sometimes as a model; sometimes they accept it, and sometimes they challenge it.[9]

The present collection of essays presents a variety of ideas about rebirth, often in competition and disagreement, but always in dialogue; for what makes Indian thought so fascinating is the constant rapprochement between opposed world views, hardly a true synthesis, but a cross-fertilization that seems to have no end, one mediation giving rise to another, each result becoming a new cause, endlessly, like karma itself. This volume might serve as a model of diversity to explain how any group of South Asians will fight (as Marriott has put it)—and, indeed, to explain how any group of Indologists will fight. For we too are actors, and how can we tell the dancers from the dance?

9. See Sheryl Daniel, "The Tool-box Approach of the Tamil to the Issues of Karma, Moral Responsibility, and Human Destiny," paper presented at the SSRC-ACLS Joint Committee on South Asia Seminar at the University of Chicago, June 9, 1977.

Part I.

Hinduism and Its Roots

1

Karma and Rebirth in the Vedas and Purāṇas

WENDY DONIGER O'FLAHERTY

The Vedic Background

The theory of rebirth does not appear in the Vedas; but the theory of re-*death* appears at a very early stage indeed. It may be that ancient Indian ideas about death predate and indeed predetermine the later theory of birth. Moreover, the idea of karma in its broader sense (including the concept of merit transfer) may well have preceded the idea of rebirth, giving strong grounds for postulating Vedic origins of the karma theory. (Throughout this paper, I shall use the term "merit transfer" to indicate the process by which one living creature willingly or accidentally gives to another a non-physical quality of his own, such as a virtue, credit for a religious achievement, a talent, or a power—often in exchange for a negative quality given by the recipient.)

In his analysis of the *śrāddha* and *sapiṇḍīkaraṇa* rites, David M. Knipe has raised a number of points relevant to the question of the origin of the theory of karma. He suggests that even the earliest recorded forms of these rites may reflect yet an older level, in which "the simpler, unsophisticated Vedic desire to *prevent* the dissolution of an after-life for the deceased" may have prevailed; the need to provide ritual food for the deceased ancestors would then be based on the desire to keep them there in some sort of heaven, not to move them on (as is the overt reason), the desire to prevent them from suffering "repeated death (*punarmṛtyu*)."[1] This ambivalence in the very earliest texts may account for a number of the persistent paradoxes, contradictions, and inconsistencies in the various karma theories—paradoxical statements about whether karma can or cannot be overruled, contradictory statements about the interaction of fate and human effort, and inconsistencies between various statements regarding the actual physical mechanism by which karma is transferred from one life to the next. Knipe's observation regarding the motivation underlying the Vedic funeral rites indicates that the tension is built in from the very beginning, a simple tension between the desire to prevent rebirth and the desire to assure rebirth.

This ambivalence appears in many forms of Purāṇic Hinduism and is usually referred to as the tension between *mokṣa* and *dharma* or between Vedic and Upaniṣadic/Vedāntic world views. It is often specifically related to the question of rebirth: one kind of immortality ("above the navel"), spiritual immortality, is destroyed by the birth of a son and the consequent ties to the world of *saṃsāra;* the other kind of immortality ("below the navel"), physical immortality, is assured by the birth of a son to perform *śrāddha* rites. That these two goals are often equated is evident from the oft-quoted maxim, "You create progeny and that's your immortality, O mortal."[2] That they are actually confused is evident from the statement of one of Carstairs' informants, who quoted the maxim defining a son as one who saves his father from hell (punnāma-narakāt trayate tat putṛ) and explained it thus: "When a man dies without a son he cannot attain *nirvana* or *mukhti* [*sic*]. . . . Because when he has no son, after his death there is no one to perform the funeral rites and for lack of these rites he can't get *nirvana*."[3] According to the classical texts, the son is necessary to assure that his father *will* be able to get another body; to be sure of being *freed* from the body forever, a man should

1. David M. Knipe, "Sapiṇḍīkaraṇa: The Hindu Rite of Entry into Heaven," pp. 111–124 of *Religious Encounters with Death, Insights from the History and Anthropology of Religions,* edited by Frank Reynolds and Earle H. Waugh (Pennsylvania State University Press, 1977), p. 112. For another analysis of *piṇḍa-dāna* as a symbolic recreation of the body, as interpreted by the priests specializing in death rituals, see Meena Kaushik, "The Symbolic Representation of Death," in *Contributions to Indian Sociology,* n.s. 10 (1976), 256–292.
2. *Āpastamba Dharmasūtra* 2.9.24.1; see Wendy Doniger O'Flaherty, *Asceticism and Eroticism in the Mythology of Śiva* (Oxford, 1973), pp. 76–77.
3. G. M. Carstairs, *The Twice-Born* (Bloomington, Indiana, 1958), p. 222.

have no son. But this Hindu confuses the two, probably equating the "trap" of *saṃsāra* with the trap of the limbo to which the man without descendants is condemned; in his view, the *śrāddha* saves the dead man from rebirth—perhaps by assuring that he will be reborn at least once in order to find his way to ultimate release, instead of stagnating forever in hell. The Purāṇic attitude toward karma is basically Vedic, and non- (or even anti-) Upaniṣadic: it advocates the *śrāddha* in order to achieve rebirth. But enough Vedāntic influence filters through to allow popular texts to equate the Vedic and Vedāntic goals.

More specifically, it is interesting to note how precisely the death rituals foreshadow the model later set forth for the creation of the embryo. As Knipe describes the ritual,

> each day of the rites results in a new portion of the *preta*'s intermediate body, the head being created on the first day, then in succession the neck and shoulders, . . . the genitals, and, on the tenth day of the offerings, the *preta* receives digestive powers so that the sufferings of hunger and thirst now experienced by the "body of nourishment" duly created may be allayed by continued offerings of *piṇḍas* and water from the living.[4]

After citing various authorities for this process, Knipe remarks:

> Incidentally, among the *saṃskāras* (Vedic-Hindu rites of passage), it is remarkable to note the parallel structures of these post-cremation *śrāddhas* and the rites at birth (*jātakarman*). In each case, following the day of birth/death there are ten days of offerings of rice, sesame, etc., ten being a homology to the human gestation period of ten (lunar) months. It may well be the case, then, that the completion of the temporary body on the tenth day is an intentional *re*birth expression.[5]

Numerous peculiarities in the classical karma doctrine begin to make good sense when viewed as developments or inversions of the process of death and the view of afterlife implicit in the *śrāddha* ritual. That it can all be put together from an assumption of the primacy of death is a genuinely Brāhmaṇic, ritualistic view; all the karma texts on rebirth *begin with death* and then proceed to describe birth. This view complements what McKim Marriott and Ronald Inden have been demonstrating in recent papers, that birth is the central symbol of Hinduism;[6] the initial unity of the model for the two processes, however one prefers to grab hold of it for a logical

4. Knipe, p. 115.
5. Ibid., p. 123, fn. 18.
6. Most recently in their article on "Caste Systems" in the *Encyclopedia Britannica*, vol. C, pp. 983 ff.

beginning, makes it possible to derive either one by rearranging the parts of the other. It is a chicken-and-egg problem: *śrāddha* is the chicken, and birth is the egg.

One linguistic clue to the manner in which the Vedic *śrāddha* system leads to the post-Vedic karma/rebirth model is the development of the word "*piṇḍa.*" The *piṇḍa* is a ball of cooked rice mixed with other ingredients such as sesame seeds, milk, butter, and honey; it is offered to the dead ancestors in limbo as a transitional food mediating between death and rebirth. Now, this ball of rice is often explicitly said to be symbolic of (a ball of) seed, as in the horse-sacrifice, where it appears in conjunction with other seed symbols (ghee and gold).[7] It is surely significant that in the *piṇḍa* offering this seed is mixed with milk (the female creative fluid) and butter (which mediates between the female fluid from which it is derived and the male fluid into which it is symbolically transmuted by churning and distillation).[8] The *piṇḍa* is thus a food strongly symbolic of the commingled substances of human procreation. Moreover, this mixture is repeated in the consecrated *cāru* of rice boiled with milk and butter that is given to women to ensure conception (preferably of a male child). Indeed, this very ceremony is directly connected with the *piṇḍa* offerings:

It is stated in the Grihya Sutra that during the ancestor-propitiation rituals the *pinda* offered to the grandfather of the householder should be eaten by his (householder's) wife if she is desirous of a son.[9]

It might be inferred that the very same substance eaten (invisibly) by the ancestors is simultaneously (visibly) eaten by the wife, and that the embryo that she conceives is in fact the new body of the deceased ancestor. In some myths, as we shall see, this is the case, but generally it is not so; for what she eats is the remainder (*ucchiṣṭa*) of the offering to the ancestors, just as a woman who wishes to become pregnant may eat the remainder (the *prasāda*) of the offerings to the gods. This is explicit in some of the earliest texts dealing with impregnation by eating the offering of rice and milk:

Aditi wished to have offspring, and so she cooked a Brahmin's rice-offering to the Sādhya gods. When they gave the remains to her, she ate it and became

7. *Śatapatha Brāhmaṇa,* Chowkhamba Sanskrit Series 96 (Benares, 1964), 13.1.1.1–4.
8. "Sexual Fluids in Vedic and Post-Vedic India," chap. 2 of Wendy Doniger O'Flaherty, *Women, Androgynes, and Other Mythical Beasts* (Chicago, 1980).
9. *Gṛhya Sūtras,* cited by Veena Das, *Structure and Cognition: Aspects of Hindu Caste and Ritual* (Delhi, 1977), pp. 101–102.

pregnant, giving birth to the four Ādityas. Then she cooked a second rice-offering, and thinking that her children would be stronger if she ate before the gods, instead of merely eating the remains, she ate first, became pregnant, and gave birth to an egg that miscarried.[10]

We will encounter other instances of the "miscarriage" of a pregnancy as a result of the eating of the rice offering in the wrong way. Here we may merely note that what the woman eats is the same substance as what the gods (or ancestors) eat, but not actually the same portion of that substance. The woman's pregnancy is *like* the ancestors' rebirth; it is not a *part* of that rebirth.

A Purāṇic myth with strange Vedic resonances plays upon the unconscious correspondence between the *cāru* given to the wife and the *piṇḍa* given to the ancestors:

A childless king was given a consecrated *cāru* of rice boiled with milk and butter to give to his wife; one of his two wives ate it and the second wife had intercourse with her in the manner of a man. The older wife became pregnant and give birth to a son; but the child "born without male semen" lacked bones and was a mere ball (*piṇḍa*) of flesh.[11]

The male/female elements of procreation are ingested, but the child is abnormal, since there is no physiological involvement of the father (who is the one believed responsible for the formation of the bones, in traditional Hindu thought; Suśruta explicitly states that a child born as the result of the mating of two females will lack bones).[12] The lack of *male* (not female) agency is deplored, for unilateral creation by men is widely accepted in the mythology; indeed, as the modern Indian editor remarks on the abnormality of the child in the myth cited above, "This is the natural consequence of the mating of females."

The abnormal child is a mere *piṇḍa*, a ball of boneless flesh—the very word that is commonly used to designate the unshaped *embryo* in Hindu medical texts. More precisely, *piṇḍa* is often used to refer to the male embryo, while the female is called *peśi*, "lump," especially in Suśruta. (*Peśi* may also describe the unformed embryo in a miscarriage, like the lump that Gandhārī brings forth and that is later

10. *Taittirīya Saṃhitā* 6.5.1; *Maitrāyaṇī Saṃhitā* 1.6.2, 4.6.9. Cf. *Śatapatha Brāhmaṇa* 3.1.3–5 for another version of Aditi's miscarriage.
11. *The Svargakhaṇḍa of the Padma Purāṇa*, edited by Asoke Chatterjee Śāstri (All-India Kashiraj Trust, Varanasi, 1972), 16.11–14.
12. *Mahābhārata*, critical edition (Poona, 1933–1960), 12.293.16–17; *Agni Purāṇa* (Ānandāśrama Sanskrit Series 41, Poona, 1957) 369.31–32; 370.19–20.

divided into a hundred sons and a single female; so, too, the sun, Mārtāṇḍa, is brought forth as a lump and then shaped into anthropomorphic form.)[13] Like the more common term for embryo (*garbha*), *piṇḍa* may refer to the womb, as in a myth in which Viṣṇu and several women take the form of *yonis* (called *piṇḍas*) to support *liṅgas*.[14] And *piṇḍa*, by virtue of its shape, may also represent male genitals: *piṇḍāṇḍau*, "ball-eggs" (dual), refers to the testicles, especially of horses. But the term *piṇḍa* is most significantly applied to the body in general, to the human form—of which the embryo is the essential aspect. Thus a word whose primary meaning is seed-food for the dead ancestors (the milk element being regarded as subservient, a necessary vehicle for the true creative force passing from son to father) comes to mean the unshaped embryo, made out of ingested food transformed into seed, or, by extension, the womb that receives the embryo and the testicles that contain seed, and finally the body which develops from seed, womb, and embryo.

A final, and highly significant, variation on the theme of *piṇḍa* appears in a Sanskrit and Tibetan Tantra.[15] Here the adept uses a meditation on the process of creation of the embryo as an explicit metaphor for his own "creation" of the visualized image of the deity with which he will identify himself. This metaphorical process is an exact parallel to the process by which the new body of the ancestor in the *śrāddha* ritual is imagined to develop like an embryo. The first stage of the embryo is a dot (*bindu*) between semen and blood; it then takes the shape of urine, then of a bubble called a *piṇḍa*, then of a lump (*peśī*) which is identified with semen, then of a mass (*ghana*) identified with menstrual blood; and finally it takes the form of flesh. Karma is said to enter the body through the seed (either the semen at the beginning of the process or, less likely, the *peśī* of the intermediary stage). The text adds, however, that the aggregate of physical qualities (skin, flesh, and blood from the mother, and tendon, marrow, and semen from the father) is called *piṇḍa*, the (globular) form of the body. Thus *piṇḍa* in this text is contrasted with both semen and menstrual blood but used to designate the final product of the embryo resulting from the combination of male and female elements.

13. *Mahābhārata* 1.107 for Gandhārī; *Śatapatha Brāhmaṇa* 3.1.3.3 for Mārtāṇḍa.
14. *Skanda Purāṇa* (Bombay, 1867) 1.1.7.20–22; 1.1.8.17–19.
15. *The Samvarodaya Tantra, Selected Chapters* [text and translation by] Shinīchi Tsuda (Tokyo, The Hokuseido Press, 1974), II.14–29. I am indebted to Charles Orzech for this passage.

Another striking example of the manner in which the funeral *piṇḍa* has been adapted, and inverted, into a sexual ritual appears in a Tantric *pūjā* to the Goddess Kālī.[16] In this ceremony, the male and female participants take in their left hands balls of food (mixed with the four Tantric "m"s) called *piṇḍas,* and they eat them in an action referred to as *tarpaṇa* ("satisfaction," the term also used to refer to the offerings of *piṇḍas* to the ancestors). This inversion is introduced not in order to change re-death into re-birth but in order to reverse death altogether, to change it into immortality through the secret ritual.

It is worthy of note that the "cognitive assumption" underlying *normal* birth processes only becomes explicit in an abnormal circumstance, as in the case of the exclusion of the father (and the substitution of a second mother) from the utilization of the milk-rice *cāru.* A similar insight into normality through the distorted lens of abnormality may be gleaned from the Dharmaśāstra prohibition against fellatio: "He who performs sexual intercourse in the mouth of his wife causes his ancestors to eat his seed for a month."[17] The sexual act which diverts human seed from performing its essential dharmic function of procreation is regarded as reversing its normal direction, traveling back to feed the previous generation instead of forward to feed the coming generation; thus the *piṇḍa* is replaced by literal human seed—though, as we have seen, it is in itself precisely a metaphor for such seed *transmuted into food*—a transmutation which is symbolically valid (and which often occurs in myths, where women swallow seed to become pregnant) but which is explicitly denied as a permissible human practice in the Dharmaśāstras. The metaphor of food in the world of the dead appears throughout the *karma-vipāka* literature in descriptions of punishments for bad deeds: sinners are forced to eat disgusting food in hell.

At this point, Jainism provides a useful negative example to pinpoint the historical development from *śrāddha* to karma. As P. S. Jaini points out, the Jainas refused to indulge in *śrāddha* ceremonies because they would not accept the illogical idea that one person's merit affects another—a basic component of the karma doctrine, and

16. Frédérique Apffel Marglin, "Types of Sexual Union and Their Implicit Meanings," paper presented at Harvard University's Center for World Religions, at the conference on "Rādhā and the Divine Consort," on June 17, 1978, pp. 17–19. Based on an unpublished manuscript entitled *Syāmapūjā Bidhi,* in Sanskrit (Oriyā script), owned and translated, with commentary, by the ritual specialist in Puri who performs this worship.

17. *Vasiṣṭhadharmaśāstra* (Bombay Sanskrit Series 23, Bombay, 1883) 12.23.

one with strong Vedic roots, roots that might already have sparked off a challenge among the early Jainas. The Cārvākas, too, found the *śrāddha* hard to swallow: "If the *śrāddha* produces gratification to beings who are dead, then here, too, in the case of travellers when they start, it is needless to give provisions for the journey [because people at home could eat and satisfy the travelers' hunger]."[18] Jainism may well have developed this distinctive non-Vedic eschatology at the same time as, or even before, the Buddhists and Upaniṣadic thinkers were developing theirs—at least as early as the time of the Buddha, the sixth century B.C. These various doctrines of karma may then have evolved at the point in history when the Jainas either anticipated or split off from the rest of Indian tradition. The Buddhists adhered more closely to the Vedic model, rejecting *śrāddha* but developing the idea of merit transfer far more strongly than the Hindus ever did themselves. The Jainas cannot explain the process of birth and rebirth at all, perhaps (as Jaini suggests) because they are too fastidious to go into the gory details, but more, I think, because all other Indian explanations of rebirth are based on a ritual image of food transfer and an underlying concept of merit transfer which the Jainas reject.

Transfer of Merit in Vedic Texts

The concept of transferred merit in its broadest sense may be traced back even behind the *śrāddha* ritual. As Knipe points out,

> It is no longer the case, as it was in Ṛgvedic eschatology, that a complete new body awaits the deceased in heaven. He requires exact assistance of the living in order to emigrate from this world to that higher one, to pass from the dangerous condition of a disembodied spirit (*preta*), to the secure role of *pitṛ* among his own *pitaraḥ*. In order to negotiate that passage he must have a proper body (or series of bodies) and regular nourishment.[19]

It is at this point that the idea of transfer (originally of food, but soon after of a combination of food and merit, a code-substance, in Marriott's terminology) must have been introduced, when rebirth in heaven was no longer a process that the individual could accomplish alone. For the descendants gave their ancestors part of their own religious merit (including the merit of having performed the *śrāddha*!) along with the ball of seed-rice; this enabled the *preta* to move "up"

18. *Sarvadarśanasaṃgraha* of Mādhava (Bibliotheca Indica, Calcutta, 1858), chap. 1; translated by E. B. Cowell (London, 1904, 4th ed.), p. 10.
19. Knipe, p. 114.

out of limbo, to the mutual benefit of the *preta* (who could now get on with the task of rebirth) and the living descendant (would could no longer be haunted by the *preta*). Thus the *śrāddha* represents an exchange of food and merit flowing in both directions: food to the *preta* (in the form of *piṇḍa*) and to the unborn descendant (in the form of embryonic substance), as well as merit to the *preta* (accruing from the ritual) and to the descendant (from the same ritual). The first assistants that the dead man required were his male children; only later was it believed that his parents also played a role in his rebirth. Thus the primacy of the Vedic model explains another puzzling aspect of the karma doctrine, the de-emphasis on the role of the parents.

Various forces that act very much like karma are transferred between sexual partners in the *Bṛhadāraṇyaka Upaniṣad.* "Good deeds" are said to be taken from a man by his female partner if he has intercourse without knowing the proper *mantra,* and he is encouraged to speak a verse guaranteed to "take away" (and transfer to himself? the text does not say) the breath, sons, cattle, sacrifices, and good deeds of his wife's lover, so that the man will die "impotent and without merit."[20] Surely this is the beginning of the idea of transfer of karma through sexual contact; though the word for "good deeds" and "merit" here is *sukṛtam,* not karma, the unity of context clearly implies that the man will transfer to himself the lover's good deeds even as a woman may take his own good deeds from him. Between these two passages occurs a third in which seed is transferred from the woman to the man; again a reversal of the natural order, and again an instance in which seed functions like karma, as the code-substance that transfers power (with which the semen is explicitly equated in this text) from a man to a woman or from a woman to a man. An even earlier, though more problematic, reference to a similar transfer may be seen in the Ṛg Vedic verse in which the goddess of dawn, Uṣas, described as a seductive dancing-girl, is said to cause the mortal to age, wearing away his life-span as a cunning gambler carries off the stakes.[21] A kind of merit transfer occurs in the *Atharva Veda* ritual involving food in the form of *ucchiṣṭa,* a ritual which may be the source of the *śrāddha* offering.[22]

20. *Bṛhadāraṇyaka Upaniṣad* (in *Upaniṣads,* with the commentary of Śaṅkara, ed. Hari Raghunath Bhagavan, Poona, 1927) 6.4.3 and 6.4.12.
21. *Ṛg Veda* with the commentary of Sāyaṇa, 4 vols. (London, 1890–92), 1.92.10.
22. Personal communication from David M. Knipe.

Transfer of merit occurs in other Vedic rituals as well. J. C. Heesterman has suggested that the sacrificer's evil was transferred to his guest, or to a rival, or even to the officiating priest.[23] Instances of karma transfer occur in the Upaniṣads, too: a dying father bequeaths his karma (among other things) to his son,[24] a rare but perhaps significant instance of the transfer from parent to child rather than (as in the Vedic ritual) from child to parent. Yet another aspect of merit transfer in the Vedic context has been suggested by Frits Staal:

> In all *śrauta* rituals there are three basic elements: *dravyam,* the substance of the oblation; *devatā,* the deity to whom the oblation is offered; and *tyāga,* the formula pronounced by the Yajamāna at the time of the oblation, by which he renounces the benefits or fruits of the ritual in favor of the deity. . . . The *tyāga* formulas, uttered by the Yajamāna, are of the form: "This is for Agni, not for me" (*agnaye idam na mama;* and analogously for the other deities). Increasingly, *tyāga* is seen as the essence of sacrifice. The term was to have a great future in Hinduism. In the *Bhagavad Gītā, tyāga* means abandoning and renouncing the fruits of all activity, and is advocated as the highest goal of life.[25]

A similar ritual process may be seen in the institution of *prasāda* in later Hinduism, in which a gift is made to the god (transferring the worshipper's devotion to the god), consecrated by the priest (the mediator), and then given back to the worshipper with added merit upon it (transferring the god's grace to the worshipper). *Prasāda* in this sense is a recycling of powers; the offering is a food (the usual medium of merit transfer) given to the god to keep him "alive" in limbo, like a *preta,* to give him the power to act; and the *prasāda* is a form of power granted to the worshipper in return. This transfer is a practical, ecologically ethical exchange.

The *piṇḍa* offering is a simultaneous transfer of flesh and merit, substance-code, to appease potentially angry or harmful ancestors, like the offerings to demons or the *prasāda* offerings to malevolent gods.[26] The *piṇḍa* of the embryo is an inversion of this transfer: the

23. J. C. Heesterman, "Vrātya and Sacrifice," in *Indo-Iranian Journal* 6, no. 1 (1962): 1–37; "Veda and Dharma," in *The Concept of Duty in South Asia,* edited by Wendy Doniger O'Flaherty (South Asia Books, 1977), pp. 80–95. Cf. Wendy Doniger O'Flaherty, *The Origins of Evil in Hindu Mythology* (University of California Press, 1976), pp. 137 and 141.

24. *Kauṣītaki Upaniṣad* 2.15; cf. *Chāndogya Upaniṣad* 4.1.4.

25. Frits Staal, *Agni: The Vedic Ritual of the Fire Altar; Part I, The Agnicayana Ritual* (Berkeley, 1980).

26. O'Flaherty (1976), pp. 89–93. For Marriott's theory of code and substance, or coded substance, see the introduction to this volume.

parents give the child both his substance (as is stated by the medical texts) and his merit, or karma (as is clear from the mythological texts), in one process. The householder (*gṛhastha*) is thus precariously balanced in the middle, supporting the male line of the past (his *piṇḍa*-consuming ancestors) and of the future (the sons who, he hopes, will feed *him* after death, and whom he must nourish with his own bodily substance before their birth).

When the theory of transmigration came to be accepted in India (whatever its source), it was superimposed upon the old system without superseding it; thus the substance-code of karma mediates between two different, contradictory theories. At this point, in the classical medical and philosophical texts, the parents are said to retain their role in providing the substance, but the merit is attributed to the soul's previous existence(s); the substance is split off from the code. The Hindus and Buddhists were now forced to postulate a series of mediating elements to connect the body (given by the parents) with its karma (given from the previous life), now that these had been split apart; hence all the *bhoga*-bodies and Gandhabbas and so forth, to mediate between spirit and matter—disunited in the interim between death and birth, and about to be reunited once again during the life-cycle after birth. Hence, too, the need for wind and breath, so prominent in the descriptions of the birth process, to mediate between fire and water in the interim between death and birth. In these various ways, Vedic ritual established the basic ground rules by which the Purāṇas were to play the karma game—and furnished several jokers for the classical deck with which it was to be played.

Karma in the Purāṇas

The doctrine of karma is a straw man in the Purāṇas: it is set up in order to be knocked down. Although the Dharmaśāstra passages rejoice in long lists of hideous tortures inevitable for various sinners, with specific causal links between karmic deeds and fruits, the narrative passages and in particular the glorifications of shrines and pilgrimage seem bent upon the very opposite goal: to show in how very many ways the workings of karma may be overcome, upset, or reversed. Though the functions of karma and the mechanisms of rebirth are discussed at great length, and though characters in tight spots often blame fate or karma, while the narrator in a tight spot hastily conjures up a previous incarnation to explain an otherwise awkward twist of the plot or inconsistency of character, the major thrust of the texts is to exhort the worshipper to undertake remedial actions in order to swim like a salmon upstream against the current of karma. The contradictory and refractory nature of the Purāṇas has often been noted in this regard: "As against the most common interpretation of the doctrine of transmigration, viz. a system of reward for the good acts and retribution of evil acts of an individual, there are stories in the Purāṇas that suggest the idea of evolutionary rebirth."[27] On a deeper level, however, the basic hydraulic analogy implicit in the karma doctrine—the reification of moral qualities into a transferable substance—is an assumption basic to the workings of Purāṇic mythology, where it is clearly manifest in the interactions between persons living or dead, as well as in the transition of an individual from one life to another.

A set piece occurs in most of the early Purāṇas and is known as *karma-vipāka,* or the ripening of karma; it is usually placed in the context of the cosmological description of the hells, and it explains how people get to hell by committing sins.[28] There is nothing particularly Indian about this set piece, though some of the fiendish tortures display an Oriental ingenuity in making the punishment fit the crime; it is the old, sad tale that we know from Dante, from Sartre, from Joyce, from our own nightmares. These passages usually say nothing about the mechanism by which the sinner comes to hell or the mechanism by which he is released; but it is worth noting that even here almost every chapter on hell is followed by a chapter on expiations, which are solemnly guaranteed to throw a monkey wrench in the karmic machine, whatever it is. These passages simply use karma

27. Mrs. Bindu C. Pandit, "*The Origin and Development of the Doctrine of Transmigration in the Sanskrit Literature of the Hindus,*" Ph.D. dissertation, University of Bombay, 1957, p. 168; cited by S. G. Kantawala, *Cultural History from the Matsya Purāṇa* (Baroda, 1964), p. 229.

28. *Viṣṇu Purāṇa* with the commentary of Śrīdhara (Calcutta, 1972) 2.6; *Vāmana Purāṇa* (Varanasi, 1968) 12; *Agni Purāṇa* 370; *Mārkaṇḍeya Purāṇa* (with commentary, Bombay, 1890) 14; *Bhāgavata Purāṇa* with the commentary of Śrīdhara (Bombay, 1832) 3.30; *Nārada Purāṇa* 1.15.31; *Samba Purāṇa* (Bombay, 1942) 84; *Garuḍa Purāṇa* (Benares, 1969) 104; also *Uttara Khaṇḍa* 46–47; *Brahmāṇḍa Purāṇa* (Delhi, 1973) 4.2; *Vāyu Purāṇa* (Bombay, 1897) 101; *Brahmavaivarta Purāṇa* (Ānandāśrama Sanskrit Series 102, Poona, 1935) 2.30, -.51–52; *Skanda Purāṇa* 1.49–51; *Varāha Purāṇa* (Calcutta, 1893) 195–212; *Padma Purāṇa* (Calcutta, 1958) 1.32; 2.15–16; 5.237, -.243, -.245; *Brahma Purāṇa* (Calcutta, 1954) 216–217; *Bhaviṣyottara Purāṇa* 4, cited by R. C. Hazra, *Studies in the Upapurāṇas; Volume II: Śākta and Non-Sectarian Upapurāṇas* (Calcutta Sanskrit College Research Series 22, Calcutta, 1963), p. 374.

as a club with which to beat the listener into a suitably contrite frame of mind; they tell us nothing about karma other than the fact that one's deeds in this life pursue one after death.

The weapon thus constructed by the "ripening of karma" chapters is then reinforced by equally formulaic phrases and paragraphs stressing the inexorable nature of karma. One such chapter, called "The Glorification of Karma" (*karma-māhātmya-kathanam*),[29] explains that karma is the cause of everything that happens in the universe. Elsewhere it is said, "The seers proclaim the karma process to be the very pedestal of the Purāṇas (*purāṇa-pīṭhā*). . . . The course of karma in a breathing creature tied to a body is deep and mysterious, hard even for the gods to comprehend; so how could men understand it?"[30]

Undaunted by this rhetorical question, some of the later Purāṇas go into considerable detail on the mechanism and function of karma, emphasizing its inevitability.[31] The content of these passages has been well summarized and discussed on several occasions;[32] for the most part, the texts merely present the major theories of the classical *darśanas* at the *Reader's Digest* level characteristic of philosophical discourse in the Purāṇas.

The Process of Death

Some Purāṇas discuss the processes of death and birth in great detail; in true Indian fashion, they begin with death and then proceed to birth, a procedure which this essay will mimic.

The sadness of death and the inability to accept it as final (sentiments which must lie very near the heart of the spirit that created the karma doctrine) are clearly reflected in several discussions of dying:

> The sages asked Vyāsa, "Who is the companion of a dying man, his father or mother or son or teacher, his crowd of friends and relations? When he leaves the body that has been his house as if it were a house of wood or mud, and goes into the world beyond, who follows him?" The sage Vyāsa replied, "Alone he is born, and alone he dies; alone he crosses the dangerous thresholds, without the companionship of father, mother, brother, son or

29. *Padma Purāṇa* 2.94.
30. *Devībhāgavata Purāṇa* (with commentary, Benares, 1960) 6.10.22a, -.34, -.41a; cf. 1.1–48, 4.2.2–7.
31. Ibid., 6.10.8–20; 6.11.20–30: 4.21.5–7; 4.21.19–28.
32. Johann Jakob Meyer, *Sexual Life in Ancient India* (New York, 1930), pp. 359–369.

teacher, without his crowd of friends and relations. When he leaves the dead body, for a brief moment he weeps, and then he turns his face away and departs. When he leaves the body, *dharma* alone follows him; if he has *dharma* he goes to heaven, but if he has *adharma* he goes to hell. Earth, wind, space, water, light, mind, intelligence, and the self (*ātman*)—these are the witnesses that watch constantly over the *dharma* of creatures that breathe on earth; together with them, *dharma* follows the *jīva*. Skin, bone, flesh, semen and blood leave the body when it is lifeless; but the *jīva* that has *dharma* prospers happily in this world and the world beyond."[33]

Another version of this text rings a few minor changes: "His relatives turn away and depart, but *dharma* follows him. . . . The body is burnt by fire, but the karma he has done goes with him."[34]

The five elements mentioned by Vyāsa and coupled with three levels of cognition are more fully expounded in other texts, which seek to distinguish between this material component of the human being and the immortal *jīva:*

Earth, wind, sky, fire, and water—these are the seed of the body of all who have bodies. The body made of these five elements is an artificial and impermanent thing which turns to ashes. The *jīva* has the form of a man the size of a thumb; this subtle body is taken on in order to experience [the fruits of karma]. That subtle body does not turn to ashes even in the blazing fire in hell; it is not destroyed in water, even after a long time, nor by weapons, swords or missiles, nor by very sharp thorns or heated iron or stone, or by the embrace of a heated image [a common torture in hell], or even by a fall from a very high place. It is not burnt or broken.[35]

This subtle body, here called the *jīva,* is the carrier of the karmic deposit; it is identical with the *liṅga-śarīra* and is also called the *ātivāhika* (or *ativāhika*) body, the body "swifter than wind."[36]

The karmic chain does not end with the *ātivāhika* body, however; several texts posit yet another stage of development, and another body to experience it in. This involves the world of the *pretas,* whom we have already encountered as central figures in the Vedic antecedents of the karma theory; it is therefore not surprising that they

33. *Brahma Purāṇa* 217.1–16.
34. *Garuḍa Purāṇa, Uttara Khaṇḍa,* 2.22–25.
35. *Brahmavaivarta Purāṇa* 2.32.27–32.
36. *Viṣṇudharmottara Purāṇa* (Bombay, no date) 116.1–12; 2.113–114; *Mārkaṇḍeya Purāṇa* 10.48b–50; -.63b–72; *Agni Purāṇa* 369.1–10; 371.6–11; *Garuḍa Purāṇa, Uttara Khaṇḍa,* 21.23ʒ3; see also Knipe, fn. 19, citing P. V. Kane, *History of Dharmaśāstra,* IV (Poona, 1953), 265–266, and Dakshina Ranjan Shastri, *Origin and Development of the Rituals of Ancestor Worship in India* (Calcutta, 1963), pp. 58 ff., for further references to the Purāṇas.

remain central to the full Purāṇic efflorescence of that theory. The duty of the living to offer oblations to the *preta* ancestors is a subject of major interest to the Brahmin authors of our texts.[37] An entire thirty-five-chapter portion of the *Garuḍa Purāṇa,* known as the *Pretakalpa,* deals with nothing but the nature of these suspended souls, the very embodiment of karmic ambivalence, literally hanging between life and death. Other texts take up the thread after the dead man has been judged by Yama:

The dead man remains in that impure *ātivāhika* body, eating the *piṇḍa* offered by his relatives; then he abandons that body and assumes a *preta* body and goes to the *preta* world for a year. A man cannot be released from his *ātivāhika* body without the *piṇḍa* for the *pretas,* but when the *sapiṇḍīkaraṇa* rite has been performed a year after his death, he gives up his *preta* body and obtains an experience body [*bhoga-deha*]. By means of the experience body he experiences the good and bad accumulated according to the ties of karma; then he is cast down, and the night-wandering demons eat that (experience) body.[38] . . . These deformed and hideous demons on earth eat that experience body when it has fallen from heaven.[39]

Not content with the *preta* body mediation of the mediation, the dialectic Paurāṇikas, always eager to subdivide anything into two of anything else, have added yet another body—the experience body, which is disposed of in a way which, we shall see, is highly significant for Purāṇic mythology. But even this does not satisfy them, and they go on to split the experience body itself into two:

There are two forms of experience body, one good and the other bad; the good one has the form of a god, but the bad one is hideous to look upon. Whatever form he used to have when he was a man, the body resembles that form somewhat. Then he leaves the experience body and goes to heaven, and when there is only a little karma left, he falls from heaven. If some evil remains, then when he has experienced heaven he takes a second experience body for evil, and having experienced the evil he then experiences heaven afterwards. (In the first instance), when he falls from heaven, he is born in the house of good, pure people. But (in the second instance), if (only a little) merit remains, then he experiences the evil (first), and when that body has been eaten he takes a good form, and when only a little karma remains, the soul is released from hell and is born in an animal womb, and there he does not experience any evil.[40]

37. O'Flaherty (1976), pp. 360–361; see also Wendy Doniger O'Flaherty, *Asceticism and Eroticism in the Mythology of Śiva* (Oxford University Press, 1973), pp. 68–70.
38. *Agni Purāṇa* 369.11–14.
39. *Viṣṇudharmottara Purāṇa* 2.113; *Garuḍa Purāṇa* 217.3–7.
40. *Agni Purāṇa* 369.15–19; *Viṣṇudharmottara Purāṇa* 2.113.1–25.

Although the sequence of action is not entirely clear, it is evident that the man of mixed karma has one experience body in heaven and another one in hell; if evil predominates, apparently he goes first to hell, then to heaven, and then from hell to an animal womb; if good predominates, he goes first to heaven, then to hell, and then from heaven again to a good birth among humans. It is highly significant that the word translated throughout these selections as "experience" (n. or v.: *bhoga, bhuj*) also has the strong connotation of "eating" or "consuming." Thus the soul in limbo eats not only the *piṇḍa* offering, its literal food, but its own past karma—its spiritual food.

The Process of Birth

This brings us then to the mechanism of birth itself. In early texts, the process is merely described, not explained, and certain questions are raised: "Every dead person consumes both his good and bad deeds; then how do they bear fruit for him? How is it that the little creature (the embryo) is not digested like a piece of food in the woman's belly where so many heavy foods are digested?"[41] The close historical connection between the transfer of merit-food to dead ancestors and to unborn descendants underlies the Indian variant of an anatomical misconception universal among children: that babies grow in the stomach. (This idea is further supported by the many Hindu myths describing conception by mouth and male anal creation.)[42] But the Sanskrit text supplies a lengthy and serious answer to the naive question:

> When he has suffered through all the hells, the sinner, through the ripening of his own karma that he committed even while inside another body, enters the animal creation, among worms, insects, and birds; among wild animals, mosquitoes, and so forth; among elephants, trees [*sic*], cattle, and horses, and other evil and harmful creatures. Then he is born as a man, a contemptible one like a hunchback or a dwarf; among Caṇḍālas, Pulkasas, and so forth. And then, accompanied by his remaining sins and merits, he enters the classes in ascending order—Śūdra, Vaiśya, king, and so forth—and then he becomes a Brahmin, a god, and an Indra. But sometimes he does it in descending order, and evil-doers fall down into hell.[43]

41. *Mārkaṇḍeya Purāṇa* 10.4–6.
42. O'Flaherty (1973), pp. 273–281; (1976), pp. 334, 343–344.
43. *Mārkaṇḍeya Purāṇa* 10.88–92.

This text then goes on to describe the process of birth as determined by karma, though unfortunately without providing a link between the *jīva* in hell and the engendered embryo:

Impregnation of a woman by a man takes place when the seed is placed in her blood; as soon as it is discharged from heaven or hell, it sets out. . . . The embryo remembers its many transmigrations, and it is distressed because of this one and that one, and therefore it becomes depressed.[44]

That the actual mechanism of birth is the union of the man's seed and the woman's blood is never challenged in these texts:

All creatures, men and animals, are bound by desire, and they have intercourse and play with one another. The blood of women, in the breast, causes the sperm to grow; for the semen of men, in the seed, grows by union with women and is nourished by the blood of the woman. At the time of the falling of the seed of the man, a portion of the *jīva (jīvāṃśa)* grows in the pregnant womb, by means of blood. From the entry of the man's *jīva* into the womb, flesh accrues.[45]

Here it is apparent that the *jīva* is given by the man and nourished by the woman, a view upheld in most of the medical and legal texts. Other Purāṇas indicate a more equal division of responsibility between man and woman: "If a person violates *dharma,* he is born in a womb made of a conjunction of semen and blood, with all the remainders of his own karmas. In the union of a woman and a man he is born."[46]

But of course things cannot remain so simple; soon we have our dialectic, now in the seed: "Leaving both heaven and hell, he takes birth in the womb of a woman, taking the form of a pair of seeds situated at the navel. The embryo is a mere bubble at first, but then blood is formed."[47] Another text divides the embryo into a different pair, sediment and juice, on the analogy of cooking rice which separates into solid and liquid in this way (and yet another echo of the rice-seed-food in the *śrāddha* ritual); it then subdivides each of these into twelve: the secretions are separated into twelve forms of impur-

44. Ibid., 11.1, -.13, -.22–24.
45. *Harivaṃśa* (Poona, 1969), appendix II *(śeṣadharmaprakaraṇa),* lines 2909–2915.
46. *Liṅga Purāṇa* (Calcutta, 1890) 88.47–48.
47. *Garuḍa Purāṇa* 217.6–7.

ity and expelled from the body, and the juice circulates in the form of twelve-fold blood which nourishes the body. Then:

Semen is born from food; and from semen the birth of the divine body takes place. When the flawless semen is placed in the womb at the fertile season, it is blown by the wind and unites with the blood of the woman. At the time of the ejaculation of the semen, the *jīva* united with the cause and enveloped and joined with its own karmas enters the womb. The semen and blood in their united form become an embryo in one day.[48]

The wind in the form of *prāṇa* (sometimes subdivided into *apāna* and *udāna*) is said to be the seat of the *jīva* that leaves the body of the dying man in the form of a sigh.[49] Now it returns to blow life back into the body, to unite the elements of fire (seed) and water (blood); this triad—wind joining fire and water—appears on the macrocosmic scale as the whirlwind between the doomsday conflagration and flood.[50] The triad appears in other descriptions of the birth process, as well:

Wind, fire, and Soma always develop the body of embodied creatures. The *jīva*, impelled by karma, enters into the embryo, taking the form of wind, abandoning all the experience bodies as it comes from heaven or hell or from an animal womb. Thus the *jīva* enters the embryo because of the power of the chain of karma.[51]

Here the wind is explicitly identified with the *jīva*, the spirit (*ātman*, the breath of life) that bridges the gap between the two primal elements of matter, fire and water, as well as between matter and substance.

Often it is said that the *jīva* becomes deluded as the embryo develops inside the womb.[52] While in the womb, the embryo remembers his former lives and is thus subject to the twin tortures of chagrin for his past misdemeanors and *Angst* over the anticipated repetitions of his stupidity (in addition to the considerable physical discomfort of confinement inside the disgusting womb). The embryo then resolves to make a better job of it this time; but like all New Year's resolutions, this one is short-lived, and at birth the *jīva* is deluded by the force of *māyā* so that (unless he is a particularly talented yogi) he forgets his former lives. The belief in the consciousness of the embryo

48. *Bhaviṣya Purāṇa* (Bombay, 1959) 4.4.9–11.
49. *Viṣṇudharmottara Purāṇa* 116.1–12; *Mārkaṇḍeya Purāṇa* 10.48–72.
50. O'Flaherty (1973), pp. 21–26; (1976), pp. 35–36, 42.
51. *Viṣṇudharmottara Purāṇa* 2.112.
52. *Brahma Purāṇa* 217.23–32.

makes possible such episodes as the tale of Bṛhaspati's rape of his pregnant sister-in-law; in the midst of the act, the embryo called out, "Hey, uncle, there isn't room enough for two here; your seed always produces a child, and I was here first." When the embryo's foot actually kicks Bṛhaspati's semen out of the womb, the enraged rapist curses the child to be born blind.[53] Thus karma can be amassed even inside the womb.

Although the newborn child is thus unaware of his accumulated karma, it is there nevertheless, together with other predetermined factors: "A creature in the mortal world is born because of his own karmas; his life-span, karma, wealth, learning, and death are born with the embodied creature in the womb. Head down and feet up, the embryo gives forth a breath, and from birth the illusion of Viṣṇu deludes the creature."[54] Another text repeats this list of five destined factors and then adds, "By his own karmas a creature becomes a god, man, animal, bird, or immovable thing."[55] The categories into which one can be born may be determined by a number of influences more complex than the mere preponderance of good or bad karma: "By good deeds one becomes a god; by bad deeds a creature is born among the animals; and by mixed deeds, a mortal. The Veda *(śruti)* is the authority for the distinction between *dharma* and *adharma*."[56]

But nothing is ever so simple, and other texts prefer to subdivide the fate of the incarnate *jīva* in other ways: "The *jīva* endowed with material substance is of three sorts, all of them devoid of knowledge and full of ignorance: the evil-doer bound for hell; the merit-maker who is bound for heaven; and the *jīva* with a mixture of these qualities."[57] Yet another division—always into two opposed categories and one mediating one—raises more complicated issues:

> In the union of seed and blood, a ball of flesh *(piṇḍa)* begins to grow in the belly, like the moon in the sky. Consciousness *(caitanya)* is always inherent in semen which has the form of seed; desire, thought, and semen become one, and then a man takes a material form in the womb of a woman. A girl is born if there is a preponderance of blood; a boy if there is a preponderance of semen; if semen and blood are equal, the embryo is a eunuch.[58]

53. *Mahābhārata* 1.98.6–18 (with insertions omitted by critical edition); *Brahmāṇḍa Purāṇa* 2.3.74.36–47.
54. *Garuḍa Purāṇa, Uttara Khaṇḍa,* 22.70–72.
55. *Padma Purāṇa* 2.94.12.
56. *Bhaviṣya Purāṇa* (Bombay, 1959) 4.4.6–8.
57. *Liṅga Purāṇa* 1.86.15–19.
58. *Garuḍa Purāṇa, Uttara Khaṇḍa,* 22.18–21.

Here the male/female opposition is added to the seed/blood, *prāṇa/apāna*, fire/water, juice/sediment, heaven/hell, god/animal dualisms—all of them subsumed under the most elementary of them all, good/evil. It is worthy of note that man appears as the mediation between god and animal (as he does between gods and demons in the mythology);[59] he is, like wind and karma, the link that explains but cannot be explained.

This text, the *Garuḍa Purāṇa*, is unique in regarding consciousness as a significant element of semen; it also places more emphasis upon the consciousness of the father himself: "Whatever a man has on his mind at the time of impregnation, a creature born of such a nature *(svabhāva)* will enter the womb."[60] This is a variant of the widespread Indian belief that whatever one thinks of at the moment of death determines one's form of rebirth; thus the tale is told of a virtuous man who, being frightened by demons at the moment of his death, thought, "Demons!" and was therefore reborn as a demon.[61] The significant variant in the *Garuḍa Purāṇa* is that it is the thought of the father, not of the reborn *jīva* itself, that determines this birth (just as, in the Upaniṣads, a man is exhorted to meditate appropriately while begetting his offspring in order to get the kind he has in mind.[62])

This brings up once more the question of the role of the karma of the parents in the process of rebirth, a role that is implicitly excluded by most of the direct discussions of the karmic process in the Purāṇas (which do not mention parental karma) but is obviously central to many of the narratives in these very same texts. There are even hints of it in some of the texts describing the karmic process: "The material substance of the embryo becomes completely dried up by karma and because of the nature of others [kalā saṃśoṣaṃ āyāti karmaṇānyasvabhāvataḥ]."[63] Who could these "others" be if not the parents? The Purāṇas state that the child's birth is affected by the karma of the father and the mother;[64] similarly, the embryo's physical makeup is contributed by both parents: the mother gives hair, nails, skin, flesh,

59. O'Flaherty (1976), pp. 78–93.
60. *Garuḍa Purāṇa, Uttara Khaṇḍa,* 22.17.
61. *Padma Purāṇa* 2.1.5.1–35; cf. O'Flaherty (1976), pp. 135–136.
62. *Bṛhadāraṇyaka Upaniṣad* 6.4.1–22.
63. *Liṅga Purāṇa* 1.86.16.
64. *Agni Purāṇa* 151.18: *pitur mātuśca karmataḥ.*

and the father gives bone, sinew, and marrow.[65] In the many Purāṇic accounts of the wicked king Vena, his evil nature is often attributed to his mother's sinful karma.[66] The actual mechanism of this karmic transfer during the process of birth is not explained in the Purāṇas, but the effect of it is certainly taken for granted; and, as we shall see, the transfer of karma in the opposite direction (from child to parent) takes place often during life and after the death of the parent.

Karma and Fate

Other factors in addition to the karma of the *jīva* itself and the karma of the parents affect the child's birth, and one of these is fate. Thus it is said, "By karma impelled by fate a creature is born in the body; taking refuge in a drop of the seed of a man he enters the belly of a woman." The commentator, Śrīdhara, glosses it thus: "By the karma that he has previously committed, with fate—that is, Īśvara [God]—as the leader or impeller, he enters; the embryo becomes a bubble made of a mixture of seed and blood."[67] Yet karma and fate are often said to work together, or even to be the same.[68] They are clearly superimposed upon each other in a myth in which a sage tries to dissuade Parāśara from killing all the demons in order to avenge his father's murder by them: "The demons did not hurt your father; it was fated to happen to him in this way. Who is killed by whom? A man experiences (the fruits of) his own deeds."[69]

The interaction of forces is more clearly evident in a similar myth in which a sage tries to dissuade Dhruva from killing all the Yakṣas in order to avenge his brother's murder by them:

"The Lord ordains the increase or decrease in the lifespan of a miserable creature [*duḥstha:* Śrīdhara glosses this as *karmādhīna,* dependent on karma, though the Lord himself is independent]. Some say this is karma; others that it is one's own nature; others that it is time; others that it is fate;

65. *Agni Purāṇa* 369.31–32; 370.19–20: cf. O'Flaherty (1976), pp. 365–366.
66. *Padma Purāṇa* 2.29–33; *Bhāgavata Purāṇa* 4.13; *Vāmana Purāṇa,* S. 26; cf. O'Flaherty (1976), pp. 324–328.
67. *Bhāgavata Purāṇa* 3.31.1–2; *Harivaṃśa, śeṣadharmaprakaraṇa* (appendix II), lines 2795–2796.
68. *Matsya Purāṇa* 30.12; Kantawala, p. 206, citing vol. I, p. 127, of the 3-vol. edition with Prākṛt commentary by Janārdanācārya and Anantācārya; *Devībhāgavata Purāṇa* 6.10.29.
69. *Liṅga Purāṇa* 1.64.109–111.

and others that it is desire. The servants of Kubera, the Yakṣas, were not the slayers of your brother; the cause of a man's birth and death is fate [*daiva:* Śrīdhara glosses it as Īśvara]. He creates this universe, and keeps it, and kills it; but because he has no egoism, he is not affected by karmas or qualities [*guṇas*]."[70]

The confusion is inherent in the very word for fate, *daiva,* which etymologically should mean "that which pertains to the gods [*devas*]." Śrīdhara glosses *daiva* as a word for God, in which case the text is saying that God is independent of karma and unaffected by it, an attitude which we will see reflected in the *bhakti* texts.

It is sometimes stated or implied that the gods are free of karma: "There are no acts prescribed or forbidden for the gods, no acts which give good or bad fruits."[71] But elsewhere a clear distinction is made between the power of fate and the power of karma, and it is said that the gods are not only separate from fate but in its sway:

In his various avatars, Viṣṇu was under a curse, and he did his various actions always in the power of fate [*daiva*].[72] . . . Brahmā, Viṣṇu, Rudra, Indra, and the other gods, demons, Yakṣas and Gandharvas, all are in the power of karma; otherwise how could they have bodies and experience happiness and sorrow as an embodied creature does? Kṛṣṇa performed all his great manly deeds [*pauruṣa*] by the power of predestination [*bhāvivaśāt*].[73]

Indra is particularly susceptible to his back-logged karma; time and again, karma is invoked as an excuse for his weakness or failure: Bali was able to usurp Indra's throne because of the evil karma that Indra had amassed by destroying the embryo in Diti's womb.[74] Often the poet remarks, "The immortals have become unhappy because of their own karma; Indra has reaped the fruit of his evil action."[75] The gods may also escape punishment for their sins by blaming this same power of karma: when Indra had raped a pregnant woman and hidden in shame, Bṛhaspati (who had committed the same act, and even with the same woman) consoled Indra by saying, "Don't worry. All this universe is in the sway of karma."[76] These apparently conflicting

70. *Bhāgavata Purāṇa* 4.11.21–25.
71. *Matsya Purāṇa* 4.6.
72. *Devībhāgavata Purāṇa* 4.20.52. cf. 3.20.36–37.
73. Ibid., 6.10.17–19, -.38b.
74. *Vāmana Purāṇa* 49–50. Cf. *Devībhāgavata Purāṇa* 6.17.40 and 9.40.70–91 for other examples of Indra's karma.
75. *Śiva Purāṇa* (Benares, 1964) 2.3.14.18–24.
76. *Skanda Purāṇa* (Bombay, 1867) 2.7.23.8–40; see O'Flaherty (1976), p. 17.

attitudes to the fate and karma of the gods may be somewhat clarified when one realizes that Śrīdhara is talking about God, the absolute, who is regarded as being either above fate or identical with it, and that the others are merely lower-case gods, who are helpless against fate and karma. Other inconsistencies result from the narrator's freedom to select whatever theory best explains the present exigencies of his plot.

In the light of these two beliefs—that God controls fate, and that the gods are controlled by it—many texts argue that man himself can do nothing to battle these inexorable forces. Yet this argument is challenged as often as it is stated without challenge. When the wicked Kaṃsa learns that he is "fated" to be killed by a child of Devakī, he boasts, "This is a matter that concerns mere mortals, and so it can be accomplished by us though we are mortal. It is known that people like me can overcome fate and turn it to advantage by the right combination of spells, and herbal medicines, and constant effort."[77] Unfortunately for Kaṃsa, his fate does not turn out to be surmountable (for the child fated to kill him is Kṛṣṇa, no "mere mortal"), and when Kaṃsa's scheme backfires he changes his tune, saying that it was not he but fate that arranged events, that he could *not* overcome fate by mere human effort. Yet the means that Kaṃsa set such store by must have been accepted by many people in ancient India—among them, the very woman whose child he was determined to destroy, Devakī, who tried to dissuade her husband, Vasudeva, from handing over the fated child:

> "Men must experience the karma that was formerly made, but can that not be worn away by pilgrimages, asceticism, and gifts? For the rites of expiation have been set forth in the *Dharmaśāstras* composed by the noble (sages) in order to destroy the evils amassed in former (lives). . . . If you decide, 'What is to be, will be,' then the medical books are in vain, and all the sacred recitations, and all effort is in vain. If everything is brought about by fate, if 'What will be, will be,' then all undertakings are without purpose, even the sacrifices that are supposed to achieve heaven. If this is so, then the authority (of the Vedas) is falsely proclaimed, and if the authority is false, why isn't *dharma* cut down? But in fact, when an effort is made, success is achieved, right before your eyes. Therefore you should investigate and determine what is to be done to protect this little boy, my little son."[78]

This argument, unlike Kaṃsa's, is vindicated by the plot, for although Vasudeva answers Devakī with a description of the inevitabil-

77. *Harivaṃśa* 47.115. 78. *Devībhāgavata Purāṇa* 4.21.5–17.

ity of karma[79] and hands over the first six children that she bears, he does make an effort to save the last son, and this effort is successful: the child, Kṛṣṇa, is saved. That he is saved by supernatural intervention, and that he himself is God, somewhat qualifies the value of this episode as proof of the efficacy of "manly effort" against divine fate. Nevertheless, it is surely significant that in proclaiming her worldly, anti-karma, non-Upaniṣadic attitude to human experience, Devakī calls upon the Vedic tradition to support her, referring to "the sacrifices that are supposed to achieve heaven"; for this is precisely the goal which David Knipe has shown to underly the *śrāddha* ritual in its archaic form, the goal of the pre-Brāhmaṇic world view that is preserved in the Purāṇic model of death and rebirth.

The argument that fate can be overcome is fully developed in other texts:

All depends upon karma. There are two destinies [*vidhāne*]: one is brought about by fate (or gods [*daiva*]) and the other by men [*mānuṣa*]. Fate cannot be fathomed; and so all activity is based upon manly effort [*pauruṣa*]. One's own karma is called fate, earned from another body; therefore wise men say that manly effort is more important. An adverse fate may be overcome by effort, by those who engage in ceremonies and strive to rise. By effort men obtain the fruit that they seek; men who have no manly energy believe in fate. Fate, what a man does, and the effects of the three times (past, present, and future)—this triad bears fruit for a man.[80]

Karma is here equated with the things that a man does, in contrast with the things that are done to him (i.e., fate); it is thus by means of karma that a man overcomes fate. An earlier variant of this text cites only the two factors, fate and the activities of man;[81] the longer text then mediates between them with a third factor, the power of time (itself a triad), which enters into the karma cycle at various points and is often cited as a cause for otherwise inexplicable action.[82] Similarly, when the medical textbooks argue about the relative weights of various causal factors, the author rejects in turn the physical elements *(dhātus),* mother and father, karma, one's own nature *(svabhāva),* and arrives at the penultimate solution: The creator, Prajāpati, made happiness and sorrow for his creatures. But, objects the text, this could not be: since Prajāpati wishes for the welfare of his creatures, he would not have burdened them with miseries as if he were a bad

79. Ibid., 4.21.5–7, 19–28.
80. *Matsya Purāṇa* 221.1–12.
81. *Agni Purāṇa* 225.23–33; 226.1–4.
82. O'Flaherty (1976), pp. 22–26. Cf. Caraka 25.16–24.

person *(asādhuvat)*. The final solution to this expression of theodicy is the traditional Indian one: time *(kāla)* is the source of a person and of his diseases. Thus time combines with fate and karma; and yet a man may try to break away.

The Conquest of Karma

If one can reverse fate, one can certainly reverse karma, a far less impersonal and more accessible force; and the texts insist that this is so. In the oldest strain of Purāṇic writings on this subject, after the usual hair-raising description of the torments of hell, the Brahmin author of the text is asked by a desperately worried listener if this is, really and truly, inevitable; the Brahmin then proceeds to narrate several chapters laying out the types of gifts to Brahmins that are certain to protect the generous sinner from the slightest danger of going to hell. In some texts, the karma theory is turned inside out against itself: by acquiring merit in certain ways, one abolishes rebirth.[83]

As the doctrines of Yoga entered the Purāṇic mainstream, Yoga became another means of deliverance; after setting up the inexorable karma process, the *Mārkaṇḍeya Purāṇa* proceeds to undermine it completely with a long chapter on the way that the practice of Yoga releases people from karma.[84] Meditation and renunciation are equally effective as karmic antidotes;[85] and later, as pilgrimage begins to usurp the Brahmin's monopoly on deliverance, the Purāṇas narrate chapter after chapter of glorifications of shrines *(tīrtha-māhātmya)*—bathing at any one of which is guaranteed to wipe out all one's past bad karma. Thus when Pārvatī asks Śiva how evil that has been accumulated in a thousand former births can be worn away, Śiva replies that this evil is worn away when one enters the Avimukta shrine at Benares.[86]

Finally, when *bhakti* is in full flower, devotion to the god is a safe-conduct through the ranks of the soldiers of Yama. The Purāṇas abound in stories in which the unrepentant sinner, about to be dragged away by the minions of Yama, is saved at the last minute by the arrival of the chariot of the servants of the sectarian god, landing

83. *Matsya Purāṇa* 57.27; 59.19; 206.17–18.
84. *Mārkaṇḍeya Purāṇa* 39.
85. *Liṅga Purāṇa* 1.86.15–21.
86. *Matsya Purāṇa* 181.10, -.17–18.

like the marines at the eleventh hour.[87] By the worship of Viṣṇu, one can "dispense" with karma; karma is conquered by those whom Kṛṣṇa loves.[88] The constricting aspects of the doctrine of karma are particularly unacceptable to the positive-thinking and vigorous devotees of contemporary gurus: thus Swami Bhaktivedanta comments on the *Bhāgavata Purāṇa* passage about karma:[89] "Under the laws of *karma* a living entity wanders within the universe under the rule of eternal time, and sometimes he becomes a mosquito and sometimes Lord Brahmā. To a sane man this business is not very fruitful. . . . But in the *Brahma-Saṃhitā* we find it said, *karmāṇi nirdahati* [lit.: "He burns away karmas"]: the Lord diminishes or vanquishes the reactions of devotees."[90]

It is thus apparent that each of the major religious systems that appear in the Purāṇas has developed a sure-fire antidote to the disease of karma; yet karma is invoked on almost every page. Why? In the first place, one must not underestimate the value of karma (and fate) as a plot device; karma ex machina explains what cannot otherwise be justified. Thus inconsistencies in character, such as an inappropriately virtuous demon, or in experience, such as the sufferings of a good man, are explained by reference to karma accumulated in unknowable previous lives—and this also gives the Paurāṇika a chance to drag in another good story, often *bei den Haarn.*[91] Karma and rebirth are even used to explain textual variants and multiforms: when the sage tells one version of a story, and the listeners object that they heard it differently, he may retort that it happened to the man twice, in two different lives.[92]

The Transfer of Karma

The karma doctrine is also put to a significant use as an expression of the identity of spirit and matter or "code and substance."[93] Karma

87. O'Flaherty (1976), pp. 231–236.
88. *Devībhāgavata Purāṇa* 9.29–30; *Varāha Purāṇa* 5; *Brahmavaivarta Purāṇa* 2.29–33; 4.74.
89. *Bhāgavata Purāṇa* 3.31.1–2.
90. A. C. Bhaktivedanta, *Śrīmad Bhāgavatam* (New York, 1975), Third Canto, Part Three, page 472.
91. O'Flaherty (1976), pp. 131–138.
92. O'Flaherty (1973), p. 19.
93. McKim Marriott, "Hindu Transactions: Diversity without Dualism," pp. 109–142 of Bruce Kapferer (ed.), *Transaction and Meaning: Directions in the Anthropology of Exchange and Symbolic Behavior,* Institute for the Study of Human Issues, Philadelphia, 1976.

is a metaphor for the effects that human beings have upon one another, in this life and even across the barrier of death. This function is based on the idea of merit transfer.[94] Although the transfer takes place between any two animate creatures (so that one may be polluted by contact with a total stranger or even an animal), it is particularly likely to arise in relation to transactions involving food and sex, the two bases of Hindu social activity and caste interactions.[95] Thus good karma accrues to anyone who feeds guests, particularly Brahmins, and bad karma to one who does not. Brahmā says, "One must never mistreat a guest, for the guest then takes the good karma of the host and leaves his own bad karma behind."[96] The feeding of a Brahmin guest is, as we have seen, a highly recommended way to get rid of one's bad karma.

The concept of the transfer of good and evil occurs throughout Indian texts on various levels of religious experience. In one view, all evil on earth is regarded as a transfer of bad karma from the Creator to mankind; in particular, Indra and Śiva wipe off their moral dirt on us.[97] In the war between the gods and demons, the good qualities and virtues of one group are constantly being transferred to the other, and back again.[98] Other qualities like ascetic power and spiritual energy (*tapas* and *tejas*) are also transferred on the karma analogy: Pārvatī transfers her *tapas* to Śiva.[99]

The most significant transfers take place within the family, between husbands and wives, siblings, and parents and children. The wife's chastity is an integral part of her husband's karma; the chaste wife can release her husband from his sin.[100] Like all karma transactions, this has a negative side as well: to destroy a man, destroy his wife's chastity:

Śiva knew that he could not kill the demon Śaṅkhacūḍa as long as the demon's wife remained faithful. He commanded Viṣṇu to take the form of Śaṅkhacūḍa and seduce her, which he did; when the good woman realized what had happened, she said, "By breaking my virtue, you have killed my husband."[101]

94. O'Flaherty (1976), p. 326.
95. Marriott, pp. 110–111.
96. O'Flaherty (1973), pp. 182–184; *Śiva Purāṇa* 4.12.26–27; *Śiva Purāṇa, Jñāna Saṃhitā* (Bombay, 1884) 42.23–45.
97. O'Flaherty (1976), pp. 139–173.
98. Ibid., pp. 67–68.
99. *Brahma Purāṇa* 35.31–60.
100. *Matsya Purāṇa* 52.23–25.
101. *Śiva Purāṇa* 2.5.40–41; *Brahmavaivarta Purāṇa* 2.16, 2.17, 2.22; O'Flaherty (1973), p. 186.

The substantive nature of this interaction is clear from a similar myth in which Śiva destroys the chastity of the wife of the demon Jalandhara: when the demon and his wife died, the spiritual energy *(tejas)* of the wife emerged from her body and entered Pārvatī, and the spiritual energy of Jalandhara entered Śiva.[102] Alf Hiltebeitel has pointed out many similar instances in the *Mahābhārata,* in myths in which a conqueror takes to himself some virtue or power of the man he conquers, as well as in the entire corpus of myths in which Śrī, the goddess of prosperity—often regarded as a "wife" of the victorious king and the incarnation of his virtues and powers—is transferred in the course of battle.[103]

The role of a wife in the transfer of karma may involve a number of complex transactions:

A demon carried off a Brahmin's wife and abandoned her in the forest. The Brahmin approached the king and said that someone had carried off his wife while he slept. The king asked him to describe her, and the Brahmin replied, "Well, she has piercing eyes and is very tall, with short arms and a thin face. She has a sagging belly and short buttocks and small breasts; she is really very ugly—I'm not blaming her. And she is very harsh in speech, and not gentle in nature; this is how I would describe my wife. She is awful to look at, with a big mouth; and she has passed her prime. This is my wife's appearance, honestly." The king replied, "Enough of her; I will give you another wife." But the Brahmin insisted that he needed to protect his own wife, "For if she is not protected, confusion of castes will arise, and that will cause my ancestors to fall from heaven." So the king set out to find her.

The king came upon her in the forest and asked her how she got there; she told him her story, concluding, "I don't know why he did it, as he neither enjoys me carnally nor eats me." The king found the demon and questioned him about his behavior: "Why did you bring the Brahmin's wife here, night-wanderer? For she is certainly no beauty; you could find many better wives, if you brought her here to be your wife; and if you took her to eat her, then why haven't you eaten her?"

The demon replied, "We do not eat men; those are other demons. But we eat the fruit of a good deed. (And I can tell you all about the fruit of a bad deed, for I have been born as a cruel demon.) Being dishonored, we consume the very nature of men and women; we do not eat meat or devour living creatures. When we eat the patience of men, they become furious; and when we have eaten their evil nature, they become virtuous. We have female demons who are as fascinating and beautiful as the nymphs in heaven; so why would we seek sexual pleasure among human women?" The king said,

102. *Śiva Purāṇa* 2.5.23–24; *Padma Purāṇa* 6.106.13–14; O'Flaherty (1973), p. 182.
103. Alf Hiltebeitel, *The Ritual of Battle: Krishna in the Mahābhārata* (Cornell University Press, 1976), pp. 141–191 (esp. p. 153), 323, and 352. Cf. also O'Flaherty (1976), p. 68.

"If she is to serve neither your bed nor your table, then why did you enter the Brahmin's house and take her away?" The demon said, "He is a very good Brahmin and knows the spells. He used to expel me from sacrifice after sacrifice by reciting a spell that destroys demons. Because of this, we became hungry, and so we inflicted this defect upon him, for without a wife a man is not qualified to perform the ritual of sacrifice."

The king said, "Since you happened to mention that you eat the very nature of a person, let me ask you to do something. Eat the evil disposition of this Brahmin's wife right away, and when you have eaten her evil disposition, she may become well behaved. Then take her to the house of her husband. By doing this you will have done everything for me who have come to your house." Then the demon entered inside her by his own *māyā* and ate her evil disposition by his own power, at the king's command. When the Brahmin's wife was entirely free of that fiercely evil disposition, she said to the king, "Because of the ripening of the fruits of my own karma, I was separated from my noble husband. This night-wanderer was (merely the proximate) cause. The fault is not his, nor is it the fault of my noble husband; the fault was mine alone, and no one else's. The demon has done a good deed, for in another birth I caused someone to become separated from another, and this (separation from my husband) has now fallen upon me. What fault is there in the noble one?" And the demon took the Brahmin's wife, whose evil disposition had been purified, and led her to the house of her husband, and then he went away.[104]

The first karmic transaction takes place when the Brahmin fears that a transfer of negative karma will cause his ancestors to fall from heaven—a significant beginning, for without legitimate children there can be no *śrāddha* to protect the ancestors. The second is implicit in the demon's wish to grant the desires of his guest (lest the slighted guest carry away the demon's good karma). The wife is ugly and evil because of the ripening of her own karma, and the demon has reached his evil circumstances as the fruits of his past misdeeds.

But the most striking transfer takes place when the demon eats the wife's evil nature (as demons eat the discarded experience-bodies of the sinners who have used them up).[105] The word used for the "eating" of her nature is *bhuj,* the same word that we encountered as it was used to designate the "experiencing" of karma, which is eaten or consumed in hell. The demon (a strict vegetarian) refuses to "enjoy" the woman in either of the normal demonic ways (as a sexual object or a square meal—the two most heavily charged karmic transfer situations, and both described by the verb *bhuj,* which often refers to

104. *Mārkaṇḍeya Purāṇa* 66.24–39; 67.1–39.
105. *Viṣṇudharmottara Purāṇa* 2.113; *Garuḍa Purāṇa* 217.3–7.

sexual enjoyment). But he eats her karma directly; and this amounts to a transfer of evil karma from the woman to the demon—who, being evil already, can easily absorb it. As Gananath Obeyesekere remarks of this process, "Only the sinner can come to harm [from demons]. This amounts to an ethicization of the actions of demons."[106] This ethicization may even be read back into the previous lives of the demons; as Mircea Eliade has pointed out, "The goddess Hariti is said to have obtained the right to eat children as a consequence of merits gained in a previous existence."[107] The good karma of demons, accumulated in a previous life, here allows them to eat good food; the evil karma of the demon that ate the evil disposition of the Brahmin's wife allows him to eat evil food (though, apparently, in this case he does not eat the woman's ugliness, as her long-suffering husband might have wished).

Another important karmic transfer takes place between brothers. In the *Mahābhārata,* Yudhiṣṭhira refuses to go to heaven and wishes to remain in hell in order to give comfort *(sukha)* to his brothers suffering there, by means of the cool breeze which his body gives off because of his virtue; at length, Dharma tells him that the scene in hell was a mere illusion produced in order to test him and to serve as a moral instruction; his brothers are in heaven, where he too goes at last.[108] The merit transfer in this episode is minimal: Yudhiṣṭhira's virtue proves useful to his brothers, and he is willing to lose something in return—heaven. But the Purāṇic expansion of this scene is far more explicit and complex:

During a brief visit to hell, to expiate one brief lapse, the virtuous king Vipaścit noticed that the air from his body was relieving the suffering of the sinners there. He therefore wished to remain there to help them, saying, "Not in heaven nor in the world of Brahmā do men find such joy as arises from giving release [*nirvāṇa*] to suffering creatures." When Indra insisted on leading him to heaven, the king said, "Men are tortured by the thousands in hell. They cry out to me, 'Save me!' and so I will not go away." Indra said, "These men of very evil karma have reached hell because of their karma; and you must go to heaven because of your own good karma. Go and enjoy your deserts in the world of the immortals, and let them wear away the conse-

106. Gananath Obeyesekere, "Theodicy, Sin and Salvation in a Sociology of Buddhism," in Edmund R. Leach (ed.), *Dialectic in Practical Religion* (Cambridge Papers in Social Anthropology, no. 5, Cambridge, 1968), pp. 7–40. Cf. O'Flaherty (1976), p. 78.
107. Mircea Eliade, "Notes de Démonologie," in *Zalmoxis* I (1938): 197–203; cf. O'Flaherty (1976), p. 78.
108. *Mahābhārata* 18.2.

quences of their own karma by means of this hell." The king said, "How can other men find delight in associating with me if these men do not become elevated in my presence? Therefore, let these sinners who are undergoing punishment be freed from hell by means of whatever good deeds I have done." Indra said, "By this you have achieved a higher place, and now you may see how these people, despite their evil karma, are released from hell." Then a rain of flowers fell upon that king, and Indra placed him in a celestial chariot and led him to heaven. And those who were there in hell were released from their punishments and entered other wombs, as determined by the fruits of their own karma.[109]

There is considerable Buddhist influence here. The virtuous king saves men who are his "brothers" only in the sense that all men are brothers; he gives them *nirvāṇa,* a Buddhist word for release (and set in a very Buddhist sentiment about the relief of suffering) in place of the mere "comfort" that Yudhiṣṭhira gave to his brothers; and he saves them all from hell not by the awkward plot device of the Epic—which simply takes it all back by declaring it an illusion—but by a very real transfer of merit in a very real hell. Even so, karma gets the last word: the sinners don't go to heaven with Vipáscit (as they do with Yudhiṣṭhira in the Epic), but are merely given release from one phase of their redemptive reincarnation, as parents are "released" from hell, to be reborn after they have been given the *piṇḍa* offering.

Parents and Children

As karma's primary function and innovation is in the realm of rebirth, it is not surprising that the most significant transfers take place between parents and children. The strange silence of the classical texts regarding the role of parents in rebirth is, as we have seen, partially explained by the post-Vedic rejection of the model which took the *śrāddha* ritual as the basis of the birth theory, a ritual in which the child "makes" the parents, and partially explained by the inversion of the birth process implicit in that very model. In the classical system, the transmigration theory bypasses the parents altogether. But Purāṇic texts tend to combine these two views. Indeed, the various types of karma, according to some systems, correspond precisely to the distinction between the parents' contribution and what we would regard as "our own" contribution to the karma bank.

To be sure, some of the philosophical texts (some Vaiśeṣika and

109. *Mārkaṇḍeya Purāṇa* 15.57–80.

Caraka texts, and perhaps even some of the Advaita) do tell us something about parents; but the parents seem to play primarily a physical role, giving the stuff (blood and semen) into which the unborn child's karma is to be infused. The Buddhists, however, suggest a primal scene which would have gladdened the heart of Sigmund Freud: the unborn child, witnessing his parents in intercourse, interacts in classically Oedipal fashion with them and is born.[110] In this model, social interaction with one's future parents precedes the birth process. The Tibetan texts, moreover, make it clear that some parental karma is transferred to the child. If we look to mythology for some of the underlying, unexpressed beliefs and cognitive assumptions of all South Asians, we find numerous examples in which the karma of the parents is transferred to the child—even as the karma of the child is transferred to the parent in the *śrāddha* ceremony.[111] This suggests that the birth process in some levels of Indian classical thought is even more complicated than our Sanskrit and Pali texts have led us to believe—unless we simplify the model by distinguishing discrete historical, chronological periods, viewing parental karma transfer as prior to, and an alternative to, the concept of reincarnated karma. The myths preserve the pre-rebirth, Vedic model of birth, and it is to the myths that we must now turn.

Numerous examples of karmic interaction between parent and child occur in the *Mahābhārata;* I should like to poach once again on Bruce Long's territory (which is so temptingly adjacent to my own) to cite a myth which strikes me as particularly archaic, even Vedic, in its attitude to karma, and which thus provides a useful foil to the full Purāṇic myths:

King Somaka had only one son, Jantu; he worried that this child might die. His priest advised him to sacrifice the child and let his one hundred wives inhale the smoke, so that they would conceive sons. Somaka did so, despite the protest of the wives, and after ten months they all had sons; Jantu was reborn as the eldest, by his original mother. When Somaka and the priest died, Somaka saw the priest boiling in a terrible hell, and asked him why. "I caused you to sacrifice, O king," said the priest, "and this is the fruit of that karma." The king said, "I will enter this (hell); let my priest be released. For he is being cooked by the fire of hell for my sake." But Dharma objected, "No one ever experiences the fruit of another's action. You see here your own fruits." When the king continued to protest that his karma was the same

110. See James McDermott's paper in this volume, citing Vasubandha's *Abhidharmakośa* 3.15, and, more elaborate, William Stablein, citing the Tibetan *Book of the Dead* and the *Caṇḍamahāroṣaṇa Tantra*.
111. O'Flaherty (1976), pp. 365 ff.

as the priest's, Dharma conceded, "If you wish this, experience the same fruit with him, for an equal length of time, and then afterwards you will both reach heaven." And so it happened.[112]

Many conflicting attitudes to karma appear in this tale. The "virtue" of the single son is somehow transferred (by personal sacrifice, the most primitive form of transfer, and by the ingestion of substance—significantly, *funeral smoke*) to a hundred others—but he is reborn among them, so that he is not truly sacrificed at all; in this first episode, the text seems to emphasize that no actual exchange need take place at all, that nothing need be lost by the one who "gives" merit, that karma is inexhaustible. This view is reinforced by Dharma's objection to the king's wish to sacrifice his good karma to get the priest out of hell—just as Dharma objects, in the *Mahābhārata,* to Yudhiṣṭhira's wish to get his brothers out of hell. The solution in this case, however, is the inverse of the solution to the sacrifice of the son: where, in that episode, no one lost anything by the transfer, so in this second episode *both* of them lose—both of them suffer the tortures of hell. In this way, the doctrine of karma is satisfied without any merit transfer—and yet ultimately everyone escapes to heaven, as they do in the Yudhiṣṭhira episode. That the suggested transfers are to take place in the form of a human sacrifice and in the transfer of merit between a king and his priest[113] are indications of the antiquity of this myth, possibly composed at a period when the concept of merit transfer was still being developed.

Elsewhere in the *Mahābhārata,* and in the Purāṇas, we find myths illustrative of the karma flow in both directions: from living children to dead ancestors (as in the tale of a sage's ancestors hanging by their fingertips in a great pit);[114] and, less often, from parents to children. A series of karmic transfers from children to parents takes place between King Yayāti and his sons and grandsons.[115] In the myth of Vena, karma flows in both directions: the evil of Vena himself is the result of the direct transfer of negative karma from his evil mother—who is evil because of the karma inherited from *her* father, death;[116] but when Vena dies, and is reborn as a leper, his good son Pṛthu saves him by going to a shrine, performing a ritual, and trans-

112. *Mahābhārata* 3.127.1–20; 128.1–19, esp. 128.13–16.

113. See Heesterman, as cited in footnote 23, above.

114. *Mahābhārata* 3.94–97; cf. O'Flaherty (1973), pp. 53–54 and 68–70.

115. O'Flaherty (1976), pp. 237–243; *Mahābhārata* 1.76–91; 5.118–120.

116. *Padma Purāṇa* 2.29–33; *Bhāgavata Purāṇa* 4.13; *Vāmana Purāṇa,* S. 26; cf. O'Flaherty (1976), pp. 324–328.

ferring that merit to his father, for his father is so impure that he would transfer his own bad karma to the shrine and thus defile it; only the devotional sacrifice of the son can save him.[117] In other texts, Vena is saved simply by the birth of his good son,[118] or, in a more primitive process, by the birth of an evil son, who draws the evil out of Vena in a direct transfer,[119] as the evil demon drew the evil nature out of the Brahmin's wife. Here, then, is the turning point in the chain of karma: evil karma is transferred from parent to child in a direct, homeopathic line, explaining the existence of evil in the present; but good karma is transferred backwards into the past and into the future, through the heteropathic devotion of the good child to the evil parent—the ritual model of the *śrāddha* offering, translated into *bhakti* mythology.

The Flow of Karma

The motif of personal devotion *(bhakti)* flows against the current of impersonal karma and the "ocean of rebirth," like a stream of fresh water flowing back out into the ocean. The fluid analogy is apt, and occurs often in the Sanskrit texts; the karma model is a very fancy bit of plumbing, a complex hydraulic system. In any social interaction, karma is transferred as by the action of a siphon when two vessels of unequal height are suddenly connected by a tube: things flow back and forth between them until they are equalized. In India, what flows is pollution (which flows up) and merit (which flows down). Things flow in and out of the body all the time in Vedic/Purāṇic Hinduism; hence the great stress placed on bodily secretions as literally creative substances: semen, blood, phlegm, tears, sweat, and so forth.[120] This also explains the Indian's great emphasis on food.

Because of this fluidity in social interaction, it is difficult, if not impossible, to pinpoint an individual's karma as distinct from that of everyone else. We have seen how the karma of parents and children merges, and that of husbands and wives; these are indeed maximal

117. *Skanda Purāṇa* 7.1.336.95–253; *Garuḍa Purāṇa* 6.4–8; *Viṣṇudharmottara Purāṇa* 1.106.5–66; O'Flaherty (1976), pp. 325–326.
118. *Brahmāṇḍa Purāṇa* 2.36.127–227; *Skanda Purāṇa* 7.1.337.72–175; *Harivaṃśa* 5.1–21; 6.1–4; *Brahma Purāṇa* 4.28–122; *Vāmana Purāṇa*, S. 26.31; *Viṣṇu Purāṇa* 1.13.7–41; O'Flaherty (1976), pp. 324–325.
119. *Bhāgavata Purāṇa* 4.13–15; *Padma Purāṇa* 2.27.19–46; O'Flaherty (1976), pp. 324–328.
120. O'Flaherty (1973), pp. 271–273.

exchange situations. But in the Indian view, every act is the result of the karma of many people; all share the responsibility for evil, though they all see it from different perspectives. Thus, as Alf Hiltebeitel has pointed out, the responsibility for the death of Droṇa is diffused, depending on the philosophy of the different heroes who examine its causes.[121] In this way, the concept of joint karma functions as a cosmological as well as a sociological principle, in which no acts of any particular figure can have any ultimacy as evil. According to this aspect of the theory of karma, the retributive function of rebirth is of secondary significance; indeed, as a Tamil Brahmin woman said to me, karma means that we are punished not *for* our actions, but *by* our actions.

Karmic forces flow constantly between people (and between gods, and animals). Two great exceptions to this rule are the realms of Hindu asceticism (where all life processes are reversed, all body substances held in[122]) and Jainism, where an extreme effort is made to reduce the flow and an almost obsessive concern with boundaries leads to a minimizing of transactions.[123] In Jainism, the soul moves up, while karma pushes down; without the basic *śrāddha* model, there can be no true exchange. In Hinduism, Vedic or Purāṇic, spirit and matter (code and substance) constantly flow in and out of each other; even in the creation myths, Prajāpati alternates between the creation of physical entities (men, beasts, trees) and abstractions—the year, and hunger, and space itself.[124] Here is true relativity, matter and energy in constant fluid transformation.

121. Personal communication from Alf Hiltebeitel, November 19, 1977. See also p. 127, n.33, and p. 253 of his *The Ritual of Battle: Krishna in The Mahābhārata* (Cornell University Press, 1976).
122. O'Flaherty (1973), pp. 261–270; (1976), p. 341.
123. Personal communication from McKim Marriott, March 1977.
124. *Viṣṇu Purāṇa* 1.5.26–65; see Wendy Doniger O'Flaherty, *Hindu Myths* (Penguin, 1975), pp. 44–46 and 316.

2

The Concepts of Human Action and Rebirth in the *Mahābhārata*

J. BRUCE LONG

Introduction

The analysis of the variety of formulations of the concepts of karma and *saṃsāra* in the *Mahābhārata* will be the sole concern in this paper. I recognize that any discussion of this subject with regard to the *MBh.* must be undertaken in medias res, given the appreciable development of these notions prior to the epic period. Even so, the enormity of the task of treating even this somewhat limited topic in the epic prohibits us from taking even a passing glance at the relevant materials in the pre-epic literature.[1] I shall also avoid the issue of the truth or falsity, adequacy or inadequacy of the principles of karma and *saṃsāra* as a general hermeneutic of the human condition, nor

1. Information on karma and *saṃsāra* in the Vedas, Brāhmaṇas and Upaniṣads may be found in the following sources: A. B. Keith, *Religion and Philosophy in the Vedas and Upanishads* (Cambridge, Mass., 1925), pp. 252 ff., 454 ff., 581–591; S. N. Dasgupta, *A History of Indian Philosophy* (Cambridge, 1922–), vol. 1; C. Sharma, *A Critical Survey of Indian Philosophy* (Varanasi, 1960); F. Edgerton, *The Beginnings of Indian Philosophy* (Cambridge, Mass., 1965), pp. 29 ff.; S. Radhakrishnan, *The Principal Upaniṣads* (London, 1953), esp. pp. 104–116; M. Hiriyanna, *The Essentials of Indian Philosophy* (London, 1949), pp. 47 ff.; R. D. Ranade, *A Constructive Survey of Upaniṣadic Philosophy* (Poona, 1926), pp. 152 ff.; and Eliot Deutsch, *Advaita Vedānta. A Philosophical Reconstruction* (Honolulu, 1969), pp. 67 ff.

shall I attempt to compare this definitive Indian world view with that of other cultures, Eastern or Western, questions treated in a suggestive article by Eliot Deutsch on "karma as a convenient fiction,"[2] and in the voluminous writings of Ian Stevenson, which represent the published findings of extensive research into possible empirical evidence for rebirth.[3]

The task before us here is at once more modest and more ambitious than those reflected in other writings on karma and *saṃsāra.* The modesty of the task rests on the intention to focus only on specific passages in the *MBh.* which speak to some aspect of the question of the nature of human action and its role in the formation of human ends. The ambitious nature of the task is determined by the intention to scrutinize a great many passages scattered throughout the *MBh.* more closely and in greater detail than has previously been attempted.[4]

The passages discussed herein reflect among themselves a remarkable (and to those who hanker after consistency, frustrating) degree of diversity, and even incongruity, of thought. At the same time, there are numerous motifs that appear time and again in passages drawn from every section of the *MBh.*, a fact that would appear to indicate that the various spokesmen on karma drew upon a common store of general notions, and at the same time exercised considerable freedom to recombine and modify those ideas according to individual and

2. "Karma as a 'Convenient Fiction' in the Advaita Vedānta," *Philosophy East and West* 15, no. 1 (1965): 3–12.

3. *Twenty Cases Suggestive of Reincarnation* (New York, 1966), and *Cases of the Reincarnation Type* (Charlottesville, Va., 1975), 2 vols.

4. Cf. other writings on karma and *saṃsāra* and related topics in the *MBh.* and the antecedents in pre-epic literature: V. M. Bedekar, "The Doctrine of the Colours of Souls in the *MBh.*," *Annals of the Bhandarkar Oriental Research Institute (ABORI)* 48–49 (1967–68): 329–338; Haridas Bhattacharya, "The Brāhmaṇical Concept of *Karma,*" *A. R. Wadia Commemoration Volume* (Bangalore, 1954), pp. 29–49; G. N. Chakravarty, "The Idea of Fate and Freedom in the *MBh.*, "*Poona Orientalist* 20 (1955) [*The Dr. H. L. Hariyappa Mem. Vol.*]; V. A. Gadgil, "*Rta and the Law of Karma,*" *All-India Oriental Conference,* 10 (Tirupati, 1940): 13–28; A. L. Herman, "Saṃsāra," *Journal of the Gangānātha Jhā Res. Inst.*, 27 (1971): 1–10; H. G. Narahari: "Karma and Reincarnation in the *MBh.*," *ABORI* 27 (1946): 102–113; "Vedic Antecedents of the Epic 'Śasarīrasvarga,'" *Indian Historical Quarterly* 28 (1952): 87–90; "Rebirth in Ancient Indian Thought," *Journal of Indian History* 43 (1965): 119–142; "Ideas About *Karma* in the Rāmāyaṇa," *Munshi Indological Felicitation Volume* (Bombay, 1963): 111–115; "Karma and Reincarnation in Classical Sanskrit Literature," *Quart. Jour. of the Mythic Society* 47 (1946–47): 68–71; Ronald M. Smith, "Birth of Thought—III. Transmigration and God," *ABORI* 35 (1954): 176–193.

sectarian predilections. I shall make every attempt to maintain a balance in the emphasis on both parallels and discontinuities among the various passages presented in order to distinguish those assumptions that appear to be common to the entire epic from those that are unique to specific passages. The focus of the present paper, on specific formulations of the doctrines of karma and *saṃsāra* in the *MBh.*, necessarily neglects the notion of karma in its "dharmic" form in the *MBh.* as a whole.[5]

The Causal Determinants of Human Destiny

In accord with its own syncretistic nature and the general propensity of Indian sages and mythographers to appeal to a multivalent range of ideas in treating almost every doctrinal topic, the *Mahābhārata* recognizes a number of different causal factors at work in arranging both immediate results and ultimate destinies. Any summary of the factors which are cited at one point or another in this great storehouse of Indian cultural lore would necessarily include the following: providential acts of God *(divya-kriyā)*,[6] divine ordinances *(divya-vidhi)*,[7] divine power or fate proper *(daiva, diṣṭa, niyati, bhāgya)*,[8] time *(kāla)*,[9] death *(mṛtyu, kṛtānta, antaka)*,[10] nature *(prakṛti)*,[11] and, finally, human action *(karma)*.[12]

The variegated nature of the palette of the ancient Indian intellectual tradition is exemplified in the initial chapter of the *Śvetāśvatara Upaniṣad* (vss. 2–3) where the sage passes in review a series of concepts of causation, then en vogue within various schools of thought: time, inherent nature, necessity, chance, the elements, the womb, the person, a combination of these, and the soul. He rejects all of these phenomena as being incapable of forming the causal basis of the

5. For this topic, see James L. Fitzgerald's "Two Brief Notes on 'Karma' Relative to the *Mahābhārata*." Presented at the ACLS-SSRC Joint Committee on South Asia–sponsored seminar, "Person and Interpersonal Relations in South Asia: An Exploration of Indigenous Conceptual Systems" at the University of Chicago, April 14, 1977.
6. Cf. 2.42.45 ff.; 3.2.6; 3.32.40; *Bhagavad Gītā* 8.21–31; 10.4–5, 33–34. [All citations of the *Mahābhārata (MBh.)* are from the Poona Critical Edition, unless otherwise noted.]
7. 3.31.3 ff.
8. 1.84.6–8; 1.89.9; 5.39.1; 2.41.1,4; 44.1; 2.17.3; 45.55 f.; 51.25–26; 56.17; 57.4; 58.18; 63.36; 64.5–6; 66.3; 67.3–4, 7; 67.7; 68.28; 72.10–11.
9. 2.40.5; 71.42; 72.8–11.
10. *Bṛhadāraṇyaka Upaniṣad* (BAU) 1.2.1 ff.; *MBh.* 13.1.50 ff.
11. *MBh.* 12.222.24 ff. (P. C. Roy trans.; hereafter referred to as PCR).
12. *Kaṭha Upan.* 2.2.7; *Maitrī Upan.* 4.2; *MBh.* 1.1.188–191; 3.148–154; 109.10–11; 12.153.12–13 (PCR); 13.207.19 f.

existence of conscious beings and contends, instead, that it is the "power of God himself, concealed in its own qualities" that controls all the forces mentioned, "from time to the soul." The importance of this passage lies in the fact that it is both a synoptic history (perhaps the earliest) of the religious philosophies of India up to the time of the late Upaniṣads (ca. 400 B.C.–) and a kind of prospectus for philosophical reflection on questions of causation and human destiny for centuries to come. The durability of this set of ideas is demonstrated by the appearance of a comparable statement made by Yudhiṣṭhira in the *Śānti-parvan:*

> Among the various groups of scholars *(viprā),* there are some who say that in the production of results, human effort *(puruṣakāra)* is primary. Some learned ones say that destiny *(daiva)* is primary and some that it is nature *(svabhāva)* that is the motivating force. Others say that acts flowing from effort (combined) with destiny, produce results, assisted by nature. Rather than taking any one of these (factors) as the sole cause of results, others say that the three in conjunction produce results. . . . These, of course, are the views of those who depend on acts with reference to goals. Those, however, whose view of things is established upon the truth, know *Brahman* to be the (primary) cause (of everything).[13]

While the epic sages drew upon this set of ideas almost exclusively in characterizing the principle of causation, they manifested a remarkable lack of consensus concerning the precise number and combination of causal factors which they believed to be operative in the world. The passage from the *Śānti–parvan* above suggests that the various schools could be classified under two rubrics: those which were committed to a life of action *(pravṛtti)* in quest of worldly goals and, perhaps, heaven after death, and those which were committed to the renunciation *(nivṛtti)* of all worldly values (including heaven) in preference for the liberative knowledge of absolute truth *(Brahma-vidyā).* The particular concept of causation and human action to which any person gave allegiance would have been dictated by the school of thought or life-ethic to which he was committed. While the philosophies of *Sāṅkhya* and *Vedānta* (both represented in a variety of subsets in the *MBh.*) provided the philosophical basis and framework for a majority of discourses on human action and destiny,

13. Consult the essay, "Action and Rebirth," by F. Edgerton in his trans. of the *Bhagavad Gītā* (New York, 1964), pp. 157 ff.; "The Nature of Karma Yoga," in E. Deutsch's trans. of the same text; and the whole of B. G. Tilak's *Śrīmad Bhagavadgītā-rahasya* (Poona, 1965).

numerous sectarian traditions (e.g., the Nārāyaṇīyas and the Pāśupatas) also made a significant imprint upon epic thought.

One conclusion that we might draw from this diversification of philosophical perspectives and the inclination to intermingle ideas drawn from a variety of schools of thought evidenced throughout the *MBh.* is that the sages and scholars failed to discover any single principle of causation that could account for all the exigencies of human life. Or, to state the matter affirmatively, like their Vedic forebears, the epic writers were prepared to embrace (or, at least, to tolerate) a diverse array of doctrines, in the conviction that while reality is one, it can be designated by many names (*Ṛg Veda* 1.164.46).

A cursory survey of a select number of passages in the *MBh.* which address some aspect of the topic of the nature of human action and its role in influencing human destiny will illuminate the range of ethico-religious ideas to which the sages appealed and the nature of the existential situations in which such questions demanded a didactic response.

KARMA

Generally speaking, the epic sages and storytellers take up their respective positions within the philosophical lineage of the Upaniṣads by accounting for the fashioning of human destiny through the medium of human action (karma). As one most succinct classical formulation of the principle of karma has it: "Even as one acts, even as he behaves, so does he become. The doer of good becomes good, the doer of evil becomes evil . . . whatever deed he performs, that he becomes [or attains]" (BAU 4.4.5). In a great many myths, legends, and didactic passages in the *MBh.*, the idea is propounded that a person reaps the results of his acts performed in previous lifetimes and comes to good- or ill-fortune as a result of his acts alone. According to one account provided by Vyāsa himself, "The acts done in former births never abandon any creature. . . . [And] since man lives under the control of karma, he must always be alert to ways of maintaining his equilibrium and of avoiding evil consequences."[14] In the *Uttarayayāti*, after Devayānī has been rescued from certain death in a deep well by King Yayāti, she is admonished by her father, Śukra, that, "by their own faults people reap sorrow and happiness. Apparently you once did some wrong which has thus been avenged" (1.73.29). Shortly thereafter, he sounds a disturbing note to Vṛṣapar-

14. 3.207.19–20. Compare 12.232.19 ff.

van, the murderer of Kaca: "The promotion of unrighteousness does not, like a cow, yield results immediately, O King. But evil does bear sure fruit, like a heavy meal on the stomach; if you do not see it ripen on yourself, it will on your sons or grandsons" (1.75.2). Along the same line, Yayāti declares that the forest-dweller who has achieved liberation from his body conducts not only himself but the ten generations on either side of him to virtuous deeds (1.86.7). In the account of the conversation between the wicked fowler and the saintly Gautamī, the question arises as to who or what is responsible for the death of Gautamī's young son, who had died as the result of a snake-bite. A series of possible culprits is passed in review in personified form: the snake itself, death, time and fate. One by one, each of the accused denies any culpability with regard to the boy's death. In the end, Gautamī, "invested with great patience and mental tranquility," divines the cause of her son's demise to be the boy's own karma in a previous lifetime and adds that she too "so acted [in the past] such that my son has died [as a consequence]."[15]

This strong confidence that each person has the capacity to influence (if not determine) his own course by his own efforts, is counterpoised with an equally compelling skepticism about the effectiveness of human action. On one occasion, Yudhiṣṭhira questions the efficacy of the law of karma: "Whether there be an effect or not of good and evil actions . . . those are the mysteries of the gods *(deva-guhyāni)*" (3.32.33). And, in numerous sections of the didactic portions of the *MBh.* (viz., the *Āraṇyaka-*, *Śānti-* and *Anuśāsana-parvans*), where the relative merits of the active life of the worldling *(pravṛtti)* and of the non-active life of the ascetic *(nivṛtti)* are debated, the party which opts for the latter way denies categorically that human acts are in any way effective in conducting men to auspicious ends.[16] An exemplary account of this ascetic position with regard to human action is provided in the story of King Vicakhu's condemnation of the animal sacrifices of the Brāhmaṇas and his assertion that non-injury

15. This is one of the meager number of instances in the *MBh.* where the notion appears that one person's karma influences both his own future and that of others who are closely related to or temporally contiguous with him. See 1.86.7 cited in the text above.

16. See esp. the "Dialogue between the Brahmin Father and His Son," 12.169 and 12.278 (PCR 175 and [169]). This same dialogue is found in *Jātaka* 509, *gāthā* 4,; *Mārk. Pur., adhy.* 10 ff. Compare also *Dhammapada* 4.47–48; and *Uttarādhyayanasūtra* 14.21–23. For critical discussions of various aspects of this story, consult the following sources: "Critical Notes," in C. E. of *MBh.* on 12.169; J. Charpentier, *ZDMG* 62 (1908): 725 ff.; and M. Winternitz, *A History of Indian Literature* (Calcutta, 1933), vol. 1, pp. 419 ff., 562 ff.

(ahiṃsā) to all creatures and a life of renunciation is the highest duty to which men can aspire *(sarvebhyo dharmebhyo jyāyasī matā).* So profound is his distaste for the life of the worldling *(gṛhastha),* established as it is upon the sacrifice, that he says, "Only the avaricious are motivated by a desire for fruit [of sacrifices]" *(kṛpanāḥ phalahetavaḥ)* and "the employment of these [sacrifices] is not prescribed in the Vedas" but "has been initiated by rascals" *(dhūrtaiḥ)* (12.257).

The most striking feature of those passages in the *MBh.* which discuss the relative merits and demerits of human action is the lack of agreement concerning the effectiveness of human action in producing results. The belief that human actions are effective stands in an unresolved state of tension with the claims that the acts of god or the machinations of blind fate are the primary causative forces at work in the world.

TIME

In the opening chapter of the *Ādi-parvan,* the bard, Sañjaya, consoles the grieving Dhṛtarāṣṭra with the declaration that all creatures pass from birth to death and thence to rebirth through the irresistible operations of time *(kāla).* It is *kāla,* he says, that ripens the creatures and then rots them (1.1.188–191; compare 12.220). In chapter three of the same *parvan,* in the course of undergoing a series of ordeals for the purpose of acquiring a pair of earrings for his guru's wife, Uttaṅka is struck by a vision of two women weaving a piece of fabric composed of black and white strands and a gigantic wheel with 360 spokes being rotated by six boys and a handsome man—all representing the creative and destructive movements of time (1.3.150–151). So inflexible is the law of time believed to be that the sages proclaimed, "Death has been decreed for all created beings. When their hour *(vidhi)* comes round, all beings are removed by law *(dharmena).*"[17] In the dialogue between the vulture and the jackal concerning the possibility of restoring the dead to life and the relative efficacy of austerities in accomplishing that end, the vulture asserts that "whether friend or foe, no one ever comes back to life having once succumbed to the power of time" (12.149.8–9). In the same passage, the fruits of karma, whether good or evil, are said to be nullified by the iron rule of time.[18]

17. 7.54 (PCR); C.E. Appendix I.8 (240–243). Cf. 12.137.45–49.
18. Vss. 44–45. For a few of the many other passages about *kāla* as the primary causative force, consult 1.3.148–175; 2.40.5; 69.44; 3.188.99; 189.25–26; 12.26.1 ff.; 149.12–13, 44–45; 213.1 ff.; 232.1 ff.; 13.1.50 ff.; 13.6; 14.17.7 ff.

FATE

Out of the wealth of materials dealing with the concept of Fate *(daiva, diṣṭa),* I shall present only a select few that illustrate the use of this concept in accounting for human destiny.[19] Like all the other concepts under investigation, the notion of fate is rendered multiphasically, by identifying it with a variety of other factors—for example, divine providence, human acts in past time, circumstantial conditions, time, and so forth. Whatever the specific meaning attributed to the idea in any given context, the term fate consistently indicates certain external forces over which the individual exercises no control, either in actualizing or deactualizing any particular state of affairs.

Yudhiṣthira rationalizes his compulsion to pursue ever-elusive success in the infamous dice-game by appealing to the invincible influence of fate. Though he knows that Duryodhana's challenge to the dicing will bring the entire family to a state of ruination, he admits, "I cannot disobey his word," because of the irresistible influence of fate (2.67.3–4). In the *Uttaryayāti,* Yayāti says, "All living creatures depend upon fate *(diṣṭa)* and their acts are wasted: regardless of what one obtains, the wise one is not concerned, knowing as he does that his fate is stronger *(diṣṭam balīyaḥ).* Whether it is good- or ill-fortune that comes to him, it is not he but fate that brings things to pass" (1.84.6–8).[20]

In many instances, fate is conceived as the instrument which the divine arranger *(Dhātṛ)* employs in working his (or its) will in the world and is frequently identified with the principle of *kāla.* In reply to Sañjaya's prophesy of the fall of the family of Dhṛtarāṣtra in retribution for their crimes against the Pāṇḍavas, Dhṛtarāṣtra avows that it is the acts of the gods (not human deeds) that bring a person to defeat. The gods delude man's mind by distorting his vision of the true nature of things and the proper order of their interrelationship, with the result that the entire system of socioreligious values is turned upside down. In this regard the old patriarch observes, "Time [or fate] does not raise a stick and clobber a man's head; the power of

19. Consult E. W. Hopkins, *Epic Mythology* (Strassburg, 1915), pp. 73 ff. for a résumé of materials on fate in the *MBh.*
20. Compare 12.15; C. Drekmeier, *Kingship and Community in Early India* (Stanford, 1962), pp. 150 ff.; H. Zimmer, *Philosophies of India,* (New York, 1951), pp. 98 ff.; and J. A. B. van Buitenen, "Some Notes on the Uttara-yayāta," *Adyar Library Bulletin* 31–32 (1967–68): 617–635.

time is just this up-ended view of things" (2.72.8–11. J. A. B. van Buitenen, trans.).[21]

GOD AS THE "ARRANGER"

The belief that both intermediate results and final destinies are predetermined by an omnipotent divine being (or principle) referred to as the "Arranger" *(Dhātṛ)* is represented in stark and unsettling terms by Draupadī in her discourse to the grieving Yudhiṣṭhira (3.31.21–39). She declares that it is god alone who establishes everything for the creatures, both happiness *(sukha)* and unhappiness *(duḥkha),* pleasure *(priya),* as well as pain *(apriya),* even before "ejaculating the seed." She represents this god as a kind of cosmic magician or "puppeteer" who "makes the body and limbs move," a "capricious blessèd Lord" who "hiding behind a disguise, assembling and breaking the creatures, plays with them as a child plays with its toys." In turn, she likens men to wooden puppets who are "propelled by the Lord" to their several destinies. Because man at no time is completely independent of the Controller's manipulative powers, he is the "master neither of himself nor of others." He knows nothing and exercises no influence whatsoever over his own happiness and misery. The entire human body, which is called a "field" *(kṣetra),* is nothing but the instrument by which god propels human beings toward their actions and corresponding results—both good and evil. Draupadī continues by arguing that since god's relation to man is more like that of a capricious and belligerent taskmaster than a benevolent and sympathetic parent, his actions must be viewed as arising from the same sort of self-serving motivations as human actions. Consequently, god, like man, is pursued by the impure fruits of his own deeds and is, therefore, vulnerable to the same moral censureship as his creatures. (Compare *Bhagavad-Gītā* 2.18–61.)

Yudhiṣṭhira, true to his nature as the "Son of Dharma," first congratulates Draupadī on the eloquence of her statement but then condemns it as utterly heretical.[22] While it is admittedly often difficult to "justify the ways of god to man," he asserts, "those of pure mind and will recognize that neither *dharma* nor the gods should be dispar-

21. Consult the following passages for additional references to the concept of fate: 1.109.10–11; 43.32; 45.55 ff.; 71.35; 67.3–4; 3.176.26 ff.; 5.159.4 (PCR); 6.76.19; 7.135.1 ff. (PCR); 8.9.3; 12.28.18 ff.; 13.6.1 ff.

22. Compare 12.161.45–46 where Yudhiṣṭhira affirms precisely the same view that he has categorically denied here.

aged, simply because the rewards [of human acts] are [in many cases] imperceptible." In other words, the inclination to revile god and *dharma* arises from a false understanding of the true nature of both, for "whoever doubts *dharma* falls into bestiality . . . [and], failing to discover a proper standard of action elsewhere, resorts to using himself as the rule, thereby falling into hell himself and bringing the world that much closer to bottomless darkness." Yudhiṣṭhira counters Draupadī's condemnation of God with essentially the same message as that delivered to Job by the voice in the whirlwind: "*Dharma* always bears (appropriate) fruit . . . [and] is never fruitless. . . . The fruition of acts, good as well as bad, their appearance and disappearance, are the mysteries of the gods." Therefore, man has no recourse but to behave in strict conformity to *dharma* and to recognize that "it is by the grace of the Supreme God that a devoted mortal becomes immortal" (3.32.29–33).

This juxtaposition of the views of Draupadī and Yudhiṣṭhira stands out as an illuminating moment in the epic treatment of karma and human destiny. Viewing each position in its starkest form, the one maintains that god alone is responsible for everything that happens in the world; the other, that either man alone or man in concert with god is responsible for the occurrence of events. This bi-polar model is often complicated all the more by introducing other factors, such as time, fate, *prakṛti*. The fact that various spokesmen in the *MBh.* designate first one then another factor as the cause of events would seem to indicate that they did not feel that the total complexity of forces at work in the world could be accounted for by reference to a single principle or agent. There is a variety of causal elements: human action, divine influence, hereditary traits, extenuating circumstances, and even potent actions of extraordinary personages such as sages, seers, magicians, and soothsayers. An example of the negative effects of such powers appears in the story of Bhīma's encounter with the gigantic serpent, which, as it turns out, is King Nahuṣa in a degraded form of existence (1.176–177). Bhīṣma inquires how he came to this terrible end, and Nahuṣa, in serpentine guise, replies that the misfortune resulted both from his own proud and belligerent behavior toward Brahmins and from the curse of Agastya. The salutary effects of the presence of gifted persons appear in another story: As Yudhiṣṭhira and his kinsmen are entering the forest, they are assured by a coterie of Brahmins that their (the Brahmins') presence in the forest would yield a beneficent effect upon the life of the Pāṇḍavas during their twelve-year exile, even though their exile is viewed as retribution for evil deeds in past time.

Indeed, numerous other passages champion the idea that multiple combinations of factors operate in the production of events. For example, Bhīṣma declares that it is "because of acts and bondage to time *(kāla-yuktena)* [that] the self revolves through repeated rounds of birth [and death]" (12.206.13). Not infrequently, divine action and time are seen as conspiring to create existing states of affairs (2.72.8–11; 14.17.7 ff.). Kṛṣṇa reveals himself to Arjuna on Kurukṣetra as the all-creating and all-destroying power of time (*BG* 10.33; cf. 11.32) and, viewed *specie sub aeternitatis,* the only actual actor within the entire universe. [Compare *BG* 9.8.] In the course of his instruction of Yudhiṣṭhira in the *Anuśāsana-parvan,* Bhīṣma asserts that a combination of destiny (understood in this context to be the cumulative effects of previous acts) and individual effort (contemporaneous resolution and its concomitant action) directs each person's earthly career. Bhīṣma contends that without the assurance that all karma bears appropriate fruit, all action would come to be viewed as meaningless, and relying on destiny alone, men would become idlers (13.6.2). Dhṛtarāṣṭra rejects this view of causation in his lamentation over the repeated defeat of Karṇa at the hands of Bhīma: "I'm convinced that fate is sovereign. Resolute effort is fruitless, given Karṇa's failure to master Bhīma despite a courageous struggle" (7.135.1, PCR).

The latitude to appeal to a number of different doctrines (some of which are ostensibly incompatible) in defining the causative forces operative within the world is exemplified nowhere more clearly than in the *Bhagavad Gītā.* In the course of instructing Arjuna concerning the nature and bases for moral action, Kṛṣṇa invokes several different notions. On the one hand, he declares that "all actions are performed by the strands *(guṇas)* alone. He is deluded by egoism that surmises, 'I am the actor'" (3.27; compare 13.20–21; 18.40). Elsewhere, he urges Arjuna to recognize "that [ritual] action arises from *Brahman* and that *Brahman* arises from the Imperishable *(akṣara)*" (ibid. 3.15). Again, Kṛṣṇa asserts that he and he alone is the source, foundation, and cause of all events within the temporal order: "I am the source of everything: from me all things spring forth" (BG 10.8a; compare 9.8). Kṛṣṇa provides experiential confirmation of this contention by revealing his universal form *(viśvarūpa)* to Arjuna. On this occasion he presents himself as the living and ever-evolving divine embodiment of all the causative forces (and their effects) in the universe (10.21–31), as the source and support of all polarized forces (10.4–5), and as the creator, maintainer, and destroyer of the entire cosmos (4.6; 7.10, 12–15; 9.8–10; 10.33–34). Finally, he complicates the situation still further by representing human action as composed of five components: body *(adhiṣṭhāna)*, agent *(kartṛ)*, instruments *(karaṇa)*, the various activities *(ceṣṭa)*, and destiny or divinity itself *(daiva)* —all this without reference to any extra-human agency (18.13–15).

Karma and Human Destiny according to Mārkaṇḍeya

While textual scholars customarily interpret a particular text by focusing attention on the ideational contents or narrative structure of the material, the hermeneutical significance of a piece can also be deciphered by taking note of its placement within the narrative and of the events or circumstances which frame it on either side. For example, in the *MBh.* a great many inquiries concerning the nature and destiny of man are introduced at moments of extreme distress, when a certain unforeseen misfortune has disrupted normal life patterns. Such crises may be precipitated by a variety of untoward events—discouragement in the face of an onerous task, a costly defeat in battle, subjection to a terminal illness, or the failure to acquire some desired boon. The crisis-event in the *MBh.* which, more than any other, calls forth instruction on the cause or causes of human destiny is Yudhiṣthira's experience of debilitating grief over the misfortunes of the Pāṇḍavas and his personal guilt for precipitating their demise by witlessly pursuing the ill-fated dicing match long after all hopes for success had vanished. At the moment of Yudhiṣthira's greatest despair, a "comforter" in the form of a deity, a sage, or a wandering mendicant, appears to reassure him and his kinsmen that their present misfortunes are the natural consequence of previous acts *(karmāni)* and, like everything else, will soon pass away. He counsels them to recognize that extended grieving over events resulting from one's own actions in past time is both a sign of ignorance and a wastage of vital energies which should be expended in more salutary ways. He assures them further that just as the current state of misfortune displaced happier states of an earlier time, even so these adversities will, in time, give place to more propitious conditions—all in strict conformity with the law of just recompense and retribution for past deeds.

At the beginning of a rather lengthy discourse to Yudhiṣthira and his kinsmen on a wide range of ethico-religious topics (3.179–221;

PCR 182–231), the sage Mārkaṇḍeya presents an elaborate formulation of the twin doctrines of karma and *saṃsāra.* As usual, Yudhiṣṭhira initiates the session by raising a number of questions regarding the nature of human acts and of the causative force or forces that influence short- and long-range "ends" in human existence. Is it a fact, he inquires, that man is the agent of his deeds, for good or ill, and that each person reaps his own reward? Or, do both acts and their effects result from the acts of god? Is it true that the results of all human acts pursue the doer during this lifetime only, or into another birth as well? By what means is the embodied soul pursued by its deeds and how is it conjoined with them, here and hereafter? And where do the acts abide when a person is deceased (3.181.6–9)?

Mārkaṇḍeya begins his discourse by delineating the history of mankind in terms of a twofold temporal schema. During the primal era, all souls were implanted in pure *(śuddha)* bodies. Being free from physical weakness and moral ambiguity, all persons were observant of holy vows, truthful and godlike. Because everyone existed in a state devoid of any kind of impurity, they enjoyed the capacity to migrate between heaven and earth at will and to perceive the multitudes of gods and seers tangibly and without the aid of any extraordinary powers of perception. They lived for thousands of years and bore an equivalent number of male offspring. But, in the course of time, they were overwhelmed by the twin vices, lust and wrath *(kāma, krodha),* became enslaved to avarice and delusion, and as a consequence of their mental confusion and moral corruption, were "cooked by all sorts of transmigrations," and were reborn innumerable times as demons, animals, and human beings. Since the time of the "fall," man, in his original, god-created body, accumulates large quantities of good and evil deeds. At death, his soul abandons his deteriorating corpse and is *instantly* reborn in a womb, "without any time intervening."[23] His past acts come to fruition, "following him like a shadow," and he is reborn with a good- or ill-fortune. The ignorant ones, blinded by their deluded views of the world and their mindless desire to perpetuate their existence on their own terms, mistakenly believe that man's destiny is controlled by death *(mṛtyu).* But the wise ones—those who have immersed themselves in sacred scripture, are resolute in their vows, are of pure birth, and are self-controlled—

23. 3.181.23–24.

know rather that the destiny of each person is determined by the "imprints" *(lakṣanaiḥ)* created by his good and bad acts. In view of the fact that a person's acts follow him throughout this life and into the next and determine the quality of his rebirth, Yudhiṣṭhira is urged to recognize that man, even in his "fallen" state, possesses the capacity to exercise a decisive influence over his fate by his own deeds in each present moment.

But the question remains whether a person can expect to reap the full harvest of his deeds, good and evil, in this world or whether the moral outcome of certain deeds will be actualized only at the moment of death or in a realm beyond this one. The answer to this question is formulated in the form of a "calculus" based on the relative degree of self-restraint and self-indulgence that marks any given lifetime. According to Mārkaṇḍeya, the law of karma requires that each person at the end of a life-span go to one or another of four different destinies: (1) persons of great wealth whose life has been filled with hedonistic self-indulgence obtain the treasures of this world but not those of the next; (2) those who study the Veda, practice austerities, adhere to Yoga, control their senses, and render aid to those who are in need earn the rewards of the other world but not this; (3) persons who live according to the dictates of *dharma* as householders, who take a wife, offer sacrificial oblations, and obtain wealth acquire the rewards of both this world and the next; (4) those ignorant and immoral persons who disdain true knowledge, give no gifts, fail to restrain their senses, and beget no offspring find happiness neither in this world nor in the next. Mārkaṇḍeya concludes his homily on human destinies by declaring that "it is by performing magnanimous deeds, practicing penances, exercising self-control, sustaining the gods, the sages, and the Manes [with auspicious rites], that those of pure mind and moral character, by their own acts, achieve the highest heaven where the souls of the blessed dwell."

It is the primary purpose of this lengthy colloquy to persuade Yudhiṣṭhira (and, by extension, all those who listen to or recite this discourse) that worldly events occur not randomly, fortuitously, or devoid of human meaning but in strict accord with the eternal principle of universal order (*dharma* or karma). The realization that events are caused solely by human acts (or in concert with other aforementioned factors, such as time, fate or divine providence) provides a person with the courage to make a firm and enduring commitment to a life of action *(karma-yoga)* and to behave in the manner commensurate with the injunctions of the sacred texts. By doing so, one may expect to have maximized his chance of coming to a good death and a good rebirth (or to a final suspension of rebirth). In addition, the assurance that the full range of effects produced by a particular act or cluster of acts does not come to fruition immediately or even during the current lifetime and that even those results that are actualized may be imperceptible to all but the most prescient sages and seers is meant to restore confidence that any given period of misfortune (of the Pāṇḍavas, in this instance) may be nothing but the prelude to a more propitious condition still to come.

The Dialogue between Kaśyapa and the Brahmin concerning Karma and *Saṃsāra*

In that section of the *Aśvamedha-parvan* commonly known as the *Anugītā* (14.16 ff.), Kṛṣṇa relates the story of a dialogue between an unidentified Brahmin and another Brahmin, named Kaśyapa, about a series of questions pertaining to the nature of human action and its effect or lack of effect on the process of birth and death.

The Brahmin initiates the conversation by giving an account of his earlier life: his early years of fortune and felicity, his subsequent fall into alternating states of felicity and misery as the result of certain sinful deeds, and his transition through numerous painful births and deaths. This autobiographical sketch is meant to provide Kaśyapa with an experiential basis for interpreting the more abstract teachings that are to follow. In quest of more information about the cause of his "fall" from felicity and his subjection to repeated births and deaths, Kaśyapa poses a number of queries: How does the body perish? How is another body constituted? How does one achieve emancipation after going through repeated rounds of rebirth? Once freed from the body, how does the *jīva* achieve another body? How does a person appropriate the fruits of his own good and evil deeds? Where do the acts reside when one is devoid of a body? It appears from the text that the Brahmin responds to no more than three of the inquiries (i.e., the death of the body, the acquisition of another body, and the mechanism of rebirth). We shall examine the sage's response to these questions in their natural order, beginning with the event of death and its aftermath and proceeding to the process of rebirth.

THE PROCESS OF CORPOREAL DISSOLUTION AT DEATH[24]

Whenever a person is haunted by a sense of his own approaching death, his mind becomes overwhelmed with fear, doubts, and despair.[25] As a result, he is diverted from the course of thought and action which he knows to be proper and conducive to a felicitous existence. As the intensity of his anxiety grows, he develops poor eating habits, with the result that he eats on an irregular basis and partakes of improper types of food. In the course of time he develops an intestinal disorder that combines with the psychological infirmity to create a disruption of the balance among the three humors *(tridoṣas)*.[26] The disequilibrium among the humors in the body provokes other severe psychosomatic infirmities and, ultimately, death, if the degenerative process is not reversed.

According to a more detailed account of this process that follows immediately in the same text, the wind[27] in the body becomes agitated in response to the combined disorders.[28] The wind disperses debilitating heat (i.e., *jvara,* or fever) throughout the organism. The free and natural movements of the vital breaths *(prāṇas)* are first restrained and then, just prior to the moment of death, halted completely.[29]

24. Compare the account of the death process recorded in BAU 4.3.35–4.4, from which the epic writer obviously derived his basic concepts.
25. *MBh.* 14.17.6–39.
26. E.g., *tridoṣa* = *vāyu,* or wind, *pitta,* or bile, and *śleṣman* or *kapha,* or phlegm. The reason that the excitation of *vāyu* in the body creates intestinal disorders is that, according to Suśruta (*Nidānasthāna* 1.8), the intestines and the rectum are the abodes of *vāyu.*
27. See BAU 3.3.2.
28. For a more technical treatment of the physio-cosmology of the wind, consult Caraka, *Sūtrasthāna,* 12, and Suśruta, *Nidānasthāna,* 1. Relevant passages of both texts are translated by J. Filliozat in *The Classical Doctrine of Indian Medicine* (Delhi, 1964), pp. 196 ff.
29. According to Caraka (ibid., 12.8) "It [the wind] becomes the determining cause of the prolongation of life when it is not excited. But when, in truth, it is excited in the body, it inflicts on the body all sorts of derangements to the detrimental forces of color, of well-being and longevity. It puts in tumult the mind, attacks all the faculties, throws down the embryos, provokes malformation, makes it go on for too long a time, engenders fright, chagrin, bewilderment, sadness, loquacity, and blocks the breaths." Filliozat, ibid., p. 200. In the teachings of Yājñavalkya (BAU 3.2.11–13; 4.3.37; 4.4.1 ff.), just prior to the moment of expiration the vital breaths *(prāṇā)* congregate within the body by moving toward the motionless center of the person, or the *ātman;* then all the sense organs are fused together into an indistinguishable mass, remaining within the body of a liberated person *(mukta)* but abandoning the body of a bound person, either through the eye, the head, or other apertures in the body.

Excited by another violent disorder, the wind inflicts upon the body an immobilizing chill and thereby dissolves the body into its five component elements.[30] In order to escape confinement within the tortured frame, the wind residing within the *prāṇa* and *apāna* frantically rushes upward and abandons the body, leaving it destitute of warmth, breath, beauty, and consciousness.[31] The channels through which the person once apprehended sense objects collapse with the loss of the support of the life breaths, the internal wind, and the *jīva.* As a result, all perception ceases.

Verses 24–28 of the same chapter provide additional information about the condition of the psychosomatic organism just prior to death. The *jīva* (here identified with the eternal *Brahman*) attracts to itself the basic elements (*dhātus* or *doṣas*) and fuses them together to form the vital organs *(marmāni).*[32] Whenever those vital parts are pierced, the *jīva,* rising up, enters the heart and immediately represses the principle of cognition *(sattva).*[33] Though still retaining the rudimentary faculty of consciousness, the individual is not conscious of anything (i.e., he is in a comatose state).[34] With the unification of the vital functions, the mind is overwhelmed with darkness *(tamasā).* Deprived of all its life-supports, the *jīva* is agitated by the wind. At this point, the person makes one long final exhalation, and the unconscious body experiences a final shudder. Deserted by the *jīva* (or *Brahman*), the person is recognized as dead.

Even though it is now separated from the body, the *jīva,* nonetheless, is surrounded on all sides by its deeds, "marked" *(aṅkita)* by auspicious and inauspicious deeds. The *jīva* is said to be imperceptible in its present condition to all except those Brahmins who, endowed with spiritual knowledge and the resolutions of the scriptures,

30. 14.17.20.

31. The four breaths according to Suśruta (ibid., 1.11 ff.) are (1) upward breath *(prāṇa),* which sustains the body and the other breaths and draws nourishment into the body; (2) downward breath *(apāna),* which governs the movements of excreta, urine, sperm, embryo, and menses; (3) concentrated breath *(samāna),* which, in cooperation with fire, digests the nourishment and separates it into various substances; and (4) diffused breath *(vyāna),* which transports the life-essence, produces perspiration, causes blood to circulate, and diffuses ills throughout the body. Compare BAU 3.9.26; 4.2.4; and *MBh.* 3.203.15–27.

32. See BAU 4.4.1–24.

33. According to Suśruta (ibid., 1.25), the wind that resides in the blood can create ulcers, that in the flesh can create painful nodes, and that in the fatty tissues can create ulcerous protuberances.

34. See Suśruta (ibid., 1.64) for a description of this state.

have the capacity to perceive the moral and spiritual quality of a person's deeds, by deciphering the "signs" that are left behind by those deeds in the post-mortem state. The soul of the deceased is said to experience pain of an identical nature at the time of both death and rebirth, caused, no doubt, by the rapid transition from one mode of being to another (i.e., from the "subtle body" to the "gross body").[35] This latter statement may refer, implicitly, to that post-mortem state of consciousness in which the *jīva* experiences rewards and punishments demanded by acts in the previous lifetime. However this may be, the assertion is made that until that time when the soul is freed completely from bondage to egotism and rebirth, each and every lifetime will be framed and suffused by suffering.

Another significant feature of the anthropology that informs this passage is the absence of any reference to a preternatural being or principle, or to any non-material factor connected with the death-process. Mental anxiety arising from the anticipation of death appears to be the sole causal factor. This text appears to draw directly upon the writings of either Caraka or Suśruta or both, where the conception of man is delineated in the terms of philosophical materialism. Nevertheless, reference is made to the influences of divine forces upon the human situation elsewhere in the *Anugītā*, and such references are juxtaposed, without being completely synthesized, with the concepts of materialistic physiology as a means of accommodating the central theistic bias of the *Anugītā* and of the *MBh.* generally.

THE MEANS OF ACQUIRING ANOTHER BODY IN THE WOMB[36]

Owing to the continuing influence of the results of previous acts, the *jīva* "reaps a harvest of both happiness and sorrow" by entering another womb. The text indicates unambiguously that the mind *(manas)* serves as the abode of the *karmaphala* and compels the *jīva* to commit itself to additional acts in quest of lasting satisfaction in one form or another. At the moment of conception, the *jīva,* marked with all its acts and enslaved to passion and wrath, enters the womb by the following means: the sperm combines with the blood of the female and enters the womb to form the "field of good and bad actions." Because of the subtlety of its nature and its unmanifested condition, the *jīva* as eternal *Brahman* remains unattached to the mind-body organism which houses and supports it. On entering the

35. 14.17.18b–19. 36. *Aśvamedhaparvan* 18.1–13.

foetus and pervading it throughout, the life-force assumes the attribute of mind and by abiding within the realm of *prāṇa* supports the body and quickens the limbs into animated activity. The *jīva* assumes whatever form is dictated by the person's previous acts. During each lifetime the *jīva* continues to cancel old "debts" and to create new ones until the embodied self *(dehin)* "achieves a true knowledge of the duties required by that contemplation which leads to liberation."[37]

THE MECHANISM OF REBIRTH[38]

Given the fact that the *jīva* is compelled to encounter the effects of its previous deeds and to assume a "mode of being that is different from [i.e., contrary to] its true nature,"[39] the question arises as to why the various *jīvas* came under the sway of corporeality in the first place. The Brahmin's explanation of the "initial incarnation" of the *jīvas* is framed by a philosophical cosmology composed of ideas drawn from both Vedānta and Sāṅkhya—a procedure commonly followed in virtually every part of the *MBh.* According to this cosmology, the Grandfather of all the creatures *(Brahma-Prajāpati)*[40] first created a body for himself and then fashioned the three worlds with both moving and still creatures. He then created *pradhāna*[41] (the material cause of the universe). *Pradhāna* pervades and constitutes everything in the cosmos and, therefore, is known by the sages to be the "chief" constituent of all phenomena. Every creature has a dualistic nature: the invisible, non-material, spiritual essence of the self is the imperishable; the visible, material, corporeal abode of the self is the perishable. Prajāpati then created all the primal elements (or crea-

37. Ibid., 18.12.
38. Ibid., 18.24–34.
39. That the embodied state of being *(dehin)* is thought to be an abnormal condition for the *jīva* is indicated by the standardized use of the term *doṣa* (impurity, fault, pollutant) in referring to the basic humors in the body.
40. Cf. *Ṛg Veda* 10.121; *Śatapatha Brāhmaṇa* 7.4.2.5.
41. Compare 12.198.16. *Pradhāna* means the "originator" or the "chief thing," and at 12.238.4, the "unmanifest" *(avyakta).* In the *Mokṣadharma* and the *Anugītā*, *pradhāna* is used synonymously with *prakṛti* (12.298.10). According to E. H. Johnston *(Early Sāṁkhya* [London, 1937], pp. 67–68), when it is employed as one of a set of sixteen *vikāras,* or "derivative modifications," the term is associated with *svabhāva,* or "inherent nature," and, as such, indicates that the twenty-four principles of the universe are derived from *svabhāva.* Cf. G. Larson, *Classical Sāṁkhya* (Delhi, 1969), p. 121.

tures = *bhūtāni*) and all the immobile creatures, after which he ordained a temporal boundary as well as transmigrations *(parivṛtti)* and a returning *(punarāvṛtti)* for all mortals.

This account of the cosmology and the establishment of the law governing birth and death differs markedly from the version presented in the subsection "The Process of Corporeal Dissolution at Death" above. This is all the more remarkable given the fact that the two accounts are, supposedly, delivered by a single person. Whereas the first account makes no mention of a supernatural agent in connection with the establishment of the cosmic-order, the second credits a personal or quasi-personal divine being with the fashioning of not only the material basis of existence *(pradhāna),* the primal elements, and the creatures of every species, but of the law of transmigration as well. The latter section makes no mention whatever of the role of karma in the determination of human destiny. This passage supports a position midway between philosophical Vedānta and devotional Kṛṣṇa-ism, by attributing all primary causative action to god while, at the same time, identifying that Creator as Brahma-Prajāpati rather than Kṛṣṇa. We might be justified in assuming that the idea of karma is the underlying assumption of every statement on human destiny in the *MBh.*, but taking this text as it stands, the responsibility for the creation of the world-order and the actualization of human destiny lies with the divine being, with no contribution of any magnitude from man himself.

The General Ideological Basis of the Conceptions of Karma and *Saṃsāra*

The Indian sages conceived of life, within both the micro- and macrocosmic spheres, not as a steady state but as a process, a continual and protracted (if not interminable) flow of life-powers, a perpetual fluctuation of forces or a coursing of energies through channels that pervade the body of the universe and the bodies of all the creatures who inhabit it. That the world and the passage of the creatures from state to state is conceived to be a transmission of power from place to place through time is clearly articulated in the Sanskrit term for metempsychosis, or rebirth. The term *saṃsāra* means literally the act of going about, wandering through, coursing along, or passing through a series of states or conditions, specifically the passage through successive states of birth, death, and rebirth.[42] The basal universal energy *(tejas, tapas, śakti)* is a kind of élan vital, which creates, supports, and (according to certain "schools of thought") constitutes *substantively* all living things. This energy is conceived to be something on the order of an electrical current or a bundle of forces fluctuating within an electromagnetic field *(kṣetra)* with good and bad, meritorious and unmeritorious deeds acting as the positive and negative charges. On other occasions, the imagery employed in both mythological and philosophical materials suggests the transmission of a fluid substance through channels or conduits running through the micro- and macrocosmic bodies: e.g., the *nāḍībandhas* or *suṣumnās* of Tantrism, the canal or trench *(kulyā)*, channel or water course *(praṇāla)* or canal *(srota)* of the narrative and medical literature.[43]

Alongside these naturalistic, abstract metaphors, there also appear images of a more organic and even personalistic nature. From the time of the Ṛg Veda, for example, the universe is conceived after the fashion of an animal (such as a goat, a cow, a horse, a bird) or as the cosmic manifestation of a primal Superman *(puruṣa)*, invested with all the physical and mental features of the primordial archetype. According to the *Puruṣasūkta (ṚV 10.90)*,[44] the cosmos was fashioned by the self-immolation of this primordial creature, with the various segments of the natural and social orders constituted of corresponding parts of his body. In the eleventh chapter of the *Bhagavad Gītā*, Kṛṣṇa reveals to Arjuna his universal form as the phenomenal manifestation of the manifold universe; the realm of *saṃsāra* is displayed as the parade of multitudinous creatures entering and leaving the thousand mouths of Viṣṇu.[45] This same cosmogony is represented in a drastically modified form in the dialogue between the Brahmin and Kaśyapa in the passage from the *Anugītā* discussed earlier. Sup-

42. The term *saṃsāra* is derived from the Sanskrit root meaning "to flow together," "wander about," or "pass through."
43. *MBh.* 14.17.23–24: "By those channels *(srotobhair)* through which he perceives sense objects, the bearer of the body no longer perceives them. It is the eternal *jīva* who creates in the body in those very channels the life-breaths that are generated by food."
44. For an illuminating commentary on this hymn, consult R. Panikkar, *The Vedic Experience* (University of California Press, 1977), pp. 72 ff.
45. It should also be noted in this connection that the twelfth-century South Indian Pāñcarātra theologian, Śrī Rāmānujācārya, employs the same "body language" in speaking of the universe as the psychophysiological abode of the eternal Godhead, Nārāyaṇa-Viṣṇu.

posedly, Prajāpati was able to turn his creative powers to the task of making the creatures only after he had fashioned a body for himself. Although the text does not say so, it is quite likely that this body served not only as the residence of the creator and the instrument of his creative acts, but was the material stuff from which the universe was shaped.

With this much material before us, we are in a position to draw a few tentative conclusions regarding the general ideational framework within which the Indian sages formulated their views of the nature and cause or causes of human destiny: (1) The universe was created or evolved by a cosmogonic power, conceived as either a personal divine being or an abstract generative principle. (2) The cosmos exists in the form of a gigantic living organism, invigorated, shaped, and supported by a gargantuan store of life-energy circulating within both the micro- and macrocosmic realms along channels or ducts. (3) That primal person or principle fashioned the creatures by projecting small quantities of his (or its) own life-essence into their bodies and investing them with his (or its) physical features and mental faculties. (4) According to the anthropomorphic view of the universe, these creatures either represent microcosmic replications of the universal organism in the form of the primal person or collectively form the numerous parts of his universal body. (5) Finally, once this cosmic life-system with its multitudinous creatures was propelled into motion, it has continued to gyrate in a cyclical pattern from death to rebirth, either under the creator's influence or by the action of fate, time, or human action, or by a combination of these factors. The universe will continue progressing in this fashion until that time when all forms of life return to perfect union with that primal entity from which they originally sprang into being.

The *MBh.* addresses a number of provocative issues pertaining to the doctrines of karma and *saṃsāra* and posits a wide diversity of answers to questions provoked by deep reflections on these ideas. At the same time, this vast reservoir of narrative tales and didactic materials leaves many of the more intellectually troublesome areas unexplored. I have found no passage that attempts to account for the exact means by which each soul finds its way into the womb and thence into the family whose moral and social standing is commensurate with the "merital" status of the *jīva.* Nor is it stated how moral entities such as good and bad acts become attached to and are transported by physical entities such as wind, fire, water, breath, sperm, and blood. Again, it is not specified in the epic whether the effects of human acts are believed to be of a moral or a physiological nature, or both. The vocabulary adapted from the world of trade and commerce to refer to good deeds as merits or assets and evil deeds as demerits or liabilities, and to the accumulation of bad karma as the acquisition of a debt, as though deeds were so many items on a financial ledger, appears to stand at odds with the description of life, death, and rebirth as the result of the transmission of a quasi-physical substance on the "back of the wind" or in the blood stream.

The silence of the Indian sages during the epic period concerning many aspects of problems relating to karma and *saṃsāra* sets us to wondering why certain queries were raised but not answered and why others were not formulated at all until later times. Perhaps the sages bypassed such issues because of their own lack of the necessary philosophical concepts or because of their recognition that discussions of a subtler and more abstract nature would exceed the limitations of their listeners' powers of comprehension. Yet another explanation might be that since the bulk of the materials in the *MBh.* concerning these two doctrines is contained in the *Mokṣadharmaparvan* where the spotlight is focused upon the nature of the path to enlightenment and liberation, some aspects of the doctrine of karma and rebirth were developed rather curiously to function as a springboard, so to speak, to the more elaborate articulation of the nature of the state of liberation and the most efficacious way or ways of achieving that sublime state.

It would appear that the intellectual needs of the time were fulfilled by distinguishing between two primary life-ethics: the religion of action *(pravṛtti),* which entails the punctilious performance of sacrifices and religious observances, and the religion of inaction or renunciation *(nivṛtti),* which demands the rejection of responsibilities for worldly action and a single-minded quest for liberative knowledge of the eternal, changeless *Brahman.* Those who adhere to the first discipline are promised that after death they may expect to go to the realm of the gods and enjoy pleasures that are sweet but transitory, and then return to this world by means of a more auspicious mode of existence. Those who adhere to the latter discipline would expect to become endowed with intelligence, faith, and courage, with the ultimate result that "even those who have an inauspicious birth, such as women, Vaiśyas, and Śūdras, could reach the highest goal."

3

Karma and Rebirth in the Dharmaśāstras

LUDO ROCHER

The beginning of the twelfth book of the *Manusmṛti* is explicitly devoted to "the ultimate retribution for (their = the four castes') deeds" (M 12.1) or "the decision concerning this whole connection with actions" (M 12.2).[1] This topic is, again explicitly, concluded at 12.82ab: "All the results, proceeding from actions, have been thus pointed out." Manu 12.82cd introduces a related but different topic: "those acts which secure supreme bliss to a Brāhmaṇa," which is concluded at 12.107ab: "Thus the acts which secure supreme bliss have been exactly and fully described." I shall take the first of these passages in "the most important Dharmaśāstra" as the basis for the following discussion. I shall supplement it with data from other passages in Manu and compare these with similar passages from other texts, in order to reconstruct the theory of karma and rebirth as it appears in Dharmaśāstra literature. On the other hand, I shall exclude from this study all data from later commentaries. In addition to the

1. Many citations in this article are from translations of Dharmaśāstras in *The Sacred Books of the East*. Even though these translations are often susceptible to improvement, they are, in general, reliable. Wherever I disagree with the existing translations, I shall either state so or replace them with my own. The following volumes of *SBE* will be referred to: vol. 2, Āpastamba, Gautama (Bühler); vol. 7, Viṣṇu (Jolly); vol. 14, Vasiṣṭha, Baudhāyana (Bühler); vol. 25 Manu (Bühler). These texts will be abbreviated as Āp, G, Vi, Va, B, and M, respectively, in addition to Y for Yājñavalkya.

fact that much of this literature, insofar as it relates to karma, remains unpublished, it is not possible at this point to present a balanced picture even of the printed commentaries in the field of *dharma*.

Manu 12.1–82 exhibits a strange mixture of general considerations on karma and *saṃsāra*, on the one hand, and different systems of reincarnation, on the other. One gets the impression that passages which originally belonged to a variety of sources—or were independent units—have been collected by the compiler of the *Manusmṛti* and put together in succession, often without the slightest transition. This procedure, which is not unknown elsewhere in Manu—and in other Dharmaśāstras—should be a warning to us when we try to describe *the* theory of karma and rebirth as it emerges from Dharmaśāstra literature. To be sure, there are a number of general underlying ideas and concepts. Yet these have been used to elaborate several very different systems, which are mutually independent but all equally within the range of *dharma*. I shall first describe the systems and then discuss some of the general ideas.

First System

As early as 12.3, Manu introduces a threefold origin of karma, corresponding to Yājñavalkya 3.131:

mind *(manas)*
speech *(vāc)*
body (*deha* (M) = *kāya* (Y))

"Action, which springs from the mind, from speech, and from the body." This threefold division of karma leads, both in Manu (12.5–9) and in Yājñavalkya (3.134–136), to a first system of rebirth.[2] Both texts give the same examples for the three types of karma:

Mental action:
  coveting the property of others
  thinking in one's heart of what is undesirable
  adherence to false (doctrines)

2. The five tables in this article provide the Sanskrit terminology on karma and rebirth in the Dharmaśāstras only. Translating many of the terms would require extensive notes. (Editor's note: Though Professor Rocher is of course perfectly right in his statement that one cannot accurately translate the names of many of the animals and things mentioned in these lists, one can translate *most* of them and make a guess at some of the others. For the benefit of the non-Sanskrit-reading masses, I have rushed in where Professor Rocher disdained to tread; the translations will give at least a general idea of the structure of the lists.)

Verbal action:
- abusing (others)[3]
- (speaking) untruth
- detracting from the merits of all men
- talking idly

Bodily action:
- taking what has not been given
- injuring (creatures) without the sanction of the law
- holding criminal intercourse with another man's wife

An important point in this system is that each of the three types of karma uniformly leads to a specific form of rebirth:

(sinful) mental action → a low caste
(evil) verbal action → a bird or a beast
(wicked) bodily action → something inanimate

Even though the "actions" are further subdivided into nine (Y) or ten (M), the three types of rebirth are not. (See Tables 1 and 2.)

Manu (12.10–11) concludes his description of the first system in an equally straightforward fashion: he who has full control over his mind, his speech, and his body is called a Tridaṇḍin; such an individual attains *siddhi,* "complete success," which is normally interpreted as synonymous with *mokṣa.*

Second System

Manu 12.24 introduces the three *guṇas* or inherent qualities of all matter: *sattva, rajas,* and *tamas* (goodness, passion, and darkness). After several stanzas dealing with aspects of the three *guṇas* which are less relevant for our purpose, stanza 12.39 introduces the transmigrations *(saṃsārāḥ)* resulting from them. Before doing so, the text (M 12.41) further subdivides each of the three *guṇas* into three levels, which have been used on numerous occasions in the Dharmaśāstras: "low, middling, and high." The following nine stanzas (M 12.42–50) list, within each of the nine subtypes, a number of possible forms of rebirth, starting from the low subtype of *tamas* up to the high sub-

3. This is the only significant difference between M and Y. M 12.6a has *pāruṣyam anṛtaṃ caiva* as two separate items of the—explicitly—fourfold "verbal action." Y 3.135a, which does not say that this type of karma is fourfold, has *puruṣo 'nṛtavādī ca* as one item in a threefold subdivision.

Table 1

act (*karma*)		
types	*subtypes*	*result (phalam)*
mental action	coveting the property of others	a low caste
	thinking in one's heart of what is undesirable	
	adherence to false (doctrines)	
verbal action	abusing (others)	a bird or a beast
	speaking (untruth)	
	detracting from the merits of all men	
	talking idly	
bodily action	taking what has not been given	something inanimate
	injuring (creatures) without the sanction of the law	
	committing adultery with another man's wife	

type of *sattva.* Even as in the first system, each of the principal categories leads to a specific type of rebirth:

sattva → the state of gods
rajas → the state of men
tamas → the condition of beasts

Differently from the first system, each of the nine subtypes is associated with a variety of possible rebirths, ranging from four to seven. (See Tables 3 and 4.)

Here again, Yājñavalkya (3.137–139), immediately after its discussion of the first system, has a similar passage, but without the subdivision into nine subtypes. It connects directly the characteristics of *sattva, rajas,* and *tamas*—which are very similar to the ones mentioned at Manu 12.31–33—with rebirth as a god, a human, or an animal, respectively. Also, Yājñavalkya (3.140) seems to suggest that only those who are subject to *rajas* and *tamas* enter into *saṃsāra.*

Table 2

act (karma)		
types	*subtypes*	*result (phalam)*
mānasam	paradravyeṣv abhidhyānam (M) paradravyāṇy abhidhyāyan (Y)	yāty antyajātitām (M) jāyate 'ntyāsu yoniṣu (Y)
	manasā aniṣṭacintanam (M) aniṣṭāni cintayan (Y)	
	vitathābhiniveśaḥ (M) vitathābhiniveśī (Y)	
vāṅmayam	pāruṣyam (M) [Y, see note 4]	yāti pakṣimṛgatām (M) mṛgapakṣiṣu jāyate (Y)
	anṛtam (M) puruṣo 'nṛtavādī (Y)	
	paiśunyam (M) piśunaḥ puruṣaḥ (Y)	
	asambaddhapralāpaḥ (M) anibaddhapralāpī (Y)	
śārīram	adattānām upādānam (M) adattādānanirataḥ (Y)	yāti sthāvaratām (M) sthāvareṣv abhijāyate (Y)
	hiṃsā avidhānataḥ (M) hiṃsako 'vidhānena (Y)	
	paradāropasevā (M) paradāropasevakaḥ (Y)	

Third System

The sequence Manu 12.52–58 again opens with two stanzas which might have served as an introduction to any treatment of karma and rebirth:

> In consequence of attachment to (the objects of) the senses, and in consequence of the non-performance of their duties, fools, the lowest of men, reach the vilest births.
>
> What wombs this individual soul enters in this world and in consequence of what actions—learn the particulars of that at length and in due order.

Table 3

	realm of goodness	
first	*second*	*highest*
	become gods	
Ascetics	Sacrificers	Brahmās
Mendicants	Seers	All-creators
Priests	Gods	Dharma
Hosts in Heavenly Chariots	Vedas	The Great
	Lights	The Unmanifest
Constellations	Years	
Demons	Ancestors	
	Realized ones	
	realm of passion	
low	*middle*	*high*
	become men	
Prize-fighters	Kings	Celestial musicians
Wrestlers	Nobles	Goblins
Dancers	Preceptors of kings	Spirits of fertility
Men who make their living with weapons	Those Best in Wars of Words	Followers of the Gods
		Celestial nymphs
Those addicted to gambling and drinking		
	realm of darkness	
low	*middle*	*high*
	become beasts	
Immovable (beings)	Elephants	Actors
Worms and Insects	Horses	Birds
Fish	Servants	Men who Cheat
Snakes	Despised Foreigners	Murderous Demons
Tortoises	Lions	Flesh-eating demons
Domestic Beasts	Tigers	
Wild Beasts	Boars	

Table 4

	sāttvikī gatiḥ	
prathamā	*dvitīyā*	*uttamā*
	devatvaṃ yānti	
tāpasāḥ	yajvānaḥ	brahmā
yatayaḥ	ṛṣayaḥ	viśvasṛjaḥ
viprāḥ	devāḥ	dharmaḥ
vaimānikā gaṇāḥ	vedāḥ	mahān
nakṣatrāṇi	jyotīṃṣi	avyaktaḥ
daityāḥ	vatsarāḥ	
	pitaraḥ	
	sādhyāḥ	
	rājasī gatiḥ	
jaghanyā	*madhyamā*	*uttamā*
	manuṣyatvaṃ yānti	
jhallāḥ	rājānaḥ	gandharvāḥ
mallāḥ	kṣatriyāḥ	guhyakāḥ
naṭāḥ	rājñāṃ purohitāḥ	yakṣāḥ
puruṣāḥ śastravṛttayaḥ	vādayuddhapradhānāḥ	vibudhānucarāḥ
dyūtapānaprasaktāḥ		apsarasaḥ
	tāmasī gatiḥ	
jaghanyā	*madhyamā*	*uttamā*
	tiryaktvaṃ yānti	
sthāvarāḥ	hastinaḥ	cāraṇāḥ
kṛmikīṭāḥ	turaṅgāḥ	suparṇāḥ
matsyāḥ	śūdrāḥ	puruṣā dāmbhikāḥ
sarpāḥ	mlecchā garhitāḥ	rākṣāṃsi
kacchapāḥ	siṃhāḥ	piśācāḥ
paśavaḥ	vyāghrāḥ	
mṛgāḥ	varāhāḥ	

However, what follows refers exclusively to the rebirth of "those who committed mortal sins" *(mahāpātaka)*, which have been enumerated at Manu 11.55:

killing a Brāhmaṇa
drinking (the spirituous liquor called) Surā
stealing (the gold of a Brāhmaṇa)
adultery with a Guru's wife

The rules for these four shall, logically, also apply to those "associating with such (offenders)" (M 11.55), and to those guilty of offenses which are "equal to" each of the four mortal sins (M 11.56–59).

Manu 12.54 (cf. Y 3.206) lays down the general rule: all those guilty of "mortal sins" will spend large numbers of years in dreadful hells and, at the end of that, enter into *saṃsāras*—hundreds (M 12.58), thousands (M 12.57). This rule is followed by four stanzas (M 12.55–58; cf. Y 3.207–208), listing several forms of rebirth for each mortal sin. These include mainly animals, a few low types of human beings, and especially for "the violator of a Guru's bed," plants (Tables 5 and 6).

The third system is different from the two previous ones in several respects. First, it deals with a very small and well-circumscribed number of activities. Second, for each of the four activities there is a list of possible rebirths in which humans, animals, and plants appear side by side indiscriminately. Third, a comparison between Manu and Yājñavalkya shows that, although the system as such was well established, the specific forms of rebirth were not: some forms of rebirth which both texts have in common are related to one "mortal sin" in Manu and to a different one in Yājñavalkya.[4]

Fourth System

The next set of stanzas in Manu (12.61–69) becomes even more specific; it deals, in great detail, with the rebirths of all kinds of thieves. There are corresponding passages in Yājñavalkya (3.213–215), and, even more closely, in Viṣṇu (44.14–43) (Tables 7 and 8).

Again, the system is very different from the preceding ones. First, it confirms something we also know from other sources: classical

4. Three of the "low types of human beings," *caṇḍāla, paulkasa,* and *vaiṇa,* also appear at Āp 2.1.2.5, but as rebirths for "theft and Brāhmaṇa murder" (? *steno 'bhiśastaḥ*), by a Brāhmaṇa, a Kṣatriya, and a Vaiśya, respectively.

India's preoccupation with theft; of all wrongdoings theft is, in this kind of text, invariably given the most exhaustive treatment. As a result, more than thirty types of theft are enumerated, each of them related to one single type of rebirth. Except for the fact that Yājñavalkya is less exhaustive than Manu and Viṣṇu, the three texts display a far greater uniformity than Manu and Yājñavalkya did in the preceding system. Does this mean anything for the particular relation between stealing object A and being reborn as animal B? There is no easy answer to this question. We might understand why a thief of grain will be reborn as a rat, or someone who steals meat, as a vulture. We may be able to appreciate, for very different reasons, why the thief of a cow *(go)* is reborn as an iguana *(go-dhā)*, or the thief of molasses *(guḍa)* as "a flying-fox" *(vāgguda)*. We can even imagine why a thief of drinking water is reborn as "a black-white cuckoo," for this bird is said to subsist on raindrops. But, in general, names of animals in Sanskrit are often uncertain, and so is their relation to the objects stolen.

Of the two concluding stanzas in this sequence (M 12.68–69, Vi 44.44–45), the first seems to summarize the whole section by stating that whoever steals something from someone else becomes an animal.[5] The second is interesting in that it specifically refers to the rebirth of women: women who are guilty of theft are reborn as the females of the animals listed in the preceding stanzas.

Fifth System

Finally, one sequence (M 12.70–72) approaches rebirth from the point of the specific duties of the four *varṇas*. In general, members of any *varṇa* who fall short of their specific duties, except in cases of emergency, "migrate into despicable bodies" and "will become the servants of the Dasyus." Next, more specific rules are laid down for the four *varṇas* separately:

Brāhmaṇa → Ulkāmukha Preta "who feeds on what has been vomited"
Kṣatriya → Kaṭapūtana (Preta) "who eats impure substances and corpses"
Vaiśya → Maitrākṣajyotika Preta "who feeds on pus"
Śūdra → Cailāśaka (Preta) "who feeds on moths" or "body-lice"

5. In reality, the stanza only partly refers to the subject of theft. It lists, together with the thief, "or [one] who has eaten sacrificial food (of) which (no portion) had been offered," which means that it had a different origin in a sacrificial context and was only secondarily inserted at this place.

Table 5

Mortal sinners	*Rebirth*	
	Manu	*Yājñavalkya*
Brahmin-killer	Dog Pig Donkey Camel Cow Goat Sheep Deer Bird Untouchable Mixed-birth Tribal	Deer Dog Pig Camel
Wine-drinker	Worm Insect Moth Birds that eat excrement Vicious creatures	Donkey Mixed-birth tribal Musician/Magician
Thief	Spiders Snakes Lizards Aquatic animals Vicious flesh-eating Demons	Worm Insect Moth
Defiler of the Guru's bed (wife)	grass shrub creeper carnivores beasts with fangs those doing cruel deeds	grass shrub creeper

Table 6

Mortal sinners	*Rebirth*	
	Manu	*Yājñavalkya*
brahmahā	śvā	mṛgaḥ
	sūkaraḥ	śvā
	kharaḥ	sūkaraḥ
	uṣṭraḥ	uṣṭraḥ
	gauḥ	
	ajaḥ	
	aviḥ	
	mṛgaḥ	
	pakṣī	
	caṇḍālaḥ	
	pukkasaḥ	
surāpaḥ	kṛmiḥ	kharaḥ
	kīṭaḥ	pulkasaḥ
	pataṅgaḥ	veṇaḥ
	viṅbhujaḥ pakṣiṇaḥ	
	hiṃsrāḥ sattvāḥ	
stenaḥ	lūtā	kṛmiḥ
	ahiḥ	kīṭah
	saraṭaḥ	pataṅgaḥ
	tiryañco 'mbucāriṇaḥ	
	hiṃsrāḥ piśācāḥ	
gurutalpagaḥ	tṛṇam	tṛṇam
	gulmaḥ	gulmaḥ
	latā	latā
	kravyādaḥ	
	daṃstriṇaḥ	
	krūrakarmakṛtaḥ	

The criterion for rebirth in this fifth system is the lack of performance, by any member of a *varṇa,* of the specific duties assigned to that *varṇa.* The same criterion is also applied in other texts, but in very different ways. Āpastamba (2.5.11.10–11) lays down the general rule that members of any *varṇa,* "if they have fulfilled their duties," move up one *varṇa* in each future existence; on the contrary, "if they

Table 7

Object stolen	*Rebirth*		
	Manu	*Yājñavalkya*	*Viṣṇu*
grain	rat	mouse	rat
yellow metal	goose	———	goose
water	aquatic bird	aquatic bird	water bird
honey	stinging insect	stinging insect	stinging insect
milk	crow	crow	crow
juice	dog	dog	dog
butter	ichneumon	———	ichneumon
meat	vulture		vulture
flesh		vulture	
fat	cormorant	———	
lard		———	cormorant
oil	"oil-eater" bird	———	"oil-eater" bird
salt	cricket	cricket	cricket
sour milk	crane	———	crane
silk	partridge	———	partridge
linen	frog	———	frog
cotton	heron	———	heron
cow	iguana	iguana	iguana
molasses	flying fox	———	flying fox

fine perfume	muskrat	muskrat	
perfume			muskrat
leafy vegetables	peacock	peacock	peacock
various cooked food	porcupine		
cooked food			hedgehog
uncooked food	porcupine	———	porcupine
fire	crane	crane	crane
household utensils	"house-maker" wasp	"house-maker" wasp	"house-maker" wasp
dyed cloth	francolin partridge	———	francolin partridge
deer or elephant	wolf	———	———
elephant	———	———	tortoise
horse	tiger	———	tiger
fruit and roots	monkey		
fruit		monkey	
fruit or flowers			monkey
woman	bear	———	bear
drinking water	black-white cuckoo	———	———
vehicles	camel	camel	camel
cattle	goat	———	goat (vulture)
garment	———	leper	———

Table 8

Object stolen	Rebirth		
	Manu	*Yājñavalkya*	*Viṣṇu*
dhānyam	ākhuḥ	mūṣakaḥ	ākhuḥ
kāṃsyam	haṃsaḥ	———	haṃsaḥ
jalam	plavaḥ	plavaḥ	jalābhiplavaḥ
madhu	daṃśaḥ	daṃśaḥ	daṃśaḥ
payaḥ	kākaḥ	kākaḥ	kākaḥ
rasaḥ	śvā	śvā	śvā
ghṛtam	nakulaḥ	———	nakulaḥ
māṃsam	gṛdhraḥ		gṛdhraḥ
palam		gṛdhraḥ	
vapā	madguḥ	———	
vasā		———	madguḥ
tailam	tailapakaḥ khagaḥ	———	tailapāyikaḥ
lavaṇam	cīrīvākaḥ	cīrī	cīrivāk
dadhi	balākā śakuniḥ	———	ba lākā
kauśeyam	tittiriḥ	———	tittiriḥ
kṣaumam	darduraḥ	———	darduraḥ
karpāsatāntavam	krauñcaḥ	———	krauñcaḥ
gauḥ	godhā	godhā	godhā
guḍaḥ	vāggudaḥ	———	vālgudaḥ

śubhā gandhāḥ	chucchundariḥ	chucchundarī	
gandhāḥ			chucchundariḥ
patraśākaḥ	barhiṇaḥ	śikhī	barhī
kṛtānnaṃ vividham	śvāvit	———	
kṛtānnam		———	sedhā
akṛtānnam	śalyakaḥ	———	śalyakaḥ
agniḥ	bakaḥ	bakaḥ	bakaḥ
upaskaraḥ	gṛhakārī	gṛhakārī	gṛhakārī
raktāni vāsāṃsi	jīvajīvakaḥ	———	jīvajīvakaḥ
mṛgebhaḥ	vṛkaḥ	———	———
gajaḥ	———	———	kūrmaḥ
aśvaḥ	vyāghraḥ	———	vyāghraḥ
phalamūlam	markaṭaḥ		
phalam		kapiḥ	
phalaṃ puṣpaṃ vā			markaṭaḥ
strī	ṛkṣaḥ	———	ṛkṣaḥ
vāri	stokakaḥ	———	———
yānāni	uṣṭraḥ	uṣṭraḥ	uṣṭraḥ
paśavaḥ	ajaḥ	———	ajaḥ (gṛdhraḥ)
vastram	———	śvitrī	———

neglect their duties," they are each time reborn in the next lower *varṇa*. It is worth noticing that these two *sūtras* have no connection whatever with the context in which they occur. They obviously represent nothing more than floating aphorisms of a very general nature, which fail to inform us, for instance, what happens upward after the Brāhmaṇa or downward after the Śūdra.

Miscellaneous Rules

In addition to the five systems described so far, Manu—and other *dharma* texts—exhibit a number of isolated rules on karma and rebirth. Some of these rules are inserted in the sections on karma and rebirth generally; others appear in very different contexts.

For instance, in between Manu's third and fourth systems there are two stanzas (M 12.59–60) which not only have nothing in common with the surrounding systems, but also have no connection whatever with each other. The first stanza enumerates four activities and four resulting forms of rebirth:

men who delight in doing hurt → carnivorous (animals)
those who eat forbidden food → worms
thieves → creatures consuming their own kind
those who have intercourse with women of the lowest castes → Pretas

The second stanza (cf. Y 3.212) is structured differently, listing three activities leading to the same result:

he who is associated with outcastes he who has approached the wives of other men he who has stolen the property of a Brāhmaṇa	→ Brahmarākṣasas

In the eleventh book Manu inserts, without any introduction, the following three stanzas on rebirth (M 11.24–26; cf. Y 1.127, Vi 59.11):

A Brāhmaṇa who begs from a Śūdra for a sacrifice	→	a Caṇḍāla
A Brāhmaṇa who, having begged any property for a sacrifice, does not use the whole (for that purpose)	→	for a hundred years a (vulture of the kind called) Bhāsa, or a crow

That sinful man, who, through covetousness, seizes the property of the gods, or the property of Brāhmaṇas	→	feeds . . . on the leavings of vultures

In the passage in Manu that deals with the duties of women, three stanzas (M 5.164–166) refer to their rebirth; the first two appear, identically but in reversed order, in the "legal" section on the duties of husband and wife (M 9.29–30). One stanza (M 5.164 = 9.30; cf. Va 21.14) is devoted to the fate of the unfaithful wife: she is "disgraced in this world, (after death) she enters the womb of a jackal, and is tormented by diseases, (the punishment for) her sins." Two stanzas (M 5.165 = 9.29, and 5.166) deal with the faithful wife "who controls her thoughts, speech, and body"—a formula reminiscent of the first system. Such a wife, besides gaining renown in this world, obtains "in the next (world) a place near her husband." This sequence, which forms a mini-system of its own, clearly illustrates the nature of Dharmaśāstra rules on rebirth—and on many other subjects. The stress in this case is definitely on the need for wives to be faithful to their husbands. Hence the opposition:

unfaithful wife → jackal
faithful wife → the world of (her) husband

The question whether the husband himself has lived the best of lives, and, therefore, whether he himself will move on to the best of worlds, is totally irrelevant. A similar stanza in Yājñavalkya (1.87) indicates the true meaning of Manu's "world of the husband"; it holds out, for the faithful wife, "the best possible destination."[6] Other isolated rules may very well have been part of similar mini-systems.

Theoretical Considerations

One cannot help being struck by the fact that, in the Dharmaśāstras, the construction and description of various systems outweigh by far the attention given to theoretical considerations and analyzing the technique of karma and rebirth.

6. Va 21.11 threatens with non-access to the *patiloka* "that woman of the Brāhmana caste who drinks spirituous liquor"; she will, instead, be "born again as a leech or a pearl-oyster."

The basic statement appears at the outset of Manu's twelfth book (M 12.3): *śubhāśubhaphalaṃ karma.* Bühler's translation: "Action . . . produces good or bad results," is misleading; the real meaning of the Sanskrit text is that actions produce "more or less" favorable results, that is, the entire gamut from very favorable to very unfavorable. Yet, the principal fact is that "action produces results."

There is no doubt that, for the typical Dharmaśāstra, the results of "sinful acts" are varied and complex. Manu (12.74–80)[7] lists them in the following order:

pain here (below) in various births
(the torture of) being tossed about in dreadful hells, Tāmisra and the rest
(that of) the forest with sword-leaved trees and the like
(that of) being bound and mangled
various torments
the (pain of) being devoured by ravens and owls
the heat of scorching sand
the (torture of) being boiled in jars, which is hard to bear
births in the wombs (of) despicable (beings) which cause constant misery
afflictions from cold and heat
terrors of various kinds
the (pain of) repeatedly lying in various wombs
agonizing births
imprisonment in fetters hard to bear
the misery of being enslaved by others
separations from their relatives and dear ones
the (pain of) dwelling together with the wicked
(labor in) gaining wealth and its loss
(trouble in) making friends and (the appearance of) enemies
old age against which there is no remedy
the pangs of diseases
afflictions of many various kinds
and (finally) unconquerable death

Although rebirth, therefore, has to be viewed within a much larger framework, there is no doubt that, for the compilers of the Dharmaśāstras, it ranked as the first and most important result of action. After the long enumeration of possible consequences of "sinful acts," Manu's conclusion (M 12.81; cf. Y 3.131–132) refers to rebirth and rebirth only:

But with whatever disposition of mind (a man) performs any act, he reaps its result in a (future) body endowed with the same quality.

7. For a similar enumeration, see M 6.61–64.

Manu (12.3) also immediately introduces another concept: *karmajā gatayo nṝṇām,* which means that a man's actions determine his *gati*—in the plural. Bühler translates: "the (various) conditions." But it is clear from several contexts in which the term occurs that *gati* has to be taken far more literally: "going, going away." Yājñavalkya 3,131, which also corresponds with Manu 12.3 in other respects, makes this even more explicit by using the verbal form *prayāti* "goes forth."

The texts give only the most elementary indications on what exactly "goes forth." Manu 12.3 merely refers to "men," and so does Manu 6.61. Elsewhere the subject of "going" is "the inner self" *(antarātman)* (M 6.73) or "the individual soul" *(jīva)* (M 12.23, Y 3.131).

Āpastamba (2.1.2.2) and Gautama (11.29–30) exhibit an interesting parallel passage on the nature of *gati,* even though they do not use the term. When a man who has duly fulfilled his own *dharma* dies, according to Āpastamba, he enjoys "supreme, unlimited happiness"; according to Gautama, "he experiences the results of his actions." Afterwards—both texts explicitly say *tataḥ*—"on his return" (Āp: *parivṛttau*), he takes birth again under the best of circumstances—good family, beauty, wisdom, and so forth. Those who have not fulfilled their own *dharma* undergo a similar fate, but in the opposite direction.

Āpastamba compares the individual's movement from this world to a world of supreme happiness—or unhappiness—and back to this world, to a wheel (*cakravat; parivṛtti* also involves the idea of rolling). Although Āpastamba does not use the word *saṃsāra,* his text reminds us of Manu 12.124: the supreme being makes all created beings "revolve like the wheels (of a chariot)" *(saṃsārayati cakravat).*

Important in both texts is the statement that rebirth occurs, after the intermediate period in which "he enjoys happiness"—or its opposite—or in which "he experiences the results of his actions," *śeṣeṇa* (G) or *karmaphalaśeṣeṇa* (Āp). Bühler translates: "by virtue of a remnant of their (merit)" (G), and "by virtue of a remainder of merit" (Āp). These translations are acceptable only with the proviso that "remnant" and "remainder" not be understood to mean mere unimportant and incidental additions to that which they are the "remnant" or "remainder" of. The term *śeṣa* in Sanskrit always indicates an important and necessary complement to something which, without it, would remain incomplete and imperfect. Hence rebirth takes place "by way of a necessary supplement to the result of actions," or "in order to bring the result of actions to completion."

The passages from Āpastamba and Gautama are exceptional in that they actually describe the results of "good action," and, subsequently, conclude with a brief note: "from this you can also gather what happens to bad action." In most cases attention is paid primarily—often uniquely—to a person's *gati* as a result of "bad action" *(karmadoṣa)*. This is obvious not only from most types of rebirth within the various systems described earlier, but also from the fact that the texts deal far more elaborately with the intervening "world of unhappiness" than they do with the "world of supreme happiness." Hells and suffering in hell are very prominent in Dharmaśāstra literature. Besides numerous shorter references in other texts, the most detailed treatment is exhibited by Viṣṇu. This text devotes an entire chapter (43) to the enumeration of twenty-one hells, to the periods of time to be spent there—one *kalpa*, one *manvantara*, one *caturyuga*, one thousand years, "a great many years"—and, finally, to a most graphic description of terrible pains and suffering.

The most revealing theoretical statement on the technique of transmigration is probably contained in Manu 12.12–23. Unfortunately, the text as we have it is susceptible to very different interpretations; the various explanations by the Sanskrit commentators are reflected in Bühler's unusually lengthy notes. The text clearly describes *ātman* or *bhūtātman* as the author of actions; the instigator of *ātman* is called *kṣetrajña*.[8] It also introduces, separately, *jīva* "through which (the *kṣetrajña*) becomes sensible of all pleasure and pain in (successive) births"; as was indicated earlier, this passage is one of those that attributes *gati*—in the plural—to *jīva*. Another concept which is clearly expressed is that, after death, another "strong body" is produced, "formed of particles (of the) five (elements)"; it is this body that is "destined to suffer the torments (in hell)," after which it is again dissolved into its elements. Any further interpretation at this point is likely to do injustice to the text.

We have seen earlier that, as a rule, action produces a result. In most cases this result is—upward or downward—*saṃsāra* or *saṃ-*

8. *Bhūtātmā = yaḥ karoti karmāṇi; kṣetrajñaḥ = yo 'syātmanaḥ kārayitā.* Compare M 12.119cd: *ātmā hi janayaty eṣāṃ karmayogaṃ śarīriṇām* "for the Self produces the connection of these embodied (spirits) with actions."

sāras, for, like *gati,* this term is often used in the plural. There are, however, exceptions, such as the Tridaṇḍin, who has been referred to in the context of the first system. The distinction is made at a more general level at Manu 6.74, in connection with the ascetic:

He who possesses true insight (into the nature of the world), is not fettered by his deeds; but he who is destitute of that insight, is drawn into the circle of births and deaths.

In other words, the distinction is between "being tied down by actions" and its opposite, which is not mentioned here, "being set free by actions."

The criterion for reaching the latter state is true insight. Thus, the ascetic is able (M 6.73), "by the practice of meditation," "to gain true insight"[9] in the *gati* of the Inner Self *(antarātman).*

The text adds (M 6.75) that ascetics can reach that level even during their lifetime:

By not injuring any creatures, by detaching the senses (from objects of enjoyment), by the rites prescribed in the Veda, and by rigorously practising austerities, (men) gain that state (even) in this (world).

But, conversely, the state of being "released while still alive" *(jīvanmukta*—the text uses the term *mukta*) can again be lost (M 6.58):

Let him disdain all (food) obtained in consequence of humble salutations, (for) even an ascetic who has attained final liberation, is bound (with the fetters of the *saṃsāra*) by accepting (food given) in consequence of humble salutations.

The idea expressed at Manu 6.73–74 returns in the second section of the twelfth book (M 12.82–107), which, for Brāhmaṇas only, examines "those acts which secure supreme bliss." The list of these activities (M 12.83; cf. Y 3.190) comes very close to that of the sixth book:

Studying the Veda, (practising) austerities, (the acquisition of true) knowledge, the subjugation of the organs, abstention from doing injury, and serving the Guru are the best means for attaining supreme bliss.

Two of these are then singled out as superior to the others and, in fact, encompassing them all: "knowledge of the soul" and "(the per-

9. There is no doubt a connection between *sam-paśyet* at M 6.73, and *samyagdarśana°*at M 6.74; the preverb *sam°* is often interpreted as synonymous with the adverb *samyak.*

formance of) the acts taught in the Veda." The remainder of the section is primarily devoted to praising the Veda. Yet there are a few elements in it that touch on the subject of rebirth. The text (M 12.88–90) distinguishes two types of acts taught in the Veda:

1. *pravṛttaṃ karma,* "acts which secure (the fulfillment of) wishes in this world or in the next," and

2. *nivrttam karma,* "acts performed without any desire (for a reward), preceded by (the acquisition) of (true) knowledge."

The difference is that he who performs *pravṛttaṃ karma* "becomes equal to the gods," whereas he who performs *nivṛttaṃ karma* "passes beyond (the reach of) the five elements." Although the term is not used here, the tradition unanimously equates this state with *mokṣa.*

Irrespective of whether a person is "tied down" in *saṃsāra* or "set free" from it, in all cases discussed so far his fate is the result of his actions. I shall conclude this article by discussing a few situations in which the correlation "action → result" seems either to have been denied, or to have become the object of some theoretical discussion.

In the first place, certain activities have explicitly been labeled "without result." Thus, whereas the fifth system above lays down specific results for members of a *varṇa* who deviate from the duties of their *varṇa,* a short sequence in Manu (11.28–30) deals in a very different way with the fate of those who live, in normal times, according to the duties that shall apply to their *varṇa* in times of distress only.

> But a twice-born, who, without being in distress, performs his duties according to the law for times of distress, obtains no reward for them in the next world; that is the opinion (of the sages).
>
> By the Viśve-devas, by the Sādhyas, and by the great sages (of the) Brāhmaṇa (caste), who were afraid of perishing in times of distress, a substitute was made for the (principal) rule.
>
> That evil-minded man, who, being able (to fulfill) the original law, lives according to the secondary rule, reaps no reward for that after death.

Similarly, whereas the performance of the two types of Vedic action *(vaidikaṃ karma)* produces the most excellent results, performance of what might be called non-Vedic action (*avaidikaṃ karma*—a term not used in the text) produces, according to Manu 12.95, no result at all.

> All those traditions and all those despicable systems of philosophy, which are not based on the Veda, produce no reward after death; for they are declared to be founded on Darkness.

Bühler's "reward" (M 11.28,30) translates Sanskrit *phalam,* and "produce no reward" (M 12.95) renders Sanskrit *niṣphalāḥ.* It is only normal that living by the wrong set of duties, or according to non-Vedic prescriptions, should not produce a "reward." What is more surprising is that the text actually denies such acts a "result."

In the second place, it is possible for individuals—exceptional individuals!—to counteract and eliminate, during their lifetime, the results of actions. One who knows the Veda is such a person. According to a simile used by Manu (12.101), he "burns down" the evil results of action.

> As a fire that has gained strength consumes even trees full of sap, even so he who knows the Veda burns out the taint of his soul which arises from (evil) acts.

It comes as no surprise that such an idea was widespread in Dharmaśāstra circles. Vasiṣṭha (27.2) has an identical stanza, except that he replaces "he who knows the Veda" *(vedajñaḥ)* by "the fire of the Veda" *(vedāgniḥ).* And "the fire of the Veda," or "the fire of knowledge" (M 11.247: *jñānāgninā)* also occurs elsewhere as the destroyer of the results of one's—sinful—actions.

The idea of "burning down" the results of actions during one's lifetime leads me to a final problem, which appears to have been of concern to the compilers of Dharmaśāstras: the relation between karma and rebirth on the one hand, and the performance of penances or expiations *(prāyaścitta)* on the other. The problem is raised in a passage which appears quasi-identically in three *dharmasūtras:* Gautama (19.2–6), Vasiṣṭha (22.1–5), and Baudhāyana (3.10.2–5). This is Gautama's text:

> Now indeed, man (in) this (world) is polluted by a vile action, such as sacrificing for men unworthy to offer a sacrifice, eating forbidden food, speaking what ought not to be spoken, neglecting what is prescribed, practising what is forbidden.
>
> They are in doubt if he shall perform a penance for such (a deed) or if he shall not do it. (Some) declare that he shall not do it, because the deed does not perish.
>
> The most excellent (opinion is), that he shall perform (a penance).

In other words, the question was disputed whether expiation was at all a worthwhile enterprise, for, according to one opinion, "action does not pass, waste away, perish," understood: in this lifetime.

To be sure, the protagonists of penance prevailed: there are numerous texts stating that the sin incurred by such or such action is cleared by such or such penance. But the ambivalence remained, as in Yājñavalkya (3.133):

Some actions ripen *(vipāka)* after death, others ripen in this world, others again either here or there; the deciding factor is the disposition *(bhāva).*

Hence conflicting texts and, within the same texts, differing views, on whether to limit penance to sins committed unintentionally. For instance, according to Manu (11.45):

(All) sages prescribe a penance for a sin unintentionally committed; some declare, on the evidence of the revealed texts, (that it may be performed) even for an intentional (offence).

More important for our present purpose is another type of uncertainty in the texts, namely with regard to a long list of physical deficiencies which are believed to be the results of wrongdoings. Manu (11.48) states the problem as follows:

Some wicked men suffer a change of their (natural) appearance in consequence of crimes committed in this life, and some in consequence of those committed in a former (existence).

The whole passage is obviously meant to exhort people to undergo the required penances immediately. Compare Manu's concluding stanzas (M 11.53–54):

Thus in consequence of a remnant[10] of (the guilt of former) crimes, are born idiots, dumb, blind, deaf, and deformed men, who are (all) despised by the virtuous.

Penances, therefore, must always be performed for the sake of purification, because those whose sins have not been expiated, are born (again) with disgraceful marks.

The intervening four stanzas (M 11.49–52) exhibit sixteen specific cases of physical consequences of wrongdoings—according to the introductory stanza: in this life or in the preceding one. It is worth noticing that the first four offenses (M 11.49) are the four "mortal sins" *(mahāpātaka)* the rebirths for which are dealt with in Manu's twelfth book—and the third system above—and which will only be introduced at Manu 11.55, after the sequence we are now dealing with. The corresponding stanza in Yājñavalkya (3.209), on the other hand, is an integral part of its sequence (Y 3.206–208) on the rebirths

10. Bühler opts for the reading °*avaśeṣeṇa,* rather than °*viśeṣeṇa.* Either one is a variant, metri causa, for °*śeṣeṇa.*

of "mortal sinners." Vasiṣṭha (20.43–44) definitely relates the illnesses to "mortal sins" committed in a previous existence:

> Now they quote also (the following verses): "Hear, (how) the bodies of those who having committed various crimes died a long time ago, and were (afterwards) born again, are (marked)"; "A thief will have deformed nails, the murderer of a Brāhmaṇa will be afflicted with white leprosy, but he who has drunk spirituous liquor will have black teeth, and the violator of his Guru's bed will suffer from skin diseases."

Viṣṇu (45.1) also leaves no doubt that the physical defects for "mortal sinners"—and many others—obtain in future existences only. This text even establishes a time sequence for passage through hells, rebirths in animal form described in its chapter 44—see the fourth system above—and subsequent rebirths in human form:

> Now after having undergone the torments inflicted in the hells, and having passed through the animal bodies, the sinners are born as human beings with (the following) marks (indicating their crime).

But even then the chapter concludes with two stanzas (Vi 45.32–33) very similar to Manu 11.52–53, exhorting people that "penances must be performed by all means."

The detailed list of offenses and resulting illnesses (M 11.49–52, Y 3.209–211, Vi 45.2–31; see Tables 9 and 10) contains at least a kernel that must have been widely accepted by the Hindu tradition. In many ways it is similar to the lists of rebirths in animal form in Table 7. For an unknown reason this type of "results of actions" was closely associated with exhortations to perform penances, so much so that at least one Dharmaśāstra, Manu, transferred it to its chapter on expiation. But everything seems to indicate that, in reality, we are dealing with yet another "system" of karma and rebirth.

Table 9

	Deficiency		
Offender	*Manu*	*Yajñavalkya*	*Viṣṇu*
transgressor	———	———	leprosy
gold-thief	diseased nails		
gold-thief		bad nails	bad nails
gold-thief			
wine-drinker	black teeth	black teeth	black teeth
Brahmin-killer	consumption	consumption	consumption
guru-wife-seducer	diseased skin	diseased skin	diseased skin
informer	foul-smelling nose	foul-smelling nose	foul-smelling nose
calumniator	foul-smelling breath	foul-smelling breath	foul-smelling breath
thief of grain	limb-deficiency	———	limb-deficiency
adulterator	limb-superfluity		
grain adulterator		limb superfluity	
grain adulterator/ thief			limb-superfluity
thief of cooked food	dyspepsia	dyspepsia	dyspepsia
thief of the word (Veda)	dumbness	dumbness	dumbness
garment-thief	white leprosy		white leprosy
horse-thief	lameness	———	lameness
reviler of gods and Brahmins	———	———	dumbness
poisoner	———	———	rolling tongue

arsonist	———	———	madness
offender of guru	———	———	epilepsy
cow-slayer	———	———	blindness
lamp-thief	blindness	———	blindness
extinguisher	one eye	———	
lamp-extinguisher		———	one eye
injurer	general disease	———	———
non-injurer	freedom from disease	———	———
oil-thief	———	oil-drinking	———
seller of tin, yak-tail, & lead	———	———	washerman
seller of whole-hoofed (animals)	———	———	hunter
one supported by son of adulterous woman	———	———	fellatio (his mouth used as vulva)
thief	———	———	bell-ringer
usurer	———	———	vertigo
solitary eater of sweets	———	———	rheumatism
promise-breaker	———	———	severe cough
semen-spiller (chastity-vow-violator)	———	———	elephantiasis
ruiner of another's livelihood	———	———	poverty
oppressor	———	———	long illness

Table 10

Offender	*Deficiency*		
	Manu	*Yājñavalkya*	*Viṣṇu*
atipātakī	———	———	kuṣṭhī
suvarṇacauraḥ	kaunakhyam		
hemahārī		kunakhī	
suvarṇahārī			kunakhī
surāpaḥ	śyāvadantatā	śyāvadantakaḥ	śyāvadantakaḥ
brahmahā	kṣayarogitvam	kṣayarogī	yakṣmī
gurutalpagaḥ	dauścarmyam	duścarmā	duścarmā
piśunaḥ	pautināsikyam	pūtināsikaḥ	pūtināsaḥ
sūcakaḥ	pūtivaktratā	pūtivaktraḥ	pūtivaktraḥ
dhānyacauraḥ	aṅgahīnatvam	———	aṅgahīnaḥ
miśrakaḥ	ātiraikyam		
dhānyamiśraḥ		atiriktāṅgaḥ	
miśracoraḥ			atiriktāṅgaḥ
annahartā	amayāvitam	amayāvī	
annāpahārakaḥ			amayāvī
vāgapahārakaḥ	maukyam	mūkaḥ	mūkaḥ
vastrāpahārakaḥ	śvaitryam	———	śvitrī
aśvahārakaḥ	paṅgutā	———	paṅguḥ
devabrāhmaṇā-krośakaḥ	———	———	mūkaḥ

garadaḥ	———	———	lolajihvaḥ
agnidaḥ	———	———	unmattaḥ
guroḥ pratikūlaḥ	———	———	apasmārī
goghnaḥ	———	———	andhaḥ
dīpahartā	andhaḥ	———	
dīpāpahārakaḥ		———	andhaḥ
nirvāpakaḥ	kāṇaḥ	———	
dīpanirvāpakaḥ		———	kāṇaḥ
hiṃsā	vyādhibhūyastvam	———	———
ahiṃsā	arogitvam	———	———
tailahṛt	———	tailapāyī	———
trapucāmara-sīsakavikrayī	———	———	rajakaḥ
ekaśaphavikrayī	———	———	mṛgavyādhaḥ
kuṇḍāśī	———	———	bhagāsyaḥ
stenaḥ	———	———	ghāṇṭikaḥ
vārdhuṣikaḥ	———	———	bhrāmarī
mṛṣṭāśy ekākī	———	———	vātagulmī
samayabhettā	———	———	khalvāṭaḥ
avakīrṇaḥ	———	———	ślīpadī
paravṛttighnaḥ	———	———	daridraḥ
parapīḍākaraḥ	———	———	dīrgharogī

4

Caraka Saṃhitā on the Doctrine of Karma

MITCHELL G. WEISS

The study of karma in the traditional Indian medical system, Āyurveda, shows how conflict between fatalistic aspects of an indigenous traditional concept must be reconciled with a practical system which necessarily assumes that the course of many human ills is not predetermined. Consequently, *Caraka Saṃhitā (Car.)* must cope with those aspects of the karma doctrine conflicting with preeminent claims of medical efficacy. *Car.* deals with karma in the context of two issues: as it relates to embryology and as it relates to the etiology of various diseases. To some extent each assumes a need for medical interventions, and the flavor of the karma doctrine advanced in *Car.* reflects that situation accordingly. Where interventions are not required, as in the explanation of the coming together of semen, blood, and the other components at the moment of conception, substantial alterations of the traditional concepts are not required. Here they are adequate, even useful, and *Car.* refers to them. Where interventions are suggested, including procedures to bring about the birth of a healthy male child or to restore a sick patient to health, these traditional ideas about karma lead to contradictions, and the adjustments made by *Car.* will be discussed.

As in the Purāṇas and elsewhere, karma and fate *(daiva)* are equated and used interchangeably. These are contrasted with actions in the present life *(puruṣakāra)*.

Fate is to be regarded as self-inflicted,
an action *(karman)* of a prior incarnation;
There is also a person's action
that he does here.[1]

Precedence by one or the other depends upon their relative strength.

Actions are either powerful, lacking power,
or both;
Thus, three types of karma are observed:
base, moderate, or superior.[2]

Weak fate is impeded
by individual action,
On the other hand, one's action
is impeded by preeminent fate.[3]

Karma is defined as an action requiring some effort,[4] and both karma and quality *(guṇa)* are inherently related to substance *(dravya)*, in which they abide.[5] Karma is required for all associations and separations, and causality stands as a fundamental precept. Causality serves as a rationale for the karma doctrine[6] and explains seemingly unexplainable situations. The principle of causality also implicitly establishes the validity of the empirical context on which the clinical practice of medicine is based.

1. *Car.*3.3.30; see also *Car.*4.2.44. *Caraka Saṃhitā of Agniveśa with the Ayurveda-Dīpikā Commentary of Cakrapāṇidatta*, ed. by Gaṅgāsahāya Pandeya in 2 vols., Kashi Sanskrit Series, no. 194 (Varanasi: Chowkhamba, 1969). *The Caraka Saṃhitā*, 6 vols., Sanskrit text with introduction and translations into Hindi, Gujarati, and English by Shree Gulabkunverba, Ayurvedic Society (Jamnagar: Gulabkunverba, 1949).
2. *Car.* 3.3.31.
3. *Car.* 3.3.33½–4.
4. *Car.* 1.1.49–56.
5. This emphasis on action, either in a past or the present life, and the rigid insistence that everything must proceed from a cause (q.v. *Car.* 2.8.41, 4.3.24) is consistent with the Nyāya-Vaiśeṣika metaphysics adopted by *Car.* at the outset. Concepts from all of the orthodox Indian philosophical systems, however, are represented in *Car.* at some point and in varying degrees of fidelity with the sources of their own traditions. Dasgupta feels that the arguments on logic in *Car.* predate and foreshadow formalized Nyāya (Dasgupta: 373–392). The term *karman* is dealt with first in an elaboration of cause *(kāraṇa)* in the Nyāya-Vaiśeṣika context. See Surendranath Dasgupta, "Speculations in the Medical Schools," ch. 13, vol. 2, pp. 273–436 in *History of Indian Philosophy*, in 5 vols. (Cambridge University Press, 1932); see also I: 213–217.
6. Cf. *Karma-māhātmya-kathanam* in which "karma is the cause of everything" (*Padma Purāṇa* 2.94), cited by Wendy O'Flaherty in this volume.

The essential conflict between the deterministic implications of the karma doctrine and the need to act, though especially salient in the medical context, has also been addressed elsewhere. Despite the implications of fatalism of karma in the Purāṇas, Dharmaśāstras, philosophical texts, and story literature, numerous means by which it may be circumvented are included, and they are often central. Wendy O' Flaherty refers to a didactic aspect of the Purāṇas which preaches, "If you decide 'What is to be, will be,' then the medical books are in vain, and all the sacred recitations and all effort is in vain."[7] And "Lazy men and those who depend upon fate never obtain their goals."[8] This view, that since fate cannot be fathomed all effort is invested in human activity, is tacitly incorporated as a basic premise in *Car.* The relationship between the passive aspect of karma (i.e., *daiva)* and the active, the deed one performs, is not explicit, although there is a sense that the latter can prevail. The use of *karman* in the active sense as a remedy is routine in the medical texts. Reference to the passive sense usually specifies the *result, fruit,* or *time* of maturation of karma, employing the genitive inflection of *karman.*[9]

The means of overcoming the effects of karma advanced in the Purāṇas, Dharmaśāstras, and the rest, namely, gifts to Brahmins, Yoga practice, pilgrimage, and so forth, have their analogues in Āyurveda. The treatment of many disorders includes *bali* sacrifices and other ritual observances in such detail as to resemble passages from Dharmaśāstra, especially for disorders attributed to exogenous *(āgantu)* factors which are less susceptible to physiological interventions.[10] As a principle it is maintained:

> Thought, word, and deed *(karman)* properly bound,
> clear-headed with sparkling judgment,
> Intent in his practice of austerities and knowledge—
> diseases do not befall such a man as this.[11]

Other passages explain the onset of specific disorders as the result of inauspicious karma.

7. *Garuḍa Purāṇa, Uttara Khaṇḍa* 2.2.2–5, q.v. Wendy O'Flaherty's discussion of "Karma and Fate" and "The Conquest of Karma," loc. cit.
8. *Matsya Purāṇa* 221.1–12, q.v. Wendy O'Flaherty, ibid.
9. See Cakrapāṇidatta's *Āyurveda-Dīpikā* commentary (in Chowkhamba edition of *Car.*) on *Car.* 4.1.98.
10. E.g., to treat insanity *(unmāda)* associated with demons *(bhūta); Suśruta Saṃhitā (Su.)* 6.60.32–37, and *Car.* 6.9.33–34.
11. *Car.* 4.2.47.

Exogenous insanity *(unmāda)* is caused by the assault of
Gods, Seers, Gandharvas, Piśācas, Yakṣas, Rākṣasas,
and Pitṛs;
And it is the result of improperly executed religious
vows and promises, and so forth, or karma in a previous life.[12]

Suśruta Saṃhita (Su.) is more reluctant to cite karma as an etiologic factor. *Su.* 1.24 is a chapter providing a detailed etiologic schema.[13] It contains many ideas also found in *Car.*, but some that are not; and it lacks some that occur in *Car. Car.* has no such chapter devoted exclusively to etiology and does not include such detail; *Su.*, however, does not include karma. A category of supernormal factors, *daivabalapravṛtta*, refers to curses, spells, and demonic wrath, and so forth, on the one hand, and lightning and natural disasters, and so forth, on the other.[14] *Daiva* here is more directly related to the Devas in contrast to *Car.*, where *daiva* is often synonymous with karma. This and the emphasis on surgical procedures characteristic of the Dhanvantari tradition represented in *Su.* distinguish it from the other early texts in the mainstream of Āyurveda, the remaining two of the so-called great three *(bṛhattrayī)*, namely, *Car.* and Vāgbhaṭa's *Aṣṭāṅgahṛdaya Saṃhitā (AHr.)*.

According to the tradition delineated in *Car.* 1.1, Indra was requested by a group of seers to deliver the medical doctrine to their representative, Bharadvāja, who then taught it to the other seers, among them Ātreya Punarvasu. Ātreya trained six disciples, including Agniveśa, Bhela, and four others. Agniveśa was the principal among these and the first to compose an instructional text to preserve the doctrine of Ātreya. Colophons of *Car.* and 6.30.289–90 indicate that the composition of Agniveśa was called the *Agniveśa Tantra* and that it was reconstructed by Caraka. Part of Caraka's revision was lost or never completed, and Dṛḍhabala completed the adumbrated version, finishing the last two of eight books and seventeen chapters of the sixth book. Dṛḍhabala may also have worked on other chapters

12. *Car.* 6.9.16; cf. *Car.* 2.7.19–20, and *Aṣṭāṅgahṛdaya Saṃhitā (AHr.)* 6.4.6.
13. Mitchell Weiss, *Critical Study of Unmāda in the Early Sanskrit Medical Literature*, Ph.D. Diss., University of Pennsylvania, 1977, p. 62. The *Suśruta Saṃhitā of Suśruta*, edited by Nārāyaṇ Rām Āchārya (Bombay: Nirṇaya Sāgara, 1945); *English Translation of The Sushruta Samhita Based on Original Sanskrit Text*, 3 vols., Chowkhamba Sanskrit Studies, vol. 30 (2nd ed.; Varanasi: Chowkhamba, 1963). The translation frequently incorporates material from Dalhana's commentary without notice and is otherwise unreliable.
14. *Su.* 1.24.7.

as well, and the question of whether he did, and if so, on which chapters remains problematic. The organization of *Car.* at the time of Dṛḍhabala is also uncertain, and so the matter of which seventeen chapters of the sixth book are indeed the last seventeen is unsettled. The date of composition and revision by Caraka is estimated to fall within the first 300 years A.D. and the revision by Dṛḍhabala at approximately A.D. 500.[15] It should be noted that whereas *Su.* is generally considered to be essentially the composition of its namesake, Caraka is believed to be the reviser rather than author of the work bearing his name. In large measure *Car.* contains the pronouncements of Ātreya frequently offered in response to questions posed by Agniveśa and the other disciples, and sometimes in response to challenges made by a Bharadvāja, not Ātreya's teacher, and others.[16] In addition to elaborations of the Ātreya doctrine by a later author(s), one finds verses, some of which may be surviving the *Agniveśa Tantra.* An adequate elucidation of the relationship of *Car.*'s component sources as they contribute to the text requires further study.

Predetermined Life Span

Dasgupta has commented on *Car.*'s facility in dealing with conflict between an immutable karma doctrine and medical efficacy.

> [Nowhere else] do we find the sort of common-sense eclecticism that we find in Caraka. For here it is only the fruits of extremely bad actions that cannot be arrested by the normal efforts of good conduct. The fruits of all ordinary actions can be arrested by normal physical ways of well-balanced conduct, the administration of proper medicines and the like. This implies that our ordinary non-moral actions in the proper care of health, taking proper tonics, medicines and the like, can modify or arrest the ordinary

15. Reasons for assigning this date and discussion of status of the controversies surrounding Dṛdhabala's contribution to *Car.* in G. J. Meulenbeld, *The Mādhavanidāna and Its Chief Commentary: Chapters 1–10, Introduction, Translation, and Notes,* Ed. & Trans. (Leiden: Brill, 1974), pp. 410–413; see also pp. 403–406. The Gulabkunverba edition of *Car.* (1949) claims to have settled the issue of determining Dṛdhabala's contribution, vol. I, pp. 96–106. See also Julius Jolly, *Medicin,* Bd. 3, H. 10, Grundriss der Indoarischen Philologie und Altertumskunde, translated by C. G. Kashikar, *Indian Medicine* (Poona: Kashikar, 1951).

16. E.g., *Car.* 4.3.15. N.b. *Car.* 1.26.8 in which a group of contemporaries of Ātreya dispute the number of *rasas.* It is unlikely that the Bharadvāja participating in these dialogues in the text could be identified as the Bharadvāja held to have delivered the corpus of Āyurveda to Ātreya in *Car.* 1.1.19–27 after receiving it from Indra. Bharadvāja Kumāraśīra is specified in *Car.* 1.26.4. See Gulabkunverba's discussion, vol. I, pp. 40–44.

course of the fruition of our karma. Thus, according to the effects of my ordinary karma I may have fallen ill; but, if I take due care, I may avoid such effects and may still be in good health. According to other theories the laws of karma are immutable.[17]

By shifting the emphasis of etiology from previous lives to the present, *Car.* effectively redefines aspects of an immutable karma doctrine as mutable. In *Car.* 3.3 on catastrophic epidemics, Ātreya confronts the essential issue. After discoursing on the increasing immorality and decreasing life span over the course of the four world ages leading to the present Kali Yuga, Ātreya is questioned by Agniveśa, who responds to the determinative implications. "Is the life span always fixed or is it not?" he asks. Ātreya replies that life span and one's power or weakness depend on both fate *(daiva)* and human effort *(puruṣakāra)*. Action *(karman)* performed in a prior existence is fate, and the other, *puruṣakāra*, is what is done here. When both are noble, life is long and happy; when both are base, it is otherwise; and when they are moderate, it causes the life to be moderate. He explains that some karma ripens in a fixed amount of time and is powerful, but some is not fixed to a time and is aroused only by motivating factors. He elaborates:

> If all life spans were fixed, then in search of good health none would employ efficacious remedies or verses, herbs, stones, amulets, *bali* offerings, oblations, observances, expiations, fasting, benedictions, and prostrations. There would be no disturbed, ferocious, or ill-mannered cattle, elephants, camels, donkeys, horses, buffalos and the like, and nothing such as polluted winds to be avoided. No anxiety about falling from mountains or rough impassable waters; and none whose minds were negligent, insane, disturbed, fierce, ill-mannered, foolish, avaricious, and lowborn; no enemies, no raging fires, and none of the various poisonous creepers and snakes; no violent acts, no actions out of place or untimely, no kingly wrath. For the occurrence of these and the like would not cause death if the term of all life were fixed and predetermined. Also, the fear of untimely death would not beset those creatures who did not practice the means for fending off fear of untimely death. Undertaking to employ the stories and thoughts of the great seers regarding the prolongation of life would be senseless. Even Indra could not slay with his thunderbolt an enemy whose life span was fixed; even the Aśvins [divine physicians] could not comfort with their medicines one who suffers; the great seers could not attain their desired life span by means of austerities; and the great seers together with the lords of the gods who know all that is to be known could not see, teach, nor perform in full measure.
>
> Furthermore, it is our power of observation that is first and foremost of all

17. S. Dasgupta, op cit. (n. 5 above), p. 403.

that is known, and it is by observing that we perceive the following: over the course of a great many battles, the life span of the thousands of men who fight compared with those who don't is not the same; similarly for those who treat every medical condition that may arise versus those who don't. There is also a discrepancy in the life span of those who imbibe poison and those who do not. Jugs for drinking water and ornamental jugs do not last the same amount of time; consequently, duration of life is based on salutary practices, and from the antithesis there is death. Also, dealing in the appropriate manner with adverse geographic locale, season, and one's own characteristics; dealing with karma and spoiled foods, avoiding over-indulgence, abstinence, or the wrong use of all things, keeping all over-indulgence in check and doing away with lack of restraint, avoiding vagabonds and haste—we perceive that proper regard for these will bring about freedom from disease. On the one hand we observe it and on the other we teach it.[18]

In response to this refutation of physiological determinism, Agniveśa asks Ātreya what is meant by the distinction of timely and untimely death if there is no fixed length of life.[19] Ātreya answers by comparing the life span of a man and that of an axle. An axle will function properly in a carriage until it wears out, and the health of a man's body remains until his original measure of strength expires in due course and he dies. That is a timely death.[20] Various problems affecting the axle will cause it to wear out prematurely. The load in the wagon may be excessive; poor roads, clumsy drivers or draft animals, poor maintenance and handling, and so forth, all might bring this about, and the same is true for a man's life span.

He comes to his end as a result of an undertaking not in accord with his strength, from eating beyond his digestive capacity, or eating bad food, from a deteriorated condition of the body, from excessive sexual intercourse, from relationships with evil men, from restraining intense urges and from not restraining intense urges that should be restrained, from the pain brought on by spirits, drugs, wind, and fire; from a beating, and from shunning food and treatment. Such is untimely death. We also observe untimely death among those who are improperly treated for an illness such as fever.[21]

Embryology: Promoting Conception

Recognition of the value of knowledgeable intervention predominates throughout *Car.*, not just with respect to maintaining health and

18. *Car.* 3.3.36.
19. *Car.* 3.3.37.
20. . . . *tathāyuḥ śarīropagataṃ balavatprakṛtyā yathāvad upacaryamāṇaṃ svapramāṇakṣayādevāvasānaṃ gacchati sa mṛtyuḥ kāle* // . . . //*Car.* 3.3.38//
21. *Car.* 3.3.38. This view is reiterated in *Car.* 4.6.28; see note 86 below. This also raises the question of the position of Dharmaśāstra with regard to malpractice.

staving off death, but also with detailed directives for promoting fertility and the birth of a healthy, intelligent male child. This is inconsistent with more rigid interpretations of the karma doctrine holding that it is the karma of the fetus remaining from previous lives, not the activities of the parents, that determines the sex and characteristics of the child. Karl Potter discusses Śaṅkara's formulation, in which karma produces certain residues *(vāsanā).* It is these karmic residues that condition the kind of birth, life span, and the nature of the experience that the *jīva* will encounter in the next incarnation.[22] This is also the mechanism specified by Patañjali in the *Yoga Sūtras.*[23]

In *Car.*, as a practical matter the influence of the parents is more important. There are directions "for the explicit purpose of establishing pregnancy and impeding obstacles to pregnancy."[24] *Car.'s* fourth book deals with "embodiment" *(Śarīrasthāna)* and is composed of eight chapters. The last of these details clinical applications and is presented as the culmination of the theory discussed in the first seven. Chapter 8 begins with procedures for dealing with infertility and establishing a pregnancy in difficult cases.[25] Preliminary procedures for purification and cleansing with emetics, purgatives, and enemas are suggested.[26] To produce a son the parents are to copulate on even days after the onset of menstruation and for a daughter on odd days, but in either case they should abstain until three days following that onset.[27] The woman is cautioned not to lie prone or on either side lest the phlegm *(śleṣman)* obstruct the passage of semen to the womb or the semen and blood be burned by bile *(pitta).*[28] A woman's overeating, excessive hunger or thirst, fear, disrespect, depression, anger, desire for sexual congress with another man, or ardent passion will render her unable to conceive, or else her offspring will be lacking in qualities. Both the man and the woman should be neither too old nor too young, nor unhealthy, and they should be well suited to each

22. See Karl Potter on "The Process of Rebirth in Some Indian Philosophical Systems," in this volume.
23. *tatas tad vipākānuguṇānām evābhivyaktir vāsanām||* "Consequently [karma (YS 4.7)] ripens solely in accordance with its qualities, and there is a manifestation of the residues" (*Yoga Sūtra* 4.8).
24. *Car.* 4.4.41.
25. *Car.* 4.8.3.
26. *Car.* 4.8.4; such preliminary treatment is commonly prescribed for many conditions.
27. *Car.* 4.8.5.
28. *Car.* 4.8.6. The three *doṣas*, i.e., pathogenic bodily elements, are generally cited as *vāta, pitta,* and *kapha. Śleṣman* is commonly substituted for *kapha.*

other.[29] Recitation of charms is suggested, special preparations of rice and barley are to be eaten, a white stallion or bull is to be gazed upon by her, and various other measures and techniques of a ritualistic nature in the character of Dharmaśāstra are described.[30]

A priest *(ṛtvij)* may be hired, who selects a spot at the northeast of the dwelling, where he strews cowdung and water about and fixes an altar. For a Brahmin he sits on the skin of a white bull, a tiger or bull for a Kṣatriya, an antelope or billy goat for a Vaiśya. He places specified articles in their proper place, lights the fire, and prepares the oblation while well-born members of the appropriate *varṇa* (i.e., Brahmin, etc., as above) are seated all about. The woman and her husband make oblations and propitiate Prajāpati and Viṣṇu: "May Viṣṇu cause this womb to be fertilized." She receives water for her general usage from the priest, circumambulates the fire three times, and eats the remains of the sacrificial ghee with her husband, and the two receive the blessing of those attending. Then they cohabit for eight days and will thus conceive the desired son.[31] For a Śudra, however, respectful salutation *(namaskāra)* to the authorities is sufficient.[32] For a woman desiring a specific type of son having certain physical and mental features, adjustments in the ritual can be made, and she is instructed regarding the diet, sport, and occupation of the kind of child she desires.[33] If these procedures are followed, conception is certain.[34]

With regard to intellectual endowments, traditional karmic influences inherent in the individual himself are also involved.

> Present mental character is a function of the nature of the intellect in all former lives, the parents' intellect, what is heard at the moment leading to pregnancy, and one's own proper behavior.[35]

Embryology: The Viable Embryo

To understand the elaboration of personality types which result from permutations of the constituents of *sattva* (i.e., mental character), the theory of conception should first be reviewed. It is believed that the *garbha* (the term for embryo and fetus) develops as a result of

29. *Car.* 4.8.6–7. 30. *Car.* 4.8.8–9. 31. *Car.* 4.8.10–11.
32. *Car.* 4.8.13. 33. *Car.* 4.8.12,14. 34. *Car.* 4.8.17.
35. *Car.* 4.8.16. See also *Car.* 4.2.27. With regard to this usage of *sattva*, see note 65.

the successful union of semen *(śukra)* and menstrual blood *(śoṇita, ārtava, rakta,* etc.). When blood predominates in the *garbha,* a girl results, with semen, a boy, and when the semen splits, there are twins.[36] Karma is invoked to explain the occurrence of a multiple birth:

> Into as many parts as it shall split,
> the semen-menstrual complex in which there is
> excessive wind *(vāta)*—
> That many parts is the number of offspring
> that she shall bear, in accordance with their karma,
> not her will.[37]
>
> As a result of karma there is unequal division
> of the semen-blood complex as it develops in the womb;
> One is larger and the second is smaller,
> and so among the twins one is distinctly larger.[38]

Eight abnormalities pertaining to sexual identity, development, and behavior are enumerated, including hermaphroditism, impotence, infertility, ectopic testis, and so forth, and each is attributed to a specific cause, such as abnormal mixture of sperm and blood, complications involving the three *doṣas*—that is, pathogenic bodily elements, wind *(vāta),* bile *(pitta),* and phlegm *(kapha)*—or the result of problems with achieving satisfactory coitus, and so forth. At the conclusion of the list, however, karma is also mentioned. "The above eight types of abnormalities are to be regarded as dependent upon karma."[39]

After conception, movements of the woman's left limbs; desire for men; feminine dreams, drinks, foods, character, and movements; feeling the *garbha* on the left side, milk from the left breast, and so forth, indicate that a female fetus will develop, and the opposite indicates a male. The importance of her thoughts at the time of conception in shaping her coming child is also emphasized.[40] It was believed that through the performance of certain *puṃsavana* rites the sex of the newly conceived *garbha* could be changed to male. Various combinations of herbs, curds, foods, and insects were employed at the proper time in a prescribed manner. One preparation of rice and flour was to be ingested through the right nostril; she might also drink two handfuls of a mixture of curds, milk, and water after

36. *Car.* 4.2.12. 37. *Car.* 4.2.14. 38. *Car.* 4.2.16.
39. *Car.* 4.2.21. 40. *Car.* 4.2.24–25.

tossing in miniature gold, silver, or iron figures of men.[41] Other procedures are also described. Measures to insure a healthy pregnancy and precautions to avoid miscarriage were advocated. Certain behaviors and habits of the expectant mother were said to be responsible for specified defects in the offspring.

Sleeping stretched out on her back might cause the umbilicus to wind around the throat of the fetus; sleeping without a cover and going about in the nude, she gives birth to insane offspring; a shrewish quarrelsome character gives birth to an epileptic; a lustful woman to an ugly and shameless or effeminate son; a woman who is perpetually upset to a fearful, emaciated, or short-lived child; a longing woman to one who causes pain to others, is jealous or effeminate; a thief to a drudge, one who inflicts great injury or who is idle; an impatient woman to one who is fierce, a cheat or a malcontent; a woman who is always asleep to a sleepyhead, a fool or a dyspeptic; a drunk to a big drinker, one who has a short memory or who is mentally disturbed; a woman who eats the meat of the large lizards to one with kidney stones, urinary retention or polyuria; a woman who eats boar meat to one who has red eyes, dyspnea and very shaggy hair; a woman who always eats fish to one who blinks infrequently or whose eyes are fixed; a woman always eating sweets to one with urinary disorder, a mute or one who is very stout; a woman always eating sour foods to one who has blood-bile sickness *(raktapitta)* or disease of skin and eyes; a woman always eating salt to one who soon becomes wrinkled and grey or bald; a woman always eating pungent foods to a son who is weak, deficient in semen or without children; a woman always eating bitter foods to one who is dehydrated, without strength or poorly developed; a woman always taking astringents to one who is dark complected, constipated or sickly—a pregnant woman, being devoted to such practices associated with the ills described above, will often bear a child with a disease causing those symptoms. Furthermore, there are defects in the semen engendered by the father along with defects produced by the mother. These are the conditions which are said to cause defects in the *garbha*.[42]

Thus, the father's semen could also be responsible for defects in the offspring, and according to Cakrapāṇidatta's commentary, the same indiscretions *(apacāra)* prior to conception are implicated.[43] In either case, this wide variety of afflictions results from parental activities with no mention of the child's karma.[44] Although parental behavior during—and possibly prior to pregnancy, for the father—is an im-

41. *Car.* 4.8.19.
42. *Car.* 4.8.21; see also *Car.* 4.4.30.
43. Cakrapāṇidatta's commentary on ibid.
44. Ibid.; see also *Car.* 4.4.30–31. *Car.* 4.3.17 represents another view when it is needed to explain observed events.

portant determinant of the condition of the offspring, other components of the *garbha* also play a major role, as we shall see.

At birth, the infant's life expectancy could be ascertained from various signs. These included the quality of hair on the head, qualities of the skin, the relative size of the head; earlobes, eyes, eyebrows, and other facial features; navel, excreta, various anatomical relationships, and so forth.[45] Other features were indicators of subsequent pathology that would develop and were attributed to fate *(daiva)*[46] and thus to karma. These were not necessarily present at birth, but were latent and might appear at any time.

Car.'s analysis of the viable embryo elucidates the relationships between specified components and accounts for a variety of stereotypical character types. As was already noted, the relative proportion of paternal semen and maternal blood determines the sex, multiplicity, and other conditions of the fetus. The *garbha* is made up of the four elements *(prabhava, bhūta)*—namely, wind, fire, earth, and water—and six types of nourishment *(rasa)*. These are also constituents of maternal blood,[47] paternal semen, food, and one's own deeds, which in turn contribute the components of the *garbha*.[48] Contributions from karma and the parents thus have a physical basis. The parental contributions to the *garbha* influence its physical and mental nature, while the mental condition is also influenced by karma from his previous incarnations, both through a material transfer of the four elements. For karma, however, this will raise a problem as the theory is developed further in the next chapter, *Car.* 4.3. There, karma is explicitly inherent in *ātman,* which is denied a physical basis in the elements; here, karma and *ātman* are construed in terms of the four elements. Additional data contribute to an explanation of such discrepancies as the failure in the integration of concepts from diverse sources. *Car.* 4.2 states:

> Due to defects of the seed, the residue of one's
> own karma *(ātma-karmā-''śaya)* and the season,
> as well as the mother's food and activities,
> The various, polluted *doṣas* produce malformations
> manifest in complexion and the senses.
>
> Just as excited waters flowing in the streams
> during the rainy season pound with sticks and stones and
> May deform a tree, the *doṣas* do the same
> to the *garbha* in the womb.

45. *Car.* 4.8.51. 46. *Car.* 5.1.7. 47. *Car.* 4.2.3. 48. *Car.* 4.2.4,26–27.

That which is borne fleet as thought goes from body to body
with the four elements and the subtle body;
A function of the nature of his karma,
its form is unseen without divine vision.

It pervades everything and supports all bodies;
it is all karma and all form;
It is consciousness, and the constituent element *(dhātu),*
but beyond the senses; it is forever fixed and imminent;
it is just that.

The elements *(bhūta)* (contained in its nourishment,
the *ātman,* mother, and father) are known to number
sixteen in the body;[49]
The four come to rest there in the *ātman*
and, correspondingly, the *ātman* in those four.

They say the elements *(bhūta)* of the mother and father
in the uterine blood and semen are the *garbha;*
The blood and semen are swollen with those elements,
and nutrient elements are added.

There are also four elements engendered by his karma
which cling to the *ātman* and enter the *garbha;*
Since the *dharmas* of the seed are all different,
they each enter into the *ātman* of the other body.

Since form is attained from its prior form,
the mind *(manas)* is of the character of its own karma,
Which then splits to form the intellectual-judgmental
faculty *(buddhi),* wherein there is *rajas* and *tamas.*
Karma is the cause.

Form is never separated from *ātman*—
not by the imperceptibles or subtle forms,
Not by karma, the mental faculty nor will,
not by one's sense of identity *(ahaṃkāra),* illness,
nor the *doṣas.*

Since the mind is restricted by *rajas* and *tamas,*
and in the absence of knowledge all the *doṣas* are there,
It is the afflicted mind *(manas)* and the force of karma
that is the reputed cause of the activities and growth
of the two [i.e., *rajas* and *tamas*].[50]

49. I.e., four elements from each of four sources. Cakrapāṇidatta embellishes with an extensive discussion of the metaphysics.
50. *Car.* 4.2.29–38.

There are four components of the viable embryo: contributions from (1) the mother, (2) the father, (3) nutrients *(rasa)* ingested by the pregnant mother, and (4) the *ātman* through which karma exerts its critical influence. This schema outlined in the preceding *śloka* verses is not, however, the last word on the matter.

As was indicated earlier, the surviving redaction of *Car.* is not without textual-critical problems.[51] The text is a mixture of prose and various types of verse, usually *ślokas* but also more complex epic meters, and there are notable substantive inconsistencies to support an argument that the text is a conglomeration of strata from several sources. From a medical perspective, the most highly sophisticated passages are frequently in prose, quoting the views of Ātreya. Summary *ślokas* commonly appear at the end of a discussion, either in the middle of a chapter or at the end, and they may also make up major portions of or even entire chapters, as in *Car.* 4.2. It was suggested earlier that some of these verses may be survivors from earlier medical texts, and the possibility that some are citations from supportive non-medical works should also be considered. This would serve to explain the inconsistencies and the occasionally tenuous links between some of these passages and the surrounding context.[52]

The prose discussion of *Car.* 4.3, quoting Ātreya, elaborates and contradicts the preceding chapter and specifies an additional component in the constitution of the *garbha,* namely, *sātmya* (i.e., constitutional integrity). The role of *sattva* becomes complex and more significant, its particular nature (now) dependent upon five components of the *garbha.*

Sperm and blood come together and settle in the womb; the *jīva* descends and, following conjunction with *sattva,* it produces the *garbha.*

This *garbha* is engendered by mother, father, *ātman, sātmya,* and nourishment *(rasa).* There is also the *sattva,* which is self-produced *(aupapāduka)* [i.e., not an externally contributed component like the others].[53]

To this Bharadvāja objects,[54] arguing that the *garbha* cannot be said to be born of these components because no single one of them can

51. See note 15.
52. See M. Weiss, op cit., pp. 68–70, 72–73, 78–81. For example, in *Car.* there is some confusion about whether demons are the cause of insanity or the manifestation of it; cf. *Car.* 2.7.11–15 and 2.7.10,19–23.
53. *Car.* 4.3.2–3.
54. See note 16.

itself produce a *garbha*.[55] Ātreya explains that this objection misses the point, that it is the combination of the five that is required,[56] and that without any one of them no *garbha* can possibly result. This also offers an opportunity for Ātreya to expound upon the nature of the five and *sattva*.[57]

Ātreya argues that there can be no conception in the absence of mother, father, *ātman*, and so forth. From the maternal contribution to the *garbha* is derived blood, flesh, fat, umbilicus, heart, lungs, liver, spleen, kidneys, bladder, rectum, stomach, and the other gastrointestinal organs. From the father's contribution comes hair, beard, nails, teeth, bones, blood vessels, sinews, other physiological channels, and semen. With *ātman* and the first two an important triad is made that receives additional discussion.

> Every instance of *ātman* may not necessarily produce the desired *garbha*, but it certainly will not without the maternal and paternal contributions. Some produce a *garbha* by their own choice, some by force of karma; sometimes there is power to bring it about, sometimes not. Where *sattva* and the rest are successfully made, there is sufficient power for producing a fetus as desired. Otherwise there is not. When there is a failure in generating a *garbha* because of defective means, the *ātman* is not the cause. According to those who know the *ātman*, the power of vision, motion, the womb, and release is *ātman*. Nothing else can produce pleasure and suffering, and from none but that is the *garbha* made and does the *garbha* itself produce. The shoot does not sprout without a seed.[58]

Contributions derived from *ātman* include the fact of arising in a particular womb, life span,[59] self-knowledge, mind *(manas)*, the senses, breathing, urges, controls, various features, voice, and complexion, pleasure and pain, desire and hate, consciousness, concentration, intellectual-judgmental faculty *(buddhi)*, memory, sense of self *(ahaṃkāra)*, and effort.[60]

Sātmya, the required balance of all the constitutional components, is also required. From its contribution sickness, lethargy, and greed desist. It provides clarity of the senses, acquisition of good voice, features, seed, and penile erection.[61]

55. *Car.* 4.3.4.
56. *Car.* 4.3.5. Bharadvāja's objections serve as a stimulant to Ātreya's discourse; see also *Car.* 4.3.15 ff. and below.
57. *Car.* 4.3.6–13.
58. *Car.* 4.3.9.
59. I.e., "predetermined" only insofar as *timely* death; see above.
60. *Car.* 4.3.10.
61. *Car.* 4.3.11.

Proper nourishment *(rasa)* is necessary for the *garbha* as well as for the health of the mother. It provides for the formation and growth of the body, maintenance of life, satiety, thriving, and strength.[62]

That *sattva* plays an important role is clear, though the exact nature of that role is somewhat elusive.[63] As the link between the spiritual and physical, and perhaps also in its role as the starting point for the individuation process producing the various mental evolutes and resulting character types,[64] it resembles the Sāṅkhya concept of *buddhi.* While it carries a connotation of mental efficacy here, it is not the *sattva* of the *guṇa* triad.[65] Its usage in *Car.* 4.4 as the term for personality indicates an application broader than the cognitive function associated with *manas.* In *Car.* 4.3, however, a passage on the nature of *sattva* identifies it with *manas:*

> The *sattva* is indeed self-produced *(aupapāduka).* In contact with the *jīva, sattva* binds it to the body. Upon confronting death, personality *(śīla)* leaves it, trust is toppled, all the senses are afflicted, strength is discharged, diseases abound, and because it is destroyed the life-breath departs. It is the perceiver of the senses and is called *manas.* We teach that there are three types: pure, impulsive, and lethargic *(śuddha, rājasa,* and *tāmasa).* Whatever shall indeed predominate in *manas,* he shall meet that in the next birth. Furthermore, when he has that pure type, he remembers even the previous incarnation, since awareness of memory is connected with the *manas* of that *ātman* and follows. Consequently, this man is called "one who remembers past life *(jātismara).*"[66]

The contributions of the *sattva* to the *garbha* include trust, character, purity, hate, memory, foolishness, apostasy, jealousy, heroism, fear, rage, lassitude, perseverence, fierceness, gentleness, seriousness, fickleness, and so forth. These are considered evolutes of *sattva* as it undergoes a differentiation process *(te sattva-vikārā yān uttara-kālaṃ sattva-bhedam).* The above traits are not all active at the same

62. *Car.* 4.3.12.
63. J. A. B. Van Buitenen, "Studies in Sāṅkhya (III): *Sattva,*" *Journal of the American Oriental Society (JAOS)* 77 (1957): 88–107.
64. *Car.* 4.4.37–39; more detail below.
65. *Rajas* and *tamas* occur in *Car.* as a dyad, singly, or with the form of *sattva* termed *śuddha,* as in the discussion which follows. This is a variation on the traditional Sāṅkhya triad inasmuch as this suggests that *rajas* and *tamas* here are modifications of the "pure" *sattva.* Thus, we have three types of *sattva* instead of *sattva* as one of the three *guṇas* constituting *prakṛti. Car.* 4.4.34 compares the debilitating effects of *rajas* and *tamas* on the mind *(sattva)* with the effects of the *doṣas* on the body.
66. *Car.* 4.3.13; see also *Car.* 4.4.36–39.

time, and the individual at a given point may be characterized by one or another.

As described, these are the five components from external sources *(mātṛja, pitṛja, ātmaja, sātmyaja, rasaja)* and the *sattva* which arises spontaneously in a given birth and departs at death.[67] Ātreya again offers the analogy of a man and a cart[68] and adds another with a tent, that is, products whose integral function depends upon the proper mutual relationships of their component parts.[69] *Sattva* influences manifestations of the *ātman* in the next birth and in its pure form may admit memory of a past birth, apparently by means of a present interaction of the *sattva* with *ātman* capable of detecting the effects on *ātman* of the prior incarnate *sattva*—which is equated to *manas* in the above account.

The influence of karma is manifest in the *ātman* and secondarily in the *sattva,* which is derived from *ātman.* Ātreya refers to this relationship to explain why the mental attributes of children differ from their parents.

> The senses are always derived of *ātman,* and destiny *(daiva)* is the cause of their development or failure to develop. Therefore the children of senseless ones, and so forth, do not resemble their father.[70]

Embryology: Character

In *Car.* 4.4 there is a detailed account of the development of the *garbha* and the characteristic changes observable in the fetus and the mother in the progressive stages from conception onward through the pregnancy. *Sattva* receives greater emphasis than before as the process of individuation is scrutinized.[71] In the developing *garbha* feelings and desires arise, and their locus is the heart. When the natural throbbing of the fetus is first perceived, it is attributed to desires carried forth from another existence, and in this condition it is said to feel

67. According to *AHr.* 2.1.1 the combination of semen and blood only is sufficient to produce *satva (sic).* Karma shapes *satva* directly and is not mediated by the *ātman.* śuddhe śukrārtave satvaḥ svakarakleśacoditaḥ / garbhaḥ sampadyate yuktivaśādagnirivāraṇau // "In accordance with its own karma and the hindrances, *satva* arises in the pure semen-menstrual blood combination. The *garbha* results as surely as fire in a kindling stick." (*AHr.* 2.1.1). In his commentary Aruṇadatta glosses *satva* by *jīva.* With regard to *kleśa,* see *Yoga Sūtras* 2.3–9.

68. See *Car.* 3.3.38.

69. *Car.* 4.3.14.

70. *Car.* 4.3.17. For a different view see notes 42–44.

71. In *Car.* 4.4.4 *sattva* is included with status equivalent to the other five in a list of

with two hearts *(dvaihṛdaya).* The *garbha* heart, a maternally engendered organ, is linked to the mother's heart, and nutrients are transmitted through the connecting channels.[72]

As was discussed, defects in the maternal or paternal contributions to the *garbha* are responsible for defects in the offspring, according to *Car.* 4.8. *Car.* 4.4.32 also includes faults stemming from the nutrients, *sātmya,* and *sattva* among these, but defects in *ātman* are not allowed.[73] Of the three types of *sattva, rājasa* and *tāmasa* are undesirable, while the *śuddha* is desirable.

> There are three types of *sattva,* viz. *śuddha, rājasa,* and *tāmasa.* The *śuddha* type is considered faultless and represents the auspicious aspect. The *rājasa* type is faulty and represents the impassioned aspect. The *tāmasa* type is also faulty and represents the foolish aspect.[74]

Various personality types are derived from each of these, and they may also be associated with certain body types, which, however, are not described.[75] For the *śuddha* type, categories are named after deities. The Brahmā type is pure, truthful, wise, and free of desire, anger, greed, and so forth. The ṛṣi type is devoted to sacrifices, study, vows, and similar concerns. The Indra type is powerful, acquisitive, heroic, virile, and concerned with his own righteousness, possessions, and pleasures. The Yama type follows what is prescribed, does what is proper, does not fight, and has a good memory, and so forth. The Varuṇa type is resolute, clean, intolerant of filth, fastidious in the performance of sacrifices, and is in control of his anger and tranquility.[76] The Kubera type commands honor, attendants, and pleasures;

the components of the *garbha.*

72. *Car.* 4.4.15.

73. *Car.* 4.4.33.

74. *Car.* 4.4.36.

75. *Car.* 4.4.37–39. Cf. a related classification of "demonic" *(bhūta)* types that produce stereotypic mental disorders in specified individuals; *Car.* 2.7.12;6.9.20–21; see Weiss, op. cit., pp. 112–133.

76. Since many of the parameters of human behavior are invariant, it is not surprising that in many of these cases the essential features are recognizable in many present-day formulations of personality type. The Varuṇa category especially is comparable to the so-called anal-compulsive character. Note also the prominence of hypomanic traits in those that follow. *Rājasa* types are comparable to various forms of narcissistic personality, which are currently the focus of much psychoanalytic theoretical interest: H. Kohut, "Thoughts on Narcissism and Narcissistic Rage," *Psychoanalytic Study of the Child,* 27 (1972): 360–400; O. Kernberg, "Contrasting Viewpoints Regarding the Nature and Psychoanalytic Treatment of Narcissistic Personalities: A Preliminary Communication," *Jour. of the Amer. Psychoanalytic Assoc.,* 22 (1974): 255–267. Such a study of comparative personality theory is of course beyond the scope of the present study.

he is emotional and enjoys his leisure. The Gandharva type is fond of laughter, dancing, music, and stories, and is well versed in Itihāsa and Purāṇa. He also likes garlands, women, leisure activities, and is contented. Although all seven of these are considered *śuddha-sattva* types, a hierarchy is indicated, with the Brahmā type at the top.

The claim of being able to remember previous lives (made for the *jātismara,* who is defined by his *śuddha-sattva)*[77] seems consistent theoretically for the Brahmin type only, since the others are for the most part reasonably normal, and the empirical strain on a theory holding that such an extraordinary capability was widespread would have been intolerable. It is more probable that *Car.* 4.3.13 and 4.4.37 represent different theoretical formulations culled from different sources, the former passage from a more grandiose scheme. The interchange there of *manas* and *sattva* may be a remnant of such a philosophically rather than medically oriented context.[78]

There are six *rājasa* types, each manifesting some degree of antisocial and otherwise undesirable behavior. The Asura type is fierce, misanthropic, lordly, deceitful, and given to rage; he is without compassion and self-serving. The Rākṣasa type is intolerant and always enraged; he is faultfinding, cruel, fond of meat, gluttonous, jealous, and lazy. The Piśāca type is gluttonous, effeminate, and likes to be alone with women; he is filthy, cowardly, a bully, and given to bad habits and diet. The Sarpa (snake) type is powerful when angry and otherwise cowardly; he is often lazy; he frightens others in the area and considers his own food and sport above all else. The Preta type likes food, has a morbid personality, is jealous and selfish. The Śakuna type is forever preoccupied with pleasure. For him food and sport come first; he is unstable and impatient, living from moment to moment.

The three *tāmasa* categories represent the fatuous aspect of *sattva.* They are the Paśu (animal), Matsya (fish), and Vanaspati (tree) types. The Paśu type is obstructive and stupid; his diet and behavior are despicable. He is a somnolent character for whom sexual intercourse is foremost. The Matsya type is cowardly and dull, and he covets food. He is fond of water, unstable, satisfied one moment and angry the next. The Vanaspati type is idle, solitary, intent on food, and bereft of all mental faculties.

77. *Car.* 4.3.13.
78. N.B. the account in *Car.* 4.1 of the differentiation of *manas* into the senses *(indriya),* etc. in *śloka* verse, especially 4.1.16–22,81.

Etiology of Disease

Car. divides all disease into two categories: *nija* (endogenous), always attributable to an imbalance of the three *doṣas,*[79] and *āgantu* (exogenous), caused by demons, poison, wind, fire, and battle injuries. The *āgantu* conditions, however, reduce to *prajñā-'parādha* (culpable insight, i.e., violations of good sense). All of the undesirable mental states *(mano-vikāra)* including jealousy, depression, fear, anger, vanity, and hate are caused by it.[80] *Nija* disorders are treated by restoring the proper physiological balance,[81] and *āgantu* disorders by giving up *prajñā-'parādha,* calming the senses, recognizing implications of geography, season, and one's own nature, and behaving in a manner consistent with them.[82]

While *Car.* admits karma as a causative factor in the etiology of disease, it tends to be included in verses of a general, theoretical nature rather than in passages with more direct clinical applicability.[83]

> Loss of concentration, resolve, and memory,
> reaching the time when karma is manifest,
> And the arrival of that which is unhealthy—
> know these to be causes of suffering.[84]

And

> For there is no significant karma whatsoever
> whose fruit is not consumed.
> Diseases produced by karma resist treatment
> until that fruit is gone; then they subside.[85]

Karma serves a dual function. Not only does it provide an explanation for those diseases that do not fit the recognizable *doṣa* patterns, but even those disorders that do fit the patterns are, when resistant to treatment, reclassifiable as *karmaja,* since that resistance is itself pathognomonic. The medical system thus copes with the characteris-

79. *Car.* 1.7.39–40.
80. *Car.* 1.7.51–52.
81. *Car.* 1.7.49–50; see also *Car.* 4.6.5–11.
82. *Car.* 1.7.53–54; see also *Car.* 4.2.39–43.
83. *Car.* 4.1.1. In 1901 J. Jolly commented on this "escape clause" feature provided the medical theory by the karma doctrine: "From the standpoint of the principle of rebirth, those diseases are considered as *karmaja,* i.e., proceeding from the misdeeds in a previous birth, for which there appears no visible cause and which resist the usual curing methods" (Jolly, op. cit. [n. 15 above], p. 72).
84. *Car.* 4.1.98.
85. *Car.* 4.1.116–117.

tically Indian drive for completeness in formulating theoretical foundations and thereby justifies an essential premise (i.e., *doṣa* theory) which can survive intact despite instances of its admitted ineffectiveness in healing certain patients. Notwithstanding this success of Āyurveda in assimilating a karma doctrine, from an etic perspective it manifests an abandoning of empirical medical methodology in the face of insurmountable illness. The system then compensates by incorporating whatever philosophical and spiritual modes of solace are available from the culture at large in order to cope with its failure. Consider the analogous situation of the present day. Although Christian Science and Western medicine are doubtlessly incompatible, physicians may none the less refer to the Will of God with impunity upon reaching the periphery of their clinical competence, and hospital architecture commonly includes a chapel, thus manifesting similar deference to the dominant cultural values.

Car. has in effect redefined the concept of karma, shifting the emphasis from past lives to present behavior in such a way as to make it clinically germane. In doing this with the concept of *prajñā-'parādha*, *Car.* adds force to its own advocacy of a salutary life style. One finds a greater willingness on the part of *Car.* to venture farther from the doctrinal escape hatch—karma—than those later texts in which medical and speculative notions became more highly intertwined in their clinical application. After refuting the proposal that the life span of every individual is predetermined, the logical inference from a more fundamentalist interpretation of the karma doctrine, Ātreya affirms:

> In this age the life span is one hundred years; perfecting one's own constitution and merits and attending to good health brings this about.[86]

Although *Car.*'s shift from the etiologic perspective dependent upon karma and spirit-possession is especially significant because the trend was moving toward a less rather than a more secular approach to medicine, in some cases the shift from karma and demonic possession to *prajñā-'parādha* is incomplete or altogether lacking. Childhood diseases have a sudden onset, produce high fever, and quickly

86. *Car.* 4.6.29–30. See also *Car.* 1.7.37–38,45. The discussion of *prajñā-'parādha* emphasizes the importance of abandoning bad habits and establishing good ones. *Car.* discusses the salutary effects of such behavior when fatalism and medicine are at odds. Cf. . . .*vāg-vastu-mātram etad vādam ṛṣayo manyante nākāle mṛtyur astīti* // " . . . The seers consider this doctrine, that there is no untimely death, to be nothing but a matter of words" (*Car.* 4.6.28).

abate. They were considered independent of the *doṣa* theory and "brought on by the anger of the gods and the rest," that is, classes of demons *(bhūta)*.[87] The exogenous mental disorders were conceived in similar terms, but here we discern a distinction between more and less sophisticated formulations of the medical theory. *Car.* 6.9.16, quoted earlier, appeals to karma and demons to explain one form of insanity, *āgantu-unmāda*. In the Nidāna section ("Pathology") this view is distinguished from and then rationalized with that of Ātreya:

> Some seek its [*āgantu-unmāda*] cause in the effect of unpraiseworthy karma committed in a previous life, but according to the great Ātreya Punarvasu, *prajñā-'parādha* is really the cause. For it is because of this *prajñā-'parādha* that one is contemptuous toward the Devas, Ṛṣis, Pitṛs, Gandharvas, Yakṣas, Rākṣasas, Piśācas, Gurus, old people, Siddhas, Ācāryas, and those worthy of honor, and thereby behaves improperly; or else he undertakes some equally unpraiseworthy activity. Once he is stricken by himself, the assaulting gods and the rest render him insane *(unmatta)*.[88]

The point may be obscured in other passages of *Car.*, but it is significant that the locus of etiologic cause had clearly shifted from outside the individual, as in the demonic accounts represented in the earlier *Atharva Veda*, to a personalized account in early Āyurveda—despite the fact that this view seems to have lost ground in the later Āyurvedic texts. Summary *ślokas* at the end of *Car.* 2.7 make it clear that it was not the demons, but the individual who was the source of his illness:

> Neither Devas nor Gandharvas nor Piśācas
> nor Rākṣasas
> Nor the others afflict the man who is
> not self-afflicted.
>
> Regarding those who turn on him
> who is afflicted by his own karma,
> His distress is not caused by them,
> since they did not bring on his apostasy.
>
> In the case of disease born of his own karma,
> the result of *prajñā-'parādha*,
> The wise man does not blame the Devas,
> Pitṛs, or Rākṣasas.

87. *Car.* 4.6.27. In *Car.* 4.1.127 the *bhūtas* are associated with improper contact with unctuous, cold, or warm objects.
88. *Car.* 2.7.10.

He should regard only himself as the cause
of his happiness and misery;
Therefore, he should keep to a salutary path
and not falter.

Honoring the Devas and the rest
and devoting himself to what is wholesome—
Whether doing these or their opposite,
it shall all reach him in the *ātman.*[89]

These *ślokas* emphasize the weight given in early Āyurveda to the shift from external to internal etiology. Demonic possession was redefined so that the problem here is not to appease the demon (cf. *Atharva Veda* 6.111) but to put one's own life in order. *Car.*'s shift in emphasis from karma to *prajñā-'parādha* similarly serves to define the root of the problem in terms of behavior pertinent to the present situation instead of previous incarnations, which the individual is actually no more able to affect in a medical context than he can a fickle demon. Unlike *Car.* (and *Bhela Saṃhitā), Su.* and *AHr.* each contain one or more separate chapters on demons *(bhūta-vidyā)* which more clearly accept the position that it is the demon rather than the individual who causes these maladies. Compare, for example, the above verses with the following admonition from *Su.* 6.60.55 which is also repeated in *AHr.* 6.5.49:

One should not move against the affliction of the
Piśāca in other than the proper manner;
They are resolute, angry, very powerful, and may
launch an attack against the physician and patient.

These texts also lack a concept of *prajñā-'parādha* and tend to see karma in more traditional rather than medical terms.

The term *aparādha* is used in *AHr.* without *prajñā,* thereby stripping the concept of its technical usage and transforming it into the violation of a more traditional moral imperative. Vāgbhaṭa, author of *AHr.* (approximately A.D. 600), posits three categories of disease, resulting (1) from the *doṣas,* (2) from karma, and (3) from a mixture of the first two. The *doṣa* disorders are associated with actions in this life and the karma disorders with a previous life.

Some arise from transgressions which are experienced,
some from prior culpability *(aparādha);*
From a mixture of these there is another,
and thus disease is known to be three-fold.

89. *Car.* 2.7.19–23.

Arising from the *doṣas* it has the corresponding
pathology; arising from karma it is
without basis [in the present life];
A malady with an intense onset when there is
slight cause is the result of *doṣas* and karma.

The first desists after treatment counteracting [the *doṣas*],
the karma type after dissipating karma,
And the disease arising from both desists
after the eradication of the *doṣas* and karma.[90]

Thus, any malady is cured when the influences of both the *doṣas* and karma are dissipated.

The zenith in the rising impact on Āyurveda of more traditional ideas about karma is best represented in an obscure monograph surviving from the later middle ages. Though unrepresentative in the extreme to which its position is taken, and so interesting for the same reason, *Jñānabhāskara* consists of a dialogue between Sūrya and his charioteer on the evils of human existence and a host of diseases—all attributed to karma. Descriptions of pathology are extensive, but therapeutics are confined to expiatory procedures. Within the scope of that presentation, however, traditional Āyurvedic topics are included, such as *vāta, pitta,* and *kapha* disorders.[91] It was, however, long before this point that Āyurveda had begun to allow its garden of empirically derived clinical insights to be invaded by weeds spreading from the more supernaturally oriented popular culture.[92]

Epidemics

In his analysis of karma in the *Mahābhārata,* J. Bruce Long notes that during times of misfortune and mental anguish the karma doctrine served as a source of meaning, encouragement, and consolation. *Car.*'s chapter on catastrophic epidemics *(Car.* 3.3: *janapado-'ddvaṃsana)* addresses itself to situations in which one might therefore expect the role of karma to be significant. In such times normal

90. *AHr.* 1.12.57–59. Vāgbhaṭa's *Aṣṭāṅgahṛdaya Saṃhitā* (Bombay: Sāgara, 1939), translated into German by L. Hilgenberg and W. Kirfel (Leiden: Brill, 1941).

91. Mss. from approximately A.D. 1500 described in *Catalogue of Sanskrit Manuscripts in the Library of the India Office, London,* compiled by E. W. O. Windisch and J. Eggeling in 2 vols., 4 pts. (London: Secretary of State for India, 1887–1935), #2719 (2030), pp. 962–964. See also M. Winternitz, *History of Indian Literature: vol. III, part II (Scientific Literature),* translated by S. Jhā (Delhi: Motilal, 1967), p. 638.

92. Personal communication from Jeremy Nobel.

medical practices and expectations are frustrated by indiscriminate and high rates of morbidity.[93] The etiologic explanation consequently shifted from the *nija* category, which could not account for these events, to the *āgantu* category. Ātreya observed that even though a diverse population may be stricken by an epidemic, there are several common denominators, namely, season, landscape, water, and wind.[94] Aberrations in any of these, such as windstorms, putrid water, changes in the wildlife or complexion of the landscape, and unseasonable weather, might produce epidemic illness.[95]

Specific cases were said to respond well to treatment, herbal remedies being especially useful, and an intelligent physician was well advised to gather the appropriate medicinal provisions while he could upon observing the natural signs of impending disaster. Cases that did not respond to treatment and ended in fatality were attributed to karma. "Most do not die, most are not of that karma."[96] Cakrapāṇidatta's commentary on this passage explains that only some karma will produce deadly illness when it matures, such as burning a village or murder. He surmises that because such events were rare, so were the fatalities. According to this view, although such fatalities are attributed to karma, it is not necessarily the karma of the victim, but potentially somebody else in the region that is ultimately responsible. Ātreya makes no such speculation, and the nature of his discussion argues against it. He seems to allow, however, for the effects of a group's karma, which may be implied by his use of *adharma*.

In answering a question put to him by Agniveśa, Ātreya responds:

> The cause of them all, Agniveśa, the misfortune that arises from the winds and the rest, is *adharma* (unrighteousness) or else previously committed bad karma *(asat-karman)*. It is nothing but *prajñā-'parādha* that nurtures them both.[97]

He cites the widespread *adharma* accruing from corrupt leaders and spiraling down the social order. Then the deities forsake the community; the seasons, winds, and waters are disturbed, and the population devastated. *Adharma* is the cause of war, and either *adharma* or some other transgressions cause the Rākṣasas and the other demonic

93. *Car.* 3.3.5.
94. *Car.* 3.3.6–7. The list here is in descending order of significance, q. v. *Car.* 3.3.10.
95. These conditions are consistent with epidemic outbreaks of cholera from contaminated water supply, malaria from Anopheles mosquito infestation, etc.
96. *Car.* 3.3.13.
97. *Car.* 3.3.19.

hordes to strike. The curses of gurus, elders, accomplished ones, and others are also caused by improper behavior rooted in *adharma.*[98] *Prajñā-'parādha* is the source of both *adharma* and *asat-karman,* which lead to catastrophy. *Adharma* may be either mediated or manifest by improper actions, and may simply refer to *asat-karman* en masse.

The following, drawn from *Car.* 4.1, elucidates the nature of *prajñā-'parādha.*

Prajñā-'parādha is considered to refer to that deed which, lacking in concentration, resolve and memory, causes harm. It provokes all the *doṣas.*[99]

Among these "violations of good sense" are the following:

forcing and suppressing the natural excretory urge
reckless behavior and too much attention to women
doing something either too late or something that should not be done *(mithyā-karman)*
violating social custom and insulting venerable men
indulging in what one knows to be unhealthy, in psychotropic drugs, and what is contrary to one's beliefs
roaming about at improper times and in improper places
friendship with those who wreak havoc
ignoring what one's senses tell him and valid experience
jealousy, vanity, fear, anger, greed, fatuation, intoxication, and confusion or a blameworthy deed *(karman)* derived from these
a blameworthy bodily activity or any other such deed *(karman)* produced by passion or fatuation—

The learned call these *prajñā-'parādha,* and they are the cause of disease. These are defective discriminations of the judgmental faculty *(buddhi),* and they bring on distress. They are known as *prajñā-'parādha* because they are in the field relating to mind *(manas).*[100]

This formulation of *prajñā-'parādha*, unique in Āyurveda, faciliated Ātreya's unparalleled emphasis on clinical empiricism over dogmatism and his subordination of supernatural etiology. While village burning and a murder committed in a prior life readily came to mind for Cakrapāṇidatta in the eleventh century as he sought to understand the significance of the term *karman* in *Car.* 3.3.13, they in fact belie Ātreya's predilection for addressing more mundane activities in the world of the present over obtuse speculation on karma rooted in the distant past.

98. *Car.* 3.3.20–23.
99. *Car.* 4.1.102. For *sarva-doṣa,* Cakrapāṇidatta includes *rajas* and *tamas* with *vāta, pitta,* and *kapha.*
100. *Car.* 4.1.103–109.

5

The Theory of Reincarnation among the Tamils

GEORGE L. HART, III

The culture of Tamilnad comes not from the Aryans of the North, though many elements from that culture were superimposed on Tamil culture, but from the megalithic culture of the Deccan. Through the oldest extant Tamil poems it is possible to gain a fairly clear picture of just what Tamil culture was like before the incursion of Aryan elements.[1] While there are, of course, many different elements that go to make up a culture, we may discern three basic features of the culture of Tamilnad before Northern influence. They are the cult of the king, the power of woman, and a corpus of conceptions about death. It is this third area that this paper will discuss.

Before the coming of the Aryan ideas, the Tamils did not believe in reincarnation. Rather, like many archaic peoples, they had shadowy and inconsistent ideas of what happens to the spirits of the dead. Their oldest belief appears to be that the spirit of the dead remains in the world ready to work mischief if it is not somehow contained and controlled. To this end, stones called *naṭukals* were erected to the spirits of especially powerful figures—heroes, kings, *satīs*—where the spirits could actually reside and be propitiated. Indeed, the Tamils believed that any taking of life was dangerous, as it released the spirits

1. See George L. Hart, III, *The Poems of Ancient Tamil: Their Milieu and Their Sanskrit Counterparts* (Berkeley and Los Angeles: University of California Press, 1975).

of the things that were killed. Likewise, all who dealt with the dead or with dead substances from the body were considered to be charged with the power of death and were thought to be dangerous. Thus, long before the coming of the Aryans with their notion of *varṇa,* the Tamils had groups that were considered low and dangerous and with whom contact was closely regulated.[2] It is important to note that these beliefs survive quite strongly even to the present. Not only are there many very low castes with whom contact is regulated (drummers, leatherworkers, barbers), there is even a low caste in Kerala called the Nāyāṭis who erect stones to their ancestors, whom they believe to inhabit the stones.[3]

Another important consequence of the indigenous Tamil notions regarding death is belief in possession. In the Sangam poems, there are many verses that show that a despondent woman was thought to be possessed by the god Murugan. Today, there are possession cults all over South India and Northern Ceylon. Whitehead described a Westerner who inadvertently witnessed a possession:

> A——was a stranger to the country and its ways. He was returning home late one night. . . . Missing his way, he strayed towards the shrine of the village goddess; and when passing the low walls of the temple his attention was suddenly arrested by a heart-rending moan, seemingly uttered by someone in great distress, inside the walled enclosure. Impelled by thoughts of rendering help to a fellow creature in distress, A—— approached the temple wall, and looking over it, saw the prostrate form of a young and handsome female, of the better class of Hindus, lying motionless as death on the stone pavement. . . . Quick as lightning, a gaunt and spectral object, almost nude, bearded to the knee, with head covered by matted tufts of hair and presenting a hideous appearance, emerged from the deep shadows around. The figure held a naked sword in one hand and a bunch of margosa leaves in the other. . . . [Upon asking a policeman the significance of what he had seen], he was told that the woman was the matron of a respectable Hindu family, who, having had no children since her marriage, had come, by the advice of her elders, to invoke the assistance of the goddess, as she was credited with the power of making women fertile. . . . The grotesque figure which had so terrified A—— was the village pūjāri, and a noted exorciser of evil spirits; and he was then exercising his art over the terrified woman in attempting to drive away the malignant spirit that had possessed her, and had thereby rendered her childless.[4]

2. Ibid., pp. 119–133.
3. See A. Aiyappan, "Social and Physical Anthropology of the Nayadis of Malabar," in *Madras Government Museum Bulletin,* general section 2, 1930–37, pp. 13–85.
4. Henry Whitehead, *The Village Gods of South India* (Calcutta: Oxford University Press, 1921), p. 120.

In Tulunad, it is believed that there are many spirits of men and women long dead who possess people and who must be propitiated in the body they have possessed.[5] The fact is that both the spirits of the dead and gods may possess people. Indeed, there is evidence that the belief in possession through the spirits of the dead is older than the belief in possession by gods.[6]

The Tamils believe that the spirit of a dead man or woman remains in the world and able to act in some mysterious way. There is relatively little to fear from spirits that have not been wronged or that are not especially powerful because of the circumstances of their life and death. However, the spirit of a king, of a great hero who died in battle, or of a woman who committed suttee, as well as the spirit of anyone unjustly killed, would lurk in the world, eager to do harm or wreak vengeance. In order to contain these powerful spirits, stones were constructed where the spirit might be contained and propitiated. These spirits might act in many ways, but one of their most dangerous manifestations was possession. It is significant that there is nothing in these beliefs that takes the view of the dead person. It is as if once dead, a man's spirit becomes existentially so alien to life that there is no use attempting to describe the world he experiences.

Even in the oldest Tamil poems, the so-called Sangam poems, there are verses describing a life after death in terms other than the above. Many poems depict a sort of Valhalla or warriors' paradise to which a man would go if he died in battle:

> How can battle rage now.
> how can warriors hold back advancing ranks?
> Touching the wounds of men who have died fighting there
> and smearing their hair with their bloody red hands,
> demon women whose forms are bright with color
> dance to the slow rhythm of the *paṟai* drum.
> The armies are being eaten up by vultures,
> and the two kings who fought furiously but justly
> have perished.

5. Peter Claus, "Possession, Protection and Punishment as Attributes of the Deities in a South Indian Village," *Man in India* 53 (1973): 231–242; Peter Claus, "The Siri Myth and Ritual: A Mass Possession Cult of South India," *Ethnology,* vol. XIV, no. 1, January, 1975, pp. 47–58.

6. See G. A. Deleury, *The Cult of Viṭhobā* (Poona, 1960), pp. 193–208. Deleury argues persuasively that the temple to Viṭhobā at Paṇḍharpūr arose around the memorial stone originally erected to a hero named Biṭṭaga.

> Their parasols droop down
> and their drums, acclaimed for their greatness, are ruined.
> In the large camp,
> where hundreds from different places were gathered
> so there was no space,
> there is no one fit to capture the field,
> and so the clamor of fighting has ceased
> suddenly, fearfully.
> Women do not eat green leaves,
> do not bathe in cool water,
> but lie there embracing the chests of their men.
> Those who have fragrant food,
> whose garlands are unwithering,
> whose eyes are unwinking,
> have guests as the world hard to get fills.
> May the fame [of the two of] you be resplendent![7]

Another poem describes the treatment of men who did not die on the field of battle:

> The mean kings there died
> and so escaped the rite that would have rid them of their infamy:
> if they had died in bed,
> their bodies would have been taken,
> and, all love for them forgotten,
> to purge them of their evil,
> Brahmins of the four Vedas and just principles
> would have laid them out on green grass
> ritually prepared
> and would have said,
> "Go to where warriors with renowned anklets go
> who have died in battle with their manliness their support,"
> and would have cut them with the sword.[8]

I do not believe that this notion of a warriors' paradise was native to South India. For one thing, several poems on this theme associate this idea with elements that are clearly Āryan, like the unwinking gods with unfading garlands in the first poem quoted above. For another, the notion of a warriors' paradise simply does not accord with the practice of erecting stones thought to be inhabited by the spirits of the dead, a practice that is clearly older than the Sangam poems.

There are several poems that describe reincarnation, of which some indicate that the belief is not well accepted. In *Puṟanāṉūṟu* 134, for

7. *Puṟanāṉūṟu* 62. See also *Puṟanāṉūṟu* 241.
8. *Puṟanāṉūṟu* 93.

example, the poet Uraiyūr Ēṇiccēri Muṭamōciyār sings about the king Āy:

> He is not a merchant dealing in the price of virtue,
> he does not think,
> "What I do in this birth I get back in the next."
> No, because it is the way of good men,
> his giving is the way it is.[9]

In *Naṟṟiṇai* 397, the heroine tells her friend that she will not die, even though her lover is away, for she is afraid that "if I die, and if there is another birth, I might forget my lover." In *Puṟanāṉūṟu* 214, a poem that appears to have been influenced by Jainism, a king gives the most detailed description in all the anthologies of the theory of reincarnation. The king is about to commit suicide by sitting towards the north and starving himself (an ancient custom evidently not related to any North Indian practice). He says,

> "Shall we do good acts?" you think,
> O you who do not cease your doubting,
> your hearts without resolve,
> your minds unclean.
> A hunter of elephants may get an elephant,
> a hunter of little birds may come back with empty hands.
> If, indeed, for those high ones who hunt the highest
> there is reward for acts they do,
> they may enjoy their recompense in an eternal world.
> Or if there is no living in enjoyment there,
> they may not have to be reborn.
> Yet even if they are not born again,
> one thing is vital:
> they must die with a faultless body
> establishing their fame like a towering peak of the Himālayas.

Presumably the elephant is entry to paradise or release from the cycle of transmigration, while the bird is remaining alive and experiencing earthly pleasures. Two points need to be made. First, the king is not starving himself to death as a Jain ascetic would, to gain release from *saṃsāra,* but rather because his two sons are coming against him in battle and he is disgraced. Second, after he died, stones were erected to him and those of his followers who sat and died with him, and

9. See also *Puṟanāṉūṟu* 141.

those stones were thought to be inhabited by the spirits of the dead, a point made eloquently by *Puṟanāṉūṟu* 221:

> He had the ample fame of giving to singers.
> He had the great love to give to dancers.
> He had a just sceptre praised by the righteous.
> He had steadfast love extolled by the able.
> To women he was gentle, to men, manly.
> He was a refuge for the high ones of the faultless revelation.
> But Death, caring nothing for his greatness and scorning his worth,
> took away his sweet life.
> Gather your grieving families and come, poets of true speech.
> We will abuse Death and say,
> "Mourning rests on the wide world,
> for he, putting on good fame,
> our protector,
> has become a stone."

So strong was the belief that the stones were inhabited by the spirits of the dead that, in *Puṟanāṉūṟu* 222, Pottiyār, who was told to go away and return to join the king in fasting to death only after his pregnant wife had borne a son, addresses the stone of the king upon his return:

> "After she who loves you,
> whose body is bright with ornaments radiant as fire,
> who no more leaves you than your shadow,
> has borne a glorious son,
> come."
> With such words you banished me from here, loveless one.
> Surely you will not remain silent, unmindful of me.
> Which place is mine,
> you who yearn for fame?

One of the finest pieces in Indian literature on the theory of reincarnation occurs in the *Puranāṉūṟu* (192). The poet accepts the theory, but not in the usual mechanistic sense. Life is so mysterious, he says, that even though a man is responsible for what happens to him he must show compassion to others:

> All lands home, all men kin.
> Evil and good come not from others,
> nor do pain and its abating.
> Death is nothing new;
> we do not rejoice thinking life sweet.

If there is hurt,
even less do we find it cause for grief.
Through the seeing of the able ones
we have come to know that hard life takes its course
as if it were a raft upon the waters of a mighty river
ever roaring and beating on rocks
after cold drops pour from flashing skies,
and so we do not wonder at those big with greatness
and still less do we despise the small.

These poems of the Sangam anthologies can be dated to the second and third centuries A.D. By about the fifth century, the influence of the Jainas and the Buddhists had grown, and the literature shows a growing acceptance of the doctrine of reincarnation. For example, sections of the *Nālaṭiyār,* a Jaina work, describe the fate of sinners in the next birth. Poem 122 speaks of those who imprison birds:

Their legs bound with iron,
slaves of strange kings,
they will work in black-earthed fields
who bring and keep in cages
partridges and quails
that live in forests resounding with bees.

Poem 243 is also interesting:

Whatever soil you plant it in,
the seed in the strychnine tree
does not grow into a coconut.
Men of the southern land, too, have entered paradise.
The next birth depends on one's efforts.
In the northern land too,
many many men are worthless.

The *Tirukkuṟaḷ,* which many believe was written by a Jain, also speaks of reincarnation. Verse 339, for example, says,

Like sleeping is death. Like waking
after sleep is birth.

Verse 5 says,

The two actions, good and bad, filled with darkness do not attach
to those who love the fame of God's truth.

In the *Cilappatikāram* the theory of karma has been grafted onto an older story, in which a *satī* whose husband was unjustly killed becomes a stone that must be propitiated and worshipped. The author of this work, Iḷaṅkō, spoils the tragic effect of the poem by attributing all the misfortunes of the hero and heroine to acts in a previous life.

It is important that in the history of the theory of reincarnation in Tamilnad, we can discern the Indian tendency to incorporate new ideas into a system by grafting them on the old, no matter how inconsistent the two may seem, rather than by discarding the old ideas. Thus the *Cilappatikāram* does not deny the older elements of the story—that Kaṇṇaki became a stone that was worshipped—but rather adds to that version the idea that she becomes a goddess in paradise. It appears that the indigenous notions of life after death were so unclear and inchoate that the theory of reincarnation, comparatively well-defined and clear, was not felt to conflict with them. Moreover, the old ideas concern the fate of the living, while the theory of reincarnation describes the fate of the dead soul. Very likely, these different viewpoints of the two systems were at least partly responsible for their not being perceived as contradictory. Thus the theory of reincarnation did not in any sense displace the older beliefs about the dangerous spirits of the dead and possession.

The history of religion in Tamilnad in the next few centuries is that of the emergence of devotional Hinduism and the disappearance of Buddhism and Jainism. I have argued that one of the most important reasons for this course of events was that Hinduism was able to adapt itself to native South Indian ideas regarding the king, woman, and death, while Buddhism and Jainism were not.[10] In this regard, it is quite important, I believe, that while devotional Hinduism pays lip service to the doctrine of reincarnation, its popular manifestations never make very much of that theory. Rather, works that appeal to the mass of Tamilians emphasize the older beliefs. A good example is the story of the great sinner from the *Tiruviḷaiyāṭaṟpurāṇam.* To a pious Brahmin and his good wife, a sinner was born "like a ship loaded full with murder and other cruel sins."

When he had grown into a youth,
the bad deeds [of former births] and lust, immense in its delusive power,
attracted him and overcame his strength of will
so that he desired her who had carried him and borne him from her womb.

He began to sleep with his mother, and one day, caught in the act of violating his mother by his father, he took a mattock and killed his

10. Hart, op. cit., pp. 71–72.

father. That night, he and his mother left the village for the wilderness. There they were surrounded by hunters, who took away the sinner's mother and money.

As if he thought, "Who will go with my son
now that robbers have taken his mother?
Now I shall be his companion," his father came
and held fast to him in the form of his great sin.

[The sin] would weep "Alas!" It would cry out,
"God, god, wretched, wretched is the punishment [for murder].
Help! Help!" Shaking its hands, it would dash them on the earth,
and, like a shadow, it would follow after him.

It would not let him come near a sacred tank or place holy to Śiva;
it kept him far from good men.
Nor would it allow the praise or the name of Śiva to come to his ears,
to come into his heart, to be uttered by his tongue.

It went before him and behind him.
It took hold of his garment and pulled him on.
With his great sin he wandered, tormented by helplessness, overcome by anguish.
Alone he went all over the earth, terrified and suffering.

Finally, "Śiva showed his grace, his sin dwindled and dwindled, and he drew near Madurai." Śiva and his wife, Aṅkayaṟkaṇṇi, appeared before him as a hunter and huntress, and Śiva asked him why he was so distressed.

> He stood pitifully and told how he had been born
> as the evil deeds he had done [in former births] bore fruit,
> how he had cuckolded his father and then killed him,
> how afterwards that sin had caught him, tormented him,
> and had not gone away no matter where he went,
> and how he had entered this city.

Śiva tells him that he can atone for his sin by performing devotions to the god Cuntarar (a form of Śiva) at Madurai, and by rolling around the temple 108 times three times a day. After the sinner departs, Śiva's wife asks him,

> "My lord, this wicked man has committed such a sin
> that he would not escape even if he fell for measureless time
> into 28 crores of hells.

Why, then, did you show him how he might escape?"
And the one who rides on the red-eyed bull that is Viṣṇu spoke:

"Even though a man is despicable, not even frightened of the sin of murder,
even though he deserves to perish with no support and no way of freeing himself,
bound by a sin he did without fear,
a sin so terrible that men are frightened even to think of it—
saving such a man is indeed saving," said he whose very form is compassion.

His wife replies, "If you wish it, then no matter what acts he has done a man can be saved. Such is the play of your grace." The sinner performs the devotions he has been instructed to do and finally merges with Śiva. The piece concludes:

It dispelled the sin of killing his Brahmin father and guru
after loving his own mother, and it gave salvation.
If it can do this, then how much more can bathing in this water
cure diabetes, leprosy, dropsy, and consumption.

When they found out that the great sin of the fallen Brahmin had been dispelled,
the king, his ministers, the people of the city, others on the earth,
and the gods in the sky were amazed, wondering,
"What is the reason that grace beyond telling and thought
was shown to this wicked one?"
They shed tears, praised the Lord of four-towered Madurai,
and were transported with bliss.[11]

It is immediately apparent that in this story, Śiva works outside the system of reincarnation. He gives salvation without any regard to a man's karma; indeed, the heinousness of the sins of the Brahmin make him, in some mysterious fashion, a more appropriate object of Śiva's grace than some other person with better karma. The religion described in this story is most emphatically not the devotion of the *Bhagavadgītā,* where one becomes unencumbered by one's acts by laying their fruits at the feet of God. Here, no effort is required of the man who is saved. The escape from his karma is a gift given spontaneously by Śiva as a part of His play. The theory of reincarnation is, in a real sense, irrelevant to the religion of devotion in Tamilnad.

I suggest that the notion of sin that is so prominent in the practice

11. Parañcōtimuṉivar, *Tiruviḷaiyāṭaṟpurāṇam, Kūṭaṟkāṇṭam* (Madras, Tirunelvēlit Teṉṉintiya Caivacittānta Nūṟpatippuk Kaḻakam, 1965), pp. 123–141.

of religion in Tamilnad was a complex phenomenon with roots in indigenous religious ideas. The ancient notions about death described above have far-reaching consequences: no one is so pure that he can protect himself from taint completely. Every man, no matter how careful he is in insulating himself from the dangerous forces carried by Harijans, menstruous women, and the like, is charged with some dangerous power that will produce negative results at some time in the future.[12] Moreover, the state of being charged with dangerous power is equated in the mind of the devotee with a state of sinfulness. That is shown clearly in the story of the great sinner, where the sin actually takes the form of the ghost of the dead father and torments the future devotee. A sin is not simply an act that one has done in the past, leaving *saṃskāras* that must bear fruit. It is a real force in the world, existentially the same as the spirit of the dead, that clings to one because he has become vulnerable to it through some act.[13] One possible response to this condition is to attempt to insulate oneself in an extreme manner, elaborately ordering every act one does in order

12. This, of course, holds only for the high castes. It is interesting that the Pariahs also have a notion of power that is dangerous to them. Dr. K. K. A. Venkatachari tells me that when he attempted to enter the huts of some Harijans in his village, they begged him not to because, being a Brahmin, he would cause their houses to burn down or some other misfortune to occur. See Edgar T. Thurston, *Castes and Tribes of Southern India* (Madras, 1909), VI: 88 ff. Because dangerous power has erroneously been called "pollution" by most students of caste, it has been assumed that caste is imposed from the top downwards, and that if one understands the attitudes of the higher castes, one can understand the caste system. I feel that the opposite is true. Caste is a social institution necessitated by the need to insulate oneself from dangerous power. Those who perform the task of insulating are the Harijans. Hence, to understand caste, one must understand the culture and the ethos of the Harijans, something no one has done to my knowledge.

13. See George L. Hart, III, "The Nature of Tamil Devotion," in *Aryan and Non-Aryan in India,* edited by Madhav M. Deshpande and Peter Edwin Hook, Michigan Papers on South and Southeast Asia, University of Michigan, 1979. That sins are tangible things that can suddenly cling to a person when his condition becomes disordered is shown by an excerpt from a Tamil version of *Śrīraṅgamāhātmyam:* When you sneeze, when you cough, when you yawn, when you spit, when a disease happens to your body, when you associate with sinners, when you say a false word, when you speak in accord with sinners, then if with cleanliness of the three organs—the body, [the mind, and speech]—you say with concentration, "Raṅgā!" then no danger will befall you. . . . And what is more, even if someone is a thousand *yojanas* away, if he thinks of that holy place, that great man and the ancestors in his line going back to the 21st generation will become persons of merit [*puṇṇiyavāṉkaḷ*], all the sins they did in former births having departed. (From *Śrīraṅka Mahātmiyam* [Madras, R. G. Pati Company, n.d.], pp. 11–12.)

to escape the disorder of dangerous forces. Indeed, such attempts were and are made by many high-caste people. Yet, even assuming that such extreme attempts to create order could be successful, they involve so much boundary-making, so much insulation from other human beings, that they appear antisocial and unethical to others in the society. Thus there is much literature in Tamil and allied languages disparaging narrow, ungenerous behavior. A good example is *Puṟanāṉūṟu* 50, in which a wandering poet has entered the king's palace and, because he is exhausted, lies down on a flower-covered table, not realizing that he is desecrating the table of the king's drum:

> Its black sides glisten,
> long straps fastened to them faultlessly.
> They shine with a garland woven of long, full peacock feathers,
> blue-sapphire dark, with bright spots,
> and they are splendid with golden shoots of *uḻiñai.*
> Such is the royal drum, hungry for blood.
> Before they brought it back from its bath
> I climbed on its bed unknowing,
> lying in the covering of soft flowers
> that was like a froth of oil poured down.
> Yet you were not angry,
> you did not use your sword whose edge cuts apart.
> Surely that was enough for all of Tamil land to learn of it.
> But you did not stop with that.
> You came near me,
> you raised your strong arm, as big around as a concert drum,
> you fanned me,
> and you made me cool.
> Did you do that act, mighty lord,
> because you have heard and understood
> that except for those whose fame here spreads over the broad earth,
> no one can stay there in the world of high estate?

It is not enough for a high-caste person to insulate himself from dangerous forces, for then he cannot show generosity and love to others. Indeed, a man who lives an excessively insulated life is a sinner in a worse sense than his counterpart who does not observe restrictions adequately, for he is responsible for the suffering of others. Thus he, too, becomes tainted:

> There is nothing more bitter than death, yet even that is sweet
> when one cannot give.[14]

14. *Tirukkuṟaḷ* 230.

In order to escape from sin, a high-caste man must both be insulated from dangerous power and be generous and compassionate.[15] The native system produces two dilemmas. First, no matter how one tries, he cannot entirely insulate himself from taint. Second, a man must be generous and compassionate in addition to being insulated from taint. Many in the past have written on the restrictions one must observe to attain respectability in South Indian society.[16] What has not been sufficiently emphasized is the corollary of this doctrine: a man must also be compassionate, generous, and a crosser of boundaries to be accorded respect.

An ideal life, then, involves a careful balance between building boundaries and crossing them: one must remain insulated from dangerous forces while helping other human beings regardless of their position in society. The solution to this ethical dilemma was, in the indigenous culture, to elevate the king to a position in which he could do what other human beings could not. Thus the king had the power to shield those who followed him and who lived in his kingdom from the taint of death incurred by killing in battle and in the course of daily life:

> If the rains should fall,
> if the harvest should diminish,
> if the unnatural should appear in mens' affairs,
> it is kings who are blamed by this world.[17]

Again and again the poems invoke the king's parasol as a symbolic agent that shields those in his kingdom from the destroying heat of the sun while emitting the cooling rays of the moon.[18] The significance of this figure is that charged dangerous power is considered hot, while auspicious safe things are cool. Thus those in the kingdom, and especially those who were devoted to the king and were willing to

15. Some will argue that there is no conflict between the need to insulate oneself from taint and the moral imperative to be generous and compassionate. To take such a position is, I feel, to misunderstand the importance attributed to generosity in South India. Generosity means not only distributing wealth to the less fortunate, but eating with them as well. It is significant that eating is both the most dangerous act one does every day and the act which, more than anything else, one must share with others.

16. M. N. Srinivas, *Religion and Society among the Coorgs of South India* (Oxford, 1952).

17. *Puṟanāṉūṟu* 35. See also *Puṟanāṉūṟu* 20, 68, 105, 117, 124, 204, 384, 386, 388, 389, 395, 397.

18. See especially *Puṟanāṉūṟu* 35, 60, 229.

sacrifice themselves for him, were in a naturally protected condition and could devote themselves to generosity. It may be remarked that the difficulty of the Brahmins throughout Tamil history has been that, unable to be warriors and beholden to northern gods and ideals, they did not submit to the king and his powers as did others in the society. Thus they had to devote themselves excessively to building boundaries and remaining insulated, as a result of which they were regarded with considerable ambivalence by others in the society throughout history. The Sanskritization and Brahmanization that some anthropologists have seen in South Indian society is an erroneous interpretation of the tendency indigenous to South Indian society to raise one's position by observing a delicate balance between building boundaries for insulation and being generous.[19] If men insulate themselves from dangerous power for the prestige they attain, they do so because of ideas that have been present in South India since before the coming of the Brahmins, not to imitate the Brahmins, who by their peculiar history have to build boundaries in a way that appears extreme even to others high in society.

With the coming of North Indian ideas in the centuries after Christ, the practice of worshipping specific gods, such as Śiva and Viṣṇu, arose and spread rapidly. Since there were no indigenous gods upon whom these imported deities could be modeled,[20] they were likened to the king. The evidence for this is extensive and, in my view, conclusive.[21] In the new system that arose, the god, like the king, was able to banish sin, or taint, in his devotees. Indeed, it was thought that sin was unable even to enter the god's temple. The only requirement was that one be a true subject of the god, that one manifest utter devotion and commitment. The sin that was removed by the god was none other than the taint of murder, often conceived in strikingly concrete terms, as in the story of the great sinner above. Nor could the new god destroy sin. Rather, he transferred it, making it inhere in something else. For example, in the *Tiruvāṉaikkāp-purāṇam,* cited by Shulman, there is a story of a Pandyan king who inadvertently kills a Brahmin. "The king's *brahmahatyā* still stands,

19. Srinivas, op. cit.

20. There was a cult of the god Murukaṉ before the coming of the Aryans, but that god was, in the oldest time, propitiated by a low-caste man called a Vēlaṉ with dancing and with sacrifices. As the Brahmins wished to be the priests of the new gods, they could not model them on Murukaṉ.

21. I have treated this at some length in the forthcoming "The Nature of Tamil Devotion."

waiting for him, at the eastern gate [of the temple], where it receives offerings of salt and spices. Complete safety exists only inside the shrine."[22] Here again, it should be noted, the sin of the king is clearly identified with the spirit of the man whom he has killed.

It was not only the live king that the new deities were modeled upon; they also derived some of their character from indigenous spirits and gods that were propitiated and contained to keep them under control. The new gods were not above being capricious or demanding blood sacrifice. Shulman cites a story about Kāmākṣī, the goddess at Kāñci: "When the chariot of the Paḷḷis was arrested at Kāñci, the sacrifice of a woman pregnant with her first child induced Kāmākṣī to make the chariot move again."[23] One of the most popular stories of devotion in South India is that of Kaṇṇappar, who tears out his eyes and places them on the liṅga to gratify Śiva.[24] It is possible that this aspect of the new gods was modeled upon the cult of the ancestors of kings.[25] Whatever the case, the new gods, like the indigenous gods and the spirits of the dead, were sometimes capricious, were associated with blood sacrifice,[26] and were able to possess the living.

It is thus in two ways that indigenous notions about the dead come into the religion of devotion. First, the god is able to banish all dead spirits and taint of death from his domain and the hearts of his devotees, and second the god is capricious, is associated with blood sacrifice, and is able to possess, like the spirits of the dead. Neither of these has any connection with reincarnation.

The ultimate goal of devotional religion differs with its adherents. In general, worship of a god provides a way out of the dilemmas and impasses created by the extremely rigid social structure of South India. An important aspect of this function has been discussed above: the god's power to remove the taint of death. It must be stressed that South Indian society is one in which social exigencies—caste restrictions, family structure, pressure to conform in undesired ways, and other restrictions whose ultimate purpose is to insulate from taint—often clash with personal desires or with a sense of what is ethical and

22. Shulman, op. cit., p. 385.
23. Ibid., p. 62.
24. See Hart, "The Nature of Tamil Devotion." For the story of Kaṇṇappaṉ, see G. U. Pope, *The Tiruvāçagam* (Oxford, 1900), pp. 141–145 n.
25. Peter Claus has suggested that some cults in Tulunad are based upon worship of a king's ancestors.
26. See Shulman, op. cit., p. 482.

moral. Indeed, this is true even of North Indian society, where the *Bhagavadgītā* solves the dilemma by an appeal to duty over everything else. In Tamilnad, no easy solution was possible, for in its society from the earliest times, ethical notions such as generosity and compassion received an emphasis that they did not have in North India with its ascetic traditions.[27] As a result, in Tamil society guilt plays a predominant role: few are able to escape totally a sense of their own inadequacy at being unable to reconcile themselves to the role that society demands of them. It is the function of the god of devotion to provide relief for such people, a relief that is psychologically effective because of the commitment and abasement shown to the god. The channel for relief is power, but not merely a generalized, inchoate power. For the sins of the devotee are conceived in ancient terms: they are ultimately made of the same stuff as the ghosts of the dead that possess, spread havoc, and create disorder. The power to remove such sins must be of the same substance (though, since it belongs to the god, it is under control and can help the devotee). Thus it, too, is a power that can possess and that can, if not carefully controlled by devotion, cause havoc.

There is, of course, a more sophisticated level at which devotional religion operates, a level reflected by such works as the Caiva Cittānta treatises, Rāmānuja's commentaries, and some Sthalapurāṇas. At this level, the aim of worship is not mainly to provide peace of mind for people caught in a difficult social system; it is actually to merge with the god. It is true that these expressions of *bhakti* appropriated the North Indian system of reincarnation; however, they have done so in such a way that it remains essentially extraneous. In its most coherent formulations in North Indian texts, the system of rebirth is a mechanical one, the acts one does inevitably determining what happens in the future. The cycle of rebirth is, of course, inescapable so long as one has *saṃskāras* produced by past deeds that must come to fruition. The way out of *saṃsāra* involves either the cessation of action (Jainism, the Ājīvikas) or a realization of the true nature of existence

27. I believe that the lack of emphasis on ethical subjects in ancient North Indian literature is at least partly occasioned by the ascetic traditions that flourished there. The *Bhagavadgītā* uses the ascetic tradition to justify the adherence to duty in the face of an ethical dilemma. There is no ancient work of North India that I know of that, like the *Tirukkuṟaḷ*, is based upon such ethical subjects as love, forbearance, and family life. It is significant that the two poems from Sangam literature that describe the life of an ascetic center about the great tragedy that must have happened to the ascetic to make him leave family life (*Puṟanāṉūṟu* 251, 252).

(the Upaniṣads, Buddhism). By the time of the *Bhagavadgītā* the solution to the dilemma of *saṃsāra* is to transfer *(sannyas)* the fruits of one's actions to God, so that they are no longer binding. While it could be argued that in all but the first of these movements, the system of reincarnation is basically foreign, it is nonetheless undeniable that it has been incorporated in a basic way into all of them. The truth of the Upaniṣads and the Buddhists, and the God of the *Bhagavadgītā,* all include in their operations the system of transmigration. For the *bhakti* movement this is not so. The relation of God to the system of transmigration is not made clear (except in a few abstruse treatises). Rather, the *bhakti* poets exclaim again and again:

I struggled in the great whirlpool
    of birth and death.
Overcome by desire, I fell into
    uniting with ornamented women.
The Lord who has a woman for part of him
    made me join his feet.
What that First One granted me
    who can receive?[28]

The system of transmigration has been adopted as an evidence of the irremediably tainted condition of man. God exists outside of it as an escape totally independent of *saṃsāra.* One's efforts are made not to escape from rebirth, but rather to attain God. Thus in a famous verse, Appar sings,

Even if I am born a worm, O kind one [*puṇṇiyā*], you must grant that I hold your feet firmly in mind.[29]

The universe is God's play for the devotee. Even though he may pay lip service to the system of transmigration, he really believes that suffering is a test sent by God, not a result of his past actions. In the story of the Little Devotee, for example, God hears of the devotee's piety and decides to test him, much as the God of the Old Testament tested Job:

In those days his [the devotee's] deeds of service went
and attained the venerable feet of the Lord who dwells on Kailāsa mountain.
That Lord who rides the bull, in order to experience his love that never fails,
came from his mountain as a fearful ascetic, his heart disposed to grace.[30]

28. *Tiruvācakam* 51.8.
29. *Tēvāram Aṭaṅkaṉmuṟai* (Madras, 1953), vol. II, poem 5078.
30. *Tiruttoṇṭar Purāṇam Eṉṉum Periyapurāṇam,* comm. C. K. Cuppiramaṇiyamutaliyār (Coimbatore, 1953), verse 3685.

As part of his vow, the Little Devotee must feed the disguised Śiva. When it turns out that the ascetic will accept only the meat of a first-born human male child, the Little Devotee and his wife kill their only son, cook him, and serve him. Finally, his devotion established, the devotee is merged with Śiva along with his wife and his son, who has been brought back to life by the God. There are many other stories in this vein, the purport of which is that life is a test to be passed through total and unswerving loyalty to God. Suffering conceived as the result of one's past actions, while mentioned on occasion (as in the story of the Great Sinner), is clearly not an indispensable part of the religion of *bhakti*. *Saṃsāra* itself is conceived not as an intricate mechanism for the recompense of one's acts, but rather as a nightmarish condition from which the only release is God. Nor can God be bought by action or even devotion. He acts in inscrutable ways and is not predictable. His grace is freely given. As Śaṅkara is supposed to have said,

> Birth again, death again,
> lying in a mother's womb again and again.
> In this *saṃsāra*, very wide, without end,
> out of compassion save me, lord Murāri.

We have been able to delineate one element that helped devotional Hinduism defeat Buddhism and Jainism in Tamilnad. The heterodox religions put great stress upon the theory of transmigration, as is shown by such Tamil works as the Jaina *Cilappatikāram* and the *Nālaṭiyār* and the Buddhist *Maṇimēkalai*. Even where such works expressed indigenous religious concepts, as when the stone for Kaṇṇaki is brought from the Himālayas in the *Cilappatikāram*, they are not made part of the Jaina or Buddhist religion. On the other hand, devotional Hinduism paid lip service to the doctrine of rebirth, but incorporated into itself and, indeed, based itself upon the vague indigenous ideas concerning death and the fate of the dead. Not only did it base the concept of sin upon the idea of the spirit of the dead; it also derived many important characteristics of the god himself from this idea. The southern religion of devotion was indeed a radically new religion in South Asia.

Part II.

Buddhism and Jainism

6

The Rebirth Eschatology and Its Transformations: A Contribution to the Sociology of Early Buddhism

GANANATH OBEYESEKERE

Introduction

This paper will inquire into the origins of the karma theory in a somewhat unorthodox manner by ignoring the Hindu-Buddhist texts in which that theory is presented and describing instead the hypothetical and ideal typical manner in which the karma-rebirth theory probably evolved. If my procedure seems outrageous it is, I submit, less hazardous and more rewarding than attempting to find the origin of the theory on the basis either of texts which have little or no reference to it (e.g., the Vedas and Upaniṣads) or of texts where the theory is in full bloom, elaborated by the speculative thought of Hindu-Buddhist-Jaina philosophers.[1] Many of the discussions of karma-

1. The first version of this paper, written in 1975, included a long preliminary section entitled "The Gangetic Religious Tradition." Basically my thesis here favors ideas developed by scholars like Kosambi and others who viewed the *sāmanic* religions (Jainism, Buddhism, and Ājīvikaism) as products of the Gangetic rather than the Indus area or the Brahmavarta, the region of East Punjab which was the locus classicus of early Vedism and Brāhmanism. The *sāmanas* were speculative thinkers who systematized diverse existing philosophical and popular religious traditions (ideas from Mohenjodaro and Harappa, Vedism, and the tribal traditions of the Ganges region) into the great religions of the sixth century B.C. I am grateful to Frank

rebirth assume that it was invented by Indian thinkers, whereas the evidence I shall submit will show that rebirth theories are very widespread, both in fantasy, as Stevenson has shown,[2] and in the institutionalized eschatology of tribal peoples in different parts of the world. In all likelihood, rebirth theories were found in ancient Indian tribal religions, probably in the Gangetic region where the great "heterodox" religions flourished.[3] The Indian religious philosophers can be credited, not with the invention of the rebirth theory, but rather with transforming the "rebirth eschatology" into the "karmic eschatology," through a process of speculative activity which I label "ethicization." Even here the Hindu-Buddhist-Jaina thinkers had competition from the Greeks of 600 B.C., notably Pythagoras and the Orphics, who produced an eschatological scheme remarkably similar to the karma theory. This essay then attempts to view rebirth theories in comparative perspective and thereby to derive, in an admittedly speculative but logically rigorous manner, the *process* whereby the rebirth eschatology is transformed into the karmic eschatology

---

Reynolds and Agehananda Bharati for comments on earlier versions of this paper. [Ed: The reader will find other related discussions of karma in Obeyesekere's article, "Theodicy, Sin and Salvation in a Sociology of Buddhism," in *Dialectic in Practical Religion,* ed. E. R. Leach (Cambridge University Press, 1968).]

2. Ian Stevenson, *Twenty Cases Suggestive of Reincarnation* (Charlottesville, Va., 1974).

3. I use the term "heterodox" advisedly. In fact, my thesis is that the great *sāmanic* religions were heterodox only vis-à-vis Brāhmanism. These religions were the orthodox traditions of the Gangetic region. It should be noted that the Kings of Magadha and Kosala were simply continuing the practice of the region when they patronized the Gangetic religions: it was a continuing religious tradition held in high regard by the people of the region. The same tradition was followed in the later history of Magadha, after it became the Maurya Empire under Chandragupta. Many scholars have had to justify the fact that Asoka became a Buddhist; they have been skeptical about the Jaina view that Chandragupta became a Jaina ascetic in his old age, or that Bindusāra was an Ājīvika. These accounts certainly fit in with our preceding discussion; the kings were personally committed to the ascetic religions, though Brāhmanism was becoming increasingly important for state ritual. That persons within the same family should give preference to one of the three religions—Buddhism, Jainism, and Ājīvikaism—is again expectable, since they were all part of an overall tradition of ascetic *sāmanas* indigenous to the region.

The tradition of shifting allegiance from one *sāmanic* religion to another or extending special patronage to one seemed to have continued till very much later. The *Silappadikaram* composed in South India sometime between the fifth and eighth centuries A.D. deals with urban merchant groups who belonged to the Gangetic religions. The author of this epic is a Jaina; the protagonists Kovalan and Kannaki are also Jaina. Yet, Kannaki's father became an Ājīvika, Madevi became a Buddhist, and her daughter, a Buddhist saint.

through the operation of the crucial causal variable known as ethicization. I shall then examine the kind of speculative activity in early Buddhist-Jaina thinkers that produced this transformation, which in turn will lead us to a discussion of some key features of the sociology of early Buddhism, Jainism, and Ājīvikaism.

The Rebirth Eschatology and Its Transformations

I shall construct a model of a simple rebirth eschatology and show how this model gets transformed into the more complex eschatologies of the great Gangetic religions. I suggest that the hypothetical processes we delineate in the model will help us to clarify actual processes that would have occurred in history. My assumption here is that religious eschatologies are not unique creations of individual religious geniuses, but are also collective representations—socially shared ideational systems—which have their genesis in the social structure and the collective historical experience of a particular social group. The three great indigenous religions of South Asia—Buddhism, Hinduism, and Jainism—have many features, particularly in the realm of ethics, psychology, and eschatology, which clearly express the views of religious geniuses like the Buddha, Mahāvīra, or Nāgārjuṇa. Religious geniuses, however, did not speculate in a socio-cultural vacuum; they are themselves products of their times, and their views are constrained by the political and social circumstances of the periods in which they lived and, above all, by their own prior cultural (ideological) heritage.

Jainism, Buddhism and later Hinduism are individual religions which nevertheless share the following common set of eschatological features:

A theory of rebirth that postulates a cyclical theory of continuity, so that death is merely a temporary state in a continuing process of births and rebirths.

A theory of karma that postulates that one's present existence is determined for the most part by the ethical nature of one's past actions.

A theory of the nature of existence known as *saṃsāra,* which includes all living things in the cycle of endless continuity.

A theory of salvation *(nirvāṇa),* the salient characteristic of which is the view that salvation must involve the cessation of rebirth, and must therefore occur outside of the whole cycle of continuity, or *saṃsāra*. Each religion may emphasize different aspects of this eschatology, and some even differ radically from others (e.g., the Hindu view of the *ātman*, or soul, and the Buddhist view of the absence of soul, or *anatta);* but the main eschatological outlines are common to these three religions of South Asia. The term karmic eschatology refers to the first three characteristics of the eschatology. The karmic eschatology, it can be presumed, constitutes the common core, or base, of the three religions on which are built their respective ideological variations and doctrinal elaborations.

The question that I pose is as follows: What is the genesis of the karmic eschatology and how did it evolve into its present form? I assume that the karmic eschatology did not emerge out of nothing, and I agree with Fürer-Haimendorf that it evolved out of a prior, simpler or primitive eschatological scheme.[4] When we examine the karmic eschatology we feel that among its three features—karma, *nirvāṇa* (salvation), and rebirth—the critical feature is rebirth. Why? When we look at eschatologies cross-culturally, we find that there are many primitive or preliterate societies that possess theories of rebirth but lack any idea of karma or *nirvāṇa* in their eschatologies. Such preliterate rebirth eschatologies occur in societies as different and geographically remote from each other as the Trobriand Islands and the Igbo of South East Nigeria. We shall assume that Indian society also had a rebirth theory of a "primitive kind," of the same type as that of Trobriand or Igbo, and that the karmic eschatology is a later development from this primitive base. We then construct a model of a rebirth eschatology which can be applicable to any society that holds a doctrine of rebirth. Thus, the model contains the fundamental structural features essential to any rebirth doctrine, minus those substantive and cross-societally variable features found in any empirical case. Having constructed a primitive rebirth eschatology, we then perform certain operations which show how this model is transformed into the more complex karmic eschatology. The term "transformation" as I use it is a sociological notion more in the tradition of Max Weber than of Lévi-Strauss or transformational linguistics. I will show how the introduction of a single causal variable—in this case a process known as ethicization—transforms the simple rebirth theory into the karmic eschatology. Existent rebirth eschatologies like other empirically manifest cultural structures show structural similarities as

4. C. von Fürer-Haimendorf, "The After-life in Indian Tribal Belief," *Journal of the Royal Anthropological Institute* 83 (1953): 37–49.

well as differences. Transformational studies cannot be performed by the use of concrete existent cases with their substantive variations; a model that draws out the structural features common to a variety of empirically existent systems must be constructed so as to show the transformational process. But the ideal model has to be contructed on our knowledge of existent systems. Therefore let me present the empirical cases that helped us construct the ideal rebirth eschatology.

NON-INDIAN REBIRTH ESCHATOLOGY: THE TROBRIAND

Trobriand have an inverted version of the conventional eschatology, for the Trobriand heaven is located in the nether world. According to Trobriand, a new life begins at the death of the individual, when his spirit, or soul *(balōma),* moves to Tuma, the Island of the Dead located "underneath." Here in Tuma the individual leads a pleasant life, analogous to the terrestrial life but much happier. Life in the other world is characterized by perpetual youth, which is preserved by bodily rejuvenation.

When the spirit, or *balōma,* sees that bodily hair is covering his skin, that his skin is getting wrinkled, or his hair grey, he simply sloughs off the old and takes on a new appearance—black locks, smooth skin, no bodily hair. The power of rejuvenation, enjoyed by spirits in Tuma (the nether world), was previously enjoyed by all humanity before it was lost through inadvertence and ill will.

When a spirit becomes tired of constant rejuvenation after a long spell "underneath," he may want to come back to life on earth. To do this, the spirit leaps far back in age and becomes a small, unborn infant. Some of Malinowski's informants explained why the spirits become tired of their heavenly abode. They said that in Tuma, as on earth, there are sorcerers. Evil sorcery is frequently practised and can reach a spirit and make him weak, sick, and tired of life; then he will go back to the human world. However, one cannot ever kill a spirit with evil magic or accident as in the human world (where sorcery is the classic interpretation of death), since "his end will always mean merely a new beginning." These rejuvenated spirits, or little preincarnated babies, or spirit children, are the only source from which humanity draws its supplies of life. The spirit finds its way back to the Trobriands and there into the womb of some woman—but always a woman of the same clan and subclan as the spirit child itself. There are different versions as to how this occurs, but no controversy about its actual occurrence. The main facts have always been "that all the spirits have ultimately to end their life in Tuma and turn into unborn infants; that every child born in this world has come into existence *(ibubuli)* in Tuma through the metamorphosis of a spirit: that the main reason and the real cause of every birth lies in nothing else but in the spiritual action."[5]

NON-INDIAN REBIRTH ESCHATOLOGY: THE IGBO

Igbo have a more complex eschatology. There are certain elements in the Igbo model that resemble the karmic eschatology, which I shall discuss later. Igbo have a polytheistic pantheon with various nature spirits, a mother goddess, ancestors, and a creator God who is *deus otiosus*. There is also a very important guardian spirit, *Chi:*

> a personal god whose role approximates to that of a guardian spirit; *Chi* determines one's fate on earth. On it is blamed one's failures. It is *Chi* who guides one to fortune or misfortune. God gives man choice, and it is one's *Chi* who leads him in the exercise of this choice.[6]

In addition to all this is a theory of rebirth.

> Reincarnation is cardinal in the religious belief of the Igbo. Its chief role is to give hope to those who feel they have failed to achieve their status goal. In the next reincarnation, it is strongly believed, a man has a chance to achieve his objectives. Transmigration, on the other hand, is conceived as the greatest punishment for the incestuous, the murderer, and the witch. "*Ilodigh uwa na mmadu*"—"may you not reincarnate in human form"—is a great curse for the Igbo.[7]

Let me present briefly the outlines of the Igbo rebirth eschatology, as described by Uchendu. Unlike Trobriand, the Igbo are fully aware of the biological facts of conception, "but other factors are also involved in pregnancy and are much more important: the consent of the deities and willingness of dead lineage members and other friendly spirits to reincarnate themselves. The absence of either of these two agents renders conception impossible, the Igbo say."[8] Thus, Igbo views on conception and birth are based on an assumption of rebirth; the ancestral soul is reincarnated in the womb of a woman (probably of the same lineage as that of the dead man, though the evidence is not clear on this point). In any rebirth theory the problem of the identity

5. B. Malinowski, *The Father in Primitive Psychology* (New York, 1966), p. 32.
6. Victor C. Uchendu, "The Status Implications of Igbo Religious Beliefs," *The Nigerian Field* 29:27–37 (1964), 35.
7. Ibid., p. 34.
8. Victor C. Uchendu, *The Igbo of Southeast Nigeria* (New York, 1965).

of the newborn in his previous birth is difficult to determine. In Trobriand, where there is a perfectly closed cycle, the identity problem is relatively clear: one is born in the same lineage and clan. But the exact kinship relationship is impossible to determine by normal human cognition. In the South Asian religions, the capacity for precognition is the gift of special virtuosi. In Igbo, the diviner helps to identify the exact kin relation of the neonate in his previous incarnation. At death the Igbo soul, guided by his guardian spirit, *Chi,* confronts the creator. The creator presents the soul with two parcels, one of which contains "the desired social positions that the individual predicted during his *Ebibi* (prereincarnation social position that the individual predicts during his lifetime on earth)." The bargain with god includes such things as long life on earth, "intelligence, wealth, 'having mouth,' that is, the power of oratory and wisdom."[9] Those who fail to make the right choice by bargaining with the creator need not despair, for they can be reborn on earth again "and hope for better luck during the next cycle."[10] Furthermore, unless he has violated a taboo the Igbo need not fear the other world, since Igbo have no conception of hell. Thus, if he has made a poor bargain with the creator, he can well afford to wait another lifetime.

What is the nature of the Igbo afterlife? Fundamental to the Igbo (and Trobriand) is the absence of a notion of heaven and hell as a means of retribution or reward. The soul joins the world of the ancestors, so that the invisible society is simply a continuation of the lineage structure of the earthly society. "In the Igbo conception, the world of the 'dead' is a world full of activities; its inhabitants manifest in their behavior and their thought processes that they are 'living.' The dead continue their lineage system; they are organized in lineages with patrilineal emphasis just as those on earth."[11]

Thus the Igbo afterworld is a reified version of the mundane social structure. After a sojourn in the afterworld the dead are reborn in the earthly social structure, except for those who have violated taboos. The latter have an inferior rebirth; they "are born feet first, or with teeth, or as members of a twin set—all of which are in themselves taboo."[12]

FORMAL FEATURES OF A PRELITERATE REBIRTH ESCHATOLOGY

I shall now construct a simplified ideal model of a rebirth eschatology typical of preliterate societies. Substantive and cross-societally

9. Ibid., p. 16. 10. Ibid., p. 17. 11. Ibid., p. 12. 12. Ibid., p. 102.

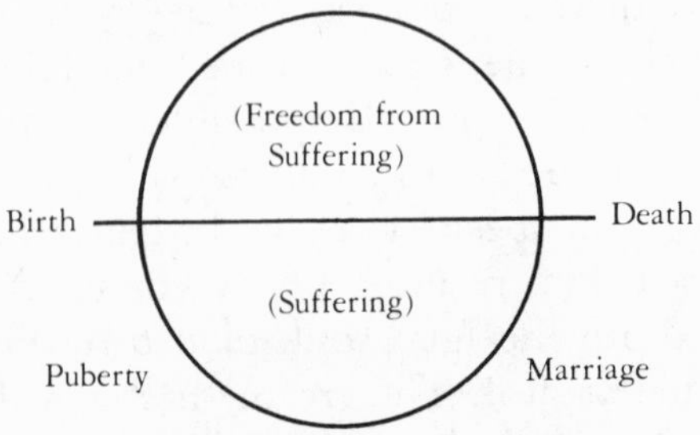

variable cultural features are eliminated from the model, so that it is a culture-free representation of the rebirth eschatology. The model can be represented as follows:

Birth transfers the individual from some otherworld (the invisible world) to the visible human world. Rites of passage at birth assist in this perilous transition. The human world into which the individual is transferred at birth is a world of suffering—in Weber's and Parson's sense of the term. During the individual's life in the human world, religious, magical, and other techniques help him cope with the problem of suffering. Especially critical are so-called life-crises, where the individual is transferred from one social status to another. Each transition tends to be viewed as a symbolic death and rebirth or, as Hertz puts it, as an *exclusion* followed by an *inclusion* in a new status.[13] When real death occurs, funeral rituals serve to transfer the individual once again to the invisible world of the dead. In some eschatologies the soul stays in the other world permanently, but in a rebirth eschatology by definition the soul's stay in the other world is temporary, for he has to be reborn in the human world at some time or other. It is indeed possible that the otherworld—in the sense of a sacred place where souls sojourn—may hardly exist or may be bypassed altogether; in this case the soul, soon after release from the body, seeks reincarnation in a new corporeal body in another earthly existence. In the ideal model of the rebirth eschatology, there is a perfectly closed cycle: a limited pool of souls moving round and round through time in a circle, as in the figure sketched above.

13. Robert Hertz, *Death and the Right Hand* (translated by R. and C. Needham, New York, 1960).

Let us now sketch in more detail the formal features of a rebirth eschatology.

The Structure of the Otherworld. Once the soul has surmounted death it may stay temporarily in some otherworld. What is the nature of that otherworld, and how is it structured? In order to construct another world human beings must perforce draw upon their experience of the earthly society in which they live. This is particularly true of small-scale preliterate societies where the experience of individuals is generally limited to their own group. The image of the otherworld is based on this world. Yet, as Hertz points out, the otherworld need not be a replica of this one. Since it is a product of the mind, human beings could express through it their fantasies of a utopia or a paradise, where suffering is eliminated. "It is or can be the realm of the ideal," says Hertz.[14] Thus, three logical possibilities regarding the structure of the otherworld should be added to our model; it should be realized that these logical possibilities are empirically realized in actual rebirth eschatologies.

The otherworld does not exist, or is a vague unstructured zone.

The otherworld is more or less a duplicate of the social structure of this world (as among the Igbo).

The otherworld is a paradise or Elysium or an idealized version of the mundane social structure (as among the Trobriand).

In all of the foregoing there could be a special evil otherworld where violators of taboos, or those who commit specially heinous crimes (e.g., sorcery) are punished. In a rebirth eschatology the paradisal or Elysium notion of the otherworld cannot be a permanent state of bliss or non-suffering, since the soul's stay there is temporary, and it must be reborn on earth, which is conditioned by "suffering." Moreover, a real problem of explanation is involved in such eschatologies, for if the otherworld is one of bliss, what motivates the individual to be reborn on earth? Malinowski's Trobriand informants realized this problem and gave him various different interpretations, such as the existence of sorcerers in their Elysium or plain boredom with paradise.

Rebirth, Transmigration, and Metempsychosis. A rebirth theory, in my usage, must involve a cultural belief in rebirth in the world of humans. The perfectly closed cycle of the preliterate rebirth model (empirical approximation: Trobriand) is broken up when, on the em-

14. Ibid., p. 79.

pirical level, the rebirth eschatology is associated with a doctrine of transmigration, where the soul sojourns in other spheres of existence outside of the human. Thus, Igbo have an addition to the rebirth eschatology, a transmigration theory to account for a class of individuals barred from human reincarnation. A transmigration theory, without rebirth, should not be confused with a rebirth eschatology.

The Absence of "Ethicization." Let me add another feature to the rebirth model sketched above: the absence of the religious evaluation of moral and ethical action, or "ethicization." Analytically viewed, morality and religion are separate spheres of action. Morality deals with the evaluation of social action in terms of "good" and "bad." I suggest that in the ideal rebirth eschatology there is no ethicization: morally wrong actions are not religiously wrong actions, and ethically good actions are not religiously good actions. The analytical distinction between ethics and religion is maintained in the ideal model. At death the individual is transferred to the otherworld irrespective of the nature of the good and bad done by him in this world. Using ethical terminology from the great religions, the otherworld is for saint and sinner alike. There is no notion of ethical compensation or reward, that is, sin and merit. "Sin" is defined as the violation of an ethical norm, which is ipso facto a religious norm; "merit" is the conformity to an ethical norm which is also a religious norm. Both are religious assessments of moral action absent from the ideal rebirth eschatology.

Ideal models or types, as Weber realized, are never duplicated in reality; only type approximation is possible. The utility of the ideal model is that it permits us, among other things, to deal with causal variables that transform the model into another type. This is what we propose doing. What are the causal variables that transform the preliterate rebirth eschatology into the karmic eschatology of the three great South Asian religions? The critical variable, I postulate, is the presence of ethicization in the latter. If the preliterate rebirth model is ethicized it *must* transform itself into the karmic eschatology. In order to show how this occurs it is necessary to spell out in more detail the concept of ethicization.

Sin and merit, we noted, are absent from the rebirth eschatology; sin, in the sense in which we have defined it, presupposes an ethicization of the religious life. Social action is always normatively sanctioned, but in the preliterate model such normative sanction is dependent on a secular rather than a religious morality. For example, it is always the case that an adulterer has violated a moral norm; but it does not follow from this that he has violated a religious norm. In the great historical religions of literate civilizations, the ethical life is systematically implicated in the religion so that any violation of an ethical or moral tenet involves simultaneously a violation of a religious tenet. This implies that the religion has been ethicized, that is, converted into an ethical system. It is likely that on the empirical level there is no religion devoid of ethical implications, but the systematic ethicization of religion is a product of evolution from a "primitive" base. How does the systematic ethicization of the religious life arise in the evolution of religion? This, it seems to me, is fundamentally due to the activities of a highly specialized priesthood engaged in speculative activity; or, as in the case of the biblical tradition, it may be due to ethical prophecy; or ethical asceticism may be operative, as in Buddhism. Literacy per se is probably of little consequence except in facilitating the process of ethicization. As far as the South Asian tradition is concerned, the intellectual climate from the period of the Upaniṣads until the time of the Buddha was conducive to religious and ethical speculation.

THE TRANSFORMATION OF THE PRELITERATE REBIRTH ESCHATOLOGY

When ethicization occurs, the rebirth eschatology must be logically transformed into a karmic eschatology in the following manner:

Since ethicization implies the religious evaluation of moral action, actions that are morally good or bad are transformed into actions that are also religiously good or bad; that is, the notions of sin and religious merit must develop.

Inasmuch as any social morality must punish (with negative sanctions) those who violate moral norms and reward those who conform, so a religious morality must also reward and punish. But in what manner? A purely social morality is concerned only with the earthly existence of humans. Since, by contrast, a rebirth eschatology entails other existences after death, religious rewards and punishments must extend to the whole eschatological sphere. This consequence of ethicization could be called "the principle of the conditionality or contingency of reward."

In the primitive rebirth eschatology the otherworld is for all; the transfer to the otherworld depends on the proper performance of the funeral rites. But when this system is ethicized, entry to the otherworld must be contingent, depending on the ethical nature of a person's this-worldly actions. What is the logical effect of the principle of the contingency of reward on the structure of the otherworld?

The otherworld must be transformed into a world of retribution and reward. If the rebirth eschatology possesses any concept of the otherworld—be it a paradisal one, as in Trobriand, or a replica of this world, as in Igbo—it must minimally split into two, a world of retribution (hell) and a world of reward (heaven). Thus, notions of heaven and hell are a part of the architecture of the otherworld where retribution and reward are meted out on the basis of an individual's this-worldly actions. The minimal logically expectable consequence of ethicization is the splitting of the otherworld into two; the actual number of mythic worlds will usually depend on the nature of the earthly social system. In Hinduism, for example, with its social structure of caste, there are multiple stratified mythical worlds of retribution and reward. When a religion is ethicized, notions such as heaven and hell must be invented. In every case heaven and hell are the just compensations for merit and sin in any ethicized religious system. The soul's stay in the otherworld is by definition temporary, or it may be bypassed altogether and the soul be reborn in a human world. But note: The earth in which the soul is reborn has already been ethicized, prior to the soul's arrival, so to speak. The earthly social structure into which the soul arrives is a place where the ideas of sin, merit, and contingency of reward have already developed as consequences of ethicization. Therefore, the operation of the principle of the contingency of reward must result in a good rebirth and a bad rebirth based on the quality of an individual's actions in this world, which inevitably must be actions during his previous lifetime. In other words, the human world itself must become a world of retribution and reward: a proto-karmic theory. What are the nature and content of these good and bad rebirths? These cannot be predicted by the manipulation of the model, but one would guess that, on the empirical level, rebirth rewards would pertain to health, wealth, and high status (all culturally defined), while retribution would involve their undesirable opposites. These types of rewards and punishments—especially status and wealth—inevitably upset the scheme found in both Trobriand and Igbo, where the individual is reborn in the very same lineage he occupied in his previous lifetime on earth (and, by definition, in all prior lifetimes). If status and wealth are allocated as rebirth rewards and punishments, he must be reborn in a position commensurate with his load of sin and merit rather than his lineage affiliations.

We noted above that the world in which the individual is reborn is, as a result of ethicization, a world of retribution and reward influenced by the nature of his actions in a previous lifetime. But, logically, his previous lifetime has been in turn influenced by a still earlier lifetime, and so on. Thus, ethicization of a rebirth eschatology, pushed to its logical extreme, links one lifetime with another in a continuing series of ethical links: which simply means that the South Asian theory of *saṃsāra* and karma has fully developed.

Ethicization results in a powerful "ontological" explanation for the necessity and nature of rebirth, a type of explanation absent in a simple rebirth eschatology.

Thus far we have seen how the ideal primitive rebirth model logically produces several elements of the karmic eschatology when the notion of ethicization is introduced into it. But the crucial concept of *nirvāṇa* or salvation is not entailed by the ethicization of the rebirth model. We have deduced an eschatology where the karma-bound "soul" wanders in *saṃsāra* in a cycle of births and rebirths: compensation for good and bad is meted out in the otherworld or the next rebirth or both. The doctrines of karma and *saṃsāra* have developed, but not the concept of *nirvāṇa*.

Nirvāṇa, therefore, cannot be derived from the ethicization of the rebirth eschatology. However, the kind of religious specialists interested in ethicization would also be interested in pushing speculation further by concerning themselves with salvation. Some of the religious virtuosi of sixth century India certainly were. If and when this occurs, the form that striving for salvation takes is entirely determined by the ethicization process described here. I define "salvation" as "a state in which suffering has been eliminated." Pure bliss results from this state. It is the ultimate status a human being achieves and the final goal of human endeavor. Says Weber: "Not every rational religious ethic is necessarily an ethic of salvation. Thus, Confucianism is a religious ethic but it knows nothing at all of a need for salvation. On the other hand, Buddhism is exclusively a doctrine of salvation";[15] and, one might add, later Hinduism and Jainism too have clearly developed notions of salvation. All these three religions

15. Max Weber, *The Sociology of Religion* (translated by Ephraim Fischoff, New York, 1963), p. 146.

may define *nirvāṇa* differently, but these definitions have one thing in common: *nirvāṇa* has to be sought outside of *saṃsāra* or the whole scheme of births and rebirths, and it must result in the cessation of rebirth and karma. I shall demonstrate that the Indian idea of salvation outside of the rebirth cycle is not particularly unique or "original," but is an inevitable logical consequence of the ethicization of a preliterate rebirth eschatology.

Nirvāṇa, or salvation, is the elimination of suffering. In many non-rebirth eschatologies suffering is eliminated in the hereafter and the soul enjoys permanent bliss. In these systems the following equation obtains: heaven or paradise = salvation = elimination of suffering. In a rebirth eschatology this equation is falsified by the fact that the souls' sojourn in heaven must perforce be temporary (not a permanent state of bliss), and by the presence of suffering in the next human rebirth. Heaven at best is an alleviation of suffering, never its elimination; and rebirth clearly implies its presence. If so, salvation must logically and inevitably occur outside of the karmic and *saṃsāric* (rebirth) process. *Nirvāṇa* is the abolition of rebirth and *saṃsāra;* logically the one cannot occur within the other. Empirically, Buddhism, for example, defines *nirvāṇa* as a "cessation of rebirth," "elimination of karma," for this very reason. There can be no other way of achieving *nirvāṇa* except outside of the rebirth cycle. In other words, if *nirvāṇa*, or salvation, is defined as a state where suffering has been eliminated (or, more positively, as a state of pure bliss), then it is logically impossible to achieve salvation within any rebirth theory. *One must abolish rebirth in order to achieve salvation.* This is not simply an idea that religious leaders have invented: they must invent it, since it is entailed by the logical structure of any rebirth theory.

PYTHAGORAS AND THE ORPHIC MYSTERIES: THE GREEK EVIDENCE

The preceding discussion could be clarified further if we move away once again from the Indian context to a comparative perspective, this time to highly developed and ethicized rebirth theories from the Greeks of the sixth century B.C. and after. Let me briefly discuss two Greek eschatologies which clearly had karma-type beliefs, though of course not the term itself. Both Pythagoreans and Orphics believed in rebirth, though the details of their eschatological doctrines have not survived. The Pythagoreans were a tight ascetic order, and in view of the founder's own contributions to Greek science and mathematics, they probably had a more intellectual religion than that of the Orphics. This is also evident in Pythagoras' positive relationship to the Apollonian cultus (he was known as "the son of Apollo"), whereas Orphism was rooted in the Dionysian mysteries.[16] Both practiced elaborate food taboos, especially "meat eating and the spread of pollution through the medium of animal skins,"[17] though the Pythagorean taboos were more elaborate. Both believed in the purification of the soul through successive births. The Orphics in particular saw the soul as the prisoner of the body; "body was the tomb of the soul."[18] According to Aristotle, the purified soul, in Pythagorean theory, may become incarnate in the philosopher and religious teacher who then raises the level of others. Like the Buddha himself, Pythagoras, as a purified being, could remember his past incarnations and maintained that in his very last incarnation he had been Euphorbus the Dardanian, who, with Apollo's help, wounded Patroclus.[19] Again utilizing the evidence in Plato's *Phaedo,* Burnet says "that there was an interval of seven generations between each rebirth, which, if we regard the myths which Plato puts in the mouth of Socrates as Pythagorean, were spent in purgatory."[20]

Regarding conceptions of ethical compensation and reward in these Greek rebirth theories, Pollard says: "The Orphic priests explained that punishments in this life were awarded for transgressions in a previous one."[21] Farnell refers to an inscription attributed to the Orphics where a notion like that of *karma-vipāka* is expressed, a series of purgative punishments whereby the soul is purified: "I have paid the penalty for unrighteous deeds." However there is no extant statement on Pythagorean ethics, though it would be surprising if one of the great speculative philosophers of all time did not develop a sophisticated ethic. It is clear, though, that both had doctrines of

16. John Pollard, *Seers, Shrines and Sirens* (London, 1965), pp. 113–114; Lewis Richard Farnell, *Greek Hero Cults and Ideas of Immortality* (Oxford, 1921), pp. 374–376.
17. Pollard, p. 96.
18. John Burnett, "Pythagoras and Pythagorianism", in Hastings' *Encyclopedia of Religion and Ethics* (New York, 1961), vol. 10, p. 526.
19. Ibid.
20. Ibid.
21. Pollard, p. 100.

salvation which had little resemblance to the early Buddhist notion of *nirvāṇa* but were not unlike more abstract conceptions like Nāgārjuna's, or the Hindu mystical notions of identity with God.

The consequences predicated by our model are found in Orphic-Pythagorean eschatology. A karma-type theory is associated with a rebirth theory, probably the result of the ethical speculation of religious groups like the Pythagoreans and the Orphics. Both Orphism and Pythagoreanism have a concept of salvation, a mystical union of an abstract sort in the former, and a more personal union in the latter. However, according to the prediction made from our model, salvation in a rebirth eschatology must logically occur outside the cycle of births and rebirths, or *saṃsāra.* Is there any evidence in the Greek eschatologies that this in fact was the case? There is no evidence as far as I could gather from Pythagorean religion, but the Orphic evidence clearly confirms our expectation. Farnell refers to an inscription on the Compagno Tablet found near Naples which reads like a statement by the Buddha himself: "I have fled forth from the wheel of bitter and sorrowful existence." A similar formula is preserved by Proclus' Commentary on the *Timaeus:* "To be released from the wheel and to gain respite from evil."[22] It is therefore clear that the Greeks had not only a theory of ethical compensation and reward like that of karma, but also a concept of salvation occurring outside the *saṃsāric* process.

EMPIRICAL OBJECTIONS

I shall now raise two serious objections to the theory stated above. First, it may be objected that the model of the preliterate rebirth eschatology is too gross a violation of empirical reality to be methodologically useful as an ideal model. Second, it may be argued that my crucial concept of ethicization as a feature of religious evolution has no empirical validity since recent studies[23] have attempted to show that preliterate religions are truly implicated in a moral universe. In other words, empirical cases do not approximate to our ideal type of an amoral religious system. I shall now consider these two objections together.

In the preceding account we have seen how the ideal model of a preliterate rebirth eschatology develops logically into a karmic one under the pressure of a social process known as ethicization. The

22. Farnell, p. 377.
23. Guy E. Swanson, *The Birth of the Gods* (Ann Arbor, Michigan, 1968).

crucial characteristic of the ideal model, from the point of view of my analysis, is the absence of ethicization and the ideas of sin and merit derived therefrom. Now, ideal models are never found in "nature" (empirical reality), and the validity of the model depends on how actual primitive eschatologies vary from the model. In actual life there will be degrees of ethicization ranging between two ideal extremes, from no ethicization (zero value) to complete or total ethicization. My view is that the rebirth eschatologies of preliterate societies occur near the "no ethicization" end of the scale, whereas Hinduism, Buddhism, and Jainism occur near the other (total ethicization) end. I have not tested this hypothesis for a sample of primitive societies, but I should like to consider some of the empirical evidence.

First, though I have used preliterate and primitive as convenient terms, the crucial distinction is between ethicized and non-ethicized in relation to rebirth eschatologies. If a rebirth eschatology is ethicized, it will produce a karmic eschatology. Thus, if Trobrianders converted their eschatology into a moral system, they would end up with a religion like Buddhism. It is irrelevant whether they are technologically primitive or civilized. However, ethicization evolves when there are specialized priesthoods, speculative activity, ethical prophecy, and other social institutions productive of speculative thinking; insofar as such institutions are relatively absent in simple societies, one would argue that, contrary to Swanson, primitive religions are characterized by a relative lack of ethical systematization of religion.

Second, in simple societies violations of the moral code are punished in this world by the legitimately sanctioned secular authority, not by some supernatural authority. However, when taboos and other ritual obligations are violated there may be immediate or automatic punishment (disease, death, or the action of an angry ancestor, ghost, or deity) or delayed punishment or both. But all moral laws—those ethical norms governing social action—are not taboos, though some taboos may involve violation of the moral code. For example, adultery rarely involves taboo, but incest often does and is also a violation of the common morality. At best, taboo is a "proto-religious ethic" which may coincidentally involve morality, but not intrinsically. I suspect that it is these fortuitous associations of morality with taboo that led Swanson to conclude that morality and religion are interwoven in primitive societies.

Third, in primitive societies at most some special acts of immorality may be singled out for otherworldly punishment, like murder or sorcery in Igbo. But there is no systematic attempt to incorporate the secular moral code into a religious one, so that certain kinds of immoral deeds like slander, lying, theft, drunkeness, and sexual misdemeanor are almost never invested with delayed supernatural punishment in most small-scale societies, though they are always ethicized in the great historical religions. It is interesting to note that when the Igbo meets his maker at death, accompanied by his guardian spirit, he has two packages—one containing his statuses in his previous (just ended) life, and another, his aspirational statuses for the next life. What he ultimately obtains at rebirth is dependent on a "market mentality"—haggling and bargaining—rather than on morality. In contemporary Buddhist peasant societies, by contrast, there is the conception of the dead man confronting Yama, the Lord of the Underworld, who has a pair of scales to weigh the good and bad actions of the dead man in his earthly life. Similarly, in Zoroastrianism the good souls at death are guided over the Bridge of the Requiter by the prophet himself and are rewarded, whereas the bad are consigned to hell. In all of these religions those who have violated the kind of everyday morality listed earlier are punished in appropriate places of hellish torment.

PRIMARY AND SECONDARY ETHICIZATION

In the previous sections I have dealt only with the conversion of a social and secular morality (i.e., social norms governing behavior and conduct) into a religious one. This aspect of ethicization has, I think, been neglected by historians of religion who have, in general, focused on the investment of preexisting religious beliefs and practices with ethical and symbolic values. They have, for example, concerned themselves with the ways in which the Buddhists converted Ṛg Vedic and indigenous deities into moral beings, upholders of righteousness, gave the Vedic sacrifice ethical and symbolic meaning, and so forth. This latter process occurs in every great religion, but I believe that the former process is the more important one. In order to highlight the importance of the former process I shall call it primary ethicization; the imposition of symbolic ethical meaning on preexisting beliefs is, in my terminology, secondary ethicization.

The Ethicization of Indian Religions

In this present section I shall examine how ethicization occurred in early Indian religion. I shall deal with three problems: First, if the karmic eschatology was indeed derived from an aboriginal belief system that was relatively unethicized, then it will be worthwhile examining contemporary tribal religions of India. If they lack ethicization now, they could surely have lacked it then. Furthermore, a lack of ethicization in these religions would substantiate our general view, contrary to Swanson and most anthropologists, that simple societies lack ethical religions in our sense of the term. I shall then consider the pre-Buddhist Vedic traditions of India in order to see whether these were ethical religions or not, since secondary ethicization of these beliefs took place in Buddhism. Then I shall deal with ethicization as a civilizational process with special emphasis on how that process occurred in the time of the great Gangetic religions.

CONTEMPORARY TRIBAL RELIGIONS

With reference to contemporary tribal religions, we are fortunate in having the foremost ethnologist of tribal India dealing with problems of "morals and merit" in a recent book.[24] Haimendorf says that those groups that are least influenced by Hindu culture have "amoral" religions. Regarding the Chenchus: "Supernatural sanctions, though not easily evaluated, came to play a comparatively small part in promoting conformity to the accepted moral standards. . . . There is little to suggest that moral lapses are subject to supernatural sanction."[25] The Reddis: ". . . the deities demand from man the observance of certain taboos . . . but the relations between man and man are to them a matter of indifference; there is no divine retribution of crime or reward for virtuous behavior."[26] "The Kamars' attitude to adultery is much the same as that of the Reddis."[27] The Daflas: "While an appeal to supernatural powers is used to strengthen a peace-pact, there is otherwise no suggestion that gods and spirits are concerned with the moral conduct of human beings."[28] "The Apa Tanis are sensitive to social approval or disapproval, and the fear of being 'shamed' is a powerful incentive to conformity. There is, on the other hand, no sense of 'sin' and no corresponding desire to acquire 'merit' in a system of supernatural rewards. . . . [Daflar and Apa Tanis] do not ascribe to their gods a general interest in the moral conduct of man."[29]

Some tribes, like the Gonds, have notions of sin, but Haimendorf thinks these are newly introduced notions.

24. C. von Fürer-Haimendorf, *Morals and Merit* (London, 1967).
25. Ibid., p. 23. 26. Ibid., p. 43. 27. Ibid., p. 45. 28. Ibid., p. 69.
29. Ibid., p. 79.

When talking of such an offense against the accepted moral order the Gonds use the word *pap,* which in several Aryan languages means "sin." There is no Gond equivalent to this word loaned from Hindi, Urdu or Marathi, and this situation suggests that Gondi ideology originally lacked the concept "sin," as distinct from an offense against the customary law upheld by the notion of village and tribal councils but unfortified by any supernatural sanction.[30]

We have shown that ethicization, or rather its lack, is not simply a feature of our ideal model, but is also a feature of at least some primitive tribal religions of India. We have no idea what the tribal or aboriginal religions were like in Buddha's own time, but it seems very likely that they lacked ethicization, like their contemporary representatives. But it should be noted that the Buddha, if not other *sāmana* groups, also helped ethicize popular Brāhmaṇic religious ideas prevailing in the Ganges region, such as the sacrifice, the gods, and, as the evidence of *Brahmajāla Sutta* and *Tevijja Sutta* indicates, the magical ideas of the Atharvavedic tradition. It will thus be important to see what the pre-Buddhist Vedic tradition was in respect to primary and secondary ethicization.

PRE-BUDDHIST VEDIC TRADITION

When we examine the eschatology of the Ṛg Veda we are confronted with an unethicized religion. In the Ṛg Veda the chief place for the dead is heaven. The soul at death, driven by a chariot or on wings, takes the route of the fathers and reaches a place of eternal rest. The notion of heaven is a paradisal one: "There is light, the sun for the highest waters, every form of happiness, the Svadhā, which is at once the food of the spirits and the power which they win by it, their self-determination."[31] The spirits enjoy material luxury, *surā,* milk, honey, ghee, and *soma,* as well as the delights of love. There is also music and singing, and a celestial fig tree where Yama drinks with the gods.

This eschatology is a paradisal, not a retributive (ethicized) one. Even Yama and Varuṇa, who sometimes may appear as ethical deities, do not "punish the dead or judge them for their sins," but rather grant a kind of unconditional pardon: "the idea of a judgement of any sort is as foreign to the Ṛg Veda as to early Iran."[32]

30. Ibid., p. 138.

31. Arthur Berriedale Keith, *The Religion and Philosophy of the Vedas and Upanishads* (Cambridge, Massachusetts, 1925), p. 407.

The notion of hell "was present in germ" in the Ṛg Veda.[33] It is a place under the earth into which Indra and Soma are to hurl evil-doers, these being the enemy, robbers or demons. The Atharva Veda has the word *narakaloka,* "evil place," in contrast with *svarga,* "heaven"; the former is a blind, black place where female goblins, sorceresses, and murderers are confined. Here persons who injure Brahmins sit in streams of blood eating their hair. There seems to be hardly any ethical view underlying these notions: special offenses are listed, not general categorical ones as in the later religions. Persons in hell are those who have committed specially heinous crimes. This is an unethicized eschatology: the otherworld is for saint and sinner alike, except for special cases of demons and criminals. Entry to the otherworld is dependent on the performance of the correct ritual, rather than on the moral nature of one's this-worldly actions.

Regarding the later Brāhmaṇas, Keith has this to say: "The most convincing evidence of all regarding the almost purely ritual character of goodness in the view of the Brāhmaṇas is that their concept of torment is inextricably bound up with the correct practice . . . of the ritual."[34] It is true that at death a man is weighed in a balance to test the good and the bad, but this is not based on a social morality, as among the present-day Sinhala-Buddhists. It is based on violations of taboo and on ritual interdictions. This comes out clearly in the vision of Bhṛgu in the *Śatapatha* and *Jaiminīya Brāhmaṇas.* There the persons punished in hell are those who cut wood without offering the *agnihotra* and those who kill and eat animals and even herbs without performing the correct ritual. In the *Kauṣītaki Brāhmaṇa* the animals take revenge upon a man in the next world unless he performs the correct ritual.[35] Clearly, we are dealing with taboo violation rather than with religious ethics or morality.

The Upaniṣads while belonging to the Vedic tradition were influenced by the speculative asceticism of the Gangetic region.[36] Yet they prove that a sophisticated speculative religion need not concern itself with morality or ethics. I shall later discuss the reasons for this lack. This absence of ethical concern has dismayed scholars who, on the basis of later historical religions, are conditioned to think that a

32. Ibid., p. 409. 33. Ibid., p. 410. 34. Ibid., p. 474.
35. Ibid., pp. 474–475.
36. A. L. Basham, *History and Doctrine of the Ājīvikas* (London, 1951), p. 242.

speculative soteriology must also entail an ethical soteriology. Thus, Paul Deussen, in his exhaustive discussion of the Upaniṣads, points out moral injunctions contained there: "The thief of gold, and the spirit drinker, the murderer of a Brahmin, and defiler of his teacher's bed: these four perish, and he who associates with them as the fifth."

But Deussen is puzzled that only special cases are cited here, rather than a systematic ethicization. His explanation is naive: "Lack of generalization, as well as the rarity of such warnings in Upaniṣad literature, proves that offenses of this character were not common."[37] He also states that ethics have no objective or external work to do in the Upaniṣads, misjudging their ethical nature, since European religious traditions emphasize external, non-subjective ethics.[38] But he forgets that both Jainism and Buddhism had an external (i.e., social) morality radically different from the subjective internal "ethics" of the Upaniṣads. The fact is that the Upaniṣadic seeker of salvation is above and beyond common everyday morality. In the *Kauṣītaki Upaniṣad* the man who attains Brahman after passing by the river of immortality casts away his good and evil deeds; he is above all morality, even above such heinous deeds as the slaying of an embryo and the murder of a father or a mother. One can therefore accept Keith's characterization of the Upaniṣads: "There is no attempt to make the theoretical philosophy a ground of morality of any sort."[39]

ETHICIZATION AS A CIVILIZATIONAL PROCESS

In this section I propose to examine the nature of the institutions that promote ethicization. I write in the sociological tradition of Max Weber, who was concerned with isolating general social processes from the flow of history.

I shall deal with two fundamental and contrasting modes of ethicization of the ancient Indo-Iranian religious tradition common to both Iran and Northwestern India. I assume with most scholars that the type of religion characteristic of the Ṛg Veda also extended to Iran. It was also the religion that was subject to the Zoroastrian reform, while the Vedic religion, in the form in which it existed in the Gangetic valley, was ethicized by religious reformers like the Buddha. The

37. Paul Deussen, *The Philosophy of the Upanishads* (London, 1906; New York, 1966), p. 366.
38. Ibid., pp. 365–366.
39. Keith, p. 585.

Buddha not only ethicized the rebirth eschatology but also gave a radical secondary ethical interpretation to popular Brāhmaṇic beliefs and institutions that prevailed in the middle Ganges. However, we are interested now not in the content of ethicization but in its vehicle and the mechanisms by which ethicization is expressed.

The Indo-Iranian religion can be seen as belonging to a single tradition; furthermore, if the preceding interpretation of the Vedic religion is correct, it was not an ethical religious tradition. The ethicization of Indo-Iranian religion took place in two radically different directions: in Iran through *ethical prophecy* as it was manifest in Zoroaster's reform, and in India through *ethical asceticism*, which was part of the speculative asceticism of the *sāmanas* and wanderers of the Gangetic region.

The Zoroastrian reform of the older Indo-Iranian religion is the typical case of ethical prophecy. Zaehner shows how the preexistent religion is rationalized to constitute a unified religious world view entirely ethical in nature. A fine example of this ethical orientation is a hymn that describes Zoroaster's vision of God, which transported him back in time to the beginning of the world: "Then, Mazdah, did I realize that thou wast holy when I saw thee at the beginning, at the birth of existence, when thou didst ordain a (just) requital for deeds and words, an evil lot for evil (done) and a good one for a good (deed)."[40]

In India the rationalization and ethicization of the preexisting religious beliefs—Vedic and non-Vedic—was through a radically different process which, for want of a better term, I label "ethical asceticism." It should be noted that all asceticism is not ethical, much of it involving magical attempts to gain power and control over man and nature, in India at the Buddha's time as well as in ours. Ethical asceticism like prophecy is speculative, involving a rationalization of religion; very often this rationalization converts the religion into a moral system. A rational speculative religious ideology can exist without a systematic moral concern, but in both ethical prophecy and ethical asceticism these two factors are inextricably interconnected. In short, one can have rationalization of religion without ethicization but not ethicization without rationalization.

40. R. C. Zaehner, *The Dawn and Twilight of Zoroastrianism* (New York, 1961), p. 44.

The spirit of the times indicates constant argument and debate among and between groups of wanderers and *sāmanas*. The *suttas* are full of references to these debates, which constituted the catalyst for speculation and religious rationalization. For example, *Mahā Sakuludāyi Sutta* refers to a debating hall "where diverse members of other sects, recluses and Brahmins were gathered together," presumably during the rainy season.[41] The substance and content of these debates are sometimes listed in Jaina and Buddhists *suttas*.

It is out of this kind of cultural background that the great speculative religions of India emerged—the Upaniṣads, Buddhism, and Jainism. Yet, speculation is different from ethicization: the Upaniṣads produced a great speculative soteriology but not an ethical religion. In reading the Buddhist and Jaina *suttas* one is struck by the fact that the Jaina and Buddhist monks often congregated during *vas*, or at resting places during their wanderings, or in a park donated by a rich devotee. In other words, the Buddhists and Jainas had a lay congregation which specially supported their own group: there were lay converts to the religion. In contrast, the other groups of wanderers, including the Upaniṣadic ascetics, had the general support of laymen, as any ascetic community would, but were not interested in lay conversion. Perhaps the real difference between *sāmanas* and wanderers may precisely have been this: the latter were concerned with the individual ascetic who has renounced the world to seek salvation; they were not interested in lay soteriology. I suggest that it is only in relation to a lay community that a systematic ethicization of a religion occurs. Let me spell this out with regard to the contrasting ethical orientations in Buddhism and the Upaniṣads.

Indian writers usually explain "*upaniṣad*" as "*rahasyam*," "secret," and Deussen agrees with this interpretation. It is an esoteric secret doctrine that the guru imparts to his pupils questing for salvation. The seeker of salvation goes to a guru and learns the secret knowledge: I suspect this orientation is true of many of the wanderer sects of the time. The secret esoteric nature of Upaniṣadic knowledge is too well known to require any documentation here.

In Buddhism and Jainism, by contrast, there was an interest in the common man, in women, and in Śūdras, that is, in a larger lay community. As Durkheim said in a classic essay, the individual cannot be

41. I. B. Horner (translator), *The Collection of the Middle Length Sayings*, vol. 2 (London, 1957), p. 206.

a moral object to himself; the ground of morality is established in a social network. Egoism and morality are fundamentally opposed; morality is established only in our relationship with others.[42] This condition hardly obtains in the Upaniṣads, where the emphasis is on the individual's quest for his own salvation rather than the welfare of the group. This is to say, not that ethics are absent in these doctrines, but that they lack systematic ethicization. Social morality is at best irrelevant for salvation, and in some instances it is a hindrance insofar as a social morality links a person to his group, whereas salvation for the Upaniṣadic ascetic is the removal of himself from the group.

Weber was wrong when he stated that in Buddhism the personal *certitudo salutis* rather than the welfare of the neighbor was the issue. Such a stance constitutes the rationale for ascetic withdrawal from the world. One could assume that retreat from the world must surely be related to personal striving for salvation. This was obviously one of the goals of early Buddhism, and perhaps the most important one. Nevertheless, another goal was conversion, proselytization, and the establishment of a lay community. But the ascetic withdrawal from the world with its goal of personal salvation must be reconciled with the establishment of communication between laity and monk. This has been a major dilemma in Buddhism and Jainism and also, as Basham has shown, in Ājīvikaism[43]—the reconciliation of personal striving for salvation with the welfare of the neighbor. One answer was the classic differentiation of monks into certain categories: *vipassanā dhura–grantha dura* (calling of meditation–calling of study); *vanavāsins–gramavāsin* (forest dwellers–community dwellers). The first category is associated with individual salvation; the latter is involved in the lay community.

While there have always been problems in reconciling the goal of the ascetic renunciation with the demands of the laity, there is not the slightest doubt that Buddhism was never an exclusive "monks' religion." The Buddha's own dilemma comes out in the early sermon, *Ariyapariyesana Sutta.*[44] There he recognized that his doctrine was difficult and for the few, and he was reluctant to preach it to the world. By not preaching he would have opted for the goal of personal salvation—in the Buddha mythology that of a *pacceka* Buddha. But after Brahmā interceded he opted for the "welfare and happiness of

42. Émile Durkheim, *Sociology and Philosophy* (New York, 1953).
43. Basham, pp. 132–138.
44. Horner (1957), pp. 203–219.

the many." The *suttas* are replete with statements that the religion is in fact for both monks and laymen. Thus, it seems to me to be incontrovertible that early Buddhism and Jainism and to a lesser extent Ājīvikaism involved the following: Preaching to the world and the establishment of communication with the lay community—not only to obtain recruits for the order but also to establish a lay following; communication with the laity facilitated by the development of monasticism. Once the order was established there were communities of monks in various parts of the middle Ganges. When the Buddha visited a city, the monks who were already there gathered to meet him. Furthermore, during the rain-retreat *(vassa)* monks resided close to human settlements, where lay supporters also were already established. The texts have many references to lay disciples in the several places where Buddha preached; they assembled to hear his teaching, and sermons were uttered during a good part of the night. Thus, a crucial feature of early Buddhism was the public sermon, which has remained to this day as a vehicle for the communication of the doctrinal tradition to the unmusical masses. These public sermons were open to all, unlike the close esoteric world of the Upaniṣadic *guru* and his pupil.

It seems clear that the laymen were part of the proselytization goals of early Buddhism. Social links between monks and laymen were established very early in Buddhism. It should be remembered that the term *bhikku* is not always to be translated as "monk," as social scientists have shown. Indeed, English-speaking Buddhists translate it generally as "priest." Difficulties in translation should not blind us to the sociological realities underlying the role of *bhikku* in the early period of the establishment of Buddhism.

THE CONTRASTING ORIENTATIONS OF ETHICAL PROPHECY AND ETHICAL ASCETICISM

The ethical asceticism that I have described is not simply a phenomenon of ancient Gangetic religion. It has also set a decisive stamp on the South Asian religious traditions that were influenced by it, much as ethical prophecy influenced the religious traditions stemming from Islam, Zoroastrianism, and Christianity. This is a huge question, and I shall only deal with a few salient characteristics of ethical asceticism as they emerge when contrasted with its polar opposite, ethical prophecy, developing Weber's argument.[45]

45. Weber, pp. 46–59.

The crux of ethical prophecy is that the prophet is the vehicle of a transcendental, unitary ethical deity whose message he communicates to the world. The ethical ascetic, by contrast, formulates his own message, derived from his own inward, contemplative speculation. Deities are external agents who at best validate or sanction the soteriological message, urging its establishment in the world.

Flowing from the foregoing is the nature of the prophet's message: It comes from God, and is therefore a proclamation of the divine will. The prophetic ethics that ensue constitute a commandment. By contrast, the ascetic's ethical message does not come from God; it is a precept to be followed because of its inherent rightness. The distinction between commandment and precept are crucial to the respective religious traditions in which ethical prophecy and asceticism are institutionalized.

Since the prophetic message is from God himself, his command brooks no compromise. Thus, ethical prophecy has an uncompromising attitude to the world. Zoroaster sees his opponents as evil incarnate; in the extreme case no mercy or quarter is shown, as in Islam or Zoroastrianism and in many sectarian traditions of Protestantism. The preexisting religion is viewed with intolerance, regarded as the worship of sticks and stones. Thus, Zoroaster denounces the *soma* drinkers: "Wilt thou strike down this filthy drunkenness with which the priests evilly delude the people."[46]

In ethical asceticism the ethical message, insofar as it comes from inward speculation, is vulnerable to compromise and revision. The rules of the monks' order were constantly being revised: the *suras* by contrast can never be revised. The attitude to lay religion is tolerant, skeptical, viewed as folly rather than as evil. Contrary to the opinion of recent scholars, Buddhism does not contain a theory of evil strictly parallel to the monotheistic one. The basic contrast is that the preexisting (or alien) religions are evil for the one, and folly for the other. This latter attitude emerges in early texts such as the *Brahmajāla Sutta* and *Tevijja Sutta* in those sections that deal with the "base arts" of the Atharva Veda and popular "superstition."

These respective attitudes characterize the tone of the religious message. The prophet's message is intense, emotionally charged, and expressed in condensed poetic language and metaphor, whereas the doctrine of ethical asceticism is ironic, reflective, and expressed in simile.

46. Zaehner, p. 38.

The uncompromising attitude of the ethical prophet often brings him into conflict with the secular order. The prophet ethicizes a preexistent religion, and this often brings him into conflict with the established priesthood and the secular authority which is legitimated by that priesthood and religion. This was true of Jesus and also of Mohammed and Zoroaster, at least in the initial period of their reforms. By contrast, ethical asceticism, lacking an uncompromising posture, does not threaten the secular order. It is neutral to that order, for it is dialectically open.

The dialectical problem of trying to reconcile difficult doctrinal concepts with lay understandings was an ongoing historical process. The sociological significance of *Milinda Pañha* (The Questions of King Milinda) is precisely this.[47] It shows this process going on five centuries after the death of the Buddha. Milinda, the King, represents *artha,* the interests of the world, while Nāgasena represents the *dhamma,* in this case the Buddhist doctrinal position. The King's dilemmas center around three basic issues. First, how to reconcile certain doctrinal concepts like *karma* and *nirvāṇa* with the realities of mundane experience. Second, how to reconcile certain features of popular lay Buddhism, such as *pārittas* already accepted at the time, with doctrinal ideas. Third, how to reconcile popular non-Buddhist lay views with doctrinal Buddhism. Nāgasena's achievement is in fact their reconciliation: the key doctrines are rendered intelligible to lay understanding and experience.

47. I. B. Horner (translator), *Milinda's Questions,* 2 vols., *Sacred Books of the East* (London, 1964).

7

Karma and Rebirth in Early Buddhism

JAMES P. McDERMOTT

On the night of his enlightenment, as he passed through a series of states of higher consciousness, the Buddha came to recognize that beings pass from existence to existence in accordance with the nature of their deeds *(kamma)*. The refrain is frequently repeated: "Thus with divine, purified, superhuman eye he sees beings passing away and being reborn *(upapajjamāne)*. He knows that beings are inferior, exalted, beautiful, ugly, well-faring, ill-faring according to (the consequences of) their *kamma*."[1] Men are heirs to what they do.

If we are fully to understand the sense in which men are considered heirs to their *kamma*, and the way in which they pass from existence to existence, brief consideration must first be given to the Buddha's understanding of the nature of man himself. According to the Pāli canon, man is made of five aggregates, or *khandhas*. These are the material body, feelings, perception, predispositions, and consciousness. At any given time man is but a temporary combination of these aggregates; for the *khandhas* are subject to continual change. A person does not remain the same for any two consecutive instants. The Buddhists deny that any of the aggregates individually or in combina-

1. *Majjhima-Nikāya (M)* 1.183. Cf. *M* 1.23; 1.482; 2.31; 3.99; etc. Sometimes the formula is placed in the mouth of the Buddha, and at others it is descriptive of him. Unless otherwise noted, all citations of the Pāli texts refer to the editions of the Pāli Text Society (PTS).

tion may be considered to be an ego, self, or soul *(attā)*. Indeed, it is erroneous to postulate any real, lasting unity behind the elements that make up an individual. The Buddha taught that belief in a self behind the *khandhas* results in egoism, attachment, craving, and hence in suffering. Thus he taught the doctrine of *anattā*, that is, the doctrine that there is no permanent self, in order to draw people away from their egoistic attachments.

Nonetheless, under certain circumstances Gotama was not so ready to deny the existence of the *attā*. Thus, in *Saṃyutta-Nikāya (S)* 4.400–401, an encounter between the Buddha and Vacchagotta is described. Vacchagotta asks whether there is a self *(attā)*. The Buddha remains silent. Then Vacchagotta asks whether this means that there is no self. Again the Buddha remains silent. Later the Buddha explains his silence to his disciple Ānanda as follows: If he had said there is a self, he would be open to the charge of siding with the eternalists. To say that there is a self does not fit with the Buddha's teaching of impermanence *(anicca)*. On the other hand, to say that there is no self is to side with the annihilationists, who rejected any idea of rebirth as untenable. Since the Buddha himself professes a concept of rebirth, the denial of the self would only tend to confuse the uneducated. Thus, the Buddha takes the middle view and remains silent.

The middle way which the *Tathāgata* treads is spelled out in greater detail at *S* 2.76. Here the interlocutor is a certain Brahmin. In response to his questions, Gotama points out the two extremes that are to be avoided: the belief that he who does the deed is he who experiences the result—this is one extreme. The other extreme is the view that he who does the deed is another individual than he who experiences the fruit. At *S* 2.19 the former of these two extremes is asserted to be the view of the eternalist *(sassata)*, the latter being the view of the annihilationist *(uccheda)*. The implication of the Buddha's response is that the being who experiences the fruits of a deed in one life is neither the same as nor different from the being who performed that deed in a previous existence. The being who is reborn is neither the same as nor different from the being who dies in a previous existence. As opposed to either of the two extremes, the Buddha teaches the doctrine of *paṭiccasamuppāda* (dependent co-origination) as the middle way between them. According to this teaching,

> aggregation *(sankhāra)* depending on ignorance, consciousness depending on aggregation, name and form depending on consciousness, the six organs of sense *(āyatana)* depending on name and form, contact depending on the

six organs of sense, sensation depending on contact, desire depending on sensation, grasping depending on desire, the process of becoming *(bhava)* depending on grasping, birth *(jāti)* depending on the process of becoming, old age and death depending on birth; sorrow, suffering, grief, and despair arise. Thus is the origin of all this aggregation of suffering.[2]

Through this causal chain a connection is made between the doing of deeds and the later experiencing of their fruits, between ignorance and craving, on the one hand, and rebirth, on the other. Rebirth thus conditions rebirth. Indeed, in the traditional interpretation the formula of dependent co-origination is taken to cover three successive existences.[3] But what is posited is a locus of points in a changing causal stream, rather than a permanent entity of any sort which could be said to transmigrate.

The post-canonical but nonetheless authoritative *Milindapañho (Miln.)* is particularly concerned to emphasize this view, using a series of similes to illustrate the point.[4] Let us cite but one example of the way in which Nāgasena deals with the question of whether one remains the same or becomes another through a series of rebirths. He holds that the process is like that undergone by fresh milk from a cow. After a time it turns to curds, then to butter, and eventually to ghee. It would be wrong to say that the milk was the same as the curds, the butter, or the ghee; yet they are produced out of it. Just as there is no sweet milk left to be found in the ghee, so there is no being *(satta)* that passes from this life to another.[5] Thus, although there is

2. The full printed text of the *paṭiccasamuppāda* is to be found at *Vinaya Pitakam (Vin.)* 1.1–2. In the PTS edition, the formula is abbreviated at *Saṃyutta-Nikāya (S)* 2.19 and 2.76. For detailed treatment of the formula, see David M. Williams, "The Translation and Interpretation of the Twelve Terms in the Paṭiccasamuppāda," *Numen* 21 (1974): 35–63. The second link in the formula is understood by the commentators to refer to rebirth-producing volitions *(cetanā)*, or "karma-formations."

3. See *Visuddhimagga (Vism)* 17.2 ff., and *Abhidharmakośa (Kośa.)* 3.20 for classical interpretations of the *paṭiccasamuppāda*. Here and in what follows references to *Vism.* will be by chapter and paragraph, following *Visuddhimagga of Buddhaghosâcariya*, edited by Henry Clarke Warren and revised by Dharmananda Kosambi, Harvard Oriental Series 41 (Cambridge: Harvard University Press, 1950). References to *Kośa.* and its self-commentary will be by chapter and verse. For the *Kośa.* I have employed the edition of Swami Dwarkidas Shastri, *Abhidharmakośa and Bhāṣya of Acharya Vasubandhu with Sphutārthā Commentary of Ācārya Yaśomitra*, 4 vols. Bauddha Bharati Series, nos. 5–7 and 9 (Varanasi: Bauddha Bharati, 1970–1973).

4. This example is taken from *Miln.* 40–41. Other illustrations of the point are at *Miln.* 46–48 and 72.

5. *Miln.* 72.

no transmigration in the strict sense of the word, *kamma* continues to be effective within the locus which defines individual existence.

Does this mean that in some sense *kamma* itself may be said to pass from one life to the next? This is the thrust of a question which King Milinda poses to the monk Nāgasena. Once again Nāgasena's response takes the form of a simile:

"What do you think about this, great King? Is it possible to point to the fruit of trees which have not yet produced fruit, saying: 'The fruit is here or there'?" "No indeed, venerable Sir." "Just so, great King, while the continuity (of life) is uninterrupted, it is not possible to point to these acts, saying: 'These acts are here or there.'"[6]

The implication of Nāgasena's illustration seems to be that once done, deeds continue to exist only through their potential to modify the continuity of life. The act *(kamma)* itself does not pass from one state to the next; it cannot be said to exist here or there. But since its potential cannot be prevented from actualizing itself in due time, it may be considered to follow a man like an unshakable shadow.

The *Visuddhimagga* is explicit in stating that "the *kamma* that is the condition for the fruit does not pass on there (to where the fruit is)."[7]

Similes such as those employed by Nāgasena to explain the rebirth process were not fully convincing, however. Even Milinda, while applauding Nāgasena's illustrations, repeatedly presses for further clarification. As Thomas Dowling notes:

The wide agreement on the principle of karmic fruition for morally qualifiable deeds stands out in marked contrast to the disagreement that characterizes the various sectarian treatments of the mechanism whereby this principle is effected. . . . The wider doctrinal positions of several of the schools can often be understood in light of the schools' unique approaches to the explanation of the link up between deed and fruit.[8]

The Puggalavādins, for example, believed that a personal entity, the *puggala,* exists. In order to avoid being accused of belief in an *attā,* they further maintained that this *puggala* was neither identical with nor different from the five aggregates. Rather, they considered the

6. *Miln.* 72.
7. *Vism.* 17.168. The translation is that of Bhikkhu Ñyāṇamoli, *The Path of Purification* (Colombo: A. Semage, 1964).
8. Thomas Dowling, "Karma Doctrine as Sectarian Earmark," unpublished paper read at the American Academy of Religion Annual Meeting at St. Louis, Missouri, on Oct. 8, 1976; p. 1.

relationship between the *puggala* and the aggregates to be ineffable *(avaktavya)*. Moreover, it was their opinion that the *puggala* transmigrates from existence to existence, thereby defining individual continuity. It provides the connecting link between one life and the next, without which the principle of *kamma* could not operate. Its existence is not a momentary state. That is, the *puggala* does not undergo constant change, dying and being reborn in each moment of consciousness. Yet it is nonetheless incorrect to hold that it remains the same from instant to instant. Again the matter is considered ineffable. The concept of the *puggala* is attacked by the Theravādin in the *Kathāvatthu (Kvu.)*.[9]

In lieu of the personal entity of the Puggalavādins, Buddhaghosa speaks of the rebirth-linking *(paṭisandhi)* of the present state with the immediately preceding state of existence—or, better, state of becoming. In the normal state of human death, the body gradually withers away like a green leaf in the sun, the sense faculties cease, and the consciousness that remains is supported by the heart-basis alone. This last moment of consciousness before death is known as the *cuti viññāna*. Immediately on its cessation, contingent upon some *kamma*, conditioned by the *cuti viññāna*, and driven by craving and ignorance not yet abandoned, there arises in the mother's womb the first stirring of consciousness of the succeeding birth. It is known as the rebirth-linking consciousness *(paṭisandhi viññāna)*. Not being carried over from the previous life, this rebirth-linking consciousness newly arises at the precise moment of conception. In other words, no transmigration of consciousness is being posited here, but rather a causally linked stream *(sota)* of discrete moments of consciousness. Buddhaghosa likens the relationship between *cuti viññāna* and *paṭisandhi viññāna* to that between a sound and its echo, or a signature-seal and its impression.[10]

According to the *Mahāṭanhāsaṅkhayasutta* of the *Majjhima Nikāya*, the conjunction of three factors is necessary for conception to take place: there must be sexual intercourse between the parents, the mother must be in the proper phase of her menstrual cycle, and a

9. See *Kvu.* 1.198 and 1.160–161. For further elaboration of both the Puggalavādin and Theravādin positions, see James P. McDermott, "The Kathāvatthu Kamma Debates," *Journal of the American Oriental Society (JAOS)* 95 (1975): 424–425. See below for a discussion of the Vaibhāṣika and Sautrāntika conceptions of the link between deed and fruit.

10. Buddhaghosa's discussion of rebirth-linking and its ramifications is to be found at *Vism.* 17.158–173.

gandhabba must be present.[11] In his commentary on this passage, Buddhaghosa explains *gandhabba* as the being about to enter the womb *(tatrūpakasatta)*, ready to exist *(paccupaṭṭhito hoti)*, being driven on by *kamma*.[12] This interpretation is not to be taken as implying the existence of an intermediate-state being *(antarā bhava)*, however; for elsewhere Buddhaghosa writes that it is the person who is confused about death and rebirth who considers it to involve a "being's transmigration to another incarnation, . . . a lasting being's manifestation in a new body."[13] Theravāda was vocal in its denial of an intermediate-state being existing between death and rebirth.[14] This being the case, Piyadassi Thera's analysis would seem to be consistent not only with the text but also with Buddhaghosa's understanding of the matter. Piyadassi Thera maintains that *gandhabba* is simply a term for the rebirth-linking consciousness *(paṭisandhi viññāna)*, rather than for a discarnate spirit of any kind.[15]

Among others, the Sarvāstivādins, the Vātsīputrīyas, and the Sammatīyas disputed the Theravādin denial of an intermediate-state being *(antarā bhava)* between death and rebirth.[16] In the *Abhidharmakośa* and its *Bhāṣya* (chap. 3), Vasubandhu argues the case for the affirmative in some detail. As he defines it in the *Bhāṣya*, the *antarā bhava* is a being which is to be found between two destinies *(gati)*. That is, it exists between the moment of death and the moment of birth, being bracketed by the five aggregates *(skandha)* of the moment of death, on the one hand, and the five aggregates of the moment of birth, on the other. The intermediate-state being itself is made up of five *skandhas* which proceed to the place of rebirth.[17] The *antarā bhava* is further said to have "the configuration of what is to be the configuration of the future being. . . . It is seen by the pure divine eye belong-

11. *M* 1.266.
12. *Papañcasūdanī Majjhimanakāyaṭṭhakathā (MA)* 2.310.
13. *Vism.* 17.113–114.
14. See *Kvu.* 8.2. The Theravādins were joined in this view by the Vibhajyavādins, Mahāsāṅghikas, and Mahīśāsakas. These groups offered no clear positive alternative to the concept of *antarā bhava.* See André Bareau, *Les Sectes Bouddhiques du Petit Véhicule* (Paris: École Française d'Extrême-Orient, 1955), p. 283.
15. Piyadassi Thera, *The Psychological Aspect of Buddhism,* The Wheel Publication no. 179 (Kandy: Buddhist Publication Society, 1972), p. 20.
16. See Bareau, *Les Sectes,* p. 283. Also note Alex Wayman, "The Intermediate-State Dispute in Buddhism," *Buddhist Studies in Honour of I. B. Horner* (Dordrecht: D. Reidel, 1974), pp. 227–237, for a discussion of the overall controversy.
17. *Kośa.* 3.10.

ing to beings of its class. It has the force of magical power or act. Its sense organs are perfect. It cannot be impeded or turned back."[18]

Vasubandhu goes on to suggest that it is this intermediate-state being to which the Buddha referred with the terms *manomaya, saṃbhavaiṣin, nirvṛtti,* and *gandharva.*[19] The name *gandharva* is explained as applying to the *antarā bhava* because of its pattern of feeding on odors *(gandhabhuk).*[20] The intermediate-state being itself is not to be classed as a destiny on the level of the five *gatis,* the *antarā bhava* being instead the access *(sagamana)* through which a being reaches its proper course of existence *(gati).* Spatially, the *antarā bhava* arises in the place where death takes place.[21]

Vasubandhu is careful to maintain that the intermediate-state being which he posits is not the same as the *ātman,* the existence of which he denies. The *ātman* is considered to be an entity which abandons the aggregates *(skandha)* of one existence, exchanging them for the aggregates of another, and which exists independently of the causal relationship between the *dharmas.*[22] By way of contrast, Vasubandhu's *antarā bhava* is itself a karmically determined combination of *skandhas,* as we have seen.

Given the existence of such an intermediate-state being, Vasubandhu proceeds to an explanation of how rebirth *(pratisaṃdhi)* takes place.[23] The Oedipal character of his analysis would do justice to Freud: driven by karma, the intermediate-state being goes to the location where rebirth is to take place. Possessing the divine eye by virtue of its karma, it is able to see the place of its birth, no matter how distant. There it sees its father and its mother to be, united in intercourse. Finding the scene hospitable, its passions are stirred. If male, it is smitten with desire for its mother. If female, it is seized with desire for its father. And inversely, it hates either mother or

18. *Kośa.* 3.13–14. The translation is that of Wayman, "Intermediate-State Dispute," p. 231.
19. *Kośa.* 3.40–41. The term *gandharva* is the Sanskrit equivalent of the Pāli *gandhabba.*
20. *Kośa.* 3.40. Cf. *Kośa.* 3.14.
21. *Kośa.* 3.4.
22. *Kośa.* 3.18. The appendix to chap. 8 (sometimes cited as chap. 9) of the *Kośa.* is a detailed refutation of the *pudgala* and *ātman* theories. This part of the *Kośa.* has been translated into English by Theodore Stcherbatsky, *The Soul Theory of the Buddhists* (Vārāṇasī: Bhāratīya Vidyā Prakāśana, 1970).
23. *Kośa.* 3.15.

father, which it comes to regard as a rival. Concupiscence and hatred thus arise in the *gandharva* as its driving passions. Stirred by these wrong thoughts, it attaches itself to the place where the sexual organs of the parents are united, imagining that it is there joined with the object of its passion. Taking pleasure in the impurity of the semen and blood in the womb, the *antarā bhava* establishes itself there. Thus do the *skandhas* arise in the womb. They harden; and the intermediate-state being perishes, to be replaced immediately by the birth existence *(pratisaṃdhi)*.

When the embryo thus formed is masculine, it clings to the right of the womb, back forward, in a crouching position; when feminine, to the left of the womb, stomach forward; when sexless, in the attitude in which the intermediate-state being envisions itself as making love. In effect, the intermediate-state being is possessed of a fully developed set of sexual organs. It enters then, masculine or feminine, and holds on as suits its sex. Developing after it thus takes rebirth in the womb, the embryo then loses its mature sexual characteristics.

In this view, as in the more psychologically oriented concept of rebirth consciousness, there is a stream of renewed existences produced in accordance with the action of karma. This is the cycle of *saṃsāra*.

The usual position of the Pāli *Nikāyas,* accepted by Vasubandhu, is that there are five possible courses, or realms of existence *(gati)*, into which sentient beings may be born. These five courses, or destinies—as the term is often translated—are listed in ascending order as (1) *niraya,* purgatory or hell; (2) *tiracchānayoni,* brute creation, the realm of animals; (3) *pettivisaya,* the world of the shades;[24] (4) *manussā,* men, human existence; (5) *devā,* the gods, heavenly existence.[25] In some passages (e.g., *D* 3.264) a sixth category, that of the *asuras* is added between the shades and mankind. When but five courses of existence are enumerated, the *asuras* are usually conceived as denizens of the world of the shades.

Of these courses of existence, *niraya* and the realms of animals, shades, and *asuras* are considered unhappy realms of existence *(apāya,* or *duggati)*. Only human and heavenly existence are considered relatively desirable courses *(sugati)*. In contrast to the

24. The term "hungry ghost," the usual translation for *peta,* is reserved for the particular class of *petas* who are distinguished by their perpetual hunger.
25. These five *gatis* are listed at *Dīgha Nikāya (D)* 3.234; *Aṅguttara-Nikāya (A)* 4.459; *M* 1.73; *Culaniddesa (Niddesa 2)* 550, etc.

Theravāda analysis on this point, the common view of the Sanskrit texts is that the *asuras* occupy the lowest desirable state of existence *(sugati).*[26]

The course into which an individual is to be born is largely determined by the nature of his acts *(kamma).* Thus, when the Buddha sees men passing from this life in accordance with their *kamma,* he thinks:

> Indeed, these venerable beings who are endowed with good conduct of body, of speech, and . . . of mind, who do not abuse noble ones *(ariya),* who are of right view, acquiring for themselves the *kamma* (which is the consequence) of the right view, after the breaking up of the body after death, they are the ones who attain happiness (or a good course, *sugati),* a heaven world *(saggaṃ lokaṃ)* . . . they are ones who attain existence among men. Indeed, these venerable beings who are endowed with misconduct of body, of speech, and . . . of mind, who abuse noble ones, who are of wrong views, acquiring for themselves the *kamma* (which is the consequence) of the wrong view, they, after the breaking up of the body after death, are ones who attain existence in the realm of the shades, . . . in an animal womb *(tiracchānayoni),* . . . who attain a state of loss *(apāya),* a miserable course *(duggati),* destruction *(vinipāta), niraya.*[27]

The gods too—and even Brahmā, the creator—are not immune to rebirth in lower states of existence. Thus, Ānanda explains to King Pasenadi of Kosala that even *devas* of the heaven of the thirty-three are subject to rebirth, and "whatever Brahmā does harm *(savyāpajjha),* that Brahmā returns to the present state of becoming *(itthatta).* Whatever Brahmā does not do harm *(abhyāpajjha),* that Brahmā does not return to the present state of becoming."[28] *Dīgha Nikāya* 1.17–18 gives an account of the beginning of a cosmic period in terms of kammic effect. According to this account, with the dissolution of each world system, most beings are reborn in a world of radiance. After a long time, that world begins to revolve. Eventually "some being because of the passing of his span of years, or because of the

26. On the *asuras* and their position in the Buddhist scheme of existence, see Alicia Matsunaga, *The Buddhist Philosophy of Assimilation* (Rutland, Vt., and Tokyo: Charles E. Tuttle, 1969), p. 51.

27. *M* 3.178–179.

28. *M* 2.132. Louis de la Vallée-Poussin, *The Way to Nirvāṇa* (Cambridge: Cambridge University Press, 1917), p. 83, observes in passing that "man and woman alone are usually regarded as being capable of sin or good deeds. The other states of existence, hells and paradises, are almost exclusively states of enjoyment, of reward or punishment." *M* 2.132 proves exception to this generalization, as do the numerous instances of good performed by the Bodhisatta in previous animal existences recorded in the *Jātakas.*

waning of his merit *(puññakkhāya),* having passed from the radiant body, is reborn *(upapajjati)* in the uninhabited Palace of Brahmā."[29] Similarly, other beings eventually fall from the world of radiance. Since Brahmā preceded them chronologically, they erroneously consider him to be their creator, a view which he also accepts because they appeared in this world system only after he had wished for company.

The beginning of the round of rebirth and, hence, of the cycle of cosmic periods is incalculable, according to the Buddha. It is like a dog on a leash running around the stake to which it is tied. There is no end to its circling.[30]

The course of one's existence, then, is crucially affected by the nature of one's *kamma.* However, *kamma* is operative not only in determining which of the *gatis* an individual will be born into but also as a causal factor with respect to certain differences between individuals. Thus, at *M* 3.202–203, it is related that Subha, Todeyya's son, asked:

> "What now, Sir Gotama, is the cause, what the reason that lowness and excellence are seen among men. . . ? For, Sir Gotama, short-lived men are seen, and long-lived ones are seen; men with many illnesses are seen, and ones free from illness are seen; ugly men are seen, and beautiful are seen; weak men are seen, and mighty are seen; men of lowly families are seen, men of high families are seen; men of little wisdom are seen, and ones possessed of insight. . . . What now, Sir Gotama, is the cause, what the reason that lowness and excellence are seen among men even while they are in human form?" "Possessed of their own *kamma,* young Brahmin, beings are heir to *kamma.* . . . Kamma distinguishes beings, that is to say, by lowness and excellence."

Appearance, health, wealth, and influence are all the result of one's past deeds. But what about one's caste? In the *Sutta Nipāta,* differences of name and clan are pronounced to be mere designations *(samannā)* settled by convention. Only the ignorant declare that one is a Brahmin by birth. "One becomes neither a Brahmin nor a non-Brahmin by birth./ One becomes a Brahmin by *kamma;* one becomes a non-Brahmin by *kamma.*"[31] In this passage the term *kamma* is used

29. *D* 1.17.
30. *S* 3.149–150. Cf. *S* 2.178f, and *S* 2.186.
31. *Sutta Nipāta (Sn.)* 650. Edited by Lord Chalmers in *Buddha's Teachings: Being the Sutta-Nipāta or Discourse Collection.* Harvard Oriental Series 37 (Harvard University Press, 1932). The rare form *kammanā,* based on the consonantal stem, appears here. The idea expressed is similar to that at *Sn.* 116–142.

with two levels of meaning. On the one hand, Gotama is saying that caste distinction is meaningless apart from the way a person acts. He alone deserves to be called a Brahmin in whom there is truth and righteousness. Even a poor man who is free from earthly attachments is, in truth, a Brahmin.[32] A second level at which I would interpret the meaning of the term *kamma* in the verse just quoted from the *Sutta Nipāta* is as a reference to past deeds working themselves out in the present (or future). That is, a man is a Brahmin in this life because of certain good works in a previous existence. The effects of *kamma* are here carefully differentiated from birth. One becomes what he is, not through birth, but rather because of his past acts. Birth or, rather, rebirth is hence but one of the effects of *kamma.* It is seen as but one element among many in the locus of instants in the round of *saṃsāra.* It is logically no more important than any other moment of existence, as is borne out by the formula of dependent co-origination *(paṭicca-samuppāda).*

Although each individual is heir to his deeds alone, the ripening of his *kamma* has consequences that reach beyond himself. That is to say, in any given situation the *kamma* of each individual involved must be in confluence with that of every other participant in the situation. Thus, for example, a fratricide could only be born of parents who because of their past *kamma* deserved the suffering that results from the violent loss of a child, who in turn deserved to suffer such a death at the hands of his brother as punishment for his own past deeds. It is a matter not simply of the *kamma* of the one son leading to his own death, but of the confluence of the *kamma* of both the parents with that of both their sons. With rare exceptions, such as in the *Viḍuḍabhavatthu* of the *Dhammapada Commentary,*[33] it is only in this sense of the confluence of the individual kammic reward and punishment of those involved in a given situation that it is possible to speak of "group *kamma*" in the classical Pāli texts.[34]

Not all pleasure, pain, and mental states that men experience are due to previous acts. In response to a question raised by one Sīvaka Moliya, Gotama replies that in addition to the effect of *kamma* *(kammavipāka),* "certain experiences *(vedayita)* . . . arise here

32. This idea is clearly expressed at *Dhammapada (Dh.)* 393 and 396. Edited and translated by S. Radhakrishnan (London: Oxford University Press, 1950).
33. *Dhammapadatthakathā (DhA.)* 1.337–361, especially 1.360.
34. See James P. McDermott, "Is There Group Karma in Theravāda Buddhism?" *Numen* 23 (1976): 67–80.

originating from bile, . . . from phlegm, . . . from wind, . . . resulting from the humors of the body, . . . born of the changes of the seasons, . . . of being attacked by adversities, . . . of spasmodic attacks."[35]

Yet where deeds are performed intentionally, their fruition in time is inexorable. *Sutta Nipāta* 666 declares that man's *kamma* is never lost *(na nassati);* it comes back to haunt him.[36] In a similar vein, *A* 5.292 strongly denies that intentional *(sañcetanika)* deeds can be wiped out once accumulated, unless their result is first experienced, in either this state of existence or another.[37] That *kamma* should not work itself out is as much an impossibility as that the mortal should not die. Not even Brahmā, on the one hand, and Māra, on the other, are able to delay the inexorable fruition of deeds in due time.[38]

The reward (or punishment) fits the deed, good deeds bringing results that are in some sense conceived to be good or pleasant, evil deeds bringing unpleasant or painful results.[39]

The *Mahākammavibhaṅgasutta* provides further definition of the way in which *kamma* inevitably works itself out.[40] In this *sutta,* Gotama rejects the view that everyone who kills, lies, steals, and so forth will be reborn in an undesirable state. Indeed, he holds that some such individuals may even be reborn in a heavenly realm. Similarly, not everyone who refrains from immoral acts will be reborn in a good course. The *sutta* goes on to explain how this view can be reconciled with belief in the inevitable working out of the effects of *kamma:* practical experience shows us that in their lifetimes individuals are capable of doing both good and evil deeds. Moreover, depending on the circumstances, actions may come to fruition either here and now or in some future state. Thus the effect of a comparatively weak deed *(dubbalakamma)* may be superseded by the effect of a comparatively strong deed *(balavakamma)* or by the accumulated effects of a series of deeds. This means that although an individual may have been a murderer, a liar, and so forth, on death he may nonetheless arise in a pleasant state if the effects of his accumulated

35. *S* 4.230–231. Cf. *A* 2.87–88, 3.131, and 5.110.
36. Cf. *Theragāthā* 143–144.
37. Similar statements occur at *A* 5.297, 299, and 300.
38. *A* 1.172.
39. The general principle is stated at *A* 1.28–30, and again at *M* 3.66–67. The canon is also full of specific examples of the operation of this principle. Among the many, one might note *M* 1.388; *S* 1.85; *A* 2.81–82 as but examples.
40. *M* 3.207–215.

good deeds are sufficient to supersede the results of his wrong doing. The fruits of the deeds which have thus been superseded will then be experienced once the fruits of the deeds which have superseded them have been exhausted.

It is in this sense that we must interpret the Buddha's analysis of *kamma* into the following four categories: (1) inoperative, apparently inoperative; (2) inoperative, apparently operative; (3) operative, apparently operative; (4) operative, apparently inoperative.[41] A deed that is clearly of slight ethical significance is called "inoperative, apparently inoperative" when its fruition is superseded, albeit temporarily, by a deed of greater ethical force. A deed, the effect of which is expected, is called "inoperative, apparently operative" when its fruition is prevented by the cultivation of another deed of the opposite character when one is on the point of death. An act of strong ethical force is called "both operative and apparently operative" when it bears fruit as expected. And, finally, if a deed, although cultivated when one is near death, is not expected to bear its fruit because of the existence of previous deeds of a different ethical character, it is called "operative, apparently inoperative" if it nonetheless comes to fruition.[42]

This interpretation points to another element in the canonical Theravāda view of *kamma,* namely, the belief that deeds done or ideas seized at the moment of death are particularly significant. Thus, in explaining how an individual who has broken one of the five precepts may nonetheless come to be reborn in a desirable course, Gotama suggests that it may be because at the time of his death he had secured the proper outlook.[43] However, this idea is not to suggest—as von Glasenapp does—that the final thoughts of a dying man "are able fundamentally to alter the value of the karma heaped up during his whole life."[44] In the balancing of accounts, a man's final outlook is given extra weight, to be sure. Nonetheless, the full force of ac-

41. *M* 3.215: atthi kammaṃ abhabbaṃ abhabbābhāsaṃ; atthi kammaṃ abhabbaṃ bhabbābhāsaṃ; atthi kammaṃ bhabbañ c'eva bhabbābhāsañ ca; atthi kammaṃ bhabbaṃ abhabbābhāsan ti.

42. This interpretation follows Buddhaghosācariya, *Papañcasūdanī Majjhimanikāyaṭṭhakathā,* edited by I. B. Horner et al. 5 vols. (London: Humphrey Milford for PTS, 1922–1938), vol. 5, p. 20.

43. *M* 3.214. Cf. *S* 4.168, 302, and 400.

44. Helmuth von Glasenapp, *Immortality and Salvation in Indian Religions,* translated by E. F. J. Payne (Calcutta: Susil Gupta India, 1963), p. 50. Von Glasenapp regards this view as parallel to certain ideas expressed in the *Bhagavad Gītā.*

cumulated *kamma* is not left out of consideration. In at least one passage, the Buddha seems to take the nature of the individual's thoughts at the moment of death merely as indicative of that person's general moral character throughout his life.[45]

A man's character as a whole is a most significant element in determining how the effects of any given act will be experienced. A trifling deed done by an individual who is generally unscrupulous in his actions will have different consequences than will a similar deed done by one who is more scrupulous about what he does. Such a deed may drag the former down to a hellish existence; whereas in the case of the latter, it may work itself out entirely in this life. The time at which the fruit of a deed ripens is thus dependent upon the circumstances.

In a section on the punishment of deeds *(kammakāraṇa)* in the *Aṅguttara Nikāya,* two classes of faults *(vajja)* are delineated: those which have their result in the present existence *(diṭṭadhammika),* and those which have their result in a future state *(samparāyika).* A man who commits a theft, is captured by the authorities, and is tortured for his crime, is an example of the former class of faults. The latter class is composed of those offenses of body, word, and thought which are rewarded through appropriate rebirth. Among these are five deeds that find retribution without delay *(kamma ānantarika).*[46] Regardless of whatever other *kamma* may have been accumulated, these lead to hellish existence in the immediately following rebirth. With the exception of these five, any deed may lie quiescent for long periods of time before it ripens. Practical experience shows that the wicked do not always suffer for their deeds in this very life.

It is also to be noted that the fruit of a deed may bud without actually ripening until much later. That is to say, a given deed may have both visible and future results, the results in this life being but a foretaste of what is to come. A liberal almsgiver thus becomes dear to many and gains a great reputation in this life, yet the results of his generosity come to full fruition only following his death when he is reborn in a heavenly realm.[47]

The great periods of time over which the rewards of a deed are said to be experienced is significant. This duration of rewards and punishments is stressed in Buddhist sermons and tales largely as a deterrent against evil, and as an inducement toward good.

45. See *Itivuttaka (It.)* 12–14.
46. These are matricide, patricide, arhaticide, intentional shedding of a Buddha's blood, and causing a schism within the *Saṃgha.* See *Vin.* 5.128; also note *Vin.* 2.193.
47. *A* 1.38–39. Cf. *S* 1.150.

As we have already seen, the state of existence in which an individual finds himself is largely determined by the nature of his past acts. *Kamma* is also active in determining the individual's moral status. Thus we might well ask whether any room is left for individual freedom. Or, is a man completely predestined in what he does? Does belief in *kamma* inevitably lead to fatalism? This is in part to raise the question of human nature.

First, it is to be noted that Gotama's understanding of existence, and hence of *kamma,* was to a certain extent based on the observation of things as they are. Thus the series of *suttas* in the *Saṃyutta Nikāya* to the effect that as the earth is greater than a speck of dust, so the number of those reborn in lower lives outnumbers those reborn as men,[48] is at once a recognition that other creatures are indeed more numerous than men, and at the same time an observation that those who regularly act selflessly are truly few in number. For these two reasons it is concluded that it is difficult to be reborn as a human being.[49]

One of the observations that Gotama made is that, by and large, people are strongly attached to life and the sense pleasures; and that this attachment frequently results in impurity. The account of Māra as plowman makes this point.[50] The evil one, it is recounted, appeared before Gotama in the guise of a plowman. He declared that each of the senses and their corresponding sense objects belongs to him. Hence all men, not even excluding the Buddha himself, must eventually fall into his clutches. The Buddha agreed that the senses do indeed belong to Māra, and insofar as they do, men are under his sway. Nonetheless, as Winston King stresses, the Buddha "claims that there *is* a way, a type of living, which is beyond the power of all sensibility and discrimination and hence free from Māra's power."[51]

What is to be distinguished here is the difference between old, or past, deeds *(purāṇakamma),* on the one hand, and new deeds *(navakamma),* on the other.[52] The eye and the other sense organs, understood as a base for feeling, are what is called *purāṇakamma.* The action which one performs now—*navakamma*—stands in contrast to past action. Man's present situation derives from old *kamma,*

48. *S* 5.474–475.
49. *Dh.* 187.
50. *S* 1.114–116.
51. Winston L. King, *In the Hope of Nibbana: An Essay on Theravāda Buddhist Ethics* (LaSalle, Ill: Open Court, 1964), p. 24.
52. This distinction is made at *S* 4.132.

but he remains free to make what he will of his present. Past *kamma* must always burn itself out; nonetheless, it is man himself who chooses among the options for present action which are presented to him. What is predetermined, then, is an individual's opportunity for certain modes of behavior, rather than either his inner moral tendencies or what he actually does.

In addition to present and past *kamma,* the Buddha also speaks of *kammanirodha* (literally cessation of action). *Kammanirodha* involves both the exhaustion of past deleterious *kamma,* and the avoidance of further action which may prove deleterious in the long run. The way that is said to lead to such cessation of action is the noble eightfold path. The fact that such a way to *kammanirodha* exists, even though the past may belong to Māra, is a clear indication of the recognition of human free will. The question of free will is not one that is explicitly asked in the Pāli canon, however. Rather, belief in the existence of free will is implicit in the notion of human responsibility, an idea which is closely connected with the whole Buddhist concept of *kamma.*

In addition to being classed as old or new, *kamma* is also classed according to the result it produces. Four categories of deeds are delineated in this manner.[53] (1) Dark with dark result. These are deeds that are harmful, that violate one or another of the precepts. They lead to an existence of unmitigated pain. (2) Bright, or pure, with bright result. Such action is harmless. Included in this category is abstention from taking life, from stealing, and the like, when these are done with a view toward obtaining a favorable rebirth. And, indeed, abstention from evil under such circumstances does lead to favorable rebirth, it is held. (3) Both dark and bright with mixed results. Such deeds are those which are at once harmful and beneficial. They result in states of existence which, like human existence, know both pleasure and pain. A significant feature of these first three categories of *kamma* is that they are each purposive. That is, they are done with a view toward attaining sensual enjoyment in this life, or a specific rebirth. (4) The fourth category of deeds is called "neither dark nor bright with neither result." Deeds of this final category lead to the consumption of past *kamma.* This category of action involves

53. The four categories are (1) kamma kaṇha kaṇhavipāka, (2) kamma sukka sukkavipāka, (3) kamma kaṇhasukka kaṇhasukkavipāka, (4) kamma akaṇhamasukka akaṇha–asukkavipāka. These are delineated several times at *A* 2.230–237. Also note their appearance at *D* 3.229 f., and *M* 1.389 f.

giving up all behavior conducive of further rebirth, whether painful or pleasant. Such action, unlike the first three categories, is selfless. Hence, from the Buddhist point of view, it alone is to be pursued.

In the *Abhidharmakośa* Vasubandhu accepts this fourfold categorization of acts. However, he notes that the third category, that of mixed karma, refers not to the character of individual acts but rather to the series of acts which defines an individual life. That is to say, there is no such thing as a black-and-white act, nor retribution which is mixed. That would imply a contradiction, according to Vasubandhu. Rather, in the same mental series some good acts are mixed with some bad acts, each with their own characteristic fruit, whether good or bad. When such a situation exists, this is referred to as mixed black-and-white karma.[54]

One of the most common classifications of *kamma* is into acts of body *(kāyakamma)*, acts of speech *(vacīkamma)*, and acts of mind *(manokamma)*.[55] Each of these produces results. Even a thought which is unaccompanied by outward action, even so much as the moving of a muscle, is considered to produce kammic effects. Actual murder no doubt has greater effect than the mere thought of murder unaccompanied by any action, yet from the Buddhist point of view, even the latter is wrong.

This classification of *kamma* into deeds of body, word, and thought is further reduced into a twofold classification at *A* 3.415. On the one hand, there is volition, mental or spiritual action. On the other, there is what is born from volition, what a person does after having willed—namely, bodily and vocal action.[56]

This twofold schema has the advantage of stressing the centrality to the early Buddhist understanding of *kamma* of what has often been translated as "volition," namely, *cetanā*. *Kamma* is virtually defined as *cetanā:* "I say, monks, that *cetanā* is *kamma;* having intended *(cetayitvā)*, one does a deed by body, word, or thought."[57] In the words of Herbert V. Guenther:

> *Cetanā,* to state it plainly, is something that corresponds to our idea of stimulus, motive, or drive. Especially this latter concept of drive, as a stimulus arousing persistent mass activity, assists in explaining the origin of

54. *Kośa.* 4.128–130.
55. This division is found at *M* 1.206, and *A* 3.415, for example, Cf. *It.* 15.
56. Cf. *Kośa.* 4.1.
57. *A* 3.415.

activity as well as that which is excitated and is forthwith active. That which is aroused to activity is the sum total of all potentialities.[58]

In other words, *cetanā* is not a matter of will alone, but also involves the impulse or drive to carry through with what is intended. Deliberate intention to do a deed plays an essential role in determining the ethical quality of that deed. Thus, a person who commits accidental manslaughter is not subject to kammic consequences as serious as those suffered by the perpetrator of a premeditated murder. In the same vein, throughout the *Vinaya Piṭaka* the penalties which are laid down for intentional violations of the monastic rules are more severe than those exacted for violations committed unwittingly. Likewise, temporary insanity is considered a mitigating circumstance by the *Vinaya*.

The *Abhidharmakośa* follows *A* 3.415 in defining "*karman*" as "intentional impulse *(cetanā)* and the act which follows upon it." It further accepts the *suttanta's* threefold classification of *kamma* into bodily, vocal, and mental acts. Vasubandhu goes on to clarify this threefold analysis in a way that is counter to the Theravādin understanding, however. He notes that the intentional impulse *(cetanā)* itself is that which is termed "mental act." Bodily and vocal acts arise from it.[59] Although any physical act supposes an intentional impulse, the actual physical act is something other than intention. For example, there is no murder without a will to kill. But the actual murder involves something more than simply the motive or drive behind the act. It also involves a certain motion or displacement of the body by means of which some living being is deprived of its life.

In contrast to the Sarvāstivādin opinion on this point, the Pāli schools consider all *kamma* to be merely *cetanā*. Mental acts are pure intentional impulse, while acts of body and voice are intentional impulses which put the body and voice in motion, not simply the actions ensuant upon such impulses.[60]

Among the more significant additions made by the Vaibhāṣikas to the conception of karma is their analysis of acts into *vijñapti* (patent; literally informative) and *avijñapti* (latent; literally non-

58. Herbert V. Guenther, *Philosophy and Psychology in the Abhidharma* (Lucknow: Buddha Vihara, 1957), p. 66.
59. *Kośa*. 4.2.
60. On this point, see Louis de la Vallée-Poussin, *La Morale Bouddhique* (Paris: Nouvelle Librairie Nationale, 1927), pp. 124–125.

informative).[61] According to the Vaibhāṣika position as described by Vasubandhu, acts of body and voice can be further divided into patent and latent. This distinction arose out of their concern to explain how the effects of an action can sometimes become manifested only long after the completion of the overt activity.

Corporal *vijñapti* karma is manifest physical action. In Western thought it is what might be loosely termed physical movement. From the Vaibhāṣika viewpoint this would be an improper interpretation, however, for all conditioned *(saṃskṛta)* elements of existence are held to be momentary. Their transitory existence is not sufficiently long to allow for the possibility of movement.[62] Thus, rather than speaking of patent bodily karma as movement, the Vaibhāṣikas describe it as a kind of appearance or condition *(saṃsthāna)* which issues from the intentional impulse and informs others of it. For example, the physical act of decapitating a man with an ax informs others of the murderous intention that initiated the murder, and would be classed as corporal *vijñapti.*

Patent vocal action consists of the pronunciation of syllables. Speech issues from an intentional impulse and informs others of it. Thus, for example, an order to commit a murder proceeds from a murderous intention and makes that intention manifest *(vijñapti).*

To use Herbert Guenther's terminology, *avijñapti* karma is "a serial continuity"[63] set up immediately after a patent *(vijñapti)* act has been performed. In other words, it is a latent potential impressed on the psycho-physical stream of the individual who initiates an ethically significant action. It is an unseen efficacy capable of producing results at some later moment of time. In some respects the Vaibhāṣika concept of *avijñapti* karma is similar to the concept of *apūrva* developed

61. For the translation of *vijñapti* and *avijñapti* as "patent" and "latent" respectively, I am indebted to Surendranath Dasgupta, *A History of Indian Philosophy,* vol. 1 (Cambridge: Cambridge University Press, 1932), p. 124. Also see K. Yamada, "On the Idea of *avijñaptikarma* in Abhidharma Buddhism" (in Japanese), *Journal of Indian and Buddhist Studies* (Tokyo), vol. 19 (1962), pp. 349–354. *Vijñapti* karma is action which makes itself known to others, while *avijñapti* karma signifies "a karmic energy which is not perceived by the five senses or made known to another" (Yamakami Sogen, *Systems of Buddhistic Thought* [Calcutta: University of Calcutta Press, 1962], pp. 149–150).

62. *Kośa.* 4.4. Vasubandhu notes that the Vātsīputriyas held the counter view that corporal *vijñapti* is displacement, or movement *(gati).*

63. Guenther, *Philosophy and Psychology in the Abhidharma,* p. 248.

by Mīmāṃsā to explain the interval between sacrificial action and its fruits.[64]

As a means to greater understanding of the concept of *avijñapti* karma, let us consider two examples. In presenting himself before the monastic community and taking the monastic vows, the prospective novice accomplishes a patent act. Insofar as it involves his presence and coming forward, it is a corporal act. Similarly, the actual recitation of the vows is vocally patent. With the performance of these patent acts, a new disposition toward self-discipline is born within the initiate. This inner disposition is an example of *avijñapti* (i.e., latent) karma. It is an internal karma, which cannot be perceived by the five senses, but which nonetheless continues to reproduce itself beyond the actual moment when the vows are recited and the accompanying ritual is performed.

A second example: Let us suppose that I hire someone to commit a murder. In giving him his orders, I commit a patent *(vijñapti)* vocal act. However, I am not yet a murderer, since no death has occurred. Nonetheless, the intent *(cetanā)* to kill continues latent within me. In obeying my orders my accomplice commits a patent corporal action of his own, namely, a murder. At that precise moment, regardless of how I am occupied, I become a murderer along with my accomplice, even though no one else may become aware of my participation in the foul deed. In the Vaibhāṣika theory there was created within me a latent *(avijñapti)* karma which by continually reproducing itself provides the connecting link between my murderous intent, on the one hand, and the actual murder and its eventual retribution, on the other.

Latent karma is said to be either corporal or vocal depending on whether it proceeds from a bodily or a vocally patent act.

Avijñapti karma is either good *(kusala)* or bad *(akusala).* It is never neutral or undefined *(avyākṛta),* for an undefined intentional impulse *(cetanā)* is weak, incapable of engendering a powerful act such as latent karma must be in order to reproduce itself after its initial cause has disappeared.[65] Since *avijñapti* karma is never undefined, it cannot be born of retribution.[66]

In contrast to latent action, however, patent *(vijñapti)* karma and

64. For a brief discussion of *apūrva* in Mīmāṃsā, see Surama Dasgupta, *Development of Moral Philosophy in India* (New York: Frederick Ungar, 1965), pp. 80–82.
65. *Kośa.* 4.30.
66. *Kośa.* 4.28.

its corresponding intentional impulse *(cetanā)* may be undefined or neutral *(avyākṛta)*, as well as good or bad.

Vasubandhu goes beyond any of the texts of the Theravāda *Tipiṭaka* in making clear in practical terms which acts fall into the undefined category. The Buddha is taken as the final authority in this matter. Any act of which the Buddha did not say that it was either good or bad, writes Vasubandhu, is undefined, or ethically neutral *(avyākṛta)*.[67] This means that any act done without grasping and which was neither specifically enjoined nor prohibited by the Buddha may be classed as *avyākṛta*. Thus the acts of everyday existence are undefined, so long as they are done without grasping *(tṛṣṇā)*.

The Sautrāntikas knew and refuted the Vaibhāṣika theory of *vijñapti* and *avijñapti* karma. Remaining closer to the position of Theravāda in this particular instance, the Sautrāntikas denied that patent karma, whether corporal or vocal, is distinct from *cetanā*. Since there is no act beyond the intentional impulse, *vijñapti* karma as defined by the Vaibhāṣikas is merely a gratuitous concept. Furthermore, since latent karma is alleged to derive from patent karma, it too must be a gratuitous concept if considered distinct from *cetanā*.[68]

The theory with which the Sautrāntikas replaced the Vaibhāṣika understanding of *vijñapti* and *avijñapti* karma may be found in the *Karmasiddhiprakaraṇa (Treatise on Karma)*.[69] In brief their view is as follows: The Sautrāntikas began with the *suttanta* principle that karma consists of the intentional impulse plus the act after having willed. They defined three such types of impulse: (1) resolution, (2) decision, (3) the motor impulse. The first two of these constitute the act of intention, or volition *(cetanākarman)*. The third is the act after having willed. The motor impulse is twofold, namely, the intentional impulse which moves the body and that which produces speech. It is these two types of motor impulse which are loosely termed corporal and vocal acts. Intentional impulses which thus bear on bodily movement and the emission of sounds are capable of

67. *Kośa*. 4.106.
68. The Sautrāntika position is outlined at *Kośa*. 4.3.
69. The *Karmasiddhiprakaraṇa* is ascribed to Vasubandhu. Bu-ston considers it an exposition of *karma* from the Yogācāra point of view. And, indeed, the text does include treatment of a notion closely resembling the Yogācāra *ālaya vijñāna*. In spite of all this, however, Étienne Lamotte concludes on the basis of internal evidence that the text is really Sautrāntika. See Lamotte, "Le Traité de l'Acte de Vasubandhu Karmasiddhiprakaraṇa," *Mélanges Chinois et Bouddhiques*, vol. 4 (1935–1936), pp. 176 ff. A translation of the treatise is to be found on pp. 207–263.

producing sui generis further impulses which the Sautrāntikas term *avijñapti*.[70]

Further differences between the Sautrāntika and Vaibhāṣika conceptions of karma arise in their respective understandings of the mechanism of reward and retribution. The question is how an act can bear fruit, how a man can be heir to his own deeds, if the individual is defined as a constantly changing series of aggregates. Let us turn first to the Vaibhāṣika answer. By way of background, it should be noted that the Vaibhāṣikas maintained that the past and future exist. Thus the act is held to exist in its own nature *(svabhāva)* in all times, past, present, and future. Only the mode of its existence varies.[71] During its present existence, that is to say, at the moment it is actually accomplished, an act projects its fruit of retribution. At that moment a potential is established which only actualizes itself much later. In projecting this potential in this way, the act becomes the cause of the fruit. By the time the potential, the fruit, is ready to actualize itself, the act has already entered into its past mode. Since the act still exists, albeit in a past mode, it provides the energy which makes the potential fruit enter into the present mode as an actuality at the appropriate time. This is the moment at which the fruit is experienced as pleasure or suffering. Thus an act projects its fruit-potential at some moment in a psycho-physical series and causes that fruit to be experienced at a later moment in that series. During the interim, however, that act has changed its mode of existence from present to past.

Moreover, in the psycho-physical series which constitutes an individual there exist certain immaterial entities *(dharma)*, unassociated with thought, which are called *prāpti* (possessions). As Thomas Dowling notes, *prāpti* "is said to be the cause that originates *(utpatti-hetu)* a specific nature in a given stream of consciousness at a given moment."[72] Every act creates in him who does it the possession *(prāpti)* of that act. So, too, a corresponding possession is created by every thought or desire. The existence of the *prāpti* is momentary. Scarcely having been born, it perishes. However, it engenders a possession *(prāpti)* similar to itself. Through a continuing process of generation of this type, we continue to possess our acts even long after the actual moment of their accomplishment. The generation of

70. This exposition of the Sautrāntika theory summarizes some of the material from *Karmasiddhiprakaraṇa,* secs. 41–50; Lamotte, "Traité de l'Acte," pp. 256–263.
71. *Kośa.* 5.58.
72. Dowling, "Karma Doctrine as Sectarian Earmark" (n. 8 above), p. 7.

the possession *(prāpti)* of any act in this way can be interrupted only by the actualization into the present of the fruit which was projected with the doing of the act. It is thus through the mechanism of possession that latent and, hence, patent karma become effective. In short, the Vaibhāṣikas posit an intermediary form of karma—*avijñapti* karma—operating through a process of the continuous generation of karma-possession as the means by which merit and demerit are rewarded.[73]

A different mechanism is posited by the Sautrāntikas. They disagreed with the Vaibhāṣikas first of all in maintaining that neither the past nor the future exists. Thus past acts do not exist and, as a result, cannot be considered efficacious in actualizing the potential fruits projected when the acts were being done. In effect, an act is considered present or past according to whether it operates or has ceased to operate. If a former act bears fruit, it is because it operates, and thus it is to be considered a present rather than a past act. All this simply means that the Sautrāntikas consider *prāpti* as defined by the Vaibhāṣikas to be one more purely gratuitous philosophical invention. It is no more valid a conception than is the Vaibhāṣika notion of latent karma as distinct from the intentional impulse. Neither possession nor *avijñapti* are things in themselves. When the Buddha affirmed the persistence of past karma, he intended only to affirm the inevitability of retribution. The Sautrāntikas, contrary to the Vaibhāṣikas, held that all acts are momentary, perishing as soon as they are born without generating new intermediary karma. However, a good or a bad act perfumes *(vāsanā)* the complex psycho-physical series which in popular parlance is termed the individual. It creates a special potentiality *(śaktiviśeṣa)* which causes the perfumed series to undergo an evolutionary process, the culminating term of which is a state of retribution called the "fruit." This potentiality, or power, is termed the *bīja* (seed).[74]

In the *Abhidharmakośa* we find a fully developed theory of what constitutes complete karma. Though a full-blown theory of this sort was never developed in the Pāli *Nikāyas,* certain precursors of such a

73. See *Kośa.* 2.179–195. Cf. la Vallée-Poussin, *Morale Bouddhique,* pp. 196–199. Also see *Karmasiddhiprakaraṇa,* secs. 15–17. Cf. Lamotte, "Traité de l'Acte," pp. 153–154, 158–160, 166–168, and 224–230.

74. See *Kośa.* 2.185 and 272; 5.63; and 9.296. Cf. *Karmasiddhiprakaraṇa,* secs. 20–26, pp. 232–239 in Lamotte, "Traité de l'Acte." Also see Padmanabh S. Jaini, "The Sautrāntika Theory of *Bīja,*" *Bulletin of the School of Oriental and African Studies, University of London,* vol. 22, pp. 236–249.

theory are to be found in the *Tipiṭaka.* In brief they are as follows: First there was the notion that for an act to have kammic consequences, it had to be done intentionally. Related to this was the idea that for a deed to have the greatest possible effect, it had to be done with consideration, not casually. Finally, there was the idea that, to a certain extent, the ethical potential of a deed, whether good or bad, can be counteracted by repentance.[75]

According to the formulation of the *Abhidharmakośa,* to be complete and really fruitful a deed must consist of three parts.[76] First, a complete act requires preparation. This part is called the *prayoga.* It is twofold, consisting of premeditation, or the intention to do the act, on the one hand, and the actual preparatory steps *(sāmantakā)* requisite to the carrying out of the act, on the other. For example, a man desiring to butcher a domestic animal rises from his bed, takes some money, and goes to market, where he buys a cow or a goat. He then takes a knife and prepares to deal the beast a blow. All these actions are preparatory to the actual killing of the beast. They constitute the *prayoga.* The second element necessary for a complete act is the principal action, called the *maula karmapatha.* To continue with our illustration, the principal action is the death-dealing blow itself. Like the *prayoga,* it too is twofold. It consists of the patent action at the moment of the animal's death, namely, the knife stroke. It also includes the latent action that arises at the precise moment of death. Finally, to be complete the principal action must be backed up. This element of an action is called the back *(pṛṣṭha).* The *pṛṣṭha* consists of consequent actions that follow upon the principal action, as well as succeeding moments in the *avijñapti.* To continue with our illustration, the *pṛṣṭha* of the butchering would include a satisfied attitude, and such acts as preparing and cutting up the carcass and selling the meat.[77]

Before we proceed further, it must be stressed that the term *karmapatha* (course of action) does not apply to trifling acts. Thus the foregoing analysis is applicable only to ethically significant acts, namely, those which if complete may be expected to produce karmic fruits. With this fact in mind, we are in a position to raise the question

75. See James P. McDermott, *Developments in the Early Buddhist Concept of Kamma/Karma,* Ph.D. dissertation, Princeton University, 1971, pp. 69–72.
76. These are delineated at *Kośa.* 4.140–141.
77. The illustration is from *Kośa.* 4.141.

of the broader implications of this theory for the principle of karma. This definition of what constitutes a complete act is of particular significance in the Sarvāstivādin understanding of the force of repentance as a factor that may modify the consequences of any given action. We have already noted the Theravādin belief that the force of an act can be counteracted to some extent by repentance. Such a belief tended to dilute belief in the inevitability of karmic retribution. The Sarvāstivādin theory of complete acts tended to reinforce this latter belief, while at the same time allowing a role for repentance. The Sarvāstivādins held that if an individual repented of an act immediately after committing the principal course of action, that act must be considered incomplete. In such a case the back *(pṛṣṭha)* is lacking. Being incomplete, the consequences of that act are vitiated. However, once an act has been carried through to its completion, once it has been backed up, whether by consequent actions or an approving mind-set, it is too late for meaningful repentance.

The Vaibhāṣikas maintain that in the sensual world *(kāmadhātu)* the preliminaries *(sāmantakā)* that prepare for a course of action *(karmapatha)* will always be patent *(vijñapti)*. These preparations may or may not also include latent *(avijñapti)* elements, depending on whether or not they are carried out while in a state of great passion. In contrast, the back, or consequential acts *(pṛṣṭha)*, necessarily involves latent elements. It is patent as well only when one continues to commit acts analogous, or secondarily related, to the principle course of action.[78]

Vasubandhu makes a further distinction between the act done *(kṛta)* and the act accumulated *(upacita)*. An act is said to be accumulated by virtue of its intentional character, its completion, the absence of regret or any counteraction, and finally its reward or retribution.[79] In thus considering action one thing and its accumulation something else, Vasubandhu is in accord with the Andhakas in their disagreement with the Theravādins,[80] who held that since the accumulation *(upacaya)* of *kamma* is the automatic concommitant of action, the two must be viewed as but different aspects of one and the same thing.

78. See *Kośa*. 4.140.
79. *Kośa*. 4.242.
80. See *Kvu*. 15.11. Also see McDermott, "Kathāvatthu Kamma Debates" (n. 9 above), p. 430.

There are three qualities which are conceived as especially contributing to the accumulation of merit. These are (1) *dāna*—liberality or munificence;[81] (2) *bhāvana*—contemplation, meditation; (3) *sīla*—moral practice.[82]

Merit can be built up and accumulated. But is it possible to transfer merit from one account to another, as it were? Taken as a whole the *Tipiṭaka* is not fully consistent on this point. On the one hand, throughout much of the Pāli canon there is a strong emphasis on the personal nature of *kamma.* One's *kamma* is said to be his own. Each being must be an island unto himself, working out his own salvation.[83] No sponsor *(pāṭibhoga)*—whether Brahmin or recluse, whether Brahmā or Māra—can protect a man against the fruit of his evil deeds.[84] Meritorious action well laid up is a treasure "not shared with others."[85] On the other hand, a doctrine of transfer of merit—apparently a popular development traceable to the Brahmanic *śrāddha* rites—finds expression in several places in the canon.[86] In the *Petavatthu,* for example, a common theme is that of the benefactor who gives a gift to the *saṃgha* and declares the act of charity to be a *peta's.* Through being ascribed to the *peta,* the act of giving becomes his in actuality; and, in this way, the *peta* acquires merit from the gift. In a similar vein, the *Mahāparinibbāna Sutta* exhorts:

> In whatever place the wise man shall make his home,
> Thence having fed the virtuous, self-controlled Brahmā-farers,
> Whatever *devatās* may be there, let him declare the gift theirs.
> Honored, they honor him; revered, they revere him.[87]

Another example of merit transference can be seen at *A* 4.63 ff, where Naṇda's mother dines an order of monks in the name of the *deva*

81. This particularly refers to almsgiving.
82. These are listed at *It.* 51; *D* 3.218; and *A* 4.241.
83. *S* 3.42; etc.
84. *A* 1.172.
85. "Khuddaka Pātha" *(Kh.)* 8.9. Edited by R. C. Childers in *Journal of the Royal Asiatic Society.* N.S. 4 (1870): 309–339.
86. On transfer of merit in the *Tipiṭaka,* see especially F. L. Woodward, "The Buddhist Doctrine of Reversible Merit," *The Buddhist Review* (London), vol. 6 (1914), pp. 38–50. The connection with *śrāddha* rites is spelled out in B. C. Law, *The Buddhist Conception of Spirits* (London: Luzac, 1936).
87. *D* 2.88. With slight variations insignificant for the question at hand, these same lines appear at *Udāna (Ud.)* 89 and *Vin.* 1.229. I. B. Horner renders these lines quite differently in her translation of *Vin.* 1.229. The crucial differences relate to line 3, the text of which reads: "Yā tattha devatā āsum [or assu] tāsaṃ dakkhiṇam ādise." My

Mahārāja Vessavaṇa, declaring: "Whatever merit *(puñña)* is in this gift, Reverend Sir, let it be beneficial for the well-being of the great king Vessavaṇa." Scattered expressions of such a doctrine are also to be found in the *Jātakas.* Thus in the *Macchuddāna Jātaka* we read that as the Bodhisatta and his brother waited on the banks of the Ganges for a boat, they ate a meal. "The Bodhisatta, having thrown the left-over food to the fish, gave the river spirit the profit *(patti).*"[88] Twice in the course of the *Jātaka* it is stated that the river spirit immediately benefited from the Bodhisatta's gift to the fish.

In light of the apparent conflict of opinion in the texts concerning the possibility of merit transference, it is worth noting that the *Sādhīna Jātaka* seems to provide evidence that acceptance of the practice of merit transference within Theravāda at times came grudgingly.[89]

Other means for aiding the departed continued to be denied. No more than prayers can raise a rock sunk in the water can they speed a man heavenward who has sunk to a lower state of existence because of his own evil actions.[90] Prayers for the dead will not alter the effects of their *kamma.* Nor can one alter his own lot by prayers, sacrifices, or rituals of other sorts.[91] A man becomes cleansed only once he has abandoned the various ways of evil action. Purificatory rites are of no avail. Thus when Puṇṇikā encounters a Brahmin performing ritual ablutions in the middle of winter, she asks him what fears lead him thus to endure the cold waters. He answers:

> "Knowing the answer, honorable Puṇṇikā, you ask
> One who doing a good deed *(kamma),* is restraining bad *kamma.* (238)
> Whether old or young, he who performs a bad deed *(kamma)*
> Is freed from bad *kamma* by a water-ablution." (239)

---

interpretation of the passage as a reference to transfer of merit is supported by the commentary to *Ud.* 89, which glosses *dakkhiṇam ādise* with *pattiṃ dadeyya,* or "give merit." For a fuller discussion of the issues and alternatives, see McDermott, *Developments* (n. 75 above), pp. 83–84, and especially p. 88, note 2.

88. Fausboll, *Jataka* no. 88, vol. 2, p. 423.

89. See James P. McDermott, "Sādhīna Jātaka: A Case Against the Transfer of Merit," *JAOS* 94 (1974): 385–387. For a conflicting interpretation, see Heinz Bechert, "Buddha-Feld und Verdienstübertragung: Mahāyāna-Ideen im Theravāda-Buddhismus Ceylons," *Académie Royale de Belgique Bulletin de la Classe des Lettres et des Sciences Morales et Politiques,* 5th series, vol. 62 (1976), pp. 42–43.

90. *S* 4.311 f.

91. The *thūpa* cult is an exception to the general rule.

To this she responds:

> "Who in ignorance told you, who did not know, that
> One is certainly freed from bad *kamma* by a water-ablution? (240)
> Is it then that all frogs, tortoises, snakes, crocodiles,
> And whatever else passes through water shall go to heaven? (241)
> Butchers of sheep, butchers of swine, fishermen, deer hunters,
> Thieves, executioners, and whatever others do bad deeds—
> Even they are freed from bad *kamma* by a water-ablution? (242)
> If these streams could carry away evil formerly done by you,
> They also could carry away your merit. By this means you would become an outsider. (243)
> That afraid of which, O Brahmin, you always descend to water—
> That do not do. Do not let the cold destroy your skin." (244)[92]

The effectiveness of Vedic sacrifice is also denied. Thus, when Gotama learns of King Pasenadi's preparations for a great animal sacrifice, he declares that such rites do not bring results. Animal sacrifices are rejected as harmful. Offerings where no goats and sheep are slain are alone acceptable.[93] Such offerings are to be in the form of gifts to the deserving, for they bear great fruit.

The Buddha also rejected self-mortification as a means to acquiring good *kamma*, and as a way to *Nibbāna*. In his own quest for enlightenment, he came to realize that austerities can be more of a hindrance than an aid. In their stead he came to favor a middle path between self-mortification and the life devoted to sensual pleasures.

For all the attention given to *kamma* in early Buddhist thought, the way to *Nibbāna*, the ultimate goal, remained—as ordinarily conceived—precisely the cessation of *kamma (kammanirodha)*.[94]

In conclusion, it remains to suggest that both the variety of early Buddhist interpretations of the karmic mechanism and the rebirth process, as well as whatever is distinctive in these interpretations, can be seen ultimately to derive from the Buddha's denial of a permanent personal entity *(attā/ātman)*.

92. *Therīgāthā* 238–244. Similarly, at *M* 1.39 the Buddha himself denies the usefulness of ritual ablution for washing away wicked deeds.
93. *S* 1.76.
94. *Kh.* 8 and *Miln.* 341 are exceptional in viewing *Nibbāna* as a possible reward for *kamma*. See James P. McDermott, "Nibbāna as a Reward for Kamma," *JAOS* 93 (1973): 344–347.

8

The Medical Soteriology of Karma in the Buddhist Tantric Tradition

WILLIAM STABLEIN

Introduction and Sources

South Asian ceremony and meditative disciplines are conditioned by a dogma of soteriology based on the idea of karma and rebirth which accommodates all possibilities for living yet dying human beings. The meaning conveyed by the hierarchy of interdisciplinary textual material dictates the ceremonial face and inner logic of Vajrāyana (i.e., Tantric) Buddhism to such a large extent that it is impossible to overlook its interlocking semantic structures. Karma cannot be understood merely by locating all the occurrences of the word *karma* (or *las,* in Tibetan) in a particular text. Since karma is the complex from which the devotee desires to be liberated, either through techniques of salvation or techniques of healing, it is reasonable to assume that the medical and salvific traditions contain structures that will provide some meaningful assumptions about karma.

From a superficial point of view, the interdisciplinary nature of this essay is based on the seeming disparity between the genres of source texts chosen for this study.[1] The most popular medical classic still

1. See Robert B. Ekvall, "Correlation of Contradictions: A Tibetan Semantic Device," in *Himalayan Anthropology* (The Hague: Mouton, 1977).

studied and practiced among Tibetan-speaking peoples is the seventeenth-century commentary on *The Four Tantras,* called the *Blue Lapis Lazuli,* which has an embryological model of karma common to the sacramentaries and the meditational texts of Tantric Buddhism. Since the *Lapis Lazuli* is a standard medical treatise, it is interesting to find similar ideas and linguistic structures in other genres of literature, such as texts in the Tantric section of the Tibetan Buddhist canon. The *Caṇḍamahāroṣaṇa* and *Mahākāla Tantras* are particularly useful for the topic of karma and rebirth, and the sixteenth chapter of the *Caṇḍamahāroṣaṇa Tantra* reiterates and interprets the dependent origination process which has bearing on the structure of karma.[2]

Some of the Tantras form quasi-medical traditions of their own with a number of healing formulas that bear a structural resemblance to similar phrases in the *Lapis Lazuli.* Among the priestly class of Buddhist Newars in Kathmandu Valley, Nepal, the deity Caṇḍamahāroṣaṇa presides over and protects the medicinal arts with prestige equal to that of the Hindu god of medicine, Dhanvantari. The Tantras, then, constitute a synthesis of the healing arts as found in the *Lapis Lazuli* and the various traditions of meditational and devotional practices. Our meditational source, chosen for its succinctness, belongs to the set of Mahākāla practices attributed to the Bkaḥ Brgyud

2. *Bai.dur.sngon.po: Being the text of Gso.ba.rig.paḥi.bstan.bcos.sman.blaḥi.-dgongs.rgyan.rgyud.bzhiḥi.gsal.bai.dur.sngon.poḥi.ma.llika.: Sde.srid.sangs.-rgyas.rgya.mtshọ's detailed synthetic treatise on the Rgyud.bzhi, the fundamental exposition of Tibetan Ayurvedic Medicine.* Reproduced from a print of the 1888–1892 blocks preserved in the Lha.sa.lcags.po.ri.rig.byed.ḥgro.phan.gling. Leh, Ladhak: S. W. Tashigangpa, 1973. This is a PL 480 acquisition: I-Tib. 73-904162. Further references will use the abbreviation *Bai.sngon.* See also Rechung Rinpoche Jampal Kunzang, *Tibetan Medicine* (Berkeley: University of California Press, 1973); William Stablein, "Textual Criticism and Tibetan Medicine," in *The Tibet Society Bulletin;* William Stablein, "Tantric Medicine and Ritual Blessings," in *The Tibet Journal: An International Publication for the Study of Tibet,* published by the Library of Tibetan Works & Archives: Special Issue, "Tibet: A Living Tradition," vol. 1, nos. 3–4 (Autumn 1976), pp. 55–69; William Stablein, "The Mahākāla Tantra: A Theory of Ritual Blessings and Tantric Medicine," Ph.D. dissertation, Columbia University, 1976; *Caṇḍamahāroṣaṇa Tantra* (Tibetan: *dpal.dtum.po.khro.bo.chen.poḥi.rgyud.*), the Tibetan Tripitaka in the collection in the Harvard University Library; Lhasa edition of the *Bkaḥ.ḥgyur* (abbreviated as *Caṇḍa*) *Rgyud,* section nga, folio 431. For an edition and translation of the first eight chapters, see Christopher George, *The Caṇḍamahāroṣaṇa Tantra: A Critical Edition and English Translation, Chapters I–VIII,* American Oriental Series, vol. 56, New Haven, 1974. See also Louis de la Vallée Poussin, "The Buddhist Wheel of Life from a New Source," *Journal of the Royal Asiatic Society of Great Britain and Ireland* (New Series), 1897, pp. 463–470.

pa lineage.[3] The passages quoted from the meditational text are all from the third and last part of the book, dealing with perfection or way of completion, which has structural similarities to the *Tibetan Book of the Dead.*[4] Indeed, the *Book of the Dead* maintains that one's success in attaining liberation after death depends on previous practice not only in devotional observances but in the specific ways of generation *(bskyed.rim)* and perfection *(rdzogs.rim).*

One aim of this essay is to restrict the discussion of karma to its flow through the continuum of the afterdeath state into the flesh and blood of an earthly being; hence our sources are limited to those which are basic to an understanding of this process, such as the *Zab.mo.nang.gi.don,* by Rang.byung.rdo.rje. This text is concerned primarily with the inner body referred to as the three channels *(rtsa.gsum),* which the Mahākāla Tantra calls the *Vajra* body *(rdo.rje.lus).*[5] This inner structure, which is important for the Tantric explanation of rebirth as well as salvation, has parallels in Hindu Tantra and yoga and offers a fully developed model of the inner body, which can be detected at various stages of sophistication in the myths and medical theories of most cultures.[6] Any discussion of the three channels or the channel-wind-drop structure *(rtsa.rlung.thig.le)* is necessarily both Tantric and medical. Hence the *Book of the Dead* assumes this structure as operative for the afterdeath being or "in-between-state-being" *(bar.doḥi.sems.can),* demonstrating its affinity with medical and meditational texts.

3. *Grub.chen.karma.pakshiḥi.man.ngag.yi.ge.med.paḥi.snyan.brgyud.ma.mgon.-zhal.sbyor.sgrub.baḥi.man.ngag.zin.bris.ngag.khrid.yod.|ḥdi.la.bskyed.rim.las.-tshogs.rdzogs.rim.mchod.sgrub.cha.tshang.lagso: This is the Oral Tradition without words in the Higher explanation of Karma Pakshi; the guiding commentary with directions for the conjugal practice of the protector Mahākāla and his mistress. Herein are the complete sacrificial practices of generation, acts, and perfection.* Gangtok: Sikkim. (Abbreviated as in the Ms.: *Mgon.*)

4. Kalsang Lhundup (editor), *Bar.doḥi.thos.grol.bzhugs.so: The Tibetan Book of the Dead* (Varanasi: E. Kalsang, Buddhist temple). (Abbreviated *Bar.do)* See also the two available translations into English: Francesca Fremantle and Chogyam Trungpa, trans., *The Tibetan Book of the Dead: The Great Liberation Through Hearing in the Bardo* (Boulder: Shambala, 1975), and W. Y. Evans Wentz, *The Tibetan Book of the Dead, the After-Death Experiences on the Bardo Plane, according to Lama Kazi Dawa-Samdup's English Rendering* (New York: Galaxy, 1960).

5. *Zab.mo.nang.gi.don.zhes.bya.bahi.gzhung.bzhugs: The Text called the Deep Inner Meaning* (Gangtok, Sikkim). (Abbreviated *Nang.don.*) For the *vajra*-body and the three channels, see Stablein, *Mahākāla,* pp. 180–181.

6. Andreas Lommel, *Shamanism: The Beginnings of Art* (New York: McGraw Hill, 1967).

The Setting, the Problem, and the Terminology

It is not surprising that a Tantric *(Vajrayāna)* priest may know a considerable number of medical techniques, or that the healer may also function as a priest. The fluidity of the literary structures certainly reflects the interplay of epistemology and empiricism that takes place in the Tantric rite itself. The above texts are all read and practiced in the Himālayan regions from Ladhak and Northern India to the borders of China; and, as we can see from the other articles in this volume, they are structurally akin to texts known throughout South Asia.

Karma is a very general notion that is applied to all phases of Buddhist praxis; on the popular and cultural levels it is an assumption that rarely takes the form of philosophical discussion and inquiry. The only major difference between Buddhists living in either a Tibetan- or a Nepalese-speaking community—both of which fall under the aegis of the Buddhist Tantric tradition—and the Buddhists of other parts of South Asia is that the former have a definite and formalized conception of an afterdeath (or in-between-being) that can be verified by canonical sources. However, karma is a very specific notion in certain contexts and defies any simple definition because it includes the various literary and cultural contexts mentioned above. The problem is to simplify the notion of karma at least to the point where we can delineate a karmic structure—in relief—in the Buddhist Tantric tradition. In no place in the literature is karma defined in such a complete and intercontextual sense; yet this study will not go beyond the texts themselves or make comparisons with Western theories of rebirth.

Our approach will be to locate "natural structures," that is, structures that are natural to the meaning of karma in its most radical formation. For example, although we shall not discuss the bodhisattva doctrine, we may refer to the seed of enlightenment as it is related to the formation of karma. We shall not be concerned with the Buddhist eightfold path, but we shall discuss the concepts of suffering and disease. The body *(lus)* and the more philosophical idea of the person will be touched upon only in the discussion of the beginnings of the body in embryological development and in meditation, where the three channels form a dominant structure. Reference to dependent origination *(rten.ḥbrel)* will be limited to the *Caṇḍamahāroṣaṇa*'s interpretations. The idea of conjugal union *(kha.sbyor)* provides a model for the purification of karma through the language of the procreative-embryological metaphor. The concept of *śūnyatā (stong.pa.ñid)* will not be considered except in the context of the wandering consciousness's attempt to become aware of its own nature and in the liturgical discourse where it forms an opposition with purity *(dag.pa)*.

One of the controversies in Buddhist circles throughout the centuries has been the significance of the afterdeath or in-between-state-being.[7] In the Tantras, the in-between-state is an imagined state of wandering, and it is this wandering that dooms one to another rebirth. Hence the word "wanderer" designates that being whose body has died and who is battling with the foes in his own karma in order to reach salvation. The term *ḥkhyam* means one who wanders with no purpose; the wanderer is beset with karmic error *(las.ḥkhrul)*. "Error" is preferable to "illusion," for "error" denotes a more causal connection with rebirth. Indeed, the wanderer is faced not with an illusion in the sense that it is simply not what he thinks it is, but with a force that, like a mirage, is something else, a contingency of *śūnyatā* that is brought about through a lack of awareness. Any differentiation between the in-between-state and the wanderer itself is purely semantic. It is somewhat misleading to say that karma moves from one place to another, transforms or stands still, but on the popular and cultural level these are certainly the prevailing ways of viewing the subject of birth, rebirth, and death.

Methodology of Oppositions: Suffering-Salvation

Karma implies a radical opposition between good *(bzang)* and evil *(ngan)* and all of their metaphors, such as clear light and dull light, virtue and non-virtue, awareness and fear. Karma and rebirth merit little attention outside the domain of soteriology; it is no accident that the *Tibetan Book of the Dead,* ostensibly a book about salvation (i.e., the certain attainment of complete and perfect Buddhahood), provides us with a panorama of descriptions of karma and rebirth.

An awareness of karma could not exist without a lucidity of con-

7. For a review of the arguments between those who adhere to the theory of intermediate state and those who do not, see Alex Wayman, "The Intermediate State Dispute in Buddhism," in *Buddhist Studies in Honour of I. B. Horner,* L. Cousins, A. Kunst, and K. K. Norman, eds. (Dordrecht, Holland: D. Reidel, 1974), pp. 227–239.

sciousness, which is expressed in the first intermediate state by the phrase "disclosing the face of the clear light in the moment-of-death-intermediate-state." Since the intermediate state is characterized by both the thought-body and the body-of-sensation, lucidity encompasses both. The carnal body, the body of flesh *(sha.lus),* despite its dualistic contrast with the thought-body *(yid.lus),* is interlocked in polarity with the thought-body through karmic impressions *(bag.chags).* Hence we have the term *bag.chags.yid.kyi.lus,* "body of thought impression." The opposition "body-mind" is then not a plus and minus but a natural structure projected to assist the listener or reader in understanding the problem at hand, which is man's suffering and liberation. Since the term "body" occurs in correlations concerning the carnal as well as the mental, the key terminology for carnality is the word flesh *(sha),* not body *(lus).* This is also true for blood *(khrag)* and semen *(khu.ba)* used in explanations of procreative embryonic development and disease etiology. "Thought-body" suggests impressions from previous lives, which are the common denominator between flesh and thought. In a strict sense, therefore, *lus* means not "body" but rather "that which is contaminated"; and, as we shall see later, contamination *(skyon)* is operational not in the body per se but in blood and semen and even more radically in the five aggregates that define the in-between-being, the wanderer. Contamination, whether it be of the humors or of the five poisons, traces karma. When the texts speak of humors they are referring to the body of flesh, but when the thought-body is discussed the texts refer to the poisons which serve as the main barrier to health, liberation, or a better rebirth. The term *dug* (poison) is used to describe the contamination left in the yogi in his highest contemplations. Hence "contamination" (i.e., "fault," *doṣa)* naturally pairs with "flesh and blood," and "poisons" with "mind," but each pair is in turn organically related to the other.

The in-between-state-being in the second part of the dying-moments-stage is able to see the setting it has come from; the priest then says: "Oh noble son, now that which is defined as 'my death' has arrived. . . . You yourself have not transcended the wandering in the world."[8] And at another moment in the rite, just before rebirth, the wanderer is told: "Because you are a thought-body, even though you have been dessicated and slaughtered, you have not at all died."[9]

8. *Bar.do,* p. 15. 9. *Bar.do,* p. 81.

We might conclude that there is no death in Tibetan Tantric Buddhism, or that the concept of death is not an absolute, or that death and no-death are equally beside the point, especially in the light of the continuum of rebirth. Our main concern, however, is the in-between-state-death *(ḥchi.khaḥi.bar.do).* In the second quote, the term *bsad* ("slaughter" or "kill") does not mean death *(ḥchi.ba).* If we take the *Book of the Dead's* example of death, that is, "that moment when the consciousness is able to see where it has come from," we can conclude that death is the ability of the wanderer to distinguish a new set of karmic appearances. Altogether there are four sets: the flesh-kinship set that the wanderer first perceives when he leaves the flesh; the dull lights of the six realms and the karmic errors; the world at large; and (if one is reborn) the flesh-kinship set once again, now with a new appearance. Death implies redeath, but this redeath occurs only if the wanderer is not aware of the metaphor "You are a thought-body." In salvific terms, the opposite of death is not life but the clear light *(ḥod.gsal).*

Karma takes on value from the language expressing the syndrome of suffering and from salvific expressions. The setting of karma can be delineated in the following general way:

1. Flesh body *(sha.lus)*	1. Thought body *(yid.lus)*
2. Suffering *(sdug.bngal)*	2. Awareness *(ngo.shes)*
3. Contamination *(skyon)*	3. *Śūnyatā (stong.pa.nyid)*
4. Impressions *(bag.chags)* and Poisons *(dug)*	4. *Dharma-, sambhoga-,* & *nirmāṇa-kāyas*
5. Duality *(gñis)*	5. Non-duality *(gñis.med)*
6. Dull light *(bkrag.med)*	6. Clear light *(ḥod.gsal)*
7. Entering the womb *(mngal.ḥjug)*	7. Buddhahood *(sangs.rgyas)*

If, instead of regarding the above oppositions as phenomena, we take advantage of the built-in zero degree (i.e., *śūnyatā* and its equivalents on the right-hand side), we have a pure value system where the meaning and value of karma are decided from both sides of the chart.

Introduction to the In-Between-States *(Book of the Dead)*

The texts that are consulted or called to memory at the time of death vary, but the dominant themes and paradigms that indicate the projection of consciousness and its contingent karma are presented in the *Book of the Dead* and in a text called the *Utkramayoga,* used in the

Nepalese communities.[10] Both texts offer instructions for raising the consciousness up from the corporeal self and liberating it or, falling short of liberation, directing it to the best possible rebirth. This entails the wandering of the consciousness principle through the in-between-states *(bar.do)* until it chooses or falls into a particular rebirth.

The term *bar.do* has the fundamental sense of those in-between states in the passage of life and consciousness that determine the individual's future pleasure and pain and redeath-rebirth experiences. It is a state where consciousness is thrust up and down between one's former and ensuing birth by karmic power *(las.dbang)*. (That is to say, the one who is of *bar.do* is a seeker of life and is thrust up and down by karmic power, as Ge.she.chosdag's *Tibetan Dictionary* defines *bar.do.ba.)* While we think of karma in the language of flesh and blood, the *Lapis Lazuli* unequivocally views the corporeal as contingent on karma:

> In the same way, the father's semen, the mother's blood with unimpaired wind, and so on (the humors), and the *bar.do* consciousness constituting one's former devotions and dependencies are by karma . . . brought into confluence.[11]

"In the same way" refers to the example in which fire is the result of the proper combination of male rubbing wood (i.e., semen), female wood that it is rubbed against (i.e., blood), dry timber, and the energies of man (i.e., the *bar.do* consciousness). Then, karma is akin to the compelling of the energies which are the ultimate cause of the fire. Even though the *bar.do* consciousness wanders without any corporeal state with its body of flesh and blood, it is precisely that state of wandering that is called the *bar.do* aggregate *(bar.doḥi. phung.po)*. This implies that the wandering being of consciousness has the qualities of form, pleasure-pain feelings, conception, aggregates, and consciousness; the wandering consciousness has momentarily lost its opportunity for complete and perfect Buddhahood and is seeking a new rebirth.

Consciousness as detached from the flesh and blood may not be contingent on form, but for the purposes of re-entry into the corporeal world where the semi-deceased maintains his individualized

10. The *Utkramayoga* is the standard procedure for performing the death rite in Nepalese society.
11. *Bai.sngon,* folio 93.

karma, the in-between-state aggregates are necessary. For example, the *Lapis Lazuli,* in its general discussion of the signs of procreation, states:

Since the two organs are united, the semen falls into the secret flower; and that which is the blood in the womb is called seed. That is to say, the semen and blood of the mother and father are said to be the seed. Because of that, it is necessary to understand the method of re-entry for the *bar.do* consciousness.[12]

And . . . since the *bar.do* aggregates have evolved and there is unimpaired (semen and blood)—as mentioned before—as well as the karmic causes for maturation *(las.kyi.rkyen),* the *bar.do* aggregates will enter the womb.[13]

The *Lapis Lazuli,* then, and presumably the rest of the Tibetan medical tradition, accept the in-between state of being as an intrinsic part of their medical lore and, as such, accept the theory of karma. How they believe it works we shall see in the next few paragraphs. The philosophical and ritual Tantras assume the *bar.do* consciousness as necessary for their praxis.

The *Book of the Dead* Structure

The three main divisions of the in-between state—the moments-of-death *(ḥchi.kha),* the re-recognition of the world *(chos.ñid),* and re-entry to the world *(srid.pa)*—are roughly analogous to the dependent origination process. The first phase of the moments-of-death *bar.do* could occur before the resetting in of nescience, which is the last opportunity to attain complete liberation without going through the ensuing phases. Here liberation is referred to as "the basic-clear-light-experience which is the unborn-vertically-penetrating-dharma-body with-no-*bar.do.*"[14] If this "basic-clear-light . . ." is not disclosed to the dying person, he gets a chance at the second *bar.do* clear-light-experience. This phase is the interim when the wheel turns to the touch of nescience. The text now mentions for the first time the force of karma *(las.kyi.nus.pa).* The omission of this expression in the discussion of the basic-clear-light-experience stage that has no *bar.do* reflects the theory of liberation as maintained by the earlier Theravādin texts. When the term *bar.do* is applied to this very beginning phase, death as the *Book of the Dead* defines it has not yet occurred. The physiological space of the *bar.do* has not developed. Hence, at

12. *Bai.sngon,* folio 109. 13. *Bai.sngon,* folio 110. 14. *Bar.do,* pp. 6–7.

this very point the possibility of a rebirth as explained in Theravādin texts becomes feasible.

In the re-recognition in-between-state phase, after the three and one-half days when one has realized the reality of death and is on the way back to rebirth, there is the appearance of karmic errors *(las.kyi.ḥkhrul.snang).* Now the consciousness principle, having departed from the body, is able to re-recognize its former immediate worldly surroundings, such as the wailing of relatives and so on. That is, even though the *Book of the Dead* discusses the initial phase of liberation in terms of the latent escape of what most people think of as the consciousness principle, the description of the first phase, the basic-clear-light-experience, does not discuss the consciousness principle but speaks rather of the inner wind *(rlung).* At this time of the subliminal dying experience, complete and perfect Buddhahood may be directly attained with no contingencies. In the second phase of the moments-of-dying, the consciousness principle departs to the outside, wondering, "Am I dead or not dead?"[15] The *Book of the Dead* clarifies this phase of reaffirming the departed consciousness not as a corporeal being but as an emotional being plagued by the vicissitudes of his own karma. The officiating priest reads: "You are now a body of thought impressions."[16]

During the fourteen-day period of this re-recognized *bar.do,* the deceased, through the medium of the ritual specialist, wages a battle with karma; he is told by the officiating priest to request to be saved from the "path of the dreadful *bar.do.*"[17] Indeed, dread, attachment, and desire are the dominant forces of karma that constitute the obstacles blocking the path of liberation.[18] For the first six days, the salvation of the wanderer depends on his awareness of the six lights associated with the six Buddhas. The lack of awareness of each light is proportionate to the wanderer's desire for the dull lights that emanate from the six realms of rebirth. On each day comes a light from one of the realms of rebirth; the former Buddha lights are called the knowledge lights, and the latter, dull lights. This is a dominant polarity throughout the rite.

Can we make an axiom for the rite? Can we say that fear of salvation and lust for fleshly attachment make up the crucial opposition

15. *Bar.do,* p. 12. 16. *Bar.do,* p. 16. 17. *Bar.do,* p. 19.
18. *Bar.do,* p. 18.

for the whole of the rite's praxis? Not exactly, except in the specific boundaries where the textual opposition occurs. It has little salvific meaning for one who understood the sign "the basic-clear-light" in the moments-of-death. In a literal sense, then, the sign is understood as the sacrament on a theological and mystical plane, but on another plane it is not understood. In the multidimensional realms of diversified codes, the wanderer's karma functions in terms of a semiotic system: a language, as we shall see, unreliable for the ordinary wanderer who does not see it in terms of radical oppositions. The *Book of the Dead* states:

> If you are frightened of the pure wisdom lights and attracted to the impure lights of the six worlds, the body of (one of) the six classes of these worlds will be acquired; and you will never be liberated from the great ocean of swirling suffering.[19]

On the seventh day one experiences the polarity, knowledge-holding-divinity-realm/beast-realm; and then from the eighth through the fourteenth day the re-recognition *bar.do* is called the wrathful *bar.do,* for at this time all the wrathful divinities in this rite make their appearance. On the fourteenth day, moreover, if the consciousness principle has not yet been liberated from *saṃsāra* the peaceful deities re-emerge in the form of the black Protector, and the wrathful deities in the form of Yama, king of the dead and of *dharma.* Since the re-recognition *bar.do* constitutes the qualities of the six sense bases, it can be said to span the categories on the wheel of life up through indulgence.

In this phase there is still the opportunity for liberation before entering a womb. Curiously, the wanderer is endowed with karmic miraculous power *(las.kyi.rdzu.ḥphrul.shugs)* which the *Book of the Dead* further qualifies by stating that it is not at all a miracle of *samādhi,* but is from the power of karma.[20] The wanderer at this point takes on the characteristics of the kind of being he will be in his next birth. He can see those beings and they can see him: "Even the complexion of his own body will take on the color of the light of whatever birth (he is destined for)."[21]

So far, the implication is that the in-between states and their configurations, though having a logic of their own, are structurally related to the dependent origination process. Since the *Caṇḍa* reflects

19. *Bar.do,* p. 37. 20. *Bar.do,* p. 74. 21. *Bar.do,* p. 88.

the theory of the *Book of the Dead,* we shall look briefly at its interpretation:

Form is endowed with the four elements: the earth which has the quality of heaviness, water which has the quality of moisture, fire which has the quality of heat, and wind which has the qualities of movement, lightness, and contraction/expansion. Therefore there are six bases of the sense: eye, ear, nose, tongue, body, and mind. They see, and so on, and so there is touch, form, sound, smell, taste, the object of touch, and the realm of the *dharma* is completely attained. And because of craving one desires happiness; and from that there is indulgence. Karma is obtained and a being enters the womb. Then birth causes the appearance of the five aggregates of indulgence, which are then born from the womb. But when the arising deathlike thoughts and their objects are suppressed, consideration of old age and death are without suffering and anguish. Yet, if (after the conscious principle is) released it laments, thinking, "I will not find the proper birth because of the obstacles of disease and so on," he will suffer. Then, because of fettering the mind over and over again there will be discontent. Indeed, he who is discontent and creates obstacles is anguished.[22]

The *Book of the Dead* can then be viewed as a partly subliminal infrastructural dependent origination cycle that is repeated in the dying and after-death moments. It is infrastructural because it extends the meaning of the original natural structure as represented by the original formula. Indeed, the possibility of salvation is inherent in the very formation of the sign, where the primary metaphors are based on the vicissitudes of emotions, procreation, and death. The goal of the praxis is to understand this formation, and any metaphor is permissible as long as it promulgates an understanding, for it is the "knowledge being itself" that accommodates the sign. Karma is obtained after indulgence, which in the *Book of the Dead* designates the wanderer's entrance into the womb and in the *Lapis Lazuli* designates the proper psycho-physical conditions for birth.

The Karmic Cycle and Sign

In the last *bar.do,* the re-entry to birth phase when one cannot see his own reflection in a mirror, there occurs the expression:

"Prolong assiduously the emanations of good karma *(bzang.po.las)*. . . . Cultivate the priest as father and mother and

22. *Caṇḍa,* folios 407–409. See also the Sanskrit text, *Buddhist Wheel,* pp. 468–469. There are certain discrepancies between the Tibetan and Sanskrit texts.

abandon jealousy."[23] Jealousy and the other contaminations appear as the primary expressions of bad karma *(las.ngan).* They stand consistently in relation to wandering. The *Book of the Dead* states in the re-recognition phase: "Alas! Through the force of the five poisons, this is the time of wandering in *saṃsāra.*"[24] As we shall see shortly, the five poisons are a dominant set of emotions in the process of completion yoga. In the *Book of the Dead,* in a similar structure, they arise in the first six days of the re-recognition phase. From a psychological and religious (and maybe ethical) point of view, this is probably the most important structure of karma for the focus of our attention.

In the second phase of the first *bar.do,* the dying stage, karma acts on the "wind principle" in such a way as to direct it through the inner nerve system and out one of the orifices of the body. This is important, for the lower the wind descends, the more bad karma it bears in the future. The *Book of the Dead* does not explain this in detail but simply states:

> After the good and bad karma moves the wind into one or the other right and left channel, it will come out from one or the other apertures; and then there will be the entering on the path of clear knowledge.[25]

As the passage suggests and as the *Book of the Dead* briefly relates in earlier passages, the movement of the wind is a concern which entails the knowledge of specialized techniques. Ideally, as in the *Utpattikramayoga* of the Nepalese, the wind is to be directed through a spot *(mastaka)* in the top of the head. This technique with its concommitant system of channels has a salvific as well as a medical value; if the technique is successful at this dying moment, as the *Book of the Dead* states,

> karma is without its bridling power. For example, it is like the light of the sun that dispels the darkness. The clear light of the path defeats the power of darkness and there is liberation.[26]

When liberation is not imminent and the signs have not been understood, the wanderer, in fleeing from them, cannot distinguish between happiness and misery. The signs, that is, the karmic errors,

23. *Bar.do,* p. 38.
24. *Bar.do,* p. 38.
25. *Bar.do,* p. 12. For a more detailed system explaining the channels, see *Nan.don.,* folio 5.
26. *Bar.do,* p. 13.

seem to take on a life of their own and to function in the thought of the wanderer as a kind of trickster. In this drama of will and fate, the wanderer may still be released and is urged by the priest to fasten himself to the flow of good karma.[27]

But what is the good karma? Or, to put it in a more precise way, where does karma receive the value "good"? The *Book of the Dead* is explicit in stating how the wanderer should fasten himself to the flow of good karma. At the time it is tempted by the copulating parents it is offered five methods by which it will not enter the womb. These methods define not only the way to link up with good karma but, as such, define good karma. That is to say, in the first method the emphasis is placed on perseverance; in the second it should cultivate the copulating male and female as one's guru in the male and female aspects without entering between them,[28] and it should perform prostrations and make offerings with the mind. In the third method, although perseverance is again mentioned, the emphasis is on the nullification of the lust and hatred that the wanderer feels for the copulating parents. In the fourth method, if the wanderer is still unsuccessful in closing the door to the womb, it is to regard all substance as false and untrue.[29] For the fifth method—the other four failing—the wanderer should cultivate the thought that "all this is the manifestation of its own mind and that the mind itself is like *māyā*—from the beginning, nothing."[30]

The sign, then, includes the appearance of devotional exercises and any indication of perseverance or of an attitude that regards all substances as false. Theoretically, every Buddhist rite is a karma sign-structure with salvific possibilities. For example, in the Mahākāla rite, ambrosia is realized through a series of signs:

> From the own nature of *śūnyatā* is a three-cornered cauldron from the (syllable) *rni;* there is a jewelled skull vessel from the (syllable) *a* and from the (syllables) *yaṁ.raṁ.laṁ.khaṁ.aṁ* (issues) bile, blood, brain marrow, flesh and bone that designate the five poisons. Then, on top, contemplate the three seed syllables *(oṁ.āḥ.hūṁ);* and after everything melts there evolves ambrosia.[31]

The above quote is a short version of a common paradigm that reoccurs in the Mahākāla rite. Since the goal of the rite is to receive

27. *Bar.do*, p. 91. 28. *Bar.do*, p. 92. 29. *Bar.do*, p. 95.
30. *Bar.do*, p. 96. 31. Stablein, *Mahākāla Tantra*, p. 51.

the powers of body, speech, and mind,[32] we have focused, albeit briefly, on the key sign-structure of karma; put in the form of a series: mind aggregates = hatred, lust, and mental confusion = *śūnyatā* (i.e., all substance is false) = syllables *(rni, a,* etc.) = images (cauldron, etc.) = syllables *(yam,* etc.) = bile, blood, etc. = the five poisons = *oṁ.āḥ.hūṁ* (Buddha's body, speech, and mind) = melting (peak moment of transsignifying) = ambrosia *(amṛta)* = body-, speech-, and mind-power *(kāyasiddhi,* etc.).

Returning now to the *Book of the Dead,* if we assume that the wanderer fails in the five methods of closing the womb door, he will choose or be driven to rebirth; at this point, we must turn to the *Lapis Lazuli* in order to complete the picture.

The wanderer receives a value of indulgence from the sign of the copulating parents who in turn are grasping because of the fundamentally identical karma. The nature of the value is the extension of flesh. The *Lapis Lazuli* says:

> After the wandering *bar.do* consciousness is set in motion by the winds of karma with whatever merit or demerit it may have, and, also, by nescience and the remaining obscurities, a basis is formed in the copulating parents. When the five elements with the semen, blood, and thought accumulate together and are suitably aggregated, it is the cause of the formation of the child in the womb.[33]

In the case of serious impairments of the semen, blood, and thought which cause sterility, the *Lapis Lazuli* quotes the commentary on the *Aṣṭāṅgahṛdayasaṃhitā,* which recommends curing ceremonies to purify each of the impairments.[34] Presumably these ceremonies are thought effective, which calls attention to the condition that, in effect, karma can be altered through the medium of ritual.

Karma, as we might expect, plays an important role in explaining the inability to reproduce, and, as such, provides us with a theory of transgenetics that allows considerable scope for philosophical explanation. The *Lapis Lazuli,* this time quoting the *sūtra* literature, states:

> That which is karma is substance arising from the aggregates of unpredictable merits and demerits which constitute the sentient being who wanders in the re-entry intermediate state; and it is the cause of acquiring a human body. If the accumulating meritorious karma is the same kind as the karma

32. Stablein, *Mahākāla Tantra,* pp. 70–71.
33. *Bai.sngon,* folio 94.
34. *Bai.sngon,* folios 94 and 95.

of the mother and father it will enter this womb. But the karma that is not reciprocal means that the consciousness will not be deposited in the parents' womb.[35]

Karma is seldom termed substance *(dngos),* but in the effort to explain the reasons for a consciousness not entering the womb, the substantive explanation seems inevitable. In this case, the question arises: does the wanderer create substance because of its own lack of awareness and inability to see the apparitions as *śūnyatā*? The question is not answered, for such an attempt in the dialogue may produce a more embarrassing question concerning the existence of self *(ātman),* a problem that seems to be taken as a moot point in the Buddhist Tantric literature.

Even though karma does not have the status of a permanent being of any kind, its value, a value of having mighty power *(las.ñid. dbang.btsan)*[36] which controls and directs the consciousness —at least in certain phases—almost betrays the no-permanent-self concept as being a mere heuristic device. This must be the reason why the texts are careful not to confuse consciousness with karma, even good karma, so that it is not only non-self that becomes a heurism but, also, karma. The above passage could be evidence that karma is a metaphor for genetics. Indeed, what we are confronted with in our study of karma is a genetic concept of the aggregates, or defiled impressions. The *Lapis Lazuli* quotes the *Garland of Vajra Tantra* in the following way:

> The cause is the *bar.do* consciousness, the mind of defiled impressions. Seen as another form, it is like an expanding bubble.[37] The meaning is not known for certain, but the wind concretizes the obscurities into a unity. After the storehouse-consciousness is drawn, the impressions are conducted to enter the womb. Then the impressions themselves control the consciousness and the blood-semen drops become mixed together with the storehouse-consciousness. It is just like one who is intoxicated with the taste of spirits.[38]

The structural connections between the *Book of the Dead* and the *Lapis Lazuli* become clear in the embryology which encompasses the same radical structure of signs that are expressed in terms

35. *Bai.sngon,* folio 96.
36. *Bai.sngon,* folio 98.
37. The form *zlub* is not clear to me.
38. *Bai.sngon,* folios 109 and 110.

of oppositions. The *Lapis Lazuli,* drawing upon the *sūtra* literature, states:

After the consciousness aggregates come to the womb, there first of all arise two kinds of mental oppositions.[39] What are the two? If at the time of copulation the wanderer is to be born as a male, lust will be generated for the mother and hatred for the father. . . . If the wanderer is to be a female, lust is generated for the father and hatred for the mother.[40]

That the medical tradition deems the poisons, hatred and lust, to be the ultimate cause of disease (as secondary growths of ignorance) confirms our position that not only is there a common structure to both Tibetan medicine and Buddhist Tantra but that their underlying conception of mental oppositions is a natural structure of karma; that is to say, karma takes its value from the concept of mental oppositions, which hence constitute a transgenetic unit of the *bar.do* consciousness. These texts make transgenetic sense out of the birth-rebirth process.

When we come to the actual moment of conception, for example, we read:

It is like the light rays of the sun that burn wood and grass through the power of a magnifying crystal. The wood does not appear to touch the magnifying crystal; and further, even though the magnifying crystal does not appear to touch the wood, it burns. In the same way, the consciousness enters the inside of the womb, and so it is said that it enters from invisible doors. Because the sentient being entering the womb is invisible it is considered not to be a foundation. . . . This is said to be similar to the place in the womb of sentient beings. For example, fire is connected with the light rays of the sun and meets with the jewel called magnifying crystal; even though the light may be obscured, it spreads to the wood through the place of the crystal. Reaching that (wood), the penetration is invisible. In the same way, even though the being of the re-entry consciousness is invisible, it reaches the place of the womb. It enters that place.[41]

Karma is given the status of bringing together the first channels (or nerves) after the being of the re-entry consciousness enters the womb: "The paths of the right and left channels of the semen and the womb (ovaries?) are connected by the power of karma."[42] Hence, in Tantric

39. This is an important term in the philosophical literature designating duality, such as attractive-unattractive: *(phyin.ci.log).*
40. *Bai.sngon,* folio 110.
41. *Bai.sngon,* folio 112.
42. *Bai.sngon,* folio 119.

meditation when it is said that the right and left channels must fuse into the middle channel it is tantamount to a purification of the power of karma. The signs, the right and left channels, take their value from karma, but with the understanding that karma takes its value from the poisons and that the poisons are *śūnyatā.* The expression "power of karma" *(las.kyi.dbang)* is employed in such a way as to focus on a hypothetical embryological structure (i.e., the original channels) which not only explains the embryo's earliest formation but provides the Tibetan Buddhist with a path to salvation in his very being. The same phrase is used in the description of the embryo's continuing development from the moment of conception:

> From the moment when the blood, semen, and thought are massed together (i.e., conception), through the first month, by means of the power of karma there evolves a life-wind from the storehouse-consciousness. One half of the life-wind becomes thoroughly mixed with all of the elements of the blood and semen, just like milk when it is churned into curds. In the same way, in the second week, after the evolution of that which is called the completely amalgamated karmic wind, it becomes a slightly oblong form which is a little thick. In the third week, after the evolution of the wind-treasury karma, the own-nature of the thickness comes into being like the actual formation of curd.[43]

Karma is vulnerable, especially up through the third week of the developing embryo, at which time the sex of the foetus is said to be subject to change through the process of center-altering. This is a ritual, the details of which are not without interest, but not central to the point of the present essay.[44]

Now that we have followed karma through the *bar.do* with its salvific possibilities into the very flesh and blood, we should be curious as to how karma or expressions closely contingent on the idea of karma, such as the five poisons, are used in relation to the new array of signs we have learned from the embryological process. We will see further how this sign-structure of karma accommodates the terminology utilized in the ritual-meditative tradition which, in turn, was partly based on a reductive conception of the body, that is, the body reduced to the three channels as a basis for a karmic being.

43. *Bai.sngon,* folio 122. 44. *Bai.sngon,* folio 122.

The Etiology of Corporeal Karma and Salvation as "Great Time"

When the *Book of the Dead*, the *Lapis Lazuli*, and the *Caṇḍa* elaborate the wanderer's lust and hatred for its future parents, and especially when the *Book of the Dead* describes karma as a force that we may liken to a trickster, clearly, at least for the moment when the wanderer succumbs to the enticement of the copulating parents, the cards are stacked against him in favor of the poisons—especially hatred and lust—the karmic nexus of the flow of suffering and disease.

The *Lapis Lazuli* in the section on physiology formulates the syndrome in terminology that enables us to extend further the sign structure of karma into blood and flesh: the structure itself is the formation of the channels.

The channels, popularly related to *cakras*, are not only significant for an understanding of esoteric meditation, but form an important structure in the Tibetan medical tradition. They help our process of understanding, not so much in the development of the physiological body, but rather in the conception of the emotional body constituting what the Buddhist Tantric tradition deems the five poisons. As such, it is not incorrect to think of this as a secondary extension of the primordial karmic body, that is, the wandering consciousness, or the aggregates of consciousness.

The basis of these channels is the life channel, which is formed gradually with the navel and produces the other channels (in the fifth week), as well as wind and drop (sperm essence).[45] The channels are not completely explained but are nonetheless mentioned as if they were a necessary step in the formation of the embryo.[46] Let us turn again to the *Lapis Lazuli:*

> The channel that generates the humors such as phlegm, the cause of the water principle, is the left one; the one that generates bile and so on, the cause of the fire principle, is the right one; and the channel that generates wind and so on, possessing the wind principle, is below the stomach.[47]. . . The brain constitutes delusion as well as phlegm; delusion is based on the brain. And since, to a very large extent, it is observed that depression and obscurity arise from the head, and because phlegm is produced from delusion, therefore cause, secondary cause, and result are found in the top part of the body. Blood, the cause of the fire principle and related to the right

45. *Bai.sngon,* folio 128. 46. *Bai.sngon,* folios 128 and 129.
47. *Bai.sngon,* folios 151 and 152.

channel, constitutes hatred and bile; hatred is based on blood and the black left channel. Because bile is produced from hatred, its cause, secondary cause, and result are found in the middle part of the body. When hatred suddenly arises, spasms can be observed to arise in the middle part of the body. Moreover, wind, the cause of the knowledge principle, guides properly the body's breath. One extremity of the wind reaching below the navel causes the principle of bliss and forms the hidden place (genitalia). The semen, then, constitutes lust and wind; lust is observed to appear in the hidden places (genitalia) of the mother and father. Since wind arises from lust, the cause, secondary cause, and result are found in the lower part of the body.[48]

To clarify the structure a little more, and to see karma in the light of its salvific dimensions, we should recall the three poisons of the mind aggregates in the dependent origination process and turn again to the *Caṇḍa*, which reiterates in a slightly different way the process of rebirth. We should keep in mind that the following passage is part of the *Caṇḍa*'s interpretation of the dependent origination process:

After the *bar.do* being acquires the basis of the six senses with nescience (and the remaining links) and sees the three worlds, it also sees the lust traces of its (potential) mother and father. Having been catapulted by one's karma of previous births, one will be born there. Because this is the birth where the wanderer sees the (erotic) delights of his mother and father, he feels their touching. Then, if the wanderer is going to be a male, he will see his own form as a baby boy; and his most intense lustful thought will arise for his mother as well as a thought possessing great hatred for his father. Through lust and hatred there will be feelings of bliss as well as suffering. Then, thinking that by joining in this conjugality he will share in the delight—even though there may be no feelings of particular suffering or bliss—the wanderer through his former lives will return (to *saṃsāric* existence). Then, because of the great thirst which catapults the wanderer by means of the winds of its former karma *(sngon.gyi.las.kyi.rlung)*, the thought arises, "I should make myself happy." Then, having considered that if born a male he would desire his own mother, the wanderer's thought, in the manner of a shooting star, enters from the path of the father's head and establishes the semen. Because the thought is established (in the father's semen), the consciousness realizes itself yearning for bliss (for the mother, the Sanskrit text adds). Hence the cause of bliss is incorporated (in this process). Then, the lust traces become one taste with the semen by means of great lust. It then issues from the father's *vajra* (genitalia) by means of the middle channel and is established in the womb-channel through its channel of the *Vajra*-principle queen who exists within the opening of the *padma* (the woman's genitalia), in the manner of trickling thought (semen), and then there is birth. . . . If the wanderer is to be born a girl, the thought-consciousness

48. *Bai.sngon*, folios 153–155. See also *Nang.don.*, folio 17.

will have lust traces for the father and hatred for the mother. The consciousness, dropping into the *padma* from the way in the mother's head and coalescing with the father's semen, establishes the channel of its birth and sees itself in the form of a woman. So it is born according to its former birth (i.e., karma, but specifically according to the moment of lust traces for the father).[49]

The three channels are a natural structure. They are a focus which introduces the psychophysical function of karma in four dimensions: embryology, rebirth, death, and salvation. This is the sense immediately grasped by a trained ritual specialist of Vajrayāna Buddhism. The channels lend absolute value to karma, and, as such, denote the salvific "perfect (or completed) way" *(rdzogs.rim),* the advanced stage of Tantric yoga. The best written example of this structure that I have seen is in an explanatory text to the Mahākāla rite:

In the middle of the five channel complexes there are: in the head, the white *oṁ,* the nature of confusion; in the neck, the red *hrīḥ,* the nature of lust; in the heart, the blue-blackish *hūṁ,* the nature of hatred; in the navel, the yellow *rāṁ,* the nature of pride; and in the genitalia region, the green *hāṁ,* the nature of envy. These five poisons, the five sacred knowledges (including the dichotomy of) knowledge-ignorance, are unified without exception. The five poisons of sentient beings and oneself are raised from everywhere through the flowing light rays (i.e., the sacred knowledge light rays); melting into the five seed syllables, they absorb all the obscurations and defilements. . . . When the breath is held because it burns down by means of the sacred knowledge, the *hāṁ* of the genitalia region will burn. After it burns upward, having burned the other four seed syllables, the defilements of the five poisons are cultivated as pure and the breath is revived and suppressed. The nature of the burned seed syllables are: in the head, a white coupling Mahākāla and consort symbolical of body, and on the thirty-two petals, white Dākinīs holding choppers and skull bowls; (similarly, couples in neck, heart, navel, and genitals).[50]

The structural connections between the medical and meditative traditions suggest a universe of signs and discourse based on the radical concepts of birth-rebirth, death-redeath, and salvation. The latter, in turn, reflects a ritual-meditative tradition beginning (in Buddhism) with the many accounts of Śākyamuni's meditation on dependent origination, which is, in essence, repeated in the *Caṇḍa.* A Buddhist attempts to be mindful of an existence based on nescience,

49. *Caṇḍa,* folios 409–410. See also the Sanskrit text, *Buddhist Wheel,* p. 469.
50. *Mgon,* folios 13–14. (See n. 3 above.)

and he aspires to the suppression of existence as leading to the suppression of nescience which is tantamount to the suppression of karma *(karmanirodha).* We have seen how the more biological aspects of existence such as blood, semen, and humors are specifically interlocked with the dependent-origination process and, further, with the Mahākāla yoga where the poisons are given absolute value as designated by the deities coupling with their consorts. The sign of suppression in the yogic context is holding the breath, which creates the heat that burns the poisons. The process is similar in all of the Buddhist Tantra meditation cycles.

The Mahākāla cycle is of particular significance because of its relation to time: "Only he whose body possesses Great Time is known as Mahākāla."[51] A goal of the praxis is to become Great Time through the yogic process. The suppression of karma in Tantra, then, is not just the suppression of each link of the chain of dependent origination but the suppression of ordinary meditation by means of the cultivation of the body, speech, and mind of the mythical perfect body—the *Vajra* body. The *Mahākāla Tantra* puts it this way:

> Even he who propounds nihilism would be making the karma of nonexistence and existence. When coupling according to one's capacity, cultivate not having mental configuration. In the world, there is no (conceived) seed without method.[52]

The procreative and embryological metaphors for karma are clear. Tantra removes karma from the possibility of heresy by relegating it to a structural metaphor which is a means and an end at the same time.

Conclusion: Pure Womb, Pure Karma

In the Tantras there is no end to the equivalencies of the world of flesh and absolute value. Yet on the level of praxis these relationships are unstable. Even on the level of sentence analysis, such polarities are not liable to generate systems of meaning reflective of the intention of the Tantras. Although we have not clearly demonstrated that the Tantras regard all things as a language, without resorting to a mind-only interpretation of our subject it is clear enough that the implied theory of karma in the Tantras rests upon the procreative and embryological metaphorical models. The language forms its own struc-

51. Stablein, *Mahākālatantra,* p. 109. 52. Idem.

ture with its own transcendent value disclosing a universe, indeed a womb, of spontaneously appearing substructures according to the nature of the practitioner.

Since the value of karma in Tantra is derived from oppositions inextricably interlocked with the womb and what it represents, not only in the embryological context but also in the discourse of mythos, we must present what is at the very heart of Tantra and is, in some sense, the most enigmatic of Tantric sentences—the opening line of numerous Tantric texts. The *Mahākāla Tantra,* for example, begins with: "Thus I have heard: at one time the Lord was dwelling in a desireless manner within the genetrix of the Goddess."[53] Thus we have from the beginning a procreative metaphor that is as poetic and mythic as it is psychological or religious. For the practitioner who follows the Tantras it is this womb that is sought; and hence, when he constructs his *maṇḍala,* regardless of the deities involved, it is the *maṇḍala* as the womb which is being projected with all of its generative possibilities. That this is the space where the Lord lives and where the sacred dialogue between him and the Goddess is recorded is also the mind of enlightenment; that is to say, the *maṇḍala* is also the semen. The body is generated as the *maṇḍala* (and womb-semen) and is constituted of body, speech, and mind. Hence, another version of the first chapter of the *Mahākāla Tantra* states: "Thus I have heard: at one time the Lord was dwelling in the tripartite principle (i.e., body, speech, and mind) of the Goddess."[54]

The problem of karma, then, is to understand the absolute value by means of the corporeal sign which is incorporated by the projection of the divine conjugal couple. The outward construction and delineation of the rite makes possible the momentary establishment of a circumference which enables the practitioner to focus on body, speech, and mind as pure substance. Ratiocination, breathing, and the poisons as the accumulations are released from their dependence, not into annihilation but into one's womb-*maṇḍala,* where they take on or begin to take on an absolute value.

The five stages of Tantric self-yoga[55] are called the pure dwellings,

53. Stablein, *Mahākālatantra,* p. 111.
54. Ibid., p. 107.
55. This self-yoga is implicit in every Mahākāla rite, but in particular it is used in the fulfillment and healing ritual performed on the twenty-ninth day of every lunar month. See William Stablein, "Mahākāla Neo-Shaman: Master of the Ritual," in *Spirit Possession in the Nepal Himalayas,* John Hitchcock and Rex Johns, eds. (England: Aris & Phillips, 1975), pp. 361–375.

or foundations; they present quite succinctly the soteriological dimension of karma that is, in essence, the womb where the Lord dwells: a dwelling of pure semen, pure blood, pure consciousness, and the principle source for the projection of absolute value. This is a metaphorical structure of oppositions that disclose an underlying fiction which, in turn, has an even deeper layer of science. The fiction is the conventional world of karma with its edifice of flesh, blood, semen, consciousness, and complex of emotions. The science is not only the observations and knowledge of this corporeal edifice but the manner in which it is incorporated in the dharmic rite which enables the Tantric Buddhist to experience the edifice as *śūnyatā,* purity, and the womb.

9

Karma and the Problem of Rebirth in Jainism

PADMANABH S. JAINI

Although nearly every religious or philosophical tradition of India has accepted the idea of karma as valid, a wide divergence exists in the extent to which various schools have developed this idea into a coherent system of doctrine. In terms of the level of interest shown in such development—a level best measured by the amount of sacred and scholastic works devoted to it—one tradition, that of the Jainas, stands clearly apart from all others. In addition to the large number of *Karma-grantha* texts found among the Śvetāmbara scriptures, Digambaras possess some thirty-eight volumes of the *Ṣaṭkhaṇḍāgama*, the *Kaṣāya-prābhṛta*, and their commentaries.[1] Portions of the latter

1. For a complete bibliography of the Śvetāmbara *Karma-grantha* literature, see Glasenapp, *The Doctrine of Karman in Jain Philosophy* (Bombay, 1942), pp. xi–xx.

The *Ṣaṭkhaṇḍāgama* is said to have been composed by Puṣpadanta and Bhūtabali (circa A.D. 200). It comprises 6,000 aphorisms *(sūtras)* in Prakrit and is divided into six parts. The first five parts have a commentary called *Dhavalā* by Vīrasena (A.D. 816), which has been edited by Hiralal Jain and published in sixteen volumes by the Jaina Sāhityoddhāraka Fund, Amaravati, 1939–59. The sixth part of the *Ṣaṭkhaṇḍāgama*, called *Mahābandha*, is better known by the alternate title *Mahādhavalā;* it has been edited by Phool Chandra Sidbhāntaśāstrī and published in seven volumes by the Bhāratīya Vidyāpītha (Benares, 1947–58). A second important scriptural work belonging to the same genre is the *Kaṣāyaprābhṛta* of Guṇabhadra (A.D. ca. 200). This text, together with its commentary *Jayadhavalā* by Vīrasena and his disciple Jinasena are said to represent the only surviving examples of the ancient *Pūrva* texts, which Digambaras suggest may even predate Mahāvīra himself. All of these materials deal in great detail with various problems relating to karma in its four aspects, namely, influx *(āsrava)*, bondage *(bandha)*, duration *(sthiti)*, and fruition *(anubhāga)*.[2]

Jainas seem to have been preoccupied with these problems from the earliest times; not only do their own scriptures pay a great deal of attention to such matters, but certain Buddhist writings in Pali attempt to discredit Jaina theories of karma, indicating that these theories were even then seen as fundamental to the overall Jaina world-view.[3]

We are not yet in a position to explain definitively the earlier and more intense interest in karma shown by Jaina thinkers (and, to a lesser extent, by those of the Buddhists) relative to their Brāhmaṇical counterparts. Perhaps the entire concept that a person's situation and experiences are in fact the results of deeds committed in various lives may be not of Āryan origin at all, but rather may have developed as part of the indigenous Gangetic tradition from which the various Śramaṇa movements arose. In any case, as we shall see, Jaina views on the process and possibilities of rebirth are distinctively non-Hindu; the social ramifications of these views, moreover, have been profound.

(A.D. ca. 800–870), has been edited by Phool Chandra Siddhāntaśāstrī and published in fifteen volumes by the Bhāratīya Digambara Jaina Granthamālā (Mathura, 1942-75). All of these Digambara works, which are of epic proportions (comprising altogether some 172,000 "ślokas" [1 śloka = 32 syllables]), have been brought to light only in the last thirty years and have not been fully studied even in India outside a small circle of Jaina scholars. Umāsvāti's *Tattvārthasūtra* and Pūjyapāda's commentary thereon called *Sarvārthasiddhi* are the two most popular works studied in the Jaina schools. For a translation of the latter work, see S. A. Jain, *Reality* (Calcutta, 1960).

2. The fact that Jainas regard karma as material *(paudgalika)*, in contrast to such relatively abstract concepts as *saṃskāra* of the Brāhmaṇical schools and *bīja* of the Buddhists, is too well known to require discussion here. For a lucid presentation of the comprehensive Jaina teaching of the karmic process, see N. Tatia, *Studies in Jaina Philosophy* (Benares, 1951), pp. 220–260.

3. . . . evaṃ vutte . . . te Nigaṇṭhā mam etad avocuṃ: "Nigaṇṭho, āvuso, Nātaputto sabbaññu sabbadassāvī aparisesaṃ ñāṇadassanaṃ paṭijānāti" . . . so evam āha: "atthi kho vo, Nigaṇṭhā, pubbe pāpakammaṃ kataṃ, taṃ imāya kaṭukāya dukkarakārikāya nijjīretha; yaṃ pan' ettha etarahi kāyena saṃvutā vācāya saṃvutā manasā saṃvutā taṃ āyatiṃ pāpassa kammassa akaraṇaṃ; iti purāṇānaṃ kammānaṃ tapasā byantibhāvā, navānaṃ kammānaṃ akaraṇā, āyatiṃ anavassavo, āyatiṃ anavassavā kammakkhayo, kammakkhayā dukkhakkhayo, dukkhakkhayā vedanākkhayo, vedanākkhayā sabbaṃ dukkhaṃ nijjiṇṇaṃ bhavissatī ti . . . " (*Majjhimanikāya* I, p. 93 [PTS]).

A significant issue in Indian philosophy concerns the actual size of the soul. Virtually all the Vedic *darśanas* assert that the soul is *vibhu*, omnipresent; Rāmānuja's theory of an atomic, dimensionless soul stands as the only orthodox exception to this view. An all-pervasive soul would of course be free from spatial limitation by the body; indeed, the very idea of "dimensions" cannot be applied to such an entity at all. Jainas, however, have consistently rejected the *vibhu* theory, arguing that since a soul cannot experience the sorrow or happiness resulting from its karma except in the context of mind, senses, and body, any existence of the soul outside that context becomes incompatible with the function of the karmic mechanism. This line of thought leads directly to the basic Jaina doctrine that a soul is exactly coterminous with the body of its current state of bondage *(svadehaparimāṇa)*.[4] Even a fully liberated soul *(siddha)*, having completely transcended contact with the material realm, is said by the Jainas to retain the shape and size of that body which it occupied at the time *mokṣa* was attained.[5] This latter doctrine is certainly a rather unexpected one, since, even in Jaina terms, total freedom from karmic bonds eliminated the necessity for any limitation upon the extent of the soul. The liberated soul, in other words, could have been seen as *vibhu* without in any way contradicting the Jaina position of the interdependence of soul and body.[6] One can only conclude that the idea of this interdependence so dominated the minds of Jaina thinkers that they were somehow reluctant to dispense with the body completely even in the case of *mokṣa*. Hence we have a doctrine in which the emancipated soul, though said to be forever free of former influences, seems to display through its shape a sort of shadowy association with the embodied state.

The Hindu doctrine of *vibhu*, as we have noted above, has some difficulty in explaining the limitation of a soul's experiences. That is, if the soul is in fact at all times everywhere, how does it come to

4. For a Jaina critique of the *vibhu* theory, see Malliṣeṇa's *Syādvādamañjarī* edited by J. C. Jain (Bombay, 1970), pp. 67–75 (henceforth referred to as *SM*).

5. anākāratvān muktānām abhāva it cen na; atītānantaraśarīrākāratvāt. *Sarvārthasiddhi*, edited by Phool Chandra Siddhāntaśāstrī (Benares, 1971), 9.4 (henceforth referred to as *SS*).

6. syān matam, yadi śarīrānuvadhāyī jīvaḥ, tad abhāvāt svābhāvikalokākāśaparimāṇatvāt tāvad visarpaṇaṃ prāpnotīti. naiṣa doṣaḥ. kutaḥ? kāraṇābhāvāt. *SS* 9.4. The Jainas allow the possibility of a soul spreading throughout the *lokākāśa* (without abandoning its body) just prior to attaining *siddah*-hood. This is called *kevalisamudghāta:* yat punar aṣṭasamayasādhyakevalisamudghātadaśāyām ārhatānām api . . . lokavyāpitvenātmanaḥ sarvavyāpakatvam, tat kādācitkam (*SM*, p. 75).

undergo the experience of only one individual being at a time? This problem is dealt with by postulation of the so-called subtle body *(sūkṣma-śarīra),* an entity said generally to be composed of eighteen[7] subtle elements and to provide the link whereby a soul may—and must—be associated with a particular "gross" (i.e., manifest) state of embodiment. The subtle body is, in other words, a sort of "agent" for the soul; while the latter "stands still," as it were, the subtle body inhabits one life-matrix (human, animal, or whatever) after another, in each case associating the soul with the experiences of that matrix. Now, since the soul can experience nothing *except* in this limited way, it might be asked why the Brāhmaṇical thinkers bothered to introduce the notion of *vibhu* in the first place; it is an attribute which certainly seems to have no practical effect upon the experiences of the soul.

The answer to this question lies in what is perhaps the most fundamental point of disagreement separating Brāhmaṇical and Jaina philosophies. For the Brāhmaṇical schools, that which is eternal (e.g., soul) cannot change, whereas for the Jainas, *all* existents, whether sentient *(jīva)* or insentient *(ajīva),* are eternal (as *dravya,* "substance") and at the same time subject to change (as *paryāya,* "modes") at every moment.[8] Thus it is possible for a soul in the Jaina system to move, to expand or contract into various shapes, and so forth. How, then, can it be said to be eternal? Because, the Jainas suggest, every existent *(sat)* possesses a quality called *agurulaghutva* ("undergoing neither gain nor loss"), whereby its total number of space-points *(pradeśa)* remains unchanged regardless of the area into which these points must be accommodated. This is described as analogous to a piece of cloth, the total material of which is the same whether it is folded or spread out flat.

Bearing in mind the Brāhmaṇical and Jaina views on the nature of the soul, we are now ready to compare the actual mechanisms of rebirth that these traditions have proposed. The most widely accepted Brāhmaṇical description of this mechanism is strongly biological in tone. We are told that after severing its connection with the human

7. pūrvotpannaṃ asaktaṃ niyataṃ mahadādisūkṣmaparyantam/
saṃsarati nirupabhogaṃ bhāvair adhivāsitam liṅgam//
Sāṅkhyakārikā of Īśvarakṛṣṇa, 40.

8. sat dravyalakṣaṇam/ utpādavyayadhrauvyayuktaṃ sat/
tadbhāvāvyayaṃ nityam/
Tattvārthasūtra 5.29–31

body, the soul dwells for some twelve days in a transitional ghostly form *(preta).* Thereafter, freed from this limbo through ritual offerings *(śrāddha)* by the son of the deceased, it travels upward to the "realm of the father" *(pitṛ-loka),* there to remain for an indeterminate period. Eventually it is brought back to earth with the rain, enters the food chain through absorption by a plant, and finally becomes associated with the seed of a male who has eaten the fruit of that plant.[9] The act of intercourse thus "introduces" this soul into the womb where its new body will grow, and the entire process begins once more. The force of karma operates here in determining which potential father will eat which plant, thus guaranteeing the soul a set of circumstances appropriate to its prior experiences.

Given their emphasis on the role of the body, we might have expected the Jainas to provide an account even more heavily oriented towards the physiological than the one given above. For some reason, however, this was not the case. To the contrary, Jaina texts make absolutely no mention whatsoever of how a soul actually enters the body of the mother-to-be. It is said only that the soul moves into a new embryo within a single moment *(samaya)* after the death of the previous body.[10] Perhaps this doctrinal assertion of so brief a period between births precluded the detailed elaboration of what actually took place during that period. It is also possible that Jaina *ācāryas* may have simply been reluctant to include sexual references in their discussions. We are, however, only speculating here; all that can be said with certainty is that the issue of the soul's physical entry into the womb is simply ignored. Indeed, Jainas even seem to have been unaware of the theories put forth by their rivals; no mention, much less any attempt at refutation, is made with regard either to the Brāhmaṇical notions already discussed or to the Vaibhāṣika theory that the transmigratory consciousness (referred to as *gandharva)*[11]

9. For details, see Paul Deussen, *The System of the Vedānta,* New York, 1973, pp. 357–398.

10. ekasamayā 'vigrahā/ (*Tattvārthasūtra* 2.29). See also note 29.

11. "trayāṇāṃ sthānānāṃ sammukhībhāvāt mātuḥ kukṣau garbhasyāvakrāntirbhavati. mātā kalyā pi bhavati, ṛtumatī ca. mātāpitarau raktau sannipatitau ca. gandharvaś ca pratyupasthito bhavati" iti. antarābhavaṃ hitvā ko' nyo gandharvaḥ. . . . naiva cāntarābhavikaḥ kukṣiṃ bhitvā praviśate, api tu mātur yonidvāreṇa. . . .taṃ deśaṃ āśliṣya . . . iti upapanno bhavati (*Abhidharmakośabhāṣya,* ed. P. Pradhan [Patna, 1967], 3.12–15).

As the following quote suggests, there was no unanimity of opinion among Vaibhāṣika teachers as to the precise amount of time spent in the *gandharva* state; the tradition of seven days' "search" for new parents has perhaps been most widely

enters the vagina at the moment of intercourse and is thus trapped therein. Their silence here is unfortunate, since critical discussions of others' views would have forced both the parties criticized and the Jainas themselves to develop their positions in a more rigorous manner. Even in the absence of such discussions, however, it is by no means impossible to infer, on doctrinal grounds, the sorts of objections that Jainas would have voiced had they chosen to do so. This may well prove to be an instructive exercise, since it will bring into focus certain of the beliefs most central to the Jaina conception of life in the universe.

Consider, for example, the Brāhmaṇical schema in which first rain, then plants, act as "vehicles" whereby a soul makes its way to its ultimate destination. For the Jainas, the realm of sentient existence is far too wide and diverse for such a thing to be possible; in their view *even the raindrops,* not to mention plant life, constitute examples of embodied souls. In this context it is possible for a soul to be *reborn* as a "water-body" *(āp-kāyika)* or as a plant *(vanaspati-kāyika),* but not for these latter entities to function simply as insentient props in the life of a soul on its way to a human existence. The general Brāhmaṇical explanation of the human rebirth process, therefore, would in Jaina terms entail at least two intermediate births in extremely low-level destinies *(gati),* a suggestion which violates Jaina rules pertaining to the operation of karma. To see how this is so, let us look in more detail at the various kinds of destinies in which the Jainas believe a soul may find itself.

In common with other Indian schools, Jainas affirm the birth-categories of gods, men, hell-beings, and *tiryañcas* ("those going horizontally," e.g., animals). Each of these categories is generally associated with a particular vertically ordered tier of the three-dimensional universe; men, for example, dwell in the centrally located *madhyaloka,* gods above them in the *devalokas,* and hell-beings below in the various infernal regions. (The case of the *tiryañcas* is somewhat more complex, as will be seen below.) The Jainas, however, have extended this system in two ways. On the one hand, they have postulated a class of emancipated souls, the "liberated ones" or

---

accepted: kiyantaṃ kālam avatiṣṭhate? nāsti niyama iti Bhadantaḥ . . . saptāhaṃ tiṣṭhatīti Bhadanta Vasumitraḥ . . . saptāhānity apare . . . alpaṃ kālam iti Vaibhāṣikāḥ. Ibid. 3, 14. For an example of the belief in a seven-week period, see *The Tibetan Book of the Dead,* edited by W. Y. Evans-Wentz (New York, 1960).

siddhas referred to earlier, who are said to have gone beyond *saṃsāra* altogether and remain forever at the very apex of the universe.[12] On the other hand, they have broken down the *tiryañca* into numerous carefully defined subcategories. While this latter move may at first glance seem to be a mere scholastic exercise, closer examination reveals that what we have here is a doctrinally significant analysis of the lower reaches of existence. The addition of this analysis, together with that of the *siddha* theory referred to above, transforms the standard "four destinies" model from a rather simplistic description of the range of life into what is, for the Jainas, a truly comprehensive statement of the possibilities available to the soul. As we shall see, moreover, there may well be implicit in the Jaina system what can only be called a theory of evolution. While the Jainas themselves subscribe to the notion of a cyclic, beginningless universe and so do not accept any such theory, their own texts seem to provide justification for such an inference. To make this point clear, let us consider more closely the specific manner in which the various *tiryañcas* have been described.

It should first be noted that "levels of existence," in the Jaina view, reflect a scale of "awareness" *(upayoga)* on the part of the soul; hence the liberated soul is omniscient *(sarvajña)*, gods have a wider range of knowledge than do men, and so on. The same system of ordering obtains within the *tiryañca* category itself. At the top of this group stand those animals, such as the lion,[13] which are said to possess five sense-faculties *(indriya)*, plus a certain capacity for reflection *(saṃjñi)*. Next are those which have five senses but *lack* the reflective capacity *(asaṃjñi)*. Moving down the list, we are told of creatures with four, three, and two senses, respectively. Finally, and most important to the present discussion, are the *ekendriyas*, single-sense beings whose whole awareness is limited to the tactile mode. Whereas the higher *tiryañcas* are of a limited number and dwell in the *madhyaloka*, *ekendriyas* are too numerous to count and may be found in every part of the universe. They consist, moreover, of five distinct types: *pṛthvī-kāyika* ("earth-bodies"), *āp-kāyika* ("water-

12. See Appendix 1 to this chapter for a diagrammatic representation of the Jaina universe.
13. It is believed that *saṃjñi* animals are capable of receiving religious instruction and also that Mahāvīra himself was awakened to the spiritual life while existing as a lion. See Guṇabhadra's *Uttarapurāṇa*, 74.167–220, (Benares, 1968).

bodies"), *tejo-kāyika* ("fire-bodies"), *vāyu-kāyika* ("air-bodies"), and *vanaspati* ("vegetable life").[14] As the names suggest, the first four of these are little more than single "molecules" of the various fundamental elements, each one a rudimentary body for some soul. The *vanaspati* are, again, of two kinds: those called *pratyeka,* which have an entire plant-body "to themselves" (i.e., one plant/one soul), and finally, the *sādhāraṇa,* or *nigoda,* those which are at so low a level that they do not even possess an individual body, but rather exist as part of a cluster or "ball" *(golaka)* of organisms of the same type. Souls in such clusters, moreover, must live and die as a group, supposedly attaining rebirth in the same state eighteen times within the space of a single human breath.[15] Not only are the *nigodas* "colonial" (in the sense that this term is applied to algae, for example), but the clusters in which they dwell may in turn occupy the bodies of *other,* higher souls, thereby achieving an almost parasitic mode of existence. *Nigodas* are said to be found in virtually every corner of the universe; only the bodies of gods, hell-beings, and the "element bodies" referred to above do not harbor them. It is further believed that these tiny creatures tend to become especially concentrated in the flesh of human beings and animals as well as in certain roots and bulbs. Such likely "hosts" are therefore banned as food for the devout Jaina, since their consumption would involve the death of an unacceptably large number of souls.[16]

It may well be asked what sort of deeds *(karmas)* one must commit in order to deserve rebirth in a state so debased as that of the *nigodas.* In the only known reference to this problem we are told how Makkhali Gośāla, leader of the Ājīvika sect, doomed his soul to just such a fate by propounding what must have been for the Jainas the ultimate heresy, namely, that knowledge was in no way efficacious in terms of

14. pṛthivyāptejovāyuvanaspatayaḥ sthāvarāḥ/ (*Tattvārthasūtra* 2.13).

15. sāhāraṇodayeṇa ṇigodaśarīrā havanti sāmaṇṇā/
te puṇa duvihā jīvā bādarasuhumātti viṇṇeyā//
sāhāraṇamāhāro sāhāraṇamāṇapāṇagahaṇaṃ ca/
sāhāraṇajīvāṇāṃ sāhāraṇalakkhaṇaṃ bhaṇiyaṃ//
jatthekka marai jīvo tattha du maraṇaṃ have aṇaṃtāṇaṃ/
bakkamai jattha ekko bakkamaṇaṃ tattha 'ṇaṃtāṇaṃ//
Gommaṭasāra (Jīvakāṇḍa) 191–193 (Agas, 1959)

16. The following plants are among those forbidden as food for a Jaina: turmeric, ginger, cardamom, garlic, bamboo, carrot, radish, beetroot, tamarind, banyan, margosa. For details, see R. Williams, *Jaina Yoga* (London, 1963), pp. 110–116.

the possibility of attaining *mokṣa.*[17] (Buddhists seem to have been equally offended by Gośāla's views; their texts suggest that not only must he have gone to hell, but for such a person there could be no possibility of enlightenment even in the future.)[18] It is clear, then, that only some shockingly evil act could send a soul to the *nigoda* realm. This idea seems to present no difficulties until we consider one further—and little-known—aspect of Jaina doctrine concerning the *nigodas.* This states that there are in fact two distinct types of souls in *nigoda:* those which have at some time been in higher states but have fallen back, as Gośāla did, and those which have *never yet* been out of *nigoda* existence. The souls in question are referred to as *itara-nigoda* and *nitya-nigoda* respectively. *Nitya* here had the sense not of "forever" but of "always up to now"; *itara* means simply "those other than" the members of the *nitya* class. These are Digambara terms; those employed by the Śvetāmbaras are very similar in meaning. The *nitya-nigoda* are, for example, called by them *avyāvahārika,* "not susceptible of specific designation," that is, having no individual forms, while the *itara-nigoda* receive, along with all higher beings, the label of *vyāvahārika,* "specifiable." Members of the *itara* group are of course also without individual bodies, but they have, at some time, at least entered the system wherein such bodies are obtained.[19]

Now, what can it mean to say that there are certain souls which have *always* been *nigodas?* If such were indeed the case, then the whole notion of placement within a given destiny on the basis of

17. See A. N. Upadhye, "Darśanasāra of Devasena: Critical text," in the *Annals of the Bhandarkar Oriental Research Institute,* 15, nos. 3–4, 198–206. Also my article, "The Jainas and the Western Scholar," in *Sambodhi* (Prof. A. N. Upadhye Commemoration Volume), L.D. Institute of Indology (Ahmedabad, July 1976), pp. 121–131.

18. "sakiṃ nimuggo nimuggo va hotī ti" . . . etassa hi puna bhavato vuṭṭhānaṃ nāma natthī ti vadanti. Makkhali-gosālādayo viya heṭṭhā narakaggīnaṃ yeva āhārā hontī ti. *Puggalapaññati-Aṭṭhakathā* 7.1. See my article, "On the Sautrāntika Theory of Bīja," *Bulletin of the School of Oriental and African Studies* vol. 22, part 2, (London, 1959), p. 246, n. 2.

19. atthi aṇaṃtā jīvā jehiṃ ṇa patto tasāṇā pariṇāmo/
bhāvakalaṃkasupaurā nigodavāsaṃ ṇa muñcanti//
Gommaṭasāra (Jivakāṇḍa), 197.

dvividhā jīvā sāṃvyāvahārikā asāṃvyāvahārikāś ceti. tatra ye nigodāvasthāta udvṛtya pṛthivīkāyikādibhedeṣu vartante te lokeṣu dṛṣṭipathamāgatāḥ santaḥ . . . vyavahārikā ucyante. te ca yady api bhūyo 'pi nigodāvasthām upayānti tathāpi te sāṃvyāvahārikā eva, saṃvyavahāre patitatvāt. ye punar anādikālād ārabhya nigodāvasthām upagatā evāvatiṣṭhante te vyavahārapathātītatvād asāṃvyāvaharikāḥ. (Quoted from the *Prajñāpanāṭīkā* in *SM,* p. 259.)

previous deeds *(karmas)* would be undermined, since these beings would clearly have had no prior opportunity to perform any karmically meaningful actions whatsoever. The very term *avyāvahārika,* moreover, supports the suggestion that the *nitya-nigodas* are in some sense beyond the operation of karma, just as are the *siddhas* at the opposite extreme. In fact, this apparent connection between the *high* and *low* points of existence is by no means accidental. Given that for Jainas the number of beings in the realm of *vyavahāra* is finite (albeit "uncountable"), the question is raised as to how it is that the steady "departure" of souls through the attainment of *mokṣa* does not eventually deplete the universe of all sentient existence. The Jainas deal with this problem by means of the *nitya-nigoda.* These beings are, unlike those of any other category, said to be *infinite (anantānanta)* in number, and thus to provide an inexhaustible reservoir of souls; as we might suspect, the rate at which members of the *nitya-nogoda* class leave their dismal condition and enter higher states for the first time is either equal to or greater than that at which human beings in various parts of the universe attain *siddha*-hood. (Such an attainment is possible only from the human condition. At least one hundred and eight souls become emancipated in each period of six months and eight moments.)[20]

This makes a convenient system, but it leaves the Jaina position open to the kind of interpretation referred to earlier, namely, that there is in fact a definite beginning and end to *saṃsāra,* and that a soul's progress from the former to the latter seems in many respects to mirror the very evolution of consciousness itself. The key point here is that no reasonable explanation has been given, in karmic terms, for the situation of the *nitya-nigoda.* Furthermore, while the Jainas have asserted that there exists a class of souls, the *abhavya,*[21] that can never attain *mokṣa,* they have *not* suggested an analogous

20. sijjhanti jattiyā khalu iha saṃvyavahārajīvarāsīo/
enti aṇāivaṇassai rāsīo tattio tammi//

iti vacanād yāvantaś ca yato muktiṃ gacchanti jīvās tāvanto 'nādinigoda-vanaspatirāśes tatrāgacchanti. na ca tāvatā tasya kācit parihāṇir nigoda-jīvānantyasyākṣayatvāt (*SM*, p. 259).

Cf. nanu aṣṭasamayādhikaṣaṇmāsābhyantare aṣṭottaraśatajīveṣu karmakṣayaṃ kṛtvā siddheṣu satsu . . . (Quoted from the *Gommaṭasāra (Jīvakāṇḍa) Keśava-varṇiṭīkā* (196) in *SM*, p. 302.)

21. See my article, "Bhavyatva and Abhavyatva: A Jaina Doctrine of 'Predestination,' " in *Bhagawān Mahāvīra and His Teachings (2500 Nirvāṇa Anniversary Volume),* Bombay, 1977, pp. 95–111.

group whose members never dwelt within the *nitya-nigoda* realm. Given the Jaina admission that *some* souls begin their existence in this rather primordial and undifferentiated state, we may not be wrong in inferring that such could be the case for *all* souls. Adding to this the fact that every soul is said to exist along a virtual continuum of consciousness, from the minimal but ineradicable trace of awareness *(nitya-udghātita-jñana)*[22] possessed by the *nigoda* to the omniscience *(ananta-*, i.e., *kevalajñāna)* of the *siddha*, we have here a model which is both linear and evolutionary in its conception.

Neither the Jainas' doctrine that souls frequently regress to lower states, nor their assertion that the *abhavyas* can proceed no higher than the *devalokas*, is incompatible with this model. Even under the restrictions noted, it is clear that souls are *in general* imagined to make slow but definite progress from minimal to maximal awareness, from what might be called "*proto-saṃsāra*" to a state beyond *saṃsāra* altogether. We may find in this kind of speculation, moreover, a rather ingenuous but interesting parallel to the modern view that the highest forms of life on our planet are, ultimately, descended from primitive micro-organisms which inhabited the ancient seas.

As we have indicated previously, Jainas will reject out of hand any suggestion that a soul's progress in the universe is either linear or evolutionary. The former notion, of course, flies in the face of their cherished belief in cyclic, beginningless operation of karma. As for the latter, it seems to have been anticipated as a potential problem; hence we find certain Jaina stories claiming that groups of souls sometimes leave *nigoda* existence and proceed directly to the human destiny, from which, with no further rebirths, they attain to *siddha*-hood.[23] (This sort of "example" is not really useful to the Jaina argument here, since it denies only *gradual* evolution.) It should be asked, therefore, how it is that these very notions, which Jainas are at such pains to deny, are according to our analysis readily inferable from some of their oldest and most basic doctrinal materials. Is it possible that, for the Jainas, the doctrine of karma represents a relatively late (albeit prehistorical) accretion, a set of ideas imposed upon

22. For several scriptural passages on this point, see N. Tatia, *Studies in Jaina Philosophy*, p. 240.

23. anādimithyādṛśo 'pi trayoviṃśatyadhikanavaśataparimāṇās te ca nityanigodavāsinaḥ . . . Bharataputrā jātās te . . . tapo gṛhītvā . . . stokakālena mokṣaṃ gatāḥ. (Quoted in Jinendra Varni's *Jainendra-siddhānta-kośa*, II, p. 318 [Bhāratīya Jñānapīṭha Publications, Varanasi, 1971].)

what was already a well-developed theoretical framework describing the operation of the universe? This framework, of course, would have been the linear-evolutionary one to which we have referred, remnants of which are discernible even now as certain seeming "inconsistencies" within Jaina doctrine (e.g., the case of the *nitya-nigoda).* Evidence that such an ancient framework did in fact exist is to be found through examination of a tradition closely associated with Jainism, that of the Ājīvikas. It is well known that Gośāla, the most famous teacher of this school, was a contemporary of Mahāvīra. Basham and others have maintained, moreover, that these two *śramaṇa* sects interacted to a large extent; one scholar has even suggested (probably erroneously) that the Ājīvikas were ultimately absorbed into the Digambara Jaina community.[24] In any case, what few references to the Ājīvikas have survived indicate the school's belief in definite limits to *saṃsāra,* with each soul passing through exactly 8,400,000 *mahākalpas* ("great aeons") before reaching *mokṣa.*[25] That the Jainas may have originally subscribed to a similar doctrine is suggested not only by the evidence already set forth, but by the fact that the number 8,400,000 has been retained in their system to the present day, although in a significantly altered context. This number is, for Jainas, the sum total of conceivable birth-situations *(yoni)* (i.e., the four destinies divided into all their sub-categories, sub-sub-categories, etc.) in which souls may find themselves, again and again, as they circle through *saṃsāra.*[26] Again, we seem to have a fragmentary holdover from an earlier doctrine. This issue need not be pursued further here; the point has been made that certain apparent anomalies in Jaina thought on karma can perhaps be best understood if we consider the possibility of a common background with the Ājīvika tradition. The important thing, for our purposes, is that in Jainism the model of a karmically ordered universe, in which the soul's posi-

24. A. F. R. Hoernle, "Ajīvakas," in *Encyclopedia of Religion and Ethics,* vol. 1, pp. 259–268; A. L. Basham's *History and Doctrines of the Ājīvikas* (London, 1951).
25. . . . cullāsīti mahākappuno satasahassāni, yāni bāle ca paṇḍite ca sandhāvitvā saṃsāritvā dukkhass' antaṃ karissanti (*Dīghanikāya,* 1.53–54 [PTS]). See Basham, ibid., p. 14.
26. sacittaśītasaṃvṛtāḥ setarā miśrāś caikaśas tad yonayaḥ/ (*Tattvārthasūtra* 2.32). tadbhedāś caturaśītiśatasahasrasaṃkhyā āgamato veditavyāḥ. uktaṃ ca:

ṇiccidaradhādu satta ya taru dasa viyaliṃdiyesu chacceva/
suraṇirayatiriya cauro coddasa maṇue sadasahassā//

SS 2.32

tion could be improved or worsened by action, did prevail over the kind of fatalistic determinism accepted by the Ājīvikas.

Our discussion of the *ekendriyas* has, it seems, led us rather far afield. The reader will recall the point that Jaina emphasis on the sentient nature of such simple beings makes it impossible for them to accept any notion of rebirth similar to that proposed by Brāhmaṇical schools. As for the Vaibhāṣika theory of the *gandharva* referred to above, this too stands in direct contradiction to a fundamental Jaina premise, namely, that the inter-birth period constitutes only a single moment in time. The fact that the *gandharva* state is said to persist for as long as seven weeks (see note 11) renders it, for Jainas, not a stage of transition at all but a whole separate destiny, in many ways reminiscent of the *preta-loka* (realm of spirits). Indeed, this same "too much time between births" objection could apply equally well to the idea of slow transmigration through rain and plants, even if this idea were not unacceptable for the quite different reasons that we have discussed. Why did the Jainas place so much emphasis on the doctrine of a momentary transition?[27] To answer this question, we must now examine their discussion of rebirth in some detail.

By conceiving of the soul as *vibhu*, Brāhmaṇical thinkers effec-

27. While Theravādin and Sautrāntika writings have set forth a doctrine of instantaneous rebirth analogous to the appearance of an image in a mirror *(bimba-pratibimba)*, this doctrine seems never to have gained so wide an acceptance among Buddhists as did the *gandharva* theory. Even if it had become the standard Buddhist view, Jainas would have rejected it on the grounds that a thing which arises and perishes within the same moment cannot undergo motion. (Recall that in the Jaina system *three* moments are actually involved: those of death, movement of the soul, and rebirth, respectively.) Indeed, the Vaibhāṣikas' awareness of this problem very likely led them to the notion of an extended transition-state in the first place.

Certain Sāṅkhya and Yoga thinkers also proposed a rebirth process occurring instantaneously or in a very short period. It must be asked, however, whether such views ever had any meaningful impact on Hindu society; even in those cases where they might have been accepted in theory, we have no evidence that the practice of *śrāddha* (rendered meaningless within such a framework) was actually abandoned. Because only one instant *(samaya)* intervenes between death and the following rebirth, it is possible for a person dying in the act of copulation to be born as his own child. The idea that a man is in some sense identical with his son is well known to Hindu literature. Thus, for example, *Manusmṛti* defines a wife as follows: "The husband, entering into the wife, becoming an embryo, is born here. For that is why the wife is called wife *(jāyā)*, because he is born *(jāyate)* again in her" (9.8). On the other hand, it is only in the Jaina literature that this belief is made literal. In fact, such an occurrence is attested to in a Jaina Purāṇa, the source of which I have unfortunately lost.

tively avoided the question of a soul's movement from one body to another. Such a soul of course pervades the physical space of *all* bodies and therefore need not "go to" one or another of them; only the mechanism of its experiential association with a particular body needs to be explained. In Jainism, however, the movement of the soul itself is fundamental to the operation of the rebirth process. We might first ask how it is that a soul, momentarily separated from a gross body, is able to undergo any motion at all. To this the Jaina will reply that movement is an *inherent property* of every soul. In its purest form, this movement proceeds directly upwards, like that of a flame; hence the *siddha,* free of all restraints, shoots like an arrow to the very top of the inhabited universe *(lokākāśa).*[28] When still under karmic influence, the soul will dart in a similar manner to its next embodiment. In both cases, the speed involved is so great that, according to the Jainas, the distance between any two points connectible by a straight line will be traversed in a single moment. (Given the multidimensional structure of the Jaina universe, certain circumstances of rebirth will require as many as two changes of direction before the appropriate *loka* and spot within it are reached. Motion along a curve is not admitted; therefore, as many as three moments may occasionally be necessary before the soul can enter its new state.)[29] It is important to recognize here that karma is not in any sense considered to *impel* the soul; it functions, rather, to channel or direct the motive force which is already present, much as a system of pipes might be used to "send" upwardly gushing water to a desired location.

Now, it should be clear that as a soul moves between two gross physical bodies, that is, during the state called *vigraha-gati,*[30] it cannot be accurately described as "totally free of embodiment"; if such were the case, it would simply fly upwards as the *siddha* does. For the system to work, in other words, the karmic "channel" must exist in

28. tad anantaram ūrdhvaṃ gacchaty ā lokāntāt/ pūrvaprayogād asaṅgatvād bandhacchedāt tathāgatipariṇāmāc ca/ (*Tattvārthasūtra* 10.5–6).
. . . tathāgatipariṇāmāt. yathā . . . pradīpaśikhā svabhāvād utpatati tathā muktātmā 'pi nānāgativakārakāraṇakarmanivāraṇe saty ūrdhvagatisvabhāvād ūrdhvam evārohati (*SS* 10.7). Beyond this point there is said to be only empty space *(alokākāśa),* where matter and even the principles of motion, rest, and time are absent. See *Tattvārthasūtra* 10.8.

29. This takes place only when there is movement to or from those realms inhabited exclusively by *ekendriyas.* See S. A. Jain, *Reality,* p. 70, n. 1.

30. vigraho dehaḥ. vigrahārthā gatir vigrahagatiḥ (*SS* 2.25).

some manifest, if subtle, form in which the soul is contained. This is in fact exactly what the Jainas have claimed; the transmigrating soul is said to be housed by a "karmic body" *(kārmāṇa-śarīra),* as well as by a so-called luminous body *(taijasa-śarīra).*[31] The former is composed of the sum total of one's karma at a given moment; the latter acts as a substratum for this karmic matter during the *vigraha-gati* and also functions to maintain body temperature during gross physical existence. Both of these invisible bodies are said to suffuse the gross and visible one during life; thus they not only "convey" the soul from one birth state to the next but constitute a real physical link between these states as well.

Committed as they were to the doctrine that the *vigraha-gati* typically occupies only a single moment, Jaina thinkers faced one major difficulty, namely, explaining how the "choice" of exactly appropriate circumstances for the next birth could possibly be made in so short a time. (Recall, in this connection, the *gandharva's* lengthy "search" for a proper birth-environment.) They have dealt with this problem by positing the existence of a unique factor, the so-called *āyuḥ-* ("longevity") *karma.* To understand the function of this factor, we must first examine certain general points of Jaina doctrine concerning the types and modes of operation of karmic matter. In addition to the four major "vitiating" *(ghātiyā)* karmas,[32] which effectively keep a soul in bondage, Jainas have delineated four minor categories said to be responsible for the mechanism of rebirth and embodiment. Among this latter group, known as *aghātiyā,* we find the following: (1) *nāma-karma,* a cover term for the collection of karmic material whose fruition determines some ninety-eight different aspects of the future body, for example, its destiny or class of existence (human, animal, etc.), its sex, color, number of senses, conformation of limbs, and the like;[33] (2) *gotra-karma,* controlling

31. yat tejonimittaṃ tejasi vā bhavaṃ tat taijasam. karmaṇāṃ kāryam kārmaṇam . . . ayaḥpiṇḍe tejo 'nupraveśavat taijasakārmaṇayor vajrapaṭalādiṣu . . . lokāntāt sarvatra nāsti pratīghātaḥ. . . . nityasambandhinī hi te ā samsārakṣayāt niraveśaṣasya saṃsāriṇo jīvasya te dve api śarīre bhavata ity arthaḥ (*SS* 2.36–42).

32. The four *ghātiyā* karmas are (1) *mohanīya* (engendering "false views" and preventing "pure conduct"; (2) *jñānāvaraṇīya* ("knowledge-obscuring"); (3) *darśanāvaraṇīya* ("perception-obscuring"); (4) *antarāya* ("restrictor of the quality of energy *(vīrya)*").

33. gatijātiśarīrāṅgopāṅganirmāṇabandhanasaṃsthānasaṃhanana sparśarasagandhavarṇānupūrvyāgurulaghūpaghātātapodyotocchvāsavihāyogatayaḥ pratyekaśarīratrasasubhagasusvaraśubhasūkṣmaparyāptisthirādeyayaśaḥkīrttisetarāṇi tīrthakaratvaṃ ca/ (*Tattvārthasūtra* 8.11).

whether the environment into which one falls is or is not conducive to the leading of a spiritual life;[34] (3) *vedanīya-karma,* producing either pleasant or unpleasant feelings in response to the environment, hence the level of happiness or unhappiness which characterizes an individual; (4) *āyuḥ-karma,* whereby the exact duration of life (ostensibly measured, among human beings, by the number of breaths to be taken) is established.

While this classification appears at first to be a simple one, it is complicated by the fact that *āyuḥ-karma,* as we have indicated above, functions in a most unusual manner. *Every other sort of karma* in the Jaina system is said to be in a constant bondage *(bandha)* and fruition *(anubhāga)* relationship with the soul; some *nāma-karma,* for example, is at every moment being bound, to come to fruition at some future time, while another is at every moment producing its result and falling away *(nirjarā)* from the soul. *Āyuḥ-karma,* however, is bound *only once* in a given lifetime, and its fruition will apply only to the very next life.[35] This specificity of application effectively places *āyuḥ-karma* in a position of primacy relative to the other *aghātiyā* karmas, since these must "fall into place" in conformity with the life-period that has been fixed. Given an *āyus* of seventy years, for example, only those *nāma-karmas* generating rebirth in a destiny where such a life-span is appropriate could conceivably come into play. Thus it is that the "selection" of the particular *aghātiyā* karmas determinative of the next existence occurs *before the moment of death.* There need be no "search" during the *vigrahagati,* since all "choices" have already been made.[36]

The peculiar characteristics attributed to *āyuḥ-karma* not only bring greater consistency to the Jaina theory of a momentary *vigraha-gati,* but have implications on the level of conduct as well.

34. This interpretation (supported by scripture) runs contrary to the popular Jaina understanding of *gotra* as "caste," etc. Jaina doctrine, of course, does not accept the notion of a caste status fixed by birth.
35. See *Jaina Jñānakośa* (in Marathi), Part 1, by Ajñāta (Aurangabad, 1972), p. 233 *(āyu).*
36. Śvetāmbara texts (Jacobi, *Jaina Sūtras,* Part 2, p. 225) contain the well-known story that the embryonic Mahāvīra underwent a transference from the womb of a Brāhmaṇa woman to that of a Kṣatriya one, the latter becoming his actual "mother." Does this suggest some breakdown in the determinative process begun by the fixing of *āyuḥ karma?* If so, it may explain the Digambara refusal to accept any such tale as valid. Śvetāmbaras, for their part, have simply labeled this event as one of the inexplicable miracles which may occur in a given aeon of time *(aṇaṃteṇa kāleṇa).* See *Sthānāṅga sūtra,* #1074.

This second aspect relates particularly to prevailing ideas concerning when the *āyuḥ-karma* may be fixed. Jaina teachers have agreed that this event cannot take place until some moment during the final third of the present lifetime, and that indeed it will often not occur until death is very nearly at hand. The determination of one's *āyuḥ-karma,* moreover, is held to be extremely susceptible to the effects of one's recent volitional activities. Thus the devout Jaina is encouraged to pay ever more strict attention to his religious vows and duties as he grows older. Activities during the first two-thirds of life are not irrelevant in this context, however, since these will have created the habits which largely define a person's behavioral tendencies as the end of his life approaches. It must be emphasized here that one is not *aware* of the moment at which the *āyuḥ-karma* is fixed; thus it will behoove him to live until his last breath as if it were still possible to influence the specific outcome of this event. This orientation is most vividly expressed in the Jaina practice of *sallekhanā,*[37] in which a mendicant of advanced age may undertake a ritual fast ending only in death. It is hoped that he will thus be enabled to face his final moments in a state of absolute tranquillity, free of the fears, desires, or other strong volitions which characterize the consciousness of the average person at this time. The fixing of *āyuḥ-karma* under such controlled and peaceful conditions is held to be extremely auspicious; not only will rebirth in lower existences be effectively precluded in this way, but the individual in question is deemed likely to find himself in an environment conducive to rapid spiritual development.

Although emphasis on the religious significance of the last moments of life is by no means unique to the Jainas (similar notions prevail among Hindus, Buddhists, and certain non-Indian communities as well), it might be said that the idea of *āyuḥ-karma,* on the basis of which Jainas rationalize this emphasis, *is* unique. But this idea itself is not a fundamental one; it seems to function, as we have seen, mainly as an explanatory adjunct to *the* distinctive Jaina doctrine pertaining to rebirth, namely, the momentariness of *vigrahagati.* The significance of this doctrine goes far beyond the context of mere scholastic dispute. Indeed, it is not unreasonable to say that the basic social distinction between Jainas and their Hindu neighbors derives mainly from the disagreement of these communities over the period of time required for transmigration to occur. Whereas Jainas

37. See Williams, *Jaina Yoga,* pp. 166–172.

have adopted many Hindu customs and ceremonies pertaining to such things as marriage, the coming of the new year, childbirth, and so forth, they have never taken up what is perhaps the most important of all rituals in Hindu society, namely, *śrāddha,* the offering of food by a son to the spirit of his dead parent. We have noted the belief that this offering is essential if the parent is to obtain a body suitable for entrance into the *pitṛ-loka,* and hence to gain the chance for eventual rebirth. It is further believed that failure of a son to perform this ritual will result in the loss of inheritance and in his wife's being rendered barren by the curse of the spirits thus stranded in the disembodied state. The *śrāddha* ritual not only represents a significant expression of the underlying parent-child tensions characteristic of the Indian family[38] but also provides perhaps the most important function of the Brāhmaṇical castes. The latter point is made in reference to the Brahmins' monopolization of the role of intermediary between the donor and the departed; only if Brahmins consume the offerings can these be "converted" into the material from which the new body of the spirit is built up.

It will be apparent that for Jainas the very idea of *śrāddha* is doctrinally invalid; a soul which goes to its next body in one moment cannot be fed, propitiated, or dealt with in any other way by those left behind. For this and other more "common sense" reasons, we find such writers as the thirteenth-century commentator Malliṣeṇa making light of the entire *śrāddha* ritual:

> Even through the performance of *śrāddha,* increase in posterity is in the case of most people not found; and . . . in the case of some, as in that of donkeys, pigs, goats, etc., even without performance thereof we see it still more. . . . And . . .
>
> "If even to dead beings the *śrāddha* is
> the cause of satisfaction,
> Then oil might increase the flame of an
> extinguished lamp."

38. It is tempting to read Freudian symbolism into this belief system: the son, though perhaps desiring to "kill" his father (by preventing his rebirth), nevertheless performs his filial duty out of fear of "castration" (the loss of property and offspring). Perhaps more to the point, however, is the fact that in Indian society the parent seems fundamentally unwilling to relinquish his control over the son, to recognize the latter's adult status; through the institution of *śrāddha,* some semblance of parental control is maintained even in death. It would be interesting to investigate whether Jainas, lacking the institutionalization of filial responsibility that *śrāddha* represents, have created some substitute ritual or social form which functions in an analogous manner.

If it is said that "What is enjoyed by the Brahman accrues to them (i.e., the ancestors)," whoever is to agree to that? Since only in the Brahman do we see the fattened bellies; and transference of these into theirs (the ancestors') cannot be espied; and because only on the part of the Brahmans is satisfaction witnessed.[39]

There is one other tenet of the Jaina system pertaining to rebirth which must be mentioned here, as it provides a further basis for the unacceptability of the practice of *śrāddha.* Whereas this practice clearly assumes that the actions of one person can affect the destiny of another, Jaina tradition has always held that an individual soul can experience results accruing only to actions which it has *itself* performed. The tenth century *ācārya* Amitagati has provided us with a forceful statement of the adamant position taken by Jainas on this matter:

Whatever karma a soul has acquired through its own prior deeds,
it will obtain the good and bad results thereof.
If one could obtain results from the deeds of others,
then surely his own deeds would be meaningless.

Except for karma earned for oneself by oneself,
no one gives anything to anyone.
Reflecting upon this fact, therefore,
let every person, unwaveringly,
abandon the perverse notion that
another being can provide him with anything at all.[40]

This emphasis on reaping the fruits only of one's own karma was not restricted to the Jainas; both Hindu and Buddhist writers have produced doctrinal materials stressing the same point. Each of the latter traditions, however, developed practices in basic contradiction to such a belief. In addition to *śrāddha,* we find among the Hindus widespread adherence to the notion of divine intervention in one's fate, while Buddhists eventually came to propound such theories as

39. *SM* XI (tr. by F. W. Thomas, pp. 69–70).
40. svayaṃ kṛtaṃ karma yad ātmana purā
phalaṃ tadīyaṃ labhate śubhāśubham/
pareṇa dattaṃ yadi labhyate sphuṭaṃ
svayaṃ kṛtaṃ karma nirarthakaṃ tadā//
nijārjitaṃ karma vihāya dehino
na ko 'pi kasyāpi dadāti kiñcana/
vicārayann evam ananyamānasaḥ
paro dadātīti vimuñcya śemuṣīm//
(*Dvātriṃśikā*) *Nitya-naimittika-pāṭhāvalī*, Karanja, 1956, p. 22.

the boon-granting *bodhisattvas,* transfer of merit, and the like. Only the Jainas have been absolutely unwilling to allow such ideas to penetrate their community, despite the fact that there must have been a tremendous amount of social pressure on them to do so.

In this discussion we have examined various aspects of the Jaina approach to rebirth. By way of conclusion, we might reiterate the important points raised thereby. The Jainas, first of all, show a remarkable tendency to associate the soul with some sort of bodily influence, whether during ordinary existence, transmigration, or even after the attainment of *siddha*-hood. In spite of this tendency, however, no biological explanation of the mechanism whereby a soul enters its new environment has been offered. The description of the possible states of rebirth includes one category, the *nitya-nigoda,* the nature of which suggests a more primitive and possibly linear concept of existence underlying the set of beliefs now taken as orthodox. Jaina views on rebirth are unique in their emphasis on the single moment involved in movement of a soul from one embodiment to the next. This emphasis, together with the less unusual but very strictly applied belief in non-transference of karma, has been reflected in the complete absence from the Jaina community of certain ritual forms typical of Brāhmaṇical society. The deeper ramifications of these issues, particularly the final one, definitely require further exploration; it is to be hoped that future researches will move in these directions.*

Appendix 1

THE JAINA UNIVERSE (LOKĀKĀŚA)

The Jaina "universe" *(loka)* is a three-dimensional structure divided into five parts. (A) The Lower World consists of seven layers and is the abode of infernal beings *(nāraki)* as well as certain demigods (demons, titan, etc.). (B) The Middle, or Terrestrial, World consists of innumerable concentric island-continents with Jambudvīpa in the center. This is the abode of humans and animals. Human beings are not found beyond the third "continent" from the center. In (C), the Higher, or Celestial, World, are found the abodes of heavenly beings *(devas).* (D) Beyond the border of the Celestial

*I should like to acknowledge the assistance of Joseph Clack in the preparation of this paper.

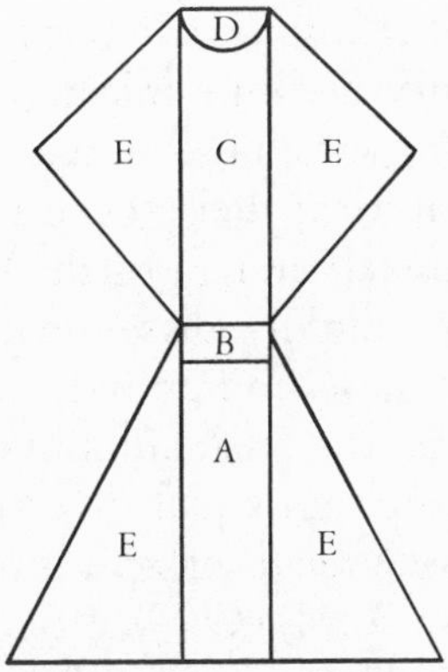

World, marked by the crescent, is the permanent abode of the Liberated Souls *(siddhas)*. This region is the apex of "World-space" *(loka-ākāśa)*. (E) Contains abodes restricted to inhabitation by *ekendriyas*. (While these single-sense organisms occupy all parts of the *lokākāśa*, *trasas* [beings having two or more senses] are restricted to areas A-C; hence we find only *ekendriyas* here.) The area surrounding this entire structure is known as "Space without Worlds" *(aloka-ākāśa)*, which is devoid of souls, matter, and time. It should be noted that there is no provision for a *pitṛ-loka* (World of Ancestors) in the Jaina cosmology.

Appendix 2

COMMUNICATION REGARDING THE PROCESS OF REBIRTH FROM SUBODH K. JAIN, PROFESSOR OF AGRONOMY AND RANGE SCIENCES, UNIVERSITY OF CALIFORNIA, DAVIS

In the theory of rebirth we assume the *karmas* to be somehow transmitted with the soul from one life to the next after rebirth. This entity of life that is transmitted we shall call "Entity" for convenience. It should have at least three properties: (1) it travels very fast (instantaneously? or as mathematicians put it, in as short a time as you please, infinitesimally); (2) it has a specific destination, i.e., the place of birth (conception); and (3) it allows very specific individuality in that a person's *karmas* are specifically attached and transfuse with the zygote of the newborn (zygote is the first cell resulting from the union of two parental germ cells). Now, what known scientific elements could hypothetically possess these three properties?

First, consider the pheromones, the chemical compounds identified in the study of animal communications. These substances are known to be produced by ants, bees, and so forth, which leave odor trails by individuals to inform their social groups about their position, distance, path of travel, and so forth. Very small quantities are needed, the odor is very rapidly disseminated, and scientists think that the complexity of these compounds can allow many specific signals. Specificity, that is, the great amount of variation among individuals transmitted through an equal diversity of pheromones (one individual–one pheromone relationship), is quite feasible. (For a discussion of pheromones, see E. O. Wilson, *Sociobiology*, Harvard University Press, 1975.) Thus, conceivably, at least higher animals including men are capable of communicating during their lifetime or at the time of death very specific individualized signals, and provide some *entity* of transmission.

A second form of this *entity* could be in *radiowaves,* released as "energy" at the time of death, which would travel at high speed, have the capacity of being received by a specific destination, and carry a specific message (or *karmas).* Now, one could easily postulate within the realm of current ideas about the origin of mutation (in genetics) (see J. D. Watson, *The Molecular Biology of the Gene,* 2nd ed., Columbia University Press, 1975) that this "energy" received by the zygote could induce changes in DNA, the genetic code of life, which when decoded during the newborn's lifetime would bring about predestined changes. Birth defects or inherited diseases, for instance, are now attributed to chance origin of mutations and expression in a suitable environment. With the present thesis, one could argue that their origin is due in part to parental genetic materials and in part to the "entity" received from the previous life.

Both of these ideas are speculative in large part, but are presented here in relation to some specific facts, which are not to be misconstrued as proofs but are merely suggestions of feasible, scientifically permissible theses. The most serious difficulty in formulating these ideas lies in our ignorance about the precise mechanism by which "destination" or "receiving station" is determined. How does a zygote receive its proper *karmas?* How do parents of a child provide for receiving it? How this entity is maintained in a zygote to unfold the consequences poses a second difficulty. Thus, at this time we are only speculating about the details of these theses. We need to understand the physical or metaphysical features of these processors of information.

Part III.

Philosophical Traditions

10

The Karma Theory and Its Interpretation in Some Indian Philosophical Systems

KARL H. POTTER

When reference is made to the Indian theory of karma and rebirth it is not usually clear what is being referred to. Since it will be important for my purposes to be as clear as possible about what *is* being referred to under such a rubric, I wish to begin with some possibly tedious distinctions.

A *theory,* as I shall use the term, is a set of connected hypotheses, involving postulation of unobservable or uncommonsensical items, that purports to predict, postdict, or otherwise explain processes in the world. Thus, for instance, we speak of particle physics as a theory, since it purports to develop an account—a set of hypotheses—to explain the behavior of bodies in a manner involving postulation of particles too small to be observed.

A *model,* as understood here, is an extended metaphor, drawn from common sense or from accepted scientific understanding, that is purported to make intelligible the workings of a theory. Thus one finds models using billiard balls or facsimiles thereof to illustrate the interaction through impact among the submicroscopic particles postulated in the theory just mentioned.

An *interpretation,* as spoken of here, is an attempt to reconstruct what must be assumed to be working in the minds of a person or persons in order to understand or explain their behavior and thought. Thus an interpretation is a second-order theory about the assumptions operative in the thinking of those who, for example, propose a first-order theory. Thus one might speculate on the conceptual assumptions which lead physicists to develop a theory of submicroscopic particles, and propose as an interpretation of their thought that the structure of the Indo-European language (say) prejudices them to think in terms of solid lumps of matter having qualities and motions, rather than in terms of some other possible model.

A very comprehensive interpretation may be termed a *conceptual scheme*.

Interpretations may be comparatively explicit or comparatively implicit, in the sense that those persons whose thought patterns are being reconstructed may be to a greater or a lesser extent aware of the assumptions suggested in an interpretation.

Theories, models, and interpretations may be either *indigenous* or not. Generally, an indigenous theory or model is one which is developed by the persons who are alleged to think in accordance with them. But there is room for ambiguity here, especially in considering an indigenous interpretation or a conceptual scheme. An interpretation or a scheme may be termed "indigenous" to community C if (1) it is attributed by someone not in C to the members of C and it is the behavior or thought of C which the interpretation is intended to explain; (2) it is recognized explicitly by all members of C as explanatory of their behavior or thought; (3) it is attributed by some members of C to all the members of C, where C is the group whose behavior or thought is alleged to be explained by the interpretation. These senses do not exhaust the possibilities.

One point of making these distinctions is to alert readers to the differing manners in which theories, models, and interpretations may be criticized. To criticize a theory—or an interpretation, which, as we saw, is a second-order theory—one may produce counterexamples, one may demonstrate inconsistency, one may show that the theoretical constructs introduced are redundant, or that the theory is empty, without explanatory force. To criticize a model one shows that the implications of the model run counter to the theory in crucial ways, that the disanalogies outweigh the analogies between the model and the theory. This is a matter of degree, since everything resembles every other thing in one respect or another, and, as it is frequently said, every analogy has its limits.

I shall be most interested here in the criticism of an interpretation. As we have just seen, interpretations may be criticized according to the same canons as other theories. However, since interpretations (unlike other theories) may be largely implicit, they may have to be unpacked, and in the process the unpacking may do injustice to the interpretation. This is especially the case if one is provided with general suggestions about an entire conceptual scheme, and then attempts (as I shall below) to unpack the suggestions into an interpretation of a certain theory, the karma theory.

Where the interpretation to be criticized is not indigenous (in one or another of the senses discriminated above) one may also criticize it by certain techniques other than the general ones applicable to theories in general. One may, for instance, point to indigenous linguistic usage as suggesting counterexamples to an interpretation. Or one may try to make explicit an implicit indigenous interpretation, arguing that though it is no better as theory than the non-indigenous one under discussion, its very indigenousness makes it a superior candidate as an explanatory device.

Now to apply some of these distinctions in the case of karma and rebirth. My starting point is the thesis that in the philosophical writings which constitute classical Yoga and Advaita Vedānta and related systems, karma and rebirth appears as a *theory* in the sense here specified. This appears most evident in the formulation found in the Pātañjala Yoga system, which I shall proceed to sketch.[1]

An act *(karman)* performed under normal circumstances—that is, with purposive intent and passion—creates *(kṛ)* a karmic residue *(karmāśaya)*, either meritorious *(dharma)* or unmeritorious *(adharma)* depending on the quality of the act. This karmic residue has or is accompanied by dispositional tendencies *(saṃskāra)* of more than one sort, including at least two kinds of traces *(vāsanā)*, one kind which, if and when it is activated, produces a memory of the originating act, the other which, if and when it is activated, produces certain afflictions *(kleśa)*. These *kleśas* are erroneous conceptions which characterize the thinking of those engaged in purposive activ-

1. The sketch is based on the *Yogasūtras* of Patañjali and the basic commentarial literature thereon, namely, the *Yogabhāṣya* of Vyāsa interpreted with the aid of Vācaspati Miśra's *Tattvavaiśāradī*. All three works are conveniently translated under one cover by James Haughton Woods in Harvard Oriental Series 17 (Cambridge, Mass.: Harvard University Press, 1914, 1927; reprinted Motilal Banarsidass: Delhi, 1966). References to this work in subsequent footnotes are indicated by "Woods."

ity, and it is they which are primarily responsible for the agent being in bondage, that is, continually creating karmic residues.

When a person dies his unactivated karmic residues including his *vāsanās* gather together within that individual's *citta*. *Citta* is Yoga's term for that *prakṛti,* or substance, composed of the three *guṇas,* whose fluctuations *(vṛtti)* constitute the thinking, willing, and feeling of sentient beings. In the Yoga view, the *citta* associated with the *puruṣa* which had "inhabited" the just-deceased body immediately passes on to a new body—presumably a foetus—and "fills in" *(āpūra)* this new body with *citta* appropriate to the kind of body that it is (if it's a cat, feline *citta* fills it in; if a human, human *citta*). The karmic residues operate within this new body to determine three things: the kind of body it is (its "birth" [*jāti*], cat or human); the length of its life *(āyus)* under normal circumstances; and the affective tone of experiences *(bhoga)* the person will have, that is, whether his experiences will be pleasurable or painful.

The foetus grows and is born as a baby complete with karmic residues and *vāsanās.* As the occasion makes possible, that is, when appropriate kinds of sense-objects are presented or other conditions are confronted, a karmic residue may mature *(vipāka)* in one of the three forms mentioned—as birth, length of life, or tone of experience. Within a given lifetime, therefore, the function of karmic residues is to provide the affective tone of experience, "good" residues producing pleasurable experiences, "bad" ones producing painful experiences. Given that the person having these experiences is a purposive agent, he will act in various ways as a part of his response to these experiences, and in so acting he will lay down another karmic residue with associated *vāsanās.*

The theory is worked out in some detail. Karmic residues, for example, may be divided into two sorts—those whose maturation will occur *(niyatavipāka)* in the present lifetime *(dṛṣṭajanman),* and those which are not thus limited and so may mature in another life *(adṛṣṭajanman).* That is to say, some actions produce residues whose maturation will occur in the same lifetime as that in which they were produced. It is generally accepted that memory activates the *smṛtivāsanās* within the same lifetime, and that in dreams the *kleśavāsanās* activate experiences relating to the originating actions; likewise, most waking experience is the direct outcome of the maturation of residues accrued in this very lifetime. But it is also the case that frequently an experience will be the outcome of *vāsanās* laid down in karmic residues produced by acts in long-past lives. For example, if one is a cat in lifetime L_1, is reborn in other types of bodies in L_2 to L_{100}, and then is reborn as a cat again in L_{101}, those *kleśavāsanās* which were laid down in L_1 and have remained stored up until now may now be activated, producing feline experiences.

The point of Yoga, as understood by Patañjali, is that it provides a way to be liberated from this karmic mechanism. I shall not try to describe the whole process, but the relevant aspect of it for our purposes is that the yogin through practice *(kriyāyoga)* tries to attenuate *(tanukṛ)* the *kleśas* through cultivation of practices opposed to them *(pratipakṣabhāvanā)*. When the *kleśas* are attenuated a certain kind of meditation *(prasaṃkhyāna)* can make them no longer operative, with the result that they do not produce any more karmic residues. Furthermore, since the very occasion for the maturation of those residues already produced requires the operation of the *kleśas,* this meditation is said to make them subtle and so no longer able to provide the necessary condition for maturation, so that those residues and their associated *vāsanās* cannot bring about any results. At this point, a process called *pratiprasava,* a kind of devolution of the manifest state of *citta* into its causal state, culminates in its returning to the unmanifest *(avyakta)* state of *prakṛti.* There are then no further fluctuations of *citta* associated with that *puruṣa.*

This, then, is the Yoga theory. It involves, as any theory in our sense must, a number of postulated entities, theoretical constructs which are not directly observable and not part of the everyday vocabulary of experience. Such constructs include *citta, kleśa, vāsanā, āśaya,* and several other items in the above account. That the account is intended to explain commonly known processes in the world is evident—memory, dreams, the pleasurable and painful qualities of daily experience, birth, length of life, and so on are alleged to be explained by the theory. But it is also evident that the explanation, like any scientific theory, goes beyond common knowledge to postulate various processes and constituents unfamiliar to the ordinary person.

To provide the ordinary person with a basis for understanding the theory of karma and rebirth Yoga authors invoke a model. The model is agricultural, which is not surprising given that India has always been an agrarian society by and large. Specifically, the Yoga texts liken the karmic process to various stages in rice farming. The major passages appear in Books 2 and 4 of the *Yogasūtras* and its commentaries by Vyāsa and Vācaspati Miśra.

In the commentaries on 2.2, the *sūtra* in which the attenuation of the *kleśas* is explained, an objector is made to ask: "If *kriyāyoga* produces attenuation of the *kleśas,* what can meditation *(prasaṃkhyāna)* accomplish?" In answer it is said:

> *Prasaṃkhyāna* makes barren *(vandhya)* the attenuated *kleśas,* which are like burned seeds *(dagdhabīja)* of winter rice *(kalāma).* If the *kleśas* are not attenuated, discrimination between *sattva* and *puruṣa* cannot even arise, much less make the *kleśas* barren. But when the *kleśas* are thinned out they can be made barren.

In 2.4 it is explained how *avidyā,* one of the five *kleśas,* is related to the other four. The *sūtra* says that *avidyā* is the "field" *(kṣetra),* that is, the "propagative ground" *(prasavabhūmi)* of the other four when those are either dormant *(prasupta),* attenuated *(tanu),* intercepted *(vicchinna),* or sustained *(udāra).* Dormancy is explained as being the "merely potential" *(śaktimātra)* state in the mind *(cetas)* which tends toward the condition of being a seed. In this state the *kleśa* is awakened when a sense-object of the appropriate sort is confronted. A questioner asks: why doesn't the person who has attained discrimination *(viveka)* still have dormant *kleśas?* The answer is that in such a person the seeds are burned by *prasaṃkhyāna* meditation, and a burned seed cannot germinate. Thus in the discriminating person we must recognize a fifth state in addition to the four mentioned in the *sūtra.* The same point is echoed in Vācaspati's comment on the tenth *sūtra* and *bhāṣya.*

Book 2.13 contains the most material for our purpose. It is the *sūtra* which declares that as long as the roots *(mūla),* that is, the *kleśas,* exist, the seeds will mature in the three forms of birth, length of life, and kind of affective experience. As Vācaspati is explaining that "*bhoga,*" or "experience," means pleasure *(sukha)* and pain *(duḥkha)* he says:

> So the soil of the self *(ātmabhūmi)* sprinkled *(viṣikta)* with the water of the *kleśas* becomes a field *(kṣetra)* producing *(prasava)* the karma-fruits *(phala).*[2]

Later, in the *Bhāṣya,* another passage runs as follows:

> Just as the rice-grains *(śālitaṇḍulā)* encased within the chaff *(tuṣāvanaddha)* when they are not burned seeds are fit for growth *(prarohasamartha),* but the winnowed chaff *(apanītatuṣā)* and the burned seed are not so fit, similarly the karmic residues when encased in the *kleśas (kleśāvanaddha)* are the subject of growth toward maturation *(vipākaprarohin),* but the winnowed *kleśas (apanītakleśa)* and the seeds burned by *prasaṃkhyāna* are not fit.[3]

2. Woods, p. 126. My translation.

3. Woods, pp. 122–123. My translation.

The agricultural analogy is once again made startlingly explicit in 4.3. The *sūtras* are discussing how evolution *(pariṇāma)* from one birth into another can occur. (The context seems to be the *siddhis,* but the explanation appears to be applicable to the general phenomenon wherever it occurs.) In 4.2 it is explained that this takes place through the filling in *(āpūra)* of *prakṛti;* commentators explain that this occurs in dependence on merit *(dharma),* and so forth, and they liken it to the way in which a spark landing on some dry grass produces a conflagration. In 4.3 the idea is developed: the occasion *(nimitta)* of this filling in is no direct overt act; rather, it happens naturally when a difference in the obstruction *(varaṇa)* of *prakṛti* occurs, says Patañjali, "like the farmer *(kṣetrikavat).*" Vyāsa explains: when the farmer wants to get water from one plot to another, he does not take it there with his hands, but cuts the barrier separating the two plots. Likewise, demerit *(adharma),* the barrier to *prakṛti*'s flow, is cut by merit, so that the *prakṛti* then flows naturally into its appropriate new form *(vikāra).* The analogy is developed even further: perhaps, it is suggested, the farmer may have trouble getting water to the roots of his plants because there are too many sprouts in the field; then, he will remove some of the seeds. Just so the *yogin* attenuates, thins out, the karmic residues so that he may exhaust them through experiencing their fruits.

A prominent feature of that *prakṛti* which functions as *citta* in Yoga is its fluidity. Indeed, in *Yogabhāṣya* on 1.12 it is explicitly referred to as a river *(nādin)* or stream, or rather as two streams, one flowing toward liberation, the other toward *saṃsāra.* There also one gets the idea that these streams are subject to obstruction.

> The stream toward objects *(viṣaya)* is dammed *(khilīkriyate)* by nonattachment *(vairāgya),* and the stream toward discrimination is opened up *(udghātyate)* by yogic practice *(abhyāsa),*

says Vyāsa, recalling the other passage about the farmer cutting the barrier separating the fields. This *citta* is composed of the three *guṇas,* we know, which are constantly changing in their relative domination of each other. *Citta* is also subject to "fluctuations" *(vṛtti),* one of which is erroneous awareness *(viparyaya),* of which the *kleśas* are instances. In this series of connections we can perhaps explain what seems otherwise odd, namely, that in Vācaspati's simile about the soil of the self being sprinkled with the water of the *kleśas,* the *kleśas* are likened to something liquid rather than (as we might expect) to some soiling dirty solid.

Water is by nature cool (pure, *sattva*), flowing (incessantly active, *rajas*) and eddying (subject to stagnation, *tamas*). However, from the point of view of a farmer, when treated in certain ways it becomes the source of nutrition and so of life and other types of energy. That process involves, we may suppose, as any type of control does, a stabilization or hardening of the stuff, at first through eddies in the stream caused by obstructions, then as more stable configurations which maintain themselves for a longer time. Furthermore, this process toward the establishment of stable configuration characteristically will proceed by the hardening of the "exterior" part which holds the configuration, or shape. Thus, as Egnor reports,[4] Indians (at least Tamilians) take the insides of things to be fluid while the outsides are solid.

In 2.13 a significant analogy appears, in which *citta* is likened to a fishnet *(matsyajāla)* having "different shapes in all places and having beginninglessly a rigid form *(sammūrchita)* fixed by the *vāsanās* caused by experience *(anubhava)* of the maturation of *karman* from the *kleśas.*" This simile fits the sketch of the liquids model in my previous paragraph, and may also help us to understand how the same *kleśas* which are liquid may also be likened in other respects to roots or even to chaff, as we saw. The cause of the "hardening" into configurations (seeds) is the tendency of water to eddy and form whirlpools because of obstructions or because of dispositions *(saṃskāra)* in the water occasioned by previous obstructions upstream. Obstructions may be good or bad depending on where the stream is heading; thus *adharma* may obstruct the passage of *citta* toward liberation, while non-attachment may dam its passage toward attraction to sense-objects.

We have, then, in the Yoga account a rather carefully worked-out theory concerning the mechanics of karma and rebirth, which is made available to the non-philosopher through appeal to the model of rice-farming. This literature seems to me among classical Indian systems the most rigorous in its treatment of these matters, but it is not the only system which deals with it extensively. Notably, Advaita Vedānta, from the Upaniṣads on, develops an account which coincides to some degree with the Yoga account but diverges from it in certain important respects.[5]

4. Margaret Trawick Egnor, "The Sacred Spell and Other Conceptions of Life in Tamil Culture," Ph.D. dissertation, University of Chicago, March, 1978.

5. The following account of Advaita's views on karma and rebirth has been reconstructed from Śaṅkarācārya's commentaries on several Upaniṣads, his *Brahmasūtrabhāṣya, Bhagavadgītābhāṣya,* and to a slight extent from Sureśvara's subcommentaries on the *Upaniṣadbhāṣyas.*

Death may be due either to "natural causes," construed in Indian thought as one's having lived through his allotted years as determined by his karma, or to violence, which interrupts the natural working out of karma. In either case, however, a man comes to the point of death endowed with several relevant bits of equipment. These include his gross body, made up of material substances; his sense organs and "action" organs (organs of speech, locomotion, sex, excretion, and grasping); his intellectual organ *(manas);* his sense of ego *(ahaṃkara);* and his internal organ (*buddhi* or *antaḥkaraṇa*), which is the basis of his ability to engage in intentional awareness and consequent activity.

In addition, he has stored up in the form of tendencies *(saṃskāra)* the residues *(anuśaya)* of acts he has performed in the life just ending, as well as residues of acts performed in previous lives which have not as yet come to "fruition" or "maturation" *(vipāka),* that is, which have not as yet produced their results. These karmic residues are of three kinds: (1) those residues which were determined at birth to work themselves out during the present life (the one just ending), called *prārabdhakarman;* (2) those residues which were produced by acts performed in a previous life, but which remain latent during this present life, called *sañcitakarman;* (3) the results of acts performed during this just-ending lifetime, which will mature in some subsequent lifetime in the normal course of events, called *sañcīyamāna* or *āgamin* karma.[6]

As karmic residues mature they cooperate with what are called "traces" or "impressions" *(vāsanā)* to determine the way in which the karmic potentials will in fact be worked out, the kind of experience *(bhoga)* which will accrue to the agent in consequence, and the future karmic residues which will be laid down by the acts so determined. These *vāsanās* appear to be decisions arrived at by the internal organ to seek certain kinds of outcomes. For instance, K. S. Iyer divides *vāsanās* into impure and pure types, and subdivides the impure into those, for example, which relate to worldly pride, those which relate to overintellectualizing (addiction to study, ritualism), and those which relate to one's body (taking the body to be one's true Self, use of cosmetics to beautify or medicine to remove blemishes from one's body).[7] At any moment in one's conscious lifetime he is guided in acting by such *vāsanās,* which develop into desires *(kāma).*[8]

6. N. Veezhinathan, "The Nature and Destiny of the Individual Soul in Advaita," *Journal of the Madras University* 47, no. 2 (1975): 19–20, understands *sañcita* to include *prārabdha* karma.

7. K. S. Iyer, "Ethical Aspect of the Vedanta," *Vedanta Kesari* 3 (1916–17): 39–41.

8. Veezhinathan, op. cit., pp. 11–12.

The Upaniṣads offer several accounts of what happens to these various things at the time of death. It is not altogether easy to rationalize all these into a consistent account. What I provide is a reconstruction which follows Śaṅkara where there are disagreements.[9] The process goes as follows:

1. The speech-function becomes absorbed into the intellectual organ, or power of thought *(manas).* The dying man stops speaking.

2. It is followed by the functions of all the other organs. Śaṅkara emphasizes that it is only the functions which merge, not the organs themselves. One must keep in mind that a sense-organ, for example, is not to be confused with its physical locus—the visual organ is different from the eyeball.

3. Then the *manas,* having absorbed these various functions, has its own functions absorbed into breath *(prāṇa).* That this is so is evidenced by the fact that dying persons—and for that matter those asleep and not dreaming—are seen to breathe although their senses and mind are not functioning.

4. Next, breath so endowed merges with the individual self *(jīva),* that is, with the internal organ as limited by the awarenesses, karmic residues, and *vāsanās* present at this moment. The man stops breathing.

5. Now the *jīva,* thus encumbered, joins the subtle elements *(tanmātra).* These are five in number, corresponding to the five gross elements—air, fire, earth, water, and *ākāśa.* These "subtle" elements are apparently conceived of as minute particles which form the seeds from which their gross counterparts grow. The cluster of the five subtle elements provides a (material) "subtle body" *(sūkṣmaśarīra)* which now encloses the *jīva* with its appurtenances, just as the gross body did during life.

6. All these factors collect in the "heart."[10] The *jīva* arrives replete with awareness (both true and false), karmic residues, *vāsanās,* desires, and internal organs, so it is perfectly capable of consciousness. However, since the external organs have stopped functioning, its consciousness at this point, like consciousness in dreams, is completely controlled by past karma. Thus at this "moment of death" the *jīva* is caused by its karma to develop a *vāsanā* which determines the

9. Śaṅkara, *Brahmasūtrabhāṣya* 4.2.1–21.

10. Indian philosophers use this term to mean the place within the body where feeling, willing, thinking, and so forth, take place. It does not necessarily denote the physical organ which goes by that name in Indian anatomy.

direction in which the subtle body will go as it leaves the "heart"—by which veins and point of egress, by what path, and to what kind of birth it will eventually proceed.

7. Thus decided, the *jīva*-controlled subtle body leaves the "heart" by one or another of the many veins and arteries, eventually gaining egress from the dead gross body by one or another aperture.

To this point, the Upaniṣadic sources appear relatively consistent in their implications. When they turn to the account of what happens immediately after death the versions diverge slightly.

Basically, the texts distinguish three paths for the subtle bodies to follow. One of these is referred to as the "northern path," the "way of the gods" *(devayāna)*, that lies through fire or light and leads to the sun. A second is the "southern path," the "way of the fathers" *(pitṛyāna)*, leading through smoke to the moon. Śaṅkara tells us that it is those who observe ritual obligations but do not have knowledge of God (i.e., Brahman with qualities, *saguṇa* Brahman) that follow the southern path; those who know God follow the northern path. Those who neither fulfilled their ritual obligations nor have knowledge follow a third path which leads to Yama's world or city, called Saṃyamana, or else they are immediately reborn as small animals, insects, perhaps plants, and so forth.[11]

How does the passage along these paths take place? In the *Bṛhadāraṇyaka Upaniṣad* we are told that the self proceeds from this body to the next like a leech or a caterpillar. Śaṅkara comments that the idea is that the self creates a link from the old body to the new by means of its *vāsanās*.[12] This serves to remind us that as the self encased in its subtle body moves along its path it is not unconscious—it is having experiences, determined by its karmic residues, as in a dream, and is forming plans and following them out as it goes along. It is thus exhausting some of its stored-up karmic residues as it proceeds, and continues doing so in the "heaven" or "hell" (sun, moon, or Saṃyamana) at which it in due course arrives.

Some details of the states along the northern path are discussed in the *Brahmasūtras*.[13] For one thing, Śaṅkara argues that by having

11. This is one of the points of divergence among the texts. Cf. Paul Deussen, *The System of the Vedanta*, translated by C. Johnston (Chicago: Open Court, 1912; reprinted New York: Dover, 1973), chaps. 20, 23.

12. Also in the *Brahmasūtrabhāṣya* on 3.1.1, commenting on the same passage in the Upaniṣad.

13. Cf. *Brahmasūtra* 4.3.

meditated on certain symbols one person may experience things appropriate to those symbols, and another other things, still there is only one "northern path." The *Chāndogya Upaniṣad* tells us that these transmigrating selves go to light, day, the waxing half of the moon, the six months when the sun is going north, the year, Āditya, the moon, lightning.[14] What sort of travel is this? Śaṅkara explains that these are references to divinities which conduct the self along the path, since in his state he is not capable of finding his own way.

The *Chāndogya* also gives us an account of the details of the southern path.[15] It leads from smoke through night, the dark fortnight, the months when the sun is moving south, to the realm of the fathers, thence to *ākāśa* and thus to the moon. Again, these are identified by Śaṅkara as deities who act as guides for the transmigrating self.

The selves of those who follow the "third path"—to Yama's world, perhaps—are "reborn" almost immediately in grains and other such things. They retain consciousness all the while, and the "hellish" experiences they earn—ascribed sometimes to instruments of torture controlled by Yama—are more plausibly construed as the natural concomitants of existing in such a state, considering the violent changes wrought on them as the grains are prepared for use in meals to be consumed by animals and human beings. These embodiments—such as plants and grains—being determined by the karmic residues of the selves which inhabit them, are rather quickly lived through, and the subtle-body-enclosed self may move on soon from one body to various others, all the while experiencing appropriate pains "as in a dream." If they are lucky they may in due course find their way into the food of humans and so get into blood and semen and eventually gain a new human birth.

As for those who arrive at the moon, the Upaniṣads tell us that they become the "food of the gods," which Śaṅkara explains means not that they are actually eaten by the gods but rather that they serve the gods. Actually, the sojourn in the moon is a period during which the meritorious residues are exhausted, and it is thus basically a happy interim. Those who have arrived there experience their just rewards in heaven for ritual observances practiced in the preceding worldly life. They do so until a small amount of karmic residue remains. They are also said to take on a watery "body" which supports the organs and allows them to generate experiences.

14. *Chāndogya Upaniṣad* 5.10.1–2.
15. *Chāndogya Upaniṣad* 5.10.3–4.

Those traveling the northern path or "way of the gods" proceed, as we have seen, through the sun (Āditya) to lightning. From there they are conducted to the realm of that which they have worshipped and meditated on. If that thing is God, they will be led to the Brahmaloka. If they meditated on some symbolic manifestation, however, they will arrive at an appropriate kind of heavenly place.[16]

It seems likely that Bādarāyaṇa, author of the *Brahmasūtras,* thought that the Brahmaloka amounted to the state of liberation. Śaṅkara, though, cannot allow that one can literally "arrive at" the higher *(nirguṇa)* Brahman, since he claims Brahman to be quite unrelated to any second thing, and so he is forced to interpret the Brahmaloka as a highest heaven, but not liberation. That raises the question whether the selves who go there return to be reborn. The Upaniṣadic text asserts that they do not return—presumably once again speaking of liberated ones—and Śaṅkara is caught in a dilemma.[17] Either he must reject Bādarāyaṇa's and the Upaniṣads' teaching on the point, or he must accept the Brahmaloka as liberation and so capitulate to the view that one can obtain liberation without knowing the nature of the Highest Brahman. The solution Śaṅkara finds is rather complex. On the one hand, he argues that the texts saying that the selves do not return from Brahmaloka mean that they do not return to rebirth in this world; they do, however, return to other forms of existence, presumably on some divine plane. On the other hand, he is willing to admit that those attaining the Brahmaloka, provided they have in the meantime attained knowledge of the Highest Brahman, will be liberated at the time of reabsorption *(pralaya). Brahmasūtrabhāṣya* 4.3.10 tells us that such selves proceed, along with the god (Hiraṇyagarbha) who rules the Brahmaloka, to "the pure highest place of Viṣṇu," and that this is what is meant by "progressive liberation" *(kramamukti),* since the Highest Brahman cannot be literally "reached."

Maṇḍana Miśra suggests still another way of resolving the dilemma. The non-returning may be only relative: it might mean that those who go to the Brahmaloka remain there until the next reabsorption, but that after that they return to bondage in the next cyclical universe.[18]

16. *Chāndogya Upaniṣad* 7 liberally illustrates the kinds of rewards intended.
17. Cf. *Brahmasūtras* 4.3.10, 22; *Bṛhadāraṇyaka Upaniṣad* 6.2.15 and Śaṅkara's comments thereon.
18. Maṇḍana Miśra, *Brahmasiddhi* with Śaṅkhapāṇi's commentary, edited by S. Kuppuswami Sastri. Madras Government Oriental Manuscript Series 4 (Madras, 1937), pp. 123–124.

Returning to those in the moon—eventually the time comes when they have exhausted their good karmic residues. At this point the watery body which had supported the organs, and so forth, during its stay on the moon dissolves, and the subtle body with its remainder of bad karma begins to fall back toward the earth. It is said to descend inversely through the stages which it ascended—through *ākāśa* to air, to smoke, into mist and cloud, and then to the earth's surface in the rain. This process does not take long, and the self is not conscious during this period, just as one loses consciousness when falling from a tree (according to one account) or because the karmic residues which remain do not become operative again until they determine the next birth.

Having arrived in the rain, the subtle body finds its way into plants. It does not get reborn in the plants, that is, it does not experience the pains of plant existence as do those who follow the "third path." Instead, the subtle body eventually attaches itself to a plant—a grain of rice, say—which is ground up, cooked, and eaten and digested by an animal. Throughout all this the attached subtle bodies remain unconscious (fortunately for them). It is pointed out by Śaṅkara that this part of the cycle is subject to multifarious accidents:[19] a subtle body might spend a long time stuck in some inaccessible place where the rainwater had carried it and then evaporated, or it may be carried around in the ecological cycle for a long time, passing through various bodies, occasionally into the ocean, back up into clouds, down again in rain, and so on.

Eventually, as it was said, the subtle body finds its way into an animal's vital juices—blood, semen—and, depending on the kind of animal it is, gets involved in the reproductive process. In the case of many animals, including humans, this means that it enters the ovum in semen. The *Aitareya Upaniṣad* notes that the *jīva* is in a sense born twice—the first time in the semen when it enters the ovum, the second when it leaves the mother's body.[20] In each case there is influence of the parent on the new gross body, through the food eaten by the parent, which interacts with the elements in the subtle body; this is why the child when born resembles its parents, both in the fact that it is a human child and not some other kind of animal, as well as in its facial features, and so forth.

19. Śaṃkara, *Chāndogyopaniṣadbhāṣya* on 5.10.6.
20. *Aitareya Upaniṣad* 4.2.3.

Not well explained in this account is what is responsible for a *jīva* destined for high-born caste status, say, getting into the bodily fluids of the right kind of parents, rather than getting a lower birth among humans or even other animals. It is perhaps not altogether speculative to suggest that this may have a good deal to do with the importance Indians place on the food they eat. The purer *jīvas* find their way into purer foodstuffs (although exactly how or why is still a mystery, it seems); then, since the higher castes eat the purer foods, and so on down the natural order, it will ordinarily work out that the right *jīvas* will be born from the right parents.

In any case, the food eaten by the mother during gestation becomes transformed into the various physical and mental substances which make up the new body, as determined by the relevant aspects carried by the subtle body.[21]

Sureśvara, like other authors, dwells on the misery of the *jīva* as it lies in the womb; here once again it has regained consciousness, and it develops its organs as the gross portions of its body corresponding to them grow.[22] Although we are not explicitly told so, it would appear that this development takes place as determined by karmic residues through the mechanism of *vāsanās.* If so, it would seem that the process of maturation of a *jīva's* karma begins again at least at the time it enters the womb, if not before.

An interesting story, corroborating some of the speculations indulged in above, is provided in the *Aitareya Upaniṣad* and its *Bhāṣya* by Śaṅkara, concerning Vāmadeva, who got liberated while in his mother's womb.[23] Vāmadeva is said to have realized the identity of his self with the Highest Self while in the womb, and he immediately got release there. The idea is that Vāmadeva was so pure and so close to enlightenment in his previous life that his liberation was accomplished before his next birth. This suggests several things. First, something must have happened to Vāmadeva while in the womb, for he was not liberated when he first got there; since this could hardly have been hearing the words of scripture or of a teacher (the immediate cause of liberation normally), we must suppose that his purity

21. Sureśvara, *Taittirīyopaniṣadbhāṣyavārttika,* edited and translated by R. Balasubramaniam (Madras: Centre for Advanced Study in Philosophy, 1974), 2.181–186, pp. 158–160.
22. Ibid., 2.189–200, pp. 162–165.
23. *Aitareyopaniṣad* with Śri Śaṅkarāchārya's *Bhāṣya,* tr. D. Venkatramiah (Bangalore: Bangalore Press, 1934), pp. 106–110.

naturally resulted in removal of ignorance without any other special cause. Second, since Vāmadeva is said to have subsequently been born and lived through a life determined by his *prārabdhakarman*, we must assume that the determination of his length of life and his experiences was in fact fixed prior to his liberation in the womb. This means, I infer, that what the *Aitareya* called the "first birth," where the subtle body enters the ovum in the semen, is the point at which the operation of karmic residues through *vāsanās* is resumed, along with the *jīva's* consciousness. Third, it suggests that the distinction between Vāmadeva's *prārabdhakarman* and his other karmic residues was already fixed prior to this "first birth," since presumably at the point of liberation all the other residues became inoperative.

All of which brings us to what we ordinarily call the birth of the child, the "second birth" of the *Aitareya*. It would seem from the foregoing that, viewed in karmic perspective, this is a relatively unimportant event, though for obvious reasons it is a critical occasion viewed from the perspective of human society. All the karmic processes are already under way, and have been for about nine months in the case of a normal child.

This child is, then, endowed with the three kinds of karmic residues noted earlier—*prārabdha*, *sañcita*, and *āgamin* karma. Śaṅkara likens *prārabdhakarman* to an arrow already in flight—it will continue until its energy is exhausted, unless something obstructs it.[24] Likewise, the child as he lives through the present life will experience the ripening of the residues of his *prārabdhakarman* unless something obstructs it, like premature death due to violence or other unnatural causes. So it is the same balance of karma of this sort which determines the length of his normal life and the type of experience he will have during that lifetime.

The process by which karmic residues affect experience needs to be discussed, since it lies at the center of supposed problems over the fatalistic or at least deterministic implications of the "Law of Karma." It seems to me that there is little cause for any such problem in the context of Advaita theory. The key to the puzzle, if any, lies in distinguishing karmic residues from *vāsanās*. A *vāsanā*, as we saw, is a man's determination to aim for certain objectives. Now such a determination is an effect of one's karmic residues—one's *vāsanās*

24. *The Bhagavad-Gītā* with the commentary of Śrī Śaṅkarāchārya, translated by A. Mahadeva Sastri (Madras: V. Ramaswamy Sastrulu & Sons, 1897, 1972), p. 365.

will be purer the purer one's karma. Further, pursuing a purer determination will get one, on balance, happier experiences, while pursuing impure determinations will get one, on balance, less happy or indeed painful experiences. It is in this sense that past actions determine future experience. But this is a very loose relation. It is not, for instance, the case that a certain act *x* in some past life specifically determines a certain event of experiencing, *y*, in this one; at best, *x* generates a determination on the agent's part to pursue a life-plan or -style which leads him to develop a desire to do something which will produce *y* if nothing interferes. Much may interfere. Furthermore, the agent, once aware of the danger of following his instincts, may perform *yoga*, and so on, to counteract the influence of his *vāsanās*. Thus the agent aware of the relation between his life-plans and his type of experience may decide to take a certain attitude toward his life as a whole. This is not another life-plan, but a way of looking at life-plans. The karmic residues must keep working themselves out—that is, a man must live some life and follow some style or plan, experiencing appropriate results—but he may remain, as it were, aloof from involvement in the process. In this second-order attitude of nonattachment lies the key to liberation.

In living one's life-plans one necessarily performs actions. Indeed, the primary meaning of the word "*karman*" is action. Actions may be classified in various ways according to Indian traditions. For example, they may be divided into bodily *(kāyika)*, vocal *(vācika)*, and mental *(mānasa)* acts. Then again, one can divide actions into ritual and non-ritual acts. Ritual acts may be divided in turn into those which are enjoined *(vidhi)* and those which are proscribed *(niṣedha)*. Of the enjoined acts there are said to be four kinds: (1) regular daily rites *(nityakarman)*, such as the baths prescribed for the Brāhmaṇa each day; (2) occasional rites *(naimittikakarman)*, observances for particular occasions, for example, to be performed at a certain point in the life-cycle, such as investiture, succoring the ancestors; (3) desired acts *(kāmyakarman)*, acts which are prescribed for one who wishes to obtain a certain result, say, heaven; (4) expiatory actions *(prayaścitta)*, acts performed to purify oneself because one has failed to do certain prescribed acts either in this life or in past lives.[25]

On Śaṅkara's view all these kinds of acts are equally capable of producing karmic residues which in turn will condition the type of

25. Cf. K. S. Iyer, op. cit., *Vedanta Kesari* 1 (1914–15): 278.

birth, length of life, and kind of experience the *jīva* will have in the next life. Some of them, indeed, may produce results in the same lifetime in which they are performed.

Which karmic residues work themselves out sooner? And which ones constitute the *prārabdhakarman* for a given lifetime as opposed to others which are *sañcita*—stored up for later fruition? Śaṅkara seems to think that in general the more intense and proximate residues, whether sinful or meritorious, tend to mature first, but that the general rule here is subject to many exceptions because there are incompatibilities among several residues which have equal claim but only one of which can mature at a given time.

How does maturation actually come about? One performs an act in lifetime A at time t, and this act is supposed to have something to do with the experience the same agent has in lifetime B at time $t+n$. In *Brahmasūtrabhāṣya* 3.2.38–41 Śaṅkara explains the difference between the views of Jaimini and Bādarāyaṇa on this score. The Mīmāṃsā view of Jaimini is that the act produces at time t something called an *apūrva,* which somehow reflects the act and presages the eventual outcome; this *apūrva* constitutes in a literal manner the "karmic residue" and works itself out automatically in lifetime B, having been passed along with the other elements of the subtle body. Bādarāyaṇa's view, as Śaṅkara interprets it, is that (1) it is clear that the act itself cannot produce the experience in lifetime B, since an act is a short-lived event; (2) although there is something like an *apūrva* (as we have seen), it cannot by itself produce the experience which constitutes its maturation, since it is an unintelligent thing, like a piece of wood, and so it cannot pick out the appropriate time and place for the pleasure or pain which constitutes the experience in question. As a result, the correct view—accepted by Śaṅkara as well as by Bādarāyaṇa—must be that God arranges things so that the resulting experiences match the merit or demerit characterizing the agent's past acts.

It will, I trust, be appreciated that bringing in God in this fashion in no way commits Bādarāyaṇa or Śaṅkara to such a strong determinism as to stifle freedom of will on the part of agents. The relation between future act, present experience, and past karma is very loose. It is possible, according to the theory, that A should do x in lifetime A, that the karmic residue should breed a *vāsanā* in lifetime B which leads him to do an act y, which is productive of great sin but immediately accompanied by pleasant experience z. Indeed, not only is that possible but presumably it happens all the time. God does not ordinarily match experience to act on the ground of the merit-value of *that* act, but rather on the ground of the merit-value of *past* acts.

The Yoga and the Advaita accounts are the two most thoroughly worked out of the theories of karma and rebirth in classical Indian philosophy. Other accounts differ in various ways from these two, but are not anywhere nearly so fully developed. As has been seen, the Yoga account is particularly strong and rigorous with respect to the karmic mechanism, while the Advaita account concentrates more fully on the actual moment-to-moment processes involved in death and rebirth. Furthermore, there is an important contrast between the two on the question of an intermediate state between death and the next birth. Yoga denies any such intermediate state, while Advaita goes into some detail about what happens during this time. The Advaita theory, therefore, involves postulation of certain items not present in Yoga, notably the subtle body.

In discussing Yoga I pointed out that the texts make consistent use of the model of rice-farming to explicate the theory. There is, as far as I can tell, no comparably consistent use made of any model in Advaita, although Śaṅkara is very fond of offering similes to explain particular points. At best, one might say that the model is built around the ecological cycle: however, this is not really a model but an integral part of the theory itself. The theory involves the hypothesis, for example, that in the rainwater there are subtle bodies embodying *jīvas* returning from sojourns in the moon, and so on, and this is no metaphor but a literal claim about the rainwater. I am not sure how important it is to push this contrast very far, however.

Although scientifically minded (mostly Western) critics have tended to view the accounts reviewed above as either very poor theories or else as myths or models themselves, it seems to me clear from the care with which the accounts are presented that their authors intended them quite literally as theories. Furthermore, it is not at all clear to me that they are any worse off with respect to the kinds of criticisms of theories sketched earlier than are theories deemed successful in Western science. The major criticism of the karma theory is that it is untestable, but similar criticisms can be made of theories in physics, for example those affected by the exigencies of quantum jumps or those which come under the restrictions suggested by Heisenberg's indeterminacy principle. Defenders of the theories in question respond that these difficulties are technical or technological, that in principle the theories are testable at least within broad limits. But surely the same can be said of the karma theory. It is not in principle untestable, though in practice it is because of technical difficulties. The difficulties arise from our inability to determine with precision which person now alive inherits which past person's karmic residues. If one complains that it is precisely the responsibility of the karma theorist to convince us that rebirth takes place at all, that there *are* any karmic residues, the parallel complaint may be recorded against the physicist who postulates unobservable microparticles. In both cases it is clear enough that what is to be explained is observable; in both cases the explanation involves postulation of unobservables. Technological advances may in time make possible testing of both types of theories—we may build bigger and better microscopes, or find theoretical ways of controlling the effects of quantum jumps or indeterminacy, and likewise we may eventually discover ways of identifying karmic residues and *vāsanās* and so of re-identifying them in another body at a later time.

Although because of their untestability the karma theories of Yoga and Advaita may properly be viewed with an attitude of suspended judgment about their truth or falsity, it seems undeniable that they do represent influential and careful statements which relate to indigenous Indian thinking about life and death. Thus they are surely relevant to attempts to provide an interpretation which captures the essential character of the (or an) Indian conceptual scheme. It is this connection which I wish to explore now.

The most substantial effort at characterizing the Indian conceptual scheme to date is that of the anthropologist McKim Marriott. Marriott interprets Indian thinking as "transactional." His major essay on the topic, he says,

> proceeds from the axiom that the pervasive indigenous assumptions of any society, such as Indian notions of the identity of actor and action and of the divisibility of the person, provide bases on which an anthropologist may construct his models of cultural behavior in that society. It applies that axiom by constructing a monistic, dividualistic general model of Indian transactions, fitting this model first to the most accessible data, which are on the interrelations and ranking of castes. It then proceeds to a wider review of the typical transactional tactics and strategies of groups and persons in India's varied moral, instrumental, and affective systems of action.[26]

26. McKim Marriott, "Hindu Transactions: Diversity without Dualism," in B. Kapferer (ed.), *Transaction and Meaning* (Philadelphia: Institute for the Study of Human Issues, 1976), p. 109. See also the introduction to this volume for a further discussion of Marriott's theory.

Marriott's interpretation features what he terms "substance-code."

> Before one begins to think of Hindu transactions, one . . . needs firmly to understand that those who transact as well as what and how they transact are thought to be inseparably "code-substance" or "substance-code."[27]

Marriott delineates a number of features of substance-code: it may be relatively gross or subtle, that is, more or less capable of transformation, such transformations conceived on analogy with the heating or cooking of foodstuffs. It is "particulate, therefore divisible, highly diverse," it "constantly circulates," and it constitutes "all natural entities," which are inevitably transformed "by combinations and separations of their substance-codes."[28] A characteristic and fundamental aspect of Indian life consists in the exchanging of substance-code, and Marriott goes on to provide an interpretation of Indian thinking about caste that distinguishes castes according to the strategies their members adopt in transacting such stuff.

In Marriott's view the Indian conceptual scheme is "monistic": there is basically one kind of stuff, called "substance-code," and Indian thought is not characterized by separations between law and nature, mind and body, spirit and matter, substance and code, and so on. The scheme is "particularistic": substance-codes are basically particles which are constantly moving from one aggregate (body) to another. These particles of substance-code range in size from gross to exceedingly subtle, and in value from negative (evil) to positive (good or pure). It is noteworthy that not only is what we (Westerners) think of as "material stuff" so constituted, but likewise "perceived words, ideas, appearances, and so forth" are also types of substance-code. Persons, in this scheme, are aggregates of particles of substance-code of various kinds, and their nature is constantly changing, owing to gain and loss of these particles. Persons are thus, in Marriott's terminology, "dividual" rather than "individual," and they are constantly exchanging some of themselves with what is in their environment, including other persons.

The connection of this general account to the interpretation of caste behavior is suggested by the following:

> Transactions, notably nonreceivings and receivings as well as initiations of action, both demonstrate and bring about natural or substantial rankings through what are thought to be the actors' biomoral losses and gains. A pattern of distributions or communications is also implied. Such communicative, distributive events are assumed to be general: one actor and his

27. Ibid., p. 110. 28. Ibid.

action are never for long quite like another actor and his action, and they all change constantly through recombinations of their parts. But actors and their interactions are never to be separated from each other; they change together.[29]

Marriott goes on with great skill to develop an analysis superior in explanatory power to previous accounts of caste behavior. I shall not summarize that analysis here, except to report that the account features a distinction of four extreme tactics which is then used to construct matrices in which an indefinite variety of behavior can be mapped. The four tactics are "optimal," which involves asymmetrical exchange in which I get more than I give; "pessimal," asymmetrical exchange in which I give more than I get; "maximal," symmetrical exchange in which I try to maximize transactions; and "minimal," symmetrical exchange in which I try to minimize transactions.

Marriott in his interpretation not only promises to make sense of the behavior reported in the data from village studies; he also spends a good deal of time developing its connection with and implications for the so-called great tradition of Hinduism. This is accomplished largely through exploring what were termed "moral, instrumental, and affective" aspects of transactions from a broader perspective. Marriott thinks of this triad as corresponding respectively to the *dharma, artha,* and *kāma* triad of values spoken of in Dharmaśāstras and other influential classical texts. He is also able to relate the four strategies to the classical account of life stages, or *āśramas,* identifying the student *(brahmacārin)* with the pessimal tactic, the householder *(gṛhasthin)* with the maximal tactic, forest-dwelling *(vānaprasthya)* with the optimal tactic, and renunciation *(saṃnyāsa)* with the minimal tactic.[30]

The reconstruction of the Indian conceptual scheme which Marriott provides, then, is conceived in broad terms and is clearly intended to provide a rationalization for a great deal of Indian thought and behavior. The question I want to raise now is whether it also rationalizes the karma and rebirth theories I sketched earlier, or whether we must find a different interpretation for them. It will be my reluctant conclusion that the latter is required. However, I shall try to show that getting clear about this may well provide the basis for much more incisive analyses of the history of Indian thought and related Indological matters.

29. Ibid., p. 112. 30. Ibid., p. 134.

The fundamental reason why Marriott's interpretation will not fit the karma theories expounded in Yoga and Advaita is that those theories do not allow for transfer of karma, while the interpretation that one naturally derives from Marriott is that they should. Karmic residues are construed as substance in these theories, and if anything can be said to be "code," these residues certainly can. Yet it seems to me we must infer that *this* kind of substance-code is not transferable.

We hear nothing about transacting or transferring karmic residues in Yoga and Advaita. The point of these theories, the motivation for developing them, derives from the philosophical concern for liberation. Indeed, Indian philosophy consists, practically by definition, of activities motivated by concern for liberation. Liberation is understood as release from bondage to the cycle of rebirth through rendering the karmic process inoperative. We saw that in Yoga this means, roughly, following practices which will result in one's acts not producing seeds of future results. In Advaita one accomplishes the same end by discovering that one doesn't really act at all; that discovery "burns the seeds" of the past, *sañcita* acts, and since one no longer acts, he acquires no new residues. That leaves only the *prārabdhakarman,* which has already begun to bear fruit, and once the liberated man has experienced the results of that karma he will not be reborn, according to Śaṅkara. In either system one's bondage or liberation is something he himself has to earn; he cannot give away his karma to someone else, even to God. The texts sometimes comment on the untenability of any view which implies that one person might experience the results of another person's actions.

Relating to this fundamental point are several corollaries which are likewise significant. For one thing, though on Marriott's account one's self is a function of one's substance-code, in Yoga and Advaita (as well as all other Hindu philosophical systems) one's self is precisely *not* substance-code, not transferable. In Yoga and its sister system Sāṅkhya the self is called *puruṣa* and is carefully distinguished from the stuff *(prakṛti)* which makes up *citta,* which is composed of the three *guṇas,* and so forth. It is the *puruṣa* which is dynamic, intelligent, and so forth. The Sāṅkhya account of bondage is that it is due to the confusion on the part of the *buddhi* stemming from its failure to discriminate the self *(puruṣa)* from the substance-code *(prakṛti,* composed of the *guṇas).* Advaita's view is similar. On Sāṅkhya, Yoga, and Advaita accounts ignorance *(avidyā)* about the relation between the self and what is not the self is the root-cause of bondage. In Advaita the true Self, the *ātman* which is *brahman*, is never really bound, never really acts, but only through ignorance appears to do so. Realization of this fact is all that is required to end the karmic process. In all the Hindu systems it is the appreciation of the distinction between the self and other things which is of the essence—this is even true in Advaita, which, though professedly a monism, celebrates the discovery that there is nothing else in reality except the self, reality being contrasted with the phenomenal world of ignorance, action, and transaction.

Another corollary relates to the nature of the renunciate, or *saṃnyāsin*, whom, as we noted, Marriott tries to explain as representing the attitude of minimal transacting. That something is amiss in this is suggested by the fact that in Marriott's reconstruction of the classical four *varṇas* (Brāhmaṇas, Kṣatriyas, Vaiśyas, and Śūdras) it is the Vaiśyas who are the minimizers ideally. Marriott explicitly notes:

> This stage [of renunciation] requires the tactic of minimal transaction in gross substance that typifies the Vaiśya. As a mendicant, the *saṃnyāsin* can no longer gain by gross and lavish giving. He sinks from the moral perfection of the forest-dweller by accepting alms in low-ranking media from all persons, but uses this tactic to reduce his attachment to any intake. He thus increases his actual independence, his freedom from external influence. To the extent that the living renouncer succeeds in minimizing his transactions, especially through developing inner powers of thought, he achieves a subtler, thus more perfect substance-code.[31]

Marriott himself seems to have doubts about this aspect of his analysis: he feels himself required to offer a few words of explanation about the parallel between *saṃnyāsin* and Vaiśya.

> If he [the *saṃnyāsin*] is sometimes respected much more than his current minimal transactions would justify—more than the comparable Vaiśya among the *varṇas*—this seems due to an assumption of a cumulative effect, explicit in the texts: the renouncer should have achieved the virtues not of a single strategic position alone, but of each previous stage that he has visited in sequence.[32]

Now it is true that the *saṃnyāsin* is expected to withdraw from transaction of worldly materials; he characteristically gives away all his possessions. But most of the rest of the passages just quoted are hard to verify from the texts. The account offered seems to describe someone who wishes to *become* a *saṃnyāsin* and chooses to demonstrate his intent by "reducing his attachment to any intake," which

31. Ibid., p. 132. 32. Ibid.

was preceded ideally by his having achieved the virtues of student, householder, and forest-dweller respectively. But a would-be *saṃnyāsin* and the real thing are quite different, and indeed it seems from the texts that one who tries to become a *saṃnyāsin* merely by attempting to withdraw from transactions will not necessarily succeed, and likewise that one who employs other tactics of transacting, such as the Brāhmaṇa's optimizing, the Kṣatriya's maximizing, or even the Śūdra's pessimizing, may be able to achieve *saṃnyāsa* more easily than by the Vaiśya's minimizing.

What seems to have happened here is that Marriott is describing the external analogue to the behavior of the *saṃnyāsin*, but has missed the inner logic, which is the exact opposite of transactional. In Sanskrit parlance we find philosophers speaking of two approaches to things, the positive approach of action *(pravṛtti)* and the negative approach of withdrawal from action *(nivṛtti)*. The *saṃnyāsin* is one who takes the latter approach. When a *saṃnyāsin* takes his vows he promises to adopt that kind of attitude. He does not promise to stop moving, speaking, eating, sleeping, and performing natural bodily functions. What he promises to do is to stop thinking transactionally, to "withdraw from the world" in the sense of losing interest in worldly transactions. On Śaṅkara's account, indeed, a *saṃnyāsin* is a *jīvanmukta*, a liberated person; in him only *prārabdhakarman* is still impelling his body, but no actions, properly speaking, are taking place at all. He has gotten this way because he has realized that transactions and worldly affairs generally are merely projections of ignorance, that in fact nothing like that really happens. With this realization that he has never acted and cannot do so now or in the future, it is clear that what are from a transactional perspective actions or failures to act are nothing of the sort: they are at best the last vestiges of the ignorance that he has now dispelled, which mean nothing at all to him now.

Marriott's interpretation, then, does not fit well when applied to matters having to do with bondage and liberation. The philosophical tradition is not the "pure" side of the transactional interpretation; it represents an entirely different indigenous interpretation. This is suggested by a moment's consideration of the Yoga model we explored earlier. It must be clear that this model of two streams meeting, eddying, and eventually being straightened out again is relevant if the streams are one person's experience, but makes no sense if the context is interpersonal. If the streams are lost in a vast ocean of other streams, the eddies will dissipate into the sea and be nobody's in particular to experience the results of, and to straighten them out doesn't necessarily bring liberation to anyone.

The textual evidence itself strongly suggests that there were from very early on in India two traditions (at least) which had dissimilar features—the transactional and the philosophical. For example, it is likely that the changing of the *trivarga* to a *caturvarga*—the adding of liberation *(mokṣa)* to the triad of *dharma, artha,* and *kāma*—represented some kind of attempt to synthesize the two traditions. Quite possibly the addition of the *saṃnyāsin* to the other three *āśramas* represents a similar attempt at synthesis. The *Bhagavadgītā,* beloved of Indians through the centuries, may have won its popularity precisely because it is such a sensitive attempt to resolve or transcend the tensions between the two traditions.[33] That the theory of karma and rebirth came late to the Vedic corpus is suggested by a passage in one of the Upaniṣads where Yajñavālkya seems to suggest that karma is a secret doctrine not to be explained to just anyone.[34] The Mīmāṃsā exegetics, whose origins must go back into Vedic times themselves, does not know of liberation and treats *dharma* as the superior way a man should choose to orient his life, a way leading to heaven, which appears to be the ultimate end conceivable for man. All of these things suggest that the karma theory did not arise from the transactional one, or vice versa, but that they represent two distinct traditions requiring reconciliation in any satisfactory world-view.

The fundamental point in all this is that the philosophical systems, in expounding the theory of karma and rebirth, do not allow transfer of karma. Yet such a notion is alluded to in various places early and later in Hindu and Buddhist texts. Other essays in this collection report such passages. The question is, what do they represent?

My notion is that they are the natural outcome of the constant attempt by Indians to reconcile the tensions between the transactional and philosophical interpretations, attempts which began as early as the karma theory was recognized and accepted and which have lasted until the present. Probably the single most important line of reconciliation was religious, better, theistic. If one can give one's

33. I am indebted for this point to James L. Fitzgerald, who pointed out the connection when a draft of the present paper was read to a seminar at the University of Chicago in 1977.
34. *Bṛhadāraṇyaka Upaniṣad* 3.2.13.

karma—one's substance-code—to God and thus be liberated from its fruition, one may escape the necessity of having to choose between *pravṛtti* and *nivṛtti.* That is the line of resolution developed in the *Bhagavadgītā* and rehearsed in medieval literature. It is the basis of the Hinduism of the last half century or more.

Other papers in this volume will explore the ramifications of and alternatives to the devotional synthesis. What seems likely, though, is that the more incisive and rigorous our understanding becomes of the nature of the tensions between the two traditions—transactional versus philosophical, *pravṛtti* versus *nivṛtti, dharma* versus *mokṣa*—the more insightful will be our understanding of the historical development of Indian thought. By developing in detail the transactional interpretation which Marriott has pioneered, by understanding more thoroughly the philosophical theories of karma and rebirth, by thus seeing more clearly just what are the points of contrast and what they may have meant to Indians of various walks of life at various points in history, the historian of ideas should be able to grasp in depth much of what has been, and to a large extent still is, the conceptual scheme governing Indian thought and behavior.

11

Karma, *Apūrva*, and "Natural" Causes: Observations on the Growth and Limits of the Theory of *Saṃsāra*

WILHELM HALBFASS

Introduction

It is one of the familiar paradoxes of the Indian religious and philosophical tradition that the theory and mythology of transmigration and karma, obviously one of the most basic and most commonly accepted premises of this tradition, is not found in its most ancient and venerable documents. "There is no trace of transmigration in the hymns of the Vedas; only in the Brāhmaṇas are there to be found a few traces of the lines of thought from which the doctrine arose."[1] We cannot and need not discuss here in detail the complex and controversial question of its origins and early developments; a few reminders may be sufficient.[2]

The available sources seem to indicate that the doctrine of rebirth, karma, and *saṃsāra* was preceded by the idea of *punarmṛtyu*, "re-death," "dying again": provided there is a continuation of our exis-

1. J. N. Farquhar, *An Outline of the Religious Literature of India* (London, 1920, repr. Delhi, 1967), p. 33.
2. On the prehistory and the earliest developments of the doctrine of karma and *saṃsāra*, cf., e.g., A. M. Boyer, "Étude sur l'origine de la doctrine du saṃsāra," *Journal Asiatique* 9:18 (1901, vol. 2), pp. 451–499.

tence after this earthly death—does it come to an end, too? What is the nature of this end? Is it unavoidable?—the notion of *punarmṛtyu* leads to that of *punarāvṛtti*, "return" into an earthly existence; the idea of cycles of death and birth, of transmigrations through many lives, of the lasting and retributive efficacy of our deeds becomes more and more prevalent in the Upaniṣads, and it wins almost universal acceptance in subsequent literature. However, its formulations in the older Upaniṣads are still tentative and partial; it is still open to basic questions and doubts, not organized and universalized into one complete and comprehensive world-view. There is an element of controversy, novelty, secrecy, illustrated by a famous passage of the *Bṛhadāraṇyaka Upaniṣad* which tells us how Ārtabhāga received this teaching from Yājñavalkya.[3] And not only here, but to a certain degree even in such texts as the *Mahābhārata*, it appears still in competition with other theories and concepts, for example, those of *kāla* and *niyati*.[4]

In contrast with its absence in the Vedic hymns and with its still controversial and somewhat tentative status in the most ancient Upaniṣads, the doctrine of karma and *saṃsāra* seems to be fully established and almost universally accepted as a comprehensive world-view in classical and later Indian thought. Only the Cārvākas and other "materialists" appear as rigorous critics of its basic premises[5]—the belief in a continued existence beyond death, in cycles of death and birth, in the retributive, ethically committed causality of our actions. For the materialists, as far as they are known to us from the reports and references of their opponents,[6] death, that is, the dissolution of our physical body, is the end. There is no inherent

3. *Bṛhadāraṇyaka Upaniṣad* 3.2.13.
4. Cf., e.g., J. Scheftelowitz, *Die Zeit als Schicksalsgottheit in der indischen und iranischen Religion* (Stuttgart, 1929); cf. also H. G. Narahari, "Karma and Reincarnation in the Mahābhārata," *Annals of the Bhandarkar Oriental Research Institute* 27 (1946): 102–113.
5. "Cārvāka" is used with more or less specific reference to a particular school, often interchangeably with the more general term "Lokāyata." The basic teachings usually attributed to the Cārvākas are also mentioned in the Buddhist canon, where they are associated with the heretic teacher Ajita Kesakambalī; cf. *Dīghanikāya* 2.23 ff.
6. Cf. G. Tucci, "Linee di una Storia del materialismo indiano," *Atti della R. Accademia Nazionale dei Lincei* (Roma), Anno 320 (1923; Ser. 5, Mem. 17), pp. 242–310; Anno 323 (1929; Ser. 6, Mem. 2), pp. 667–713. E. Frauwallner, *Geschichte der indischen Philosophie* (2 vols., Salzburg, 1953–1956; Eng. trans. by V. Bedekar: *History of Indian Philosophy*, 2 vols., Delhi, 1973), pp. 295–309 (trans. pp. 215–226); S. N. Dasgupta, *A History of Indian Philosophy*, vol. 3 (Cambridge, 1940, repr. 1961), pp. 512–550.

power of retribution attached to our deeds. There is no goal or value beyond earthly pleasure. "The elements are earth, water, fire, and air. Wealth and pleasure are the sole aims of man. The elements move through original impulse. There is no other world. Emancipation is death."[7] "Dharma and adharma don't exist; there is no result of good and bad actions."[8] "As long as we live, let's have a pleasant life."[9] The awareness of this basically different approach, this materialistic and hedonistic denial of the foundations of the karma theory, is to a certain extent kept alive by the traditions of the Hindus as well as of the Jainas and Buddhists, in particular in doxographic literature. Haribhadra's *Ṣaḍdarśanasamuccaya,* Mādhava's *Sarvadarśanasaṃgraha,* the *Sarvasiddhāntasaṃgraha* falsely attributed to Śaṅkara, and various other works of this type all present the Cārvāka view as one of the traditional world-views and as a fully established *darśana;* other texts deplore the growing influence of materialistic and hedonistic ways of thinking.[10]

However, the doxographic presentation of the Cārvākas is usually highly stereotyped. Their position is far from being a living philosophical challenge to the authors of later times; it appears rather fossilized in its contents and argumentation. There is no "dialogue" between the materialists and their opponents. Their criticism of the ideas of immortality and retribution, which are basic premises of the theory of karma, is preserved by the tradition; but it is not much more than a relic from the distant past. As a matter of fact, what the doxographic accounts present as the explicit target of this criticism is in most instances not the theory of karma and *saṃsāra* as such, but rather the belief in immortality and retribution in general or in its older forms. Vedic sacrifices, which relate to the "other world" *(paraloka),* to a continued existence of our ancestors, and so forth, are ridiculed, particularly the *śrāddha* ceremony: There is no "other world," nobody in it for whom our sacrificial activities might be useful.[11] It is this criticism of doctrines and practices of the Vedas and

7. Kṛṣṇamiśra, *Prabodhacandrodaya,* ed. and trans. S. K. Nambiar (Delhi, 1971), pp. 40–41 (act II).
8. Haribhadra, *Ṣaḍdarśanasamuccaya,* v. 80.
9. Mādhava, *Sarvadarśanasaṃgraha* (Poona, Ānandāśrama Sanskrit Series [ASS], 1906), p. 5: yāvaj jīvet sukhaṃ jīvet. This is also quoted in various other texts.
10. E.g., the *Prabodhacandrodaya.*
11. Cf. *Sarvadarśanasaṃgraha,* pp. 2, 5; *Prabodhacandrodaya,* pp. 40–41 (v. 21). According to the Cārvākas, sacrificial performances are nothing but a means of livelihood for the performing priests.

Brāhmaṇas which is carried through the centuries by the doxographic tradition; "materialistic" arguments which relate, in a specific sense, to later developments of the doctrine of karma and *saṃsāra* are very rare.[12]

Apart from the Cārvākas and certain other "materialists" and "fatalists,"[13] virtually nobody in the classical and later traditions of Indian religion and philosophy has questioned the basic principles of the theory of karma. There seems to be no explicit awareness and hardly any reflection of the initial absence of the theory in the oldest period of thought, although the texts which document this absence are carefully preserved. The doctrine of karma and *saṃsāra* is projected into the most ancient texts, including the Vedic hymns;[14] it is always taken as their indispensable background and presupposition. Concepts and theories which were initially used independently of and without reference to the karma theory, and which, in its earlier phases, appear side by side with it and as its possible rivals, are reinterpreted in the light of the karma theory, are accommodated to or identified with it. *Daiva, niyati,* and so forth, no longer represent an impersonal cosmic "fate," but are constituted by one's own past actions; *kāla,* "time," is no longer seen as an independent ordaining principle, but becomes a function of karma.[15] Karma explains the causes of our present fate[16] by means of what has been regarded as "one underlying fundamental intuition."[17] But although it may be argued that karma is directed toward a single all-comprehensive world-view,[18] we cannot disregard the concrete historical varieties

12. A specific criticism of the transfer of a *jīva* from one body into a new one is found in the Lokāyata chapter of Śāntirakṣita's *Tattvasaṃgraha,* ed. E. Krishnamacharya (Baroda, Gaekwad's Oriental Series [GOS], 1926, with Kamalaśīla's *Pañcikā*), vv. 1861 ff.

13. The most notorious fatalists in the Indian tradition are the Ājīvikas, headed by Makkhali Gosāla; cf. A. L. Basham, *History and Doctrines of the Ājīvikas* (London, 1951).

14. Cf. *Ṛg Veda* 4.27 (Vāmadeva in the womb).

15. Cf. J. Scheftelowitz (see n. 4), pp. 21 ff.

16. H. von Glasenapp, *The Doctrine of Karman in Jaina Philosophy,* trans. G. B. Gifford (Bombay, 1942), p. 30. (German original: Leipzig, 1915; Diss. Bonn). Cf. also Sri Aurobindo, *The Problem of Rebirth* (Pondicherry, 1969), p. 14. In a negative perspective, Christian and other critics have often emphasized the all-inclusive character of karmic causality; e.g., T. E. Slater, *Transmigration and Karma* (London and Madras, 1898), p. 36: "Thus Karma or Adrishta becomes the one and only law of the universe."

17. R. Panikkar, "The Law of Karman and the Historical Dimension of Man," *Philosophy East and West* 22 (1972): 26.

18. See notes 111–114 below, on the universalization of karma.

and deep-rooted tensions and ambiguities which remain with the theory even in its fully developed "classical" versions.[19]

There are symptomatic border problems, "grey zones," questions and ambiguities concerning the scope and limits of karmic causality. It is by no means simply taken for granted that the whole world is just a stage for ethically committed or soteriologically meaningful events, or that natural processes are necessarily governed by or subordinate to retributive causality. The realm of cosmology and even that of biology is not *eo ipso* coextensive with the realm of *saṃsāra,* that is, of retribution and of possible soteriological progression. There are various ways of specifying and delimiting karma and *saṃsāra* and of relating karmic causality to other contexts of causality.

The theory of karma and *saṃsāra* is not, and certainly has not always been, *the* Indian way of thinking. It does not represent one basically unquestioned pattern and premise of thought, and it would be quite inadequate to try to find one master key, one single hermeneutic device which would allow us to understand it all at once and once and for all. As a matter of fact, the understanding of the karma theory has often been hampered by an exclusive and thus misleading search for *one* basic principle or pattern of thought, *one* essential meaning, *one* "underlying intuition," by an exclusive interest in its core and its essence, disregarding its perimeter and its limits, its conflicts and its tensions.[20]

In its concrete totality, the doctrine of karma and *saṃsāra* is a very complex phenomenon, both historically and systematically. It functions at various levels of understanding and interpretation, as an unquestioned presupposition as well as an explicit theory, in popular mythology as well as in philosophical thought. In its various contexts and applications, it has at least three basically different functions and dimensions: karma is (1) a principle of causal explanation (of factual occurrences); (2) a guideline of ethical orientation; (3) the counterpart and stepping-stone of final liberation. These three functions are balanced, reconciled, and integrated in various manners; they do not form a simple and unquestioned unity.

In the following, I shall try to describe and to analyze some of the basic and exemplary problems which arise from the encounter and juxtaposition of karma and other contexts of causation. The perspec-

19. See the introduction to this volume for a survey of these varieties.
20. Attempts to categorize karma definitively "as such" as a law, principle, power, theory, belief, etc., have inevitably been futile.

tive will be historical; I shall focus on cases which reflect historical changes in this area, which illustrate the differences and tensions between older and later levels of thought, and which exemplify the processes of adjustment of pre-karmic and extra-karmic ways of thinking to the theory of karma and *saṃsāra.* I shall first discuss the Mīmāṃsā concept of *apūrva,* specifically its interpretation by Kumārila; then I shall deal with some basic problems of the Vaiśeṣika concept of *adṛṣṭa.* A short "epilogue" will refer to Śaṅkara's retrospective consummation of the theory of karma.

Karma and the Mīmāṃsā Concept of *Apūrva*

The Mīmāṃsā, more properly Pūrvamīmāṃsā or Karmamīmāṃsā, presents itself as the advocate of the Vedic foundations against criticisms, changes, and reinterpretations. Divided into various schools, it carries the exegesis and defense of the Vedic sacrificial *dharma* into the period of the classical philosophical systems, into their framework of methods and presuppositions. It carries with it a set of pre-Upaniṣadic notions and ways of thinking which may appear obsolete in the new atmosphere. On the other hand, it disregards or rejects ideas or doctrines which have become basic premises for the other systems. Final liberation *(mokṣa),* commonly accepted as a leading theme or even as the basic concern of philosophical thought, does not play any role in the older literature of the system; Mīmāṃsā deals with *dharma,* not with *mokṣa.*[21] Familiar ideas like the cyclical destruction of the world *(mahāpralaya),* "yogic perception" *(yogipratyakṣa),* the "Lord" *(īśvara),* and so forth, remain excluded even in its later literature.[22] For our present discussion, the following is of peculiar significance: the Mīmāṃsā carries the heritage of the "prekarmic" past of the Indian tradition into an epoch for which karma and *saṃsāra* have become basic premises. As well as their counterpart, *mokṣa,* the concepts of karma and *saṃsāra* do not play any role in the *Mīmāṃsāsūtra* and remain negligible in its oldest extant commentary, Śabara's *Bhāṣya.* These texts do not deal with "works" or "deeds" in general, and they do not refer to or presuppose any general theory of an ethically committed, retributive causality inherent in

21. The Mīmāṃsā neglect of the idea of final, irreversible liberation is still reflected in the teachings of Dayānanda Sarasvatī, the founder of the Ārya Samāj; he recognizes only temporary "paradises," or states of bliss.
22. We do not here consider later, syncretistic tendencies.

such deeds. They deal only with the specific efficacy of the Vedic sacrificial works.

However, with the transformation of Mīmāṃsā into a comprehensive, fully developed philosophical system, karma and *saṃsāra*, as well as *mokṣa*, become more significant and manifest in its thought and argumentation, not so much as explicit themes, but as tacitly accepted presuppositions or as points of reference and orientation.[23] This is exemplified in a very peculiar and complex manner by the writings of Kumārila, the most successful systematizer of the Mīmāṃsā tradition. Kumārila's basic concern in this connection is to explicate and to justify the specific Mīmāṃsā ideas about the efficacy of the Vedic rituals, which are considered to be the core of *dharma*. He has to do this in the context and atmosphere of ways of thinking for which karma and *saṃsāra* have not only become basic premises but which have also developed sophisticated theoretical models and a keen sense of problems in this area and with reference to causality in general. Kumārila's procedure presents a remarkable example of a highly specialized and idiosyncratic line of thinking which nevertheless illustrates some of the most basic problems of the functioning of karma and of causality in general. The efficiency of the Vedic rituals entails its own special and "trans-karmic" (or rather, "proto-karmic") causality; the encounter of this type of causality with the wider causal context of karma and *saṃsāra* leads to symptomatic questions of correspondence and mutual adjustment. The discussion of these problems centers around the concept of *apūrva*, for Kumārila that particular "potency" which gathers and stores the efficacy of the Vedic rituals and makes it possible for transitory sacrificial performances to have lasting effects in the distant future.

There is no explicit reference to *apūrva* in Jaimini's *Mīmāṃsāsūtra*. We find it only in Śabara's *Bhāṣya* and its commentaries and subcommentaries. We cannot discuss here the background and prehistory of the Mīmāṃsā usage of this concept (in particular its role in Bhartṛhari's *Vākyapadīya*, a text with which Kumārila is well acquainted), or the question whether or to what extent it relates to its

23. Cf. Kumārila, *Mīmāṃsāślokavārttika* with *Nyāyaratnākara* of Pārthasārathimiśra, ed. R. S. Tailanga (Benares, Chowkhamba Sanskrit Series [CCS], 1898–1899; henceforth abbreviated ŚV), Sambandhākṣepaparihāra, vv. 108 ff. "Previous births" *(janmāntara)* are also accepted by Śabara on Jaimini's *Mīmāṃsāsūtra* (MS) 1.3.2, where he speaks about the non-remembrance of what has been experienced in a previous life.

usage in grammatical literature, as characterizing the "prescriptive rules" *(vidhi)*, which teach something "new," not said before. The way in which it is discussed by Śabara and his commentators leaves no doubt that, even within Mīmāṃsā, it is a very controversial concept. It is presented in basically different interpretations and at various levels of thematization and reification. Śabara's brief remarks are commented upon in two widely divergent sections in Prabhākara's *Bṛhatī* and in Kumārila's *Tantravārttika.*[24] Prabhākara's comments are even shorter than Śabara's own remarks; in their brevity, they remain cryptic and deliberately elusive as far as the ontological status of *apūrva* is concerned; for more explicit statements we have to refer to the writings of Prabhākara's follower and commentator Śālikanāthamiśra.[25] Kumārila's commentary, on the other hand, is very elaborate, and it goes far beyond Śabara's own statements; the *apūrvādhikaraṇa* of the *Tantravārttika* is the most important and most comprehensive discussion of the topic in classical Mīmāṃsā.

At the beginning of this section, a lengthy *pūrvapakṣa* is presented, according to which the assumption of *apūrva* is quite unnecessary and unfounded. Kumārila's refutation is a special application of the epistemological device of *arthāpatti,* "circumstantial inference" or "negative implication": Vedic injunctions would be meaningless or misleading if the connection between the sacrificial acts and their future results were not established; *apūrva* is this indispensable connecting link. *Apūrva* is a potency produced by the sacrifice which makes it possible that its fruits be reaped at a later time; it is a bridge between the actions and their promised results. In this context, *apūrva* appears as a specific device to account for a specific exegetic problem. Yet Kumārila himself leaves no doubt that it has wider and

24. The decisive section is on MS 2.1.5. It relates to an objection already discussed by Śabara on MS 1.1.5—that as long as the sacrifice takes place, it does not produce its fruit, and when the fruit occurs, the sacrifice is no longer there. Another relevant section is found in the Vyākaraṇādhikaraṇa of Kumārila's *Tantravārttika* (henceforth TV), in *Mīmāṃsādarśana* (Jaimini, Śabara, Kumārila), ed. K. V. Abhyaṅkara and G. S. Jośī (Part I, on 1.2.1–2.1.49, Poona, ASS, 1927, Poona^2, 1970) on MS 1.3.24–29. On the use of *apūrva* in grammar, cf. Patañjali, *Mahābhāṣya* on Pāṇini 1.4.3. Bhartṛhari's *Vākyapadīya* uses the word in 2.119 (quoted by Kumārila, TV 241 ff); 3.7.34; 3.1.69.

25. Cf. his commentary, *Ṛjuvimalāpañcikā,* on Prabhākara's *Bṛhatī* (Bṛh) (Part 3, ed. S. Subramanya Sastri, Madras, 1962) and his systematic monograph *Prakaraṇapañcikā.* In Prabhākara's interpretation, the word *ārambha* used in Jaimini's *Sūtra* is much more important. On the contrasting interpretations, cf. G. Jha (Jha), *Pūrva-mīmāṃsā in Its Sources* (Benares,^{2} 1964), pp. 226 ff.

more general implications and ramifications: basically, the same problem for which the concept of *apūrva* is supposed to provide a solution exists also in the case of ordinary, "secular" activities such as farming, eating, studying:[26] the results cannot be expected right after the completion of the acts, but only some time in the future. A certain storable "power" *(śakti)* is necessary as a connecting and mediating principle between act and result. This is a rule which applies to all cases of instrumentality and to the causal efficiency of actions in general.[27] The actions as such are sequences of vanishing moments. They can gain totality, coherence, and future efficacy only if, in spite of their temporal disparity and constant disintegration, their causal power is accumulated and integrated and remains present up to the completion of the appropriate results. This is even more obvious in the case of complex activities which combine various actual performances at various times and occasions; a favourite example in the sacrificial field is the new and full moon sacrifice, *darśapūrṇamāsa.*[28]

We cannot and need not enlarge here on the technical details and scholastic developments of the theory of *apūrva.* One of the main issues is how subdivisions in the realm of *apūrva* are supposed to correspond to the complexities of the rituals and the Vedic pronouncements by which they are enjoined, how certain subordinate, auxiliary actions have or produce their own specific units of *apūrva,* and how these contribute to the final and comprehensive *apūrva* of the complete sacrifice, which in turn corresponds to the unity and totality of the result, for example, heaven, *svarga.*[29] Basically, *apūrva* comes in "units" of higher and lower order; incomplete acts do not produce any *apūrva* at all; and the subordinate *apūrvas* of the auxiliary parts of the sacrifice do not accomplish anything independently, if the whole sacrifice is not completed.[30] On the other hand, the distinguishability of the various *apūrvas* or "units" of *apūrva* accounts for the multiplicity and variety of the results.[31]

26. TV, p. 365.
27. TV, p. 366: sarvasādhanānām iṣṭaphalapravṛttāv āntarālikavyāpārāvaśyabhāvitvāt.
28. TV, pp. 364–365.
29. Cf. Jha, pp. 240 ff. The most familiar handbook of the later period is Āpadeva, *Mīmāṃsānyāyaprakāśa (Āpadevī),* ed. and trans. F. Edgerton (New Haven, 1929).
30. On the structural analogy between *apūrva* and the concept of *sphoṭa* as used in speculative grammar, cf., e.g., Maṇḍana, *Sphoṭasiddhi,* v. 10 (trans. M. Biardeau, ed. N. R. Bhatt, Pondicherry, 1958), pp. 29, 83.
31. TV, p. 367: yasya tv apūrvāṇi kriyante, tasya pratikarma pratiyogaṃ ca tadbhedād upapanne phalanānātvavaicitrye.

In trying to locate *apūrva*, to account for its lasting presence after the disappearance of the sacrificial act as a physical act, Kumārila ultimately resorts to the soul of the sacrificer—although *apūrva* remains for him a potency *(yogyatā)* generated by, and in a sense belonging to, not the sacrificing person, but the principal sacrifice *(pradhānakarman)* itself. The causal potencies created and left behind by the sacrificial acts remain present as traces or dispositions *(saṃskāra)* in the person who has performed them; according to Kumārila, there is no other possible substratum in which they could inhere.[32]

Throughout his discussion, Kumārila takes it for granted that in its basic dimensions his discussion of *apūrva* responds to problems which concern acting in general, in particular the relationship of acts to such results that occur only in the distant future. In a sense, it appears as a case study on the causal efficiency of acts in general. Yet the dividing line which separates *apūrva* from other types of causal potency remains clear and irreducible. *Apūrva* is unique insofar as it results exclusively from the execution of Vedic injunctions; and its separation from and juxtaposition with other, "secular" types of acting and of causal potency leads to peculiar though mostly implicit problems of coordination and of possible interference.

There seems to be a basic assumption that if Vedic rites, including all subsidiary acts, are performed in strict accordance with the Vedic rules, they will not fail to produce their proper results. Sacrificial, "*apūrvic*" causality seems to operate within a finite and well-defined set of conditions, a kind of closed system, in which it seems to be secure from outside interference: in bringing about its assigned result, the power of the sacrifice, that is, *apūrva*, will prevail over other possible influences, including those which might arise from the general karmic status of the sacrificer.[33]

The standard example of a sacrificial result in Kumārila's discussion is the attainment of heaven *(svarga)*; in this case it is obviously impossible to challenge empirically the efficacy of the sacrifice, that is, its power to produce the result. However, there are other cases where the actual occurrence of the result is not relegated to a future life or a transempirical state of being. The most notable among these is the

32. TV, p. 369: yadi svasamavetā-eva śaktir iṣyeta karmaṇām, tadvināśe tato na syāt, kartṛsthā tu na naśyati.
33. On the other hand, it is held that if a particular result is assigned to a particular sacrifice by the Veda, only this, and no other results, will be accomplished; cf. ŚV, Citrākṣepaparihāra, v. 16.

citrā ceremony,[34] which is supposed to lead to the attainment of cattle *(paśu)* and thus presents itself as an easy target of criticism and ridicule, already referred to and discussed in Śabara's *Bhāṣya*.[35] Kumārila devotes one chapter of his *Ślokavārttika* to presenting the arguments against the *citrā* ceremony *(Citrākṣepa)* and another one to refuting these arguments *(Citrākṣepaparihāra)*. In his refutation, he does not resort to any extra-*apūrvic* factors, such as the bad karma of the sacrificer, to account for the obvious irregularities in the appearance of the assigned result. It is simply the nature of the *citrā* sacrifice that there is no specified and exactly predictable temporal sequence between its performance and the occurrence of the result. The desired result, the attainment of cattle, may very well occur not in this but in a future life; on the other hand, cases of the acquisition of cattle which are not preceded by empirically ascertainable *citrā* performances should be seen as results and indicators of performances of this ritual in a previous existence, and the invisible causal agency of *apūrva* should be taken as directing the visible sequence of events.[36]

In the case of the "rain-producing" *kārīrī* sacrifice, however, relegation of the result to an indefinite future seems to be much less acceptable, since what is at stake here is the production of rain in the immediate future. In this case, Kumārila cannot avoid referring to adverse *apūrvic* influences, to the counterproductive efficacy of other Vedic actions, which, at least temporarily, prevent the result of the *kārīrī* ceremony (rain) from appearing. Kumārila's commentator Pārthasārathi adds that we are dealing here with acts prohibited by the Veda, the result of which stands in opposition to the production of rain; at any rate, the obstructive influence should itself be rooted in specific acts enjoined or prohibited by the Veda, not in any general karmic circumstances.[37]

Kumārila's discussion of *apūrva* remains for the most part restricted to "optional rites" *(kāmyakarman)* and rites for specific occasions, which are aimed at the fulfillment of specific desires and needs and presented in terms of positive injunctions *(vidhi)*. The question whether there is an *apūrva* corresponding to the violation of

34. The defense of the *citrā* sacrifice is one of the most symptomatic cases of Mīmāṃsā apologetics, and it became one of the starting points of Mīmāṃsā epistemology.
35. On MS 1.1.5.
36. Cf. ŚV, Citrākṣepaparihāra, vv. 11–12.
37. ŚV, v. 26; cf. Pārthasārathi in ŚV, p. 688.

prohibitions *(pratiṣedha)*, that is, resulting from such actions which according to the Veda will lead to punishments or undesirable consequences, is only briefly referred to by Kumārila.[38] Basically, he is ready to accept such a negative counterpart of the positive potential resulting from proper sacrificial enactments: there is an *apūrva* resulting from violating the prohibition to kill a Brahmin, and it will accomplish the punishment of the violator in hell *(naraka)*. Yet it is not surprising that Kumārila does not further enlarge on this point. He has obviously reached a rather delicate border area of his theory of *apūrva* which would make it difficult for him to avoid various conceptual entanglements and to keep his discussion within the limits of a specifically Vedic context of causality and from lapsing into the general field of "karmic," that is, retributive causality: what, for example, is the mechanism governing a violator of a Vedic prohibition who is not entitled to the study of the Veda and thus cannot derive any *apūrva* from it? What happens to a Śūdra killing a Brahmin?

Another point which is not really clarified is the *apūrvic* status of the "permanent rites" *(nityakarman)*, regular performances which are not designed for the attainment of specific results. In the *Ślokavārttika*,[39] Kumārila mentions them casually in connection with the theme of final liberation, which is not really his own concern; their value consists in their contribution to eliminating past demerit and to keeping off such demerit which would result if they were not performed. The systematic implications of these suggestions are not pursued.

Apūrva is a conceptual device designed to keep off or circumvent empirically oriented criticism of the efficacy of sacrifices, to establish a causal nexus not subject to the criterion of direct, observable sequence. Yet, in trying to safeguard metaphysically the *apūrvic* sanctuary of sacrificial causality, Kumārila repeatedly emphasizes that its basic problems are parallel to those of "ordinary," "secular" causality and action: the "empiricists" are not safe on their own ground; even there they cannot get along without some durable and coordinating "potency" *(śakti)*, which must be analogous to that of *apūrva*.[40]

Kumārila commits himself much more deeply to developing a

38. TV, pp. 368–369; cf. Someśvara, *Nyāyasudhā* (on TV), ed. Mukunda Sastri (Benares, CSS, 1909), p. 604.
39. ŚV, Sambandhākṣepaparihāra, vv. 110 ff.; cf. also M. Hiriyanna, *Outlines of Indian Philosophy* (London,[6] 1967), p. 330.
40. See above, p. 274.

comprehensive metaphysical *theory* of *apūrva* than his rival Prabhākara, and he goes much more clearly and resolutely beyond Śabara's statements. In presenting the *ātman* as the "substratum" *(āśraya)* of *apūrva*, which inheres in it as a *saṃskāra*, he opens himself, as I shall discuss later, to the influence of models of thought developed in Nyāya and Vaiśeṣika and presented in Vātsyāyana's *Nyāyabhāṣya* and elsewhere. Prabhākara not only avoids locating *apūrva* as a *saṃskāra* in the sacrificer; he also avoids any comparable theoretical commitment. For him, the basic question raised by the concept of *apūrva* is not that of a causal mechanism functioning toward the accomplishment of a desired result *(phala)*, but that of the unconditional authority and imperative power of the Veda: what is "to be done" *(kārya)* according to the Vedic injunctions has not merely and not even primarily an instrumental value, and it need not be explained or justified in terms of a coherent theory of its causal efficacy; nor does the Veda have to derive any additional motivating power from such a theory.[41] As Rāmānujācārya's *Tantrarahasya* explains in an eloquent summary of the Prābhākara views on this matter, "duty" *(kāryatā)* and "instrumentality" *(sādhanatā)* are essentially different, and the fulfillment of the Vedic injunctions *(vidhi)* is a purpose in itself.[42] Here, the "optional rites" are themselves interpreted in the light of the "permanent rites," which are not motivated by the expectation of a desired result.

As we noted earlier, Kumārila, though emphasizing the parallels between *apūrva* and other "stored effects" of actions, does not integrate his notion of *apūrva* into the general context of the theory of karma, nor does he discuss problems of interaction, overlapping, or conflict between these two types and contexts of causality. There can be no doubt that Kumārila is fully aware of the karma theory and, moreover, that he recognizes it as a generally accepted and basically acceptable presupposition of philosophical thought.[43] Yet his way of dealing with it remains, in spite of a few explicit statements, casual and elusive.

While Kumārila is far from questioning the basic validity of the theory in general, he does reject certain symptomatic applications, specifically in the field of cosmology, and he points out some funda-

41. Cf. Bṛh, pp. 319 ff; Hiriyanna, pp. 328 ff.
42. Rāmānujācārya, *Tantrarahasya* (TR), ed. R. Shama Shastry. 2nd ed. by K. S. Ramaswami Sastri (Baroda, GOS, 1956), pp. 57, 59.
43. Cf. ŚV, Sambandhākṣepaparihāra, vv. 94 ff.

mental difficulties which arise in this context. In accordance with the Mīmāṃsā refusal to accept the doctrine of periodic world destructions and subsequent regenerations, he rejects the attempt of the Vaiśeṣika school to explain these cosmic processes by presenting the retributive power of past deeds, together with the controlling agency of the "Lord," as their efficient cause:[44] karma cannot be the moving force behind the whole world process in the theistic Vaiśeṣika or in the "atheistic" Sāṅkhya context.

On the other hand, it is obvious that the way of thinking which is exemplified by the Vaiśeṣika concept of *adṛṣṭa*—the retributive potency of past deeds stored as a quality of the soul *(ātman)*—has served as a model for the explication of *apūrva* by Kumārila and by subsequent authors. *Apūrva* and *adṛṣṭa* are often found in close relationship. They may be used almost interchangeably, or *adṛṣṭa* may function in specifically sacrificial contexts as a concept which includes *apūrva*.[45] We may also refer here to Śaṅkara who uses *apūrva* in such a way that it relates to karma, that is, what is called *adṛṣṭa* in Vaiśeṣika, in general.[46] However, in this context Kumārila himself uses not the term *adṛṣṭa* but *saṃskāra,* which in Vaiśeṣika is restricted to other functions. A possible source for the use of *saṃskāra* in Kumārila's discussion of *apūrva* would be the "examination of the fruit" *(phalaparīkṣā)* in the *Nyāyabhāṣya*.[47] This section responds directly to the basic concern of the *apūrva* discussion: how can actions, specifically sacrificial performances but also actions in a general sense, produce results which occur a long time after the completion and disappearance of the actions? The *Nyāyabhāṣya* answers that the actions leave certain dispositions *(saṃskāra),* namely, *dharma* and *adharma,* in the soul and that these make it possible that the fruit, such as heaven *(svarga),* is reaped at a much later time. Even in the choice of its examples, the *Nyāyabhāṣya* sometimes comes close to Kumārila's presentation. It is noteworthy that the interpretation of

44. Ibid., vv. 70 ff. Cf. Pārthasārathi, *Śāstradīpikā,* ed. L. S. Dravid (Benares, CSS, 1916), pp. 320 ff, 327 ff. Although the Sāṅkhya is more in the focus of this argumentation, it seems that the idea which is rejected here was not originally at home in Sāṅkhya; see below, n. 71.
45. Cf. Maṇḍana, *Sphoṭasiddhi* (see n. 30), v. 11 (p. 84); Pārthasārathi, *Śāstradīpikā,* p. 14; also the "Glossarial Index" in F. Edgerton's *Āpadevī* (see above, n. 29).
46. On Bādarāyaṇa's *Brahmasūtra* (BS) 3.1.6; 3.2.38 ff.
47. On Gautama's *Nyāyasūtra* (NS) 4.1.44 ff., in *The Nyāyasūtras with Vātsyāyana's Bhāṣya,* ed. G. S. Tailanga (Benares, Vizianagram Sanskrit Series, 1896). On *saṃskāra* cf. also *Yogasūtra* 3.9 ff; 4.8 ff. *(vāsanā).*

apūrva as a *saṃskāra* is introduced only in the *Tantravārttika;* it is not found in Kumārila's *Ślokavārttika,* which precedes the *Tantravārttika* and deals with *apūrva* in a more casual manner.

While Kumārila cautiously adopts for his own context what he finds useful in the Nyāya or Vaiśeṣika discussions, representatives of these systems in turn try to cope with the Mīmāṃsā theory of sacrificial causality or specifically with Kumārila's explication of *apūrva.* Examples may be found in Śrīdhara's *Nyāyakandalī* and in Jayanta's *Nyāyamañjarī;* a pre-Kumārila version of the theory of *apūrva,* basically amounting to the idea of a substrateless and impersonal power which is invoked and manifested by the sacrificial performance, was already discussed and refuted by Uddyotakara in his *Nyāyavārttika* on Sūtra 1.1.7. A major difficulty which Śrīdhara sees in Kumārila's *apūrva* is the way in which it is still supposed to belong to the sacrifice itself and not just to the sacrificer. For him, no real quality or potency can inhere in or belong to an action.[48] A shorter, less specific discussion is found in Vyomaśiva's Vaiśeṣika commentary,[49] in which he still refers primarily to the older view that there is a "dharma without substratum" *(anāśrito dharmaḥ).* In accordance with the main direction of the karma theory, *adṛṣṭa* as understood in Vaiśeṣika is not only stored in, but also belongs to and is caused by, the acting person *(puruṣa):* we are the responsible causes of our actions, of which we have to bear the consequences as traces in our own soul. In Mīmāṃsā, only the *utsarga,* the official act of initiating the sacrifice, has to be done by the sacrificer; the actual performances themselves may be left to "paid agents." Although Kumārila maintains that the soul *(ātman)* of the sacrificer is the subject or the "doer" of the sacrificial action, the question of personal authorship and responsibility is less important here: what produces *apūrva* is rather the impersonal power of the sacrifice itself, which is only unleashed, activated during the actual performance of the sacrifice. *Apūrva* may be stored and coordinated in the soul; yet it is not merely and not even primarily a quality or subordinate ingredient of the soul; it is and remains

48. *Nyāyakandalī* (NK) by Śrīdhara, in *Bhāshya of Praśastapāda,* together with the *Nyāyakandalī,* ed. V. P. Dvivedin (Benares, Vizinagram Sanskrit Series, 1895), pp. 273 ff; Śrīdhara quotes from the *apūrvādhikaraṇa* of TV; he also refers to Maṇḍana, Vidhiviveka.

49. *Vyomavatī* (Vy) by Vyomaśiva, in *Praśastapādabhāṣyam* . . . with comm. *Sūkti* by Jagadīśa Tarkālaṅkāra, *Setu* by Padmanābha Miśra, and *Vyomavatī* by Vyomaśivācarya, ed. Gopinath Kaviraj (Benares, CSS, 1924–1930), pp. 639 ff.; this passage does not indicate any acquaintance with TV.

the effect and the stored power of the sacrifice.[50] Although Kumārila has made various adjustments to the way of thinking exemplified by the Vaiśeṣika doctrine of categories and to the theories of *saṃskāra* and *adṛṣṭa*, the magico-ritualistic world-view of the Brāhmaṇa texts, which presupposes an impersonal mechanism of forces to be invoked by the rituals, remains present as an underlying factor in his discussion of *apūrva*.

In his *Nyāyamañjarī*, Jayanta discusses the problems of sacrificial causality in accordance with the Nyāya tradition of Vedic apologetics. He is far from questioning the specific role and efficacy of Vedic rituals; in a rare case of concrete biographical information in Indian philosophical literature, he mentions an immediately successful *sāṃgrahaṇī* ceremony performed by his own grandfather; yet he does not accept the Mīmāṃsā strategy of defense.[51] Jayanta quotes repeatedly from the sacrificial discussions in Kumārila's *Ślokavārttika;* however, he does not give any indication that he is aware of the *apūrvādhikaraṇa* of the *Tantravārttika*. In his criticism of the Mīmāṃsā theory of sacrificial causality, he constantly refers to a view which, unlike the theory of *Tantravārttika*, does not recognize the storage of sacrificial effects, of *apūrva*, as a *saṃskāra* of the soul. The "saṃskāric" view *(saṃskriyāpakṣa)* is presented as a specialty of the Nyāya school.[52]

Jayanta places the theory of sacrificial efficacy more resolutely in the general framework of the theory of karma and *saṃsāra*. He does not accept the Mīmāṃsā restriction to specific and exclusively sacrificial contexts of causality, but sees a much more open field of possible interaction and interference with other karmic influences. The possibility of "defects in the sacrificer" *(kartṛvaiguṇya)* is seen as much more relevant and as a potential cause of delay for the reaping of the

50. TV, pp. 366 ff.: the *puruṣa* is not the *sādhana* of the results; pp. 369 ff.: the soul is indispensable as an *āśraya*, but remains comparable to a mere carrier (cf. the simile of the camel, p. 370). A curious discussion of the question of personal authorship in sacrificial performances is found in Śaṅkaramiśra's Upaskāra on *Vaiśeṣikasūtra* (VS), 6.1.5.; available in many editions (first Calcutta *Bib. Ind.* 1861); trans. by N. Sinha (Allahabad, Sacred Books of the Hindus, 1911). Śaṅkaramiśra obviously misunderstands the *pūrvapakṣa* in MS 3.7.18 (rejected MS 3.7.19 ff., with Śabara) as Jaimini's own view.

51. Cf. *Nyāyamañjarī* (NM) of Jayanta Bhaṭṭa, ed. S. N. Śukla, 2 vols. (Benares, Kashi Sanskrit Series, 1934–1936), pp. 248 ff.; the *sāṃgrahaṇī* ceremony, which was followed by the acquisition of the village Gauramūlaka, is mentioned on p. 250.

52. NM, p. 255. ŚV, Citrākṣepaparihāra, v. 26, is quoted twice; cf. also ŚV on Sūtra 2, vv. 195 ff.

sacrificial results. Since the varying degrees of immediacy and regularity in the appearance of sacrificial results can be explained by referring to various factors of merit and demerit, it becomes unnecessary for Jayanta to assume, as Kumārila does, any basic distinction in the nature of the sacrifices themselves.[53] Thus, without renouncing the special role of sacrificial causality, Jayanta tries to integrate it into the general framework of karma and *saṃsāra*.

Finally, we may mention here a section in Vācaspati's *Tattvavaiśāradī* on *Yogasūtra* 2.13, where the relationship between the dominant *apūrva* of the *jyotiṣṭoma* (the means of attaining heaven) to the negative potential of the act of killing which is subordinate to this sacrifice is discussed in a way which is characteristically different from Kumārila's way of dealing with this question[54]—that is, integrated into a general theory of merit, demerit, and retributive causality.

Karma, *Adṛṣṭa*, and "Natural" Causality

In the development of the Mīmāṃsā concept of *apūrva*, in particular in Kumārila's presentation, we found the encounter of Vedic exegesis and of the theory of the sacrifice with the general theory of karma, the attempt to defend and to explicate the uniqueness of sacrificial causality and at the same time to cope with more general and basic problems of causality and action. The Vaiśeṣika concept of *adṛṣṭa* ("unseen," "invisible"), on the other hand, exemplifies the encounter of a system of cosmology, philosophy of nature, and categorial analysis with soteriological ideas and the attempt to explicate and to justify within its own conceptual framework the theory of karma and *saṃsāra*.

In classical Vaiśeṣika, as represented by Praśastapāda, *adṛṣṭa* is a comprehensive term for *dharma* and *adharma*, "merit" and "demerit," two of the twenty-four qualities *(guṇa)* enumerated in the list of "categories" *(padārtha)* of the system. However, the basic text of the school, the *Vaiśeṣikasūtra* attributed to Kaṇāda, has only a list of

53. The threefold division of sacrifices into those which bear fruit after death (e.g., *jyotiṣṭoma*), those which bear fruit irregularly (e.g., *citrā*), and those which bear fruit in this life (e.g., *kārīrī*) is Jayanta's direct target of criticism (NM, p. 252). On the *vaiguṇya* theory, which is rejected as a general explanation by Kumārila, TV, p. 368, cf. the *Nyāyabhāṣya* (NBh) (in NS [see n. 47 above]) on 2.1.57 ff. At any rate, the sacrifice is not supposed to perish without any fruition at all (*adattaphala*, NM, p. 254).

54. ŚV on Sūtra 2, vv. 239 ff., 249 ff.

seventeen *guṇas* which does not include *dharma* and *adharma;* and there is no reason to accept the later claim that they were implicitly considered as *guṇas,* that is, as qualities of the soul.[55] The integration of *dharma* and *adharma* into the list of *guṇas* is a symptomatic step in the process of the final systematization of Vaiśeṣika and of its attempted merger of soteriology and "physics."

Although the *Vaiśeṣikasūtra* does not list *adṛṣṭa* among the "qualities," the term and concept is nevertheless quite familiar in this text. Most of the occurrences of *adṛṣṭa* are found in a section[56] which deals with various causes of mostly physical movements (karman in the technical meaning of Vaiśeṣika, i.e., the third "category," *padārtha*): *adṛṣṭa* moves objects in ordeals and magnetic processes; it causes extraordinary movements of earth and water, the circulation of water in trees, the upward flaming of fire, the horizontal blowing of wind or air, the initial movements of atoms and "minds" (*manas,* in the process of forming new organisms). Another section[57] uses *adṛṣṭa* and *dharma/adharma* in a more religious and ethical perspective, referring to the "invisible" results and purposes of ritual and ethical activities, to their "merit" and "demerit." *Dharma* is further mentioned as a causal factor in dreams, in the extraordinary type of cognition known as *ārṣa,* and so forth.[58] It is obvious that *adṛṣṭa* covers at least two different sets of problems and implications, and it may be questioned whether or to what extent there is an original conceptual unity in these two usages. As far as the physical and cosmological usage of *adṛṣṭa* is concerned, its primary function seems to be to account for strange and extraordinary phenomena in nature which would not be explicable otherwise (magnetism, upward movement of fire, etc.), as well as for phenomena which seem to be signs or to contain an element of reward and punishment; according to Candrānanda's *Vṛtti,* the oldest extant commentary on the *Vaiśeṣikasūtra,* such events as earthquakes are indicators of good and evil *(śubhāśubhasūcana)* for the inhabitants of the earth.[59] Although there

55. The Jaina author Jinabhadra (probably sixth century and apparently not familiar with Praśastapāda's work) states explicitly that the number of qualities in Vaiśeṣika is seventeen; cf. *Viśeṣāvaśyakabhāṣya,* ed. D. Malvania (Ahmedabad, 1966–1968), vv. 2972 ff. with commentary.

56. VS 5.1.15; 5.2.2, 4, 8, 14, 19. Cf. also VS 4.2.5: *dharma* causing the movement of atoms toward the formation of bodies.

57. VS 6.2.1 ff.; 6.2.1 is repeated as 10.20 (10.2.8 of the Upaskāra version).

58. VS 9.24, 28 (9.2.9; 28 Upaskāra).

59. Candrānanda on VS 5.2.2; if this were to be expressed in terms of the karma theory, it would obviously imply some kind of "group karma."

is an obvious ethical implication in the second group of cases, the *Sūtra* text does not indicate in any way that the *adṛṣṭa,* which is supposed to cause these events, is to be understood as inhering in souls *(ātman).* This assumption would seem to be even more remote in cases like the upward flaming of fire, for which no ethical, retributive, or psychological implications are suggested.[60] In cases like this, *adṛṣṭa* appears simply side by side with other causes of physical motions like "gravity" *(gurutva)* or "fluidity" *(dravatva),* which inhere in those material substances which they affect; like *adṛṣṭa,* "gravity" and "fluidity" are explicitly classified as "qualities" only in the later list of twenty-four *guṇas.* The most momentous function of *adṛṣṭa* seems to be referred to in the statement that it causes the initial movements of atoms and "minds"—the function of a "prime mover" when after a period of *mahāpralaya,* during which the whole world process has come to a complete rest, the regeneration of our universe starts again. On the other side and in an obviously different perspective, *adṛṣṭa* or *dharma/adharma* is introduced to ensure the retributive efficacy of actions which have a ritual or moral significance. In this sense, it shows a close analogy with *apūrva;* Śaṅkaramiśra, the author of the *Upaskāra* on the *Vaiśeṣikasūtra,* repeatedly uses the word *apūrva* in this context.[61]

The *Vaiśeṣikasūtra* does not state that the unseen physical power behind such phenomena as the upward flaming of fire and the retributive power of past deeds stored in the soul are identical, nor does it state that they are different. We do not know when the identity, which is taken for granted by Praśastapāda and later Vaiśeṣika, was first established in an explicit and definite manner. Already the *Nyāyabhāṣya* of Vātsyāyana has a more unified concept of *dharma/adharma* as being inherent in the soul; and the connection between the retributive efficacy of deeds, stored as "dispositions" *(saṃskāra)* of the soul, and certain physical processes has been made more explicit.[62] However, it does not consider the specific kinetic functions of *adṛṣṭa* mentioned in the *Vaiśeṣikasūtra;* and it does not use the term *adṛṣṭa* as a synonym of *dharma/adharma.* Instead the term is used with reference to a theory which is rejected by the *Nyāyabhāṣya* and

60. Candrānanda's and Śaṅkaramiśra's attempts in this direction are not very convincing; Śaṅkaramiśra on 5.2.13 (14 Candrānanda) suggests that only first movements of flaming, etc., at the beginning of a new world period are meant.
61. Cf. also his comments on VS 6.1.5, with lengthy remarks on Mīmāṃsā.
62. NBh on NS 3.2.63 ff.; cf. also 4.1.44 ff.

which maintains that there is an "invisible force" *(adṛṣṭa)* in the material atoms *(aṇu)*, also in the "mind" *(manas)*, which gives them the kinetic impulse needed for the formation of bodies, and so forth; in this view, *adṛṣṭa* seems to function primarily as a principle of physicalistic, naturalistic explanation, and its ethical and soteriological implications remain at least very obscure.[63] The theory that *adṛṣṭa* resides in the atoms and not in the *ātman* is also referred to and rejected by Praśastapāda's commentator Vyomaśiva.[64]

In the tradition of the Vaiśeṣika school, its final systematizer, Praśastapāda, leaves no doubt concerning the unity of *adṛṣṭa* in its various physical, ethical, and religious functions. He universalizes its application as an indispensable factor functioning in the processes of life and consciousness: *dharma* and *adharma* are supporting causes and conditions of life in general *(jīvanasahakārin)*, of its basic condition of breathing as well as of mental processes like desire and cognition.[65] In particular, Praśastapāda emphasizes the role of *adṛṣṭa* in the cosmic processes of the periodic destruction and regeneration of the whole universe.[66] There is no doubt that *adṛṣṭa (dharma/adharma)* has now become all-pervasive and that it functions as the key factor in re-interpreting the "natural" world as *saṃsāra*, that is, as a mechanism of reward and punishment, or karmic retribution. Yet, even the great systematizer Praśastapāda has not been able to harmonize completely or cover the ambiguities and dichotomies inherited from the *Vaiśeṣikasūtra*. There remains a tendency to separate the contexts of physical or cosmological explanation and of ethics,

63. NBh on 3.2.73; the word *adṛṣṭa* is introduced at NS 3.2.72. There is no good reason to accept the suggestion of Vācaspati's *Nyāyavārttikatātparyaṭīkā* that this is a Jaina view. It may rather be a view which at a certain time had its proponents within Vaiśeṣika or Nyāya itself. The question of the causality of atomic motion is highly ambiguous in Jaina thought; although *dharma* and *adharma* function as media of motion and rest and may even be called their causes (Kundakunda, *Pañcāstikāyasāra*, v. 102: *gamaṇaṭṭhidikāraṇāṇi*), they are not supposed to be efficient (ibid., v. 95), but only conditional and auxiliary causes (*upagraha;* Umāsvāti, *Tattvārthasūtra* 5.17), and a certain spontaneous causality is left to the movable things themselves (cf. Kundakunda, v. 96).

64. Vy, pp. 638 ff.

65. *Praśastapādabhāṣya* (PB), in NK (see n. 48 above), pp. 308 ff. On the role of *adṛṣṭa/dharma* in the process of sense perception, cf. p. 186; in dreams, p. 184; *adharma* as a factor in the occurrence of doubt, p. 175; also generally in the explanation of phenomena like desire, aversion, pleasure, etc. VS 4.1.9, which deals with the conditions of perception and corresponds to PB, p. 186, does not mention *dharma*.

66. PB, pp. 48 ff. We cannot discuss here the question of the influence of the "Great Lord" (Maheśvara) in this process.

soteriology, and Vedic apologetics. The physical functions of *adṛṣṭa,* in particular the specific examples given by the *Sūtra,* are left out of consideration in the section on *dharma* and *adharma* within the systematic survey of the qualities; this section focuses, quite in accordance with the more popular connotations of *dharma,* on socio-religious duties and their karmic implications. Instead, it is a section in the chapter on "motion" (i.e., *karman* in its technical Vaiśeṣika meaning) which presents *adṛṣṭa* in its more specifically physical and biological role and which refers to the peculiar kinetic functions attributed to it in the *Sūtra.*[67]

Praśastapāda says that, apart from its other functions, *adṛṣṭa* has to account for such phenomena in the merely material, physical realm of the elements *(mahābhūta)* which do not have an otherwise ascertainable cause *(anupalabhyamānakāraṇa)* and which can be beneficial or harmful *(upakārāpakārasamartha)* to us.[68] This twofold condition illustrates a basic ambiguity in the meaning of *adṛṣṭa:* on the one hand, it serves as a kind of gap-filler in the realm of physical causality, providing a principle of explanation where other, "visible" and therefore preferable causes fail. On the other hand, it serves as a device to interpret the world process as *saṃsāra,* in terms of reward and punishment, of what is beneficial and harmful to us, thus not simply supplementing, but potentially replacing the whole context of "natural" physical causality; as we have seen, Praśastapāda tends to universalize the presence and influence of dharmic, retributive causality, also trying to integrate the "Lord," *īśvara.*

E. Frauwallner, to whom we owe the most penetrating and reliable analysis of the Vaiśeṣika system, has suggested that in its origins the Vaiśeṣika was a "pure" philosophy of nature, theoretical in its orientation, interested in the explanation of natural phenomena, not in soteriological schemes and methods of liberation from *saṃsāra.*[69] Whatever the original status of the Vaiśeṣika may have been—whether we accept Frauwallner's stimulating, yet inevitably speculative thesis or not—it remains undeniable that the soteriological orientation is not genuinely at home in Vaiśeṣika. This was clearly felt even within the Indian tradition; the dharmic commitment and the soteriological relevance of the Vaiśeṣika doctrine of categories were

67. PB, pp. 308 ff.
68. Ibid. There is a rule in Vaiśeṣika that "invisible" causes should not be invoked as long as "visible" causes are available.
69. Cf. Frauwallner 2, p. 90 (trans., p. 60).

repeatedly questioned. Praśastapāda's procedure, as well as that of the final redactors of the *Vaiśeṣikasūtra,* may in part be understood as a response to such charges, found in the *Nyāyabhāṣya* and other texts.[70] *Adṛṣṭa,* which may primarily have been a gap-filler in the causal explication of the universe, subsequently offered itself as a channel for a much more decidedly dharmic and soteriological reinterpretation of the Vaiśeṣika theory of the universe. At the same time, this theory of the universe and of the categories of reality was presented as a framework and basis for explicating in a theoretically coherent manner the status and functions of retributive causality, to account for karma in terms of a comprehensive metaphysics and categoriology. Insofar as *adṛṣṭa* is presented as a potentially all-pervasive factor in the universe, in particular as the moving force of its periodic regenerations, a karmic framework has been provided for the functioning of "natural" causality; on the other hand, *dharma/adharma,* or what is called karma in most of the other systems, has found its theoretical accommodation in a context which remains primarily that of a philosophy of nature and a doctrine of categories. This is a balance which is at the same time a compromise, and it has obviously contributed to the scholastic petrification of the Vaiśeṣika. As we have noticed earlier, this use of karma/*adṛṣṭa* as a principle of cosmological explanation was rejected by the Mīmāṃsā; it found, however, a more positive response in a school which has a much more genuinely soteriological orientation than the Vaiśeṣika: the Sāṅkhya.[71]

We need not discuss here in detail the more technical problems of how *adṛṣṭa* is supposed to function in the contexts of physical and mental causation. Our main concern is its status in the general field of causality, the question of how it relates to or interacts with other causal factors. The most common suggestion in Praśastapāda's work is that of a causal aggregate in which *adṛṣṭa* functions as one among other causes *(kāraṇa):* its absence or presence, just like the absence or presence of other factors, may decide whether an effect, be it an act of perception or a physiological process, takes place or not; or it may add to or subtract from what other causes may bring about.[72] How-

70. NBh on 1.1.9 contrasts the Vaiśeṣika categories, as mere neutral objects of knowledge, with the soteriologically relevant Nyāya category of *prameya.* In the presentation of its soteriological claim, NBh shows the influence of Buddhist thought.
71. Cf. Frauwallner 1, pp. 404 ff (trans., pp. 318 ff.).
72. See above, p. 285.

ever, sometimes it seems to represent not so much one causal factor among others, but rather another level of causality, or something like a medium and condition of causal efficacy, which may unleash, neutralize, or counteract causal influences in the mental as well as in the physical sphere. In this sense, its function would come closer to that of the "category" of "potency," *śakti,* which is included in the categorial systems of the Prābhākara school and of Candramati's *Daśapadārthī,* but is rejected in classical Vaiśeṣika.[73]

An important condition of the understanding of *adṛṣṭa* is that its substrata, the souls, are supposed to be omnipresent *(vibhu).* Its efficacy is thus not at all restricted to that particular body which is attached to its underlying *ātman* as an instrument of *saṃsāric* experience. Since any *ātman* is omnipresent, its *adṛṣṭa* can function anywhere and affect all those entities which may become relevant for it in terms of karmic reward and punishment. An illustration of this is given in Uddyotakara's *Nyāyavārttika:* if somebody waters a tree, the success of his action, that is, the process of fertilization and growth, may be influenced by the karma of the person who at a later time will eat the fruits of the tree; it becomes the function of the tree, directed by the karmic potential of a soul which may or may not be that of the person who watered the tree, to provide an opportunity of retributive experience, of enjoyment.[74]

Although any soul's *adṛṣṭa* may potentially function anywhere, it has, of course, a specific jurisdiction over the particular body which serves as a vehicle of retribution for that soul which is the *adṛṣṭa's* "own" underlying substratum. The body, together with the sense-organs and the "mind" *(manas),* provides the *ātman* with its karmic rewards and punishments, and the *adṛṣṭa* regulates their appropriate distribution.

The necessity of merit and demerit for the explanation of organic processes and structures is already a theme in the *Nyāyasūtra,* and the *Nyāyabhāṣya* and its subcommentaries give us elaborate and formalized "proofs" for this necessity: there have to be vehicles, in-

73. Cf. Frauwallner 2, p. 154 (trans., p. 109). *Śakti* is rejected by Vy, p. 194, and NK, pp. 144 ff.

74. *Nyāyavārttikam* (NV) of Udyotakara Miśra, ed. V. Dvivedin (Calcutta, Bibliotheca Indica, 1887–1914), on 4.1.47: mūlasekādikarmakṛtam bhoktuḥ karmāpekṣaṃ pṛthivyādidhātum anugṛhṇāti. NV on 3.2.67 calls the functions of karma with reference to the body "restrictive" *(niyāmaka).*

struments of retributive experience; and the complex instrumental character of organic bodies *(śarīra)* would remain unexplained if they were not seen as fulfilling this very function and as being shaped by the retributive causality of *dharma* and *adharma*.[75] Karmic causality may affect material, physical processes in general; in the realm of life, however, it appears as the most basic and decisive factor, as that which distinguishes living organisms from lifeless matter. The implication seems to be that there is no life without karma, that life and *saṃsāra*, the realms of biology and of soteriology, are exactly coextensive.

A diametrically opposed view is presented and rejected in the *Nyāyabhāṣya*—the theory that there is no basic distinction between mere matter and living organisms, that all forms of life are just spontaneous configurations of matter, that there is no need to postulate karma as the formative principle of organisms.[76] This radical materialistic denial of karmic causality remains, as we have noted earlier, far from being a living challenge to the general acceptance of the karma theory in classical Indian thought, and its rejection is common to the Hindu, Buddhist, and Jaina schools. Yet there are certain questions and ambiguities concerning the demarcation line between the realms of life and lifeless matter; and it is not always simply taken for granted that life and *saṃsāra* are exactly coextensive. The special case of Jainism, which includes even minerals in its horizon of living, saṃsāric existence, need not concern us here. Even within Hinduism, there has been some room for questions and disagreements and for historical changes in this matter.

The standard idea of *saṃsāra*, of transmigratory existence and of retributive causality, is that it comprises the whole sphere "from Brahmā to the tufts of grass" *(brahmādistambaparyanta)*. Yet, the inclusion of the plants or vegetables has not always been accepted in all the philosophical schools of Hinduism. In Praśastapāda's systematization of Vaiśeṣika, vegetables are not classified as living organisms *(śarīra)*, that is, as receptacles of experience, but as mere "objects" *(viṣaya)*; just like stones, they are nothing but special configurations of the element earth.[77] The *Vaiśeṣikasūtra* itself remains

75. Nbh on 3.2.63 ff. The definition of *śarīra* is given in 1.1.11.
76. Ibid. This *pūrvapakṣa* is already referred to in NS 3.2.63: Bhūtebhyo mūrtyupādāvat tadupādānam.
77. PB, p. 27.

ambiguous and poses, moreover, peculiar philological problems in this connection.[78] In later Vaiśeṣika texts, the whole issue is tacitly dropped or its treatment is adjusted to the more comprehensive view of *saṃsāra,* which includes the vegetables. An explicit discussion of the problem is found in Udayana's *Kiraṇāvalī:* although trees are seats of experience, although they have all the basic attributes of living, experiencing beings, Praśastapāda chose not to include them in the class of *śarīra,* because their internal awareness is extremely faint *(atimandāntaḥsaṃjñatā)* and because they are mostly mere subsidiaries to other living beings.[79] Udayana still argues for what his successors usually take for granted. Certain border-line problems are also found in the case of the lowest animals, such as worms and insects, creatures which are called *kṣudrajantu, svedaja,* and so forth in the Indian tradition. The most familiar type of biological or zoological classification in India follows the criterion of the origin, the kind of "birth" of the various creatures. In two different versions, this scheme is already found in two of the oldest Upaniṣads, the *Chāndogya* and the *Aitareya.* According to the *Chāndogya Upaniṣad,*[80] all living beings are either "born of an egg" *(aṇḍaja),* "born alive" *(jīvaja),* or "sprout-born" (*udbhijja,* born from something that bursts, splits). Instead of this threefold scheme, the *Aitareya Upaniṣad*[81] has a fourfold one: "egg-born," "sprout-born" *(udbhinnaja),* "born with an embryonic skin" (*jāruja,* later usually *jarāyuja* and corresponding to *jīvaja*), and finally "sweat-born" (*svedaja,* in a more general sense: born from warmth and moisture). The two Upaniṣads neither explain nor exemplify exactly what they mean by these classifications. However, we find these schemes, predominantly the fourfold one, with certain variations in many later texts of differ-

78. The Sūtra which divides the products of earth into organisms, sense organs, and objects is found only in the Upaskāra version (4.2.1).

79. *Praśastapādabhāṣyam* with the comm. *Kiraṇāvalī* of Udayanācārya, ed. J. N. Jetly (Baroda, GOS, 1971), p. 39 Cf. pp. 39–40: vṛkṣādayaḥ pratiniyatabhoktrādhiṣṭhitāḥ, jīvanamaraṇasvapnaprajāgaraṇarogabheṣajaprayogabījasajātīyānubandhānukūlopagamapratikūlāpagamādibhyaḥ prasiddhaśarīravat: trees, etc., are inhabited by particular experiencers, since they show all the characteristics such as living, dying, sleep, waking, disease, curability, seeds, attachment to their own species, seeking what is favorable, avoiding what is unfavorable, which we find also in the case of what is generally accepted as *śarīra.* In a different context, the question is referred to by Vyomaśiva (Vy, p. 404). Cf. also Śaṅkaramiśra, Upaskāra on VS 4.2.5. Śrīdhara in NK, p. 83, denies souls in trees, etc.

80. *Chāndogya Upaniṣad* 6.3.1.

81. *Aitareya Upaniṣad* 3.3.

ent branches of Indian learning, in philosophy, in medicine, in *dharma* literature.[82] We need not discuss here the implications of the *aṇḍaja* (birds, fish, etc.) and *jīvaja* groups (viviparous, mostly mammals), nor even of the more problematic group of the *udbhijja* creatures (which are not always simply understood as plants or vegetables, but occasionally also as animals coming from a larva, etc.). The group which is of primary interest in the present context is that of the "sweat-born" creatures.

The class of "sweat-born" or "heat-born" creatures often coincides more or less with what in other contexts is called *kṣudrajantu*, "little, insignificant creatures." The expression *kṣudrāṇi bhūtāni* is already found in the *Chāndogya Upaniṣad*,[83] where we are told that these creatures live according to the rule "be born and die" and do not enter the "way of the fathers," which is a cycle leading back to an earthly existence, nor the "way of the gods," which is without return to earth. It has been suggested that this means that their existence is a merely ephemeral one and that they do not take any part in the processes of transmigration and retribution.[84] Such an interpretation would go beyond the ambiguous statement of the Upaniṣad, and it would not have the support of the parallel version of this text in the *Bṛhadāraṇyaka Upaniṣad*.[85] It seems that we are dealing here not with completely extra-transmigrational forms of life, but rather with a form of soteriological failure which would relegate these creatures to an endless repetition of their state of being, not giving them any opportunity for soteriological ascent.

At any rate, the biological and soteriological status of the creatures known as *kṣudrajantu* and *svedaja* seems to be rather precarious in several texts, and more than once the possibility of a spontaneous, non-karmic origin of these forms of life suggests itself. Worms, maggots, lice, and similar creatures are supposed to originate in various

82. Cf., for example, Manu 1.43 ff. A classification of four types of birth *(yoni)* is also found in Buddhism: *aṇḍaja, jalābuja, saṃsedaja, opapātika (Majjhimanikāya* 12, ed. V. Trenckner [London, 1888], vol. 1, p. 73). *Opapātika* refers to the "sudden" origination of gods, and so forth. On Jaina classifications, cf. Frauwallner 2, pp. 266 ff. (trans., pp. 193 ff.). Still helpful as a general survey, but to be used with caution: B. N. Seal, *The Positive Sciences of the Ancient Hindus* (London, 1915); on plant life: G. P. Majumdar, *Vanaspati* (Calcutta, 1927).

83. *Chāndogya Upaniṣad* 5.10.8. Cf. Pāṇini 2.4.8: *kṣudrajantavaḥ;* Patañjali has various suggestions on the exact meaning of the term. Cf. Vy, p. 229: *kṣudrajantavo yūkādayaḥ*.

84. Cf. H. von Glasenapp, *Indische Geisteswelt* (Baden-Baden s.a.), vol. 2, p. 209.

85. *Bṛhadāraṇyaka Upaniṣad* 6.2.1–16; esp. 6.2.16.

disintegrating materials, in rotting food, in corpses, in pus, in excrement, and from other kinds of organic warmth and moisture;[86] we even have the curious case of the small worms *(kṛmi),* which according to some writers on the science of erotics *(kāmaśāstra)* are produced from blood *(raktaja, rudhirodbhava)* in the female sex organs and cause there the "itching" *(kaṇḍūti)* of sexual passion.[87] None of these texts gives us a theory of the spontaneous, non-karmic origination of certain forms of life; on the other hand, there is no indication of an agency of "souls" and their karma in these processes.

It is not surprising that the appearance of maggots in rotting materials was used by the Cārvākas and other materialists in their argumentation for a non-karmic, spontaneous origination of life from mere matter. In the canonical writings of the Buddhists as well as of the Jainas, we hear about a materialistic king by the name of Pāyāsi (Prakrit form: Paesi), who conducts various "experiments" to demonstrate the non-existence of the soul and the soulless origination of living creatures.[88] For example, he has a person executed whose corpse is put in an iron pot which is then sealed up. When the pot is opened again some time later, the corpse is full of maggots. For Pāyāsi/Paesi, this means: no souls could get into the pot, since it had been sealed; so there must have been soulless, spontaneous origination of life. And if this is possible in the case of worms, why not also in the case of humans?

The materialistic reference to the allegedly spontaneous origination of life in rotting materials is still mentioned in the *pūrvapakṣa* sections of various later texts such as Jayanta's *Nyāyamañjarī;* in Jayanta's own view, there can be no doubt that it is the presence of souls *(ātman)* and the efficacy of their karma which transforms parts of rotting substances, such as rotting sourmilk, into the bodies of worms, thus creating peculiar vehicles of karmic retribution.[89] The Jaina commentator Guṇaratna even turns the appearance of worms in corpses into a direct argument *against* materialism.[90] In such classical

86. Cf., e.g., Patañjali, *Mahābhāṣya* on Pāṇini 1.4.30: a casual reference to the origination of "dung-beetles" *(vṛścika)* from cow-dung. On the same "phenomenon," cf. Śaṅkara (also Bhāskara) on BS 2.1.6. Other examples may be found in medical literature.

87. R. Schmidt, *Beiträge zur indischen Erotik* (Berlin,[2] 1911), p. 257 (quoting from the *Ratirahasya* and the *Anaṅgaraṅga*).

88. Cf. Frauwallner 2, pp. 297 ff. (trans., pp. 216 ff.).

89. NM 2, p. 13: *śukrasoṇitādivad dadhyavayavān vikṛtān upādāsyate. . . .*

90. *Tarkarahasyadīpikā* on Haribhadra's *Ṣaḍdarśanasamuccaya,* v. 49, ed. M. K. Jain (Calcutta, Jñānapīṭha Mūrtidevī Jaina Granthamālā, 1969), pp. 224 ff. Cf. *Ācārāṅgasūtra* 1.1.6.

and later sources, there is, in fact, an increasingly systematic and rigid superimposition of religious and soteriological schemes and perspectives upon biological, zoological, cosmological observations, and a gradual evaporation of the spirit of observation, of the empirical openness for natural phenomena. The old schemes of biological and zoological classification are not further developed or empirically supplemented.[91] The interest in such classifications is more and more overshadowed by the interest in the ways and levels of *saṃsāra;* the old schemes of classification are reduced to, or replaced by, soteriological hierarchies.

We have discussed earlier how karmic causality, specifically in Vaiśeṣika, interacts with other causes, how it influences or controls physical and other natural processes, how its sovereignty is extended and stabilized in the development of Vaiśeṣika thought. To conclude this discussion, it may be an appropriate experiment to reverse our perspective and to ask whether or to what degree the efficacy of physical and other "natural," non-karmic causes may extend into what should be the domain of karmic retribution. Since retribution takes place in the realm of awareness, of the experience *(bhoga)* of pleasure or pain, we may formulate this question as follows: is there anything in the realm of experience, of pleasant and unpleasant states of awareness, which is controlled not by karma but by the intrusion of non-karmic factors? Is there, for example, the possibility of "undeserved" suffering caused by "merely" natural causes? In his presentation of "pleasure" *(sukha)* and "pain" *(duḥkha)* as two "qualities" *(guṇa)* of the soul, Praśastapāda states that they arise "in relation to dharma" *(dharmādyapekṣa);*[92] apart from this, not much explicit attention is paid to the problem in Vaiśeṣika literature. There is certainly nothing that might be compared to the very pronounced and explicit way in which some Buddhist texts, specifically of the Theravāda tradition, address this question.

In the *Saṃyuttanikāya,* Moliyasīvaka asks whether it is true that all pleasant, painful, and neutral feelings are caused by past deeds *(pubbekatahetu).* The Buddha responds by enumerating eight different causes of diseases; the "ripening of karma" *(kammavipāka)* is only one of these.[93] The conclusion is that the view referred to by

91. We are not considering certain developments in medical literature. On the Vaiśeṣika way of including the biological materials in mythical soteriological schemes, cf. Frauwallner 2, pp. 41 ff. (trans., p. 23).
92. PB, pp. 259–260. In the case of *duḥkha* (p. 260), reference is made to *adharma.*
93. *Saṃyuttanikāya* 26.21, ed. L. Feer, vol. 4 (London, 1894), pp. 230 ff.

Moliyasīvaka is not tenable. The *Milindapañha* quotes this passage from the *Saṃyuttanikāya* and relates it to the question of whether there can still be painful experiences for the Tathāgata whose stock of karma has been eliminated.[94] The answer is that there can be such experiences, caused by physical events like the falling of a stone, and that he is still subject to such diseases which are not due to karmic factors. Remarkable debates on the scope and limits of karmic causality are also found in the *Kathāvatthu;* they illustrate the controversial status of this theme as well as the basic contrast which was seen between the "private" and experiential processes of the "ripening of karma" and such "public" and cosmic processes as the formation of the earth.[95]

There has been a tendency to disregard or reinterpret the view expressed in the *Milindapañha,* and it has certainly not become the prevailing view in Theravāda orthodoxy.[96] This view may, in fact, show a certain lack of universality and a rigidity in the application of the karma principle; yet in the way in which it exposes even the Buddha to "ordinary," "natural," "neutral" causality, it opens a dimension of freedom, of indifference towards karma and its peculiarly "selfish" and "private" causality. At the very least, it illustrates a problem which was usually disregarded or simply precluded by definition.

Epilogue: The "Way of the Fathers" and the Theory of Karma in Śaṅkara's Advaita Vedānta

Both the *Chāndogya Upaniṣad* and the *Bṛhadāraṇyaka Upaniṣad* contain, with certain variations, a chapter which P. Deussen has called "the most important and most explicit text on the theory of transmigration which we have from the Vedic period."[97] The text first presents the "five-fire doctrine" *(pañcāgnividyā),* which is supposed to answer, among other questions, the question why the "other world,"

94. *The Milindapañha,* ed. V. Trenckner (London, 1880; repr. 1962), pp. 134 ff.
95. *Kathāvatthu* 7.7–10, specifically 7.7: paṭhavī kammavipāko ti? 7.10 establishes a sharp distinction between *kamma* and *kammavipāka.*
96. Cf. the statements of leading Sinhalese authorities referred to by Nyānatiloka, *Die Fragen des Milindo,* vol. 1 (Leipzig, 1919), pp. 216 ff. (n. 121).
97. *Sechzig Upanishads des Veda* (Leipzig,[3] 1921, repr. 1963), p. 137. The two sections are found in *Chāndogya Upaniṣad* 5.3–10 and *Bṛhadāraṇyaka Upaniṣad* 6.2 (=*Śatapatha Brāhmaṇa* 14.9.1).

in spite of so many creatures dying and passing into it, does not become full, that is, how and why there is return from that world into this earthly sphere. In the sacrificial language of the Brāhmaṇas, we learn that man, in his return, has to pass through five stages or transformations which are all considered to be sacrificial fires, or as taking place within the context of sacrificial fires: man (i.e., deceased man) is "sacrificed" by the gods in "that world" as *śraddhā*, "faith"; then he becomes *soma*, rain, food, semen, from which he will again arise as a human being. Subsequently, this doctrine is combined with the distinction between the "way of the fathers" *(pitṛyāna)* and the "way of the gods" *(devayāna)*. The "way of the gods" is the way of those who, through their knowledge and faith, reach the "world of brahman," beyond the sun, and liberation from earthly existence. The "way of the fathers," on the other hand, is the way of those who have done pious and sacrificial works and have enjoyed the reward resulting from these deeds in heaven, but have ultimately been unable to avoid the return into an earthly existence. A "third abode" *(tṛtīyaṃ sthānam)* is also referred to; it means existence as low animals and is for those who do not reach the "way of the gods" or the "way of the fathers." According to the *Kauṣītaki Upaniṣad*, all those who die proceed at least to the moon from where they may be turned back. The doctrines of the "five fires" and of the "two paths" obviously do not form an original unity; in fact, the "two paths" found outside this combination, for example, in the *Kauṣītaki Upaniṣad*, and, side by side with the combined version, in the *Jaiminīya Brāhmaṇa*.[98] We cannot and need not enlarge here on the specific problems and highly controversial issues connected with the interpretation of these doctrines.[99] Our primary concern is the character of the sequence of events which constitutes the "way of the fathers," its type and pattern of regularity, and the way in which man is seen as participating in it.

The downward part of the "way of the fathers" coincides basically with the sequence of the "five fires." However, it is more naturalistic in its presentation, describing the sequence of events as a series of natural transformations rather than a sacrificial series: there is trans-

98. *Kauṣītaki Upaniṣad* 1.1 ff. *Jaiminīya Brāhmaṇa* 1.18; the "combined" version: 1.45 ff.The *Jaiminīya* versions differ in various ways from the other versions. On the transformation into water, food, seed, cf. *Śatapatha Brāhmaṇa* 3.7.4.4

99. For a good survey, cf. H. W. Bodewitz, *Jaiminīya Brāhmaṇa* 1.1–65. Translation and Commentary (Leiden, 1973), pp. 243 ff.

formation into ether, wind, rain, and food—that is, nourishing vegetables; these, being eaten and transformed into semen, may lead the one who has gone through these stages back into human or possibly animal existence.[100] Natural cycles, recurrent, seasonal phenomena are used as vehicles of the migrations or transformations of the human being between its earthly existences. Death and birth, ascent and return—the phases and phenomena of man's existence relate to or even coincide with natural, cosmic, meteorological events, such as the ascent of smoke to the sky, the phases of the moon, the seasons, the seasonal rains. The goal is to get beyond these cyclical, seasonal processes, to a permanent heaven or to the world of brahman. In several ancient texts, the moon is the lord of the seasons, those regularities which imply the recurrence of life and death, which determine the scope and the limits of the "way of the fathers." He is the guardian of heaven. In the *Kauṣītaki Upaniṣad,* he examines the knowledge of those who ascend to him after their death, and he decides whether they may proceed to those spheres where they are free from the seasonal cycles and the repetition of their earthly existence. In the versions of the *Chāndogya* and *Bṛhadāraṇyaka Upaniṣads,* no such function is assigned to the moon; the division of the "two ways" takes place already here on earth. In the *Jaiminīya Brāhmaṇa,* the seasons themselves appear as guardians and conduct the decisive examination.[101]

There are only a few stations in the succession of events where knowledge and merit become relevant. They decide whether one remains confined to the "way of the fathers" or reaches the "way of the gods"; within the "way of the fathers," the merit of past deeds, primarily sacrificial acts, decides how long one is allowed to stay in the realm of the moon. Apart from this, entering upon the "way of the fathers" means to be subject to a succession of events and transformations which follows its own "natural" order and is not directed or kept in motion by the retributive causality of our deeds. To be sent into a plant, a vegetable, is not in itself a form of retribution and punishment; it is just the ordinary, "natural" way of returning to the earth. The texts under discussion are still far from a clear and

100. The version of the *Chāndogya Upaniṣad* is more detailed, introducing several additional stages of transformation.

101. *Kauṣītaki Upaniṣad* 1.1; *Jaiminīya Brāhmaṇa* 1.18, 46, with the notes by H. W. Bodewitz, pp. 55 ff., 117 ff. On the connection between life and death and day and night, the phases of the moon, and so forth, cf. *Bṛhadāraṇyaka Upaniṣad* 3.1.3 ff.

thorough conception of karmic, retributive causality; other passages in the *Bṛhadāraṇyaka Upaniṣad* may indeed come much closer to such a conception.[102] Problems of the continuity and coherence of act and retribution or of the durability and identity of the subject in the various processes of transformation do not become explicit; the question "who or what transmigrates?" is not really asked.

A transition which seems particularly delicate and problematic, most notably in the version of the *Chāndogya Upaniṣad*, is the transfer from the vegetable being into the organism and to the level of being of its eater, its consumption and appropriation by a human being or by an animal. While natural processes take care of the transportation up to the vegetable existence, the next step is obviously of a different order. The *Chāndogya Upaniṣad* emphasizes that it is a very difficult transition.[103] As a matter of fact, it seems to be left to mere chance which kind of living being will consume a particular vegetable, extract its essence, transform it into the semen of a new creature, its own offspring, and thus raise it to its own level of being. The most exemplary account of the formation of the semen, a "second *ātman*" in the body of the father, and of the processes of conception and birth, is found in the *Aitareya Upaniṣad*,[104] and it has been taken for granted by the traditional commentators that this has to be understood in the context of the "way of the fathers."

Only the version of the *Chāndogya Upaniṣad* tries to establish a relationship between one's type of birth and the preceding good or bad conduct *(caraṇa)*, in a passage which appears somewhat abruptly and seems to be a later addition.[105] Later systematizers, in particular Śaṅkara, refer specifically to this problematic transition, trying to harmonize and to reconcile, but at the same time making explicit the differences and tensions between this scheme of thought and the later, fully developed theory of karma.

The most explicit and most coherent discussion of karma and transmigration which we find in Śaṅkara's writings, *Brahmasūtrabhāṣya* 3.1.1–27, deals primarily with the exegesis of the "two ways" and the "five fires," specifically the "way of the fathers." Śaṅkara emphasizes that only *śruti* is a really authoritative source for our knowledge and understanding of the processes of karma and

102. Cf. *Bṛhadāraṇyaka Upaniṣad* 3.2.13; 4.4.3 ff.
103. *Chāndogya Upaniṣad* 5.10.6.
104. *Aitareya Upaniṣad* 2.1 ff. (= *Aitareya Āraṇyaka* 2.5.1 ff.).
105. *Chāndogya Upaniṣad* 5.10.7.

transmigration: attempts to explain this matter in terms of assumptions produced by human thought alone *(puruṣamatiprabhavāḥ kalpanāḥ)* are inevitably futile; the various theories and conceptualizations presented by the Sāṅkhya or the Vaiśeṣika, by the Buddhists or the Jainas, are contradicted by one another as well as by *śruti.*[106] Nevertheless, Śaṅkara develops a rather elaborate scheme of reasoning designed to harmonize and systematize the teachings of *śruti,* to reconcile the pattern of the "way of the fathers" with that understanding of transmigration which is expressed in the metaphor of the caterpillar,[107] an understanding which seems to imply a much more direct transition from one body into the next one, without such a long and complicated interlude as the *pitṛyāna.* In his explanation and apologetics, Śaṅkara also uses a peculiar interpretation of the theory of *apūrva;* it states that subtle ingredients or transformations of the sacrificial oblations, specifically of the sacrificial water, constitute the *apūrva* which "envelops" the soul of the sacrificer, accompanies it to the heavenly spheres, and keeps it there as long as the sacrificial merit lasts.[108] Following an interpretation which had already been suggested by Bādarāyaṇa's predecessor Kārṣṇājini, Śaṅkara states that once a transmigrating soul *(jīva)* has been led back to earth by the "way of the fathers," into the condition of a vegetable, its karmic residue *(anuśaya)* will determine its further development. The assumption of such a residue which remains after the processes of enjoyment and cancellation of karma in the heavenly spheres is explained and justified in an elaborate discussion. In this way, Śaṅkara tries to bridge what might appear as a gap in the causal sequence, to establish that the transition from the vegetable to its "eater" is not left to mere chance.[109]

It is a familiar phenomenon and need not further concern us here that Śaṅkara in his interpretation and apologetics presupposes and employs doctrines and conceptual devices developed at a much later time than the texts he is dealing with. For our present discussion, it is more significant that his exegesis of the "five fires" and the "way of the fathers" ultimately and explicitly demonstrates the unreconciled

106. On BS 3.1.1.
107. As used in *Bṛhadāraṇyaka Upaniṣad* 4.4.3.
108. On BS 3.1.6. This or a similar theory is already referred to and rejected by Prabhākara, Bṛh, p. 323. On BS 3.2.38 ff.,Śaṅkara criticizes the Mīmāṃsā *apūrva.*
109. Cf. on BS 3.1.8 ff. Bādarāyaṇa refers to Kārṣṇājini in BS 3.1.9.

disparity of these old Upaniṣadic models and the later systematic understanding of karma and transmigration. Following the lead of Bādarāyaṇa, he arrives at a curious juxtaposition of two different transmigrating entities *(jīva)* in one and the same organism.

The rain which falls to earth nourishes the plants, but it does not give them their life-principle. A *jīva* which is sent down to earth by, or in the form of, rain is thus attached to an organism which is already occupied and operated by a *jīva* of its own. It cannot really be embodied in such an organism; it is only located in it as a kind of "guest *jīva.*" Śaṅkara is very explicit on this distinction of different jīvas in one vegetable organism: for the *jīva* that has been "born into" and is embodied in a vegetable, this means a form of karmic retribution, the allocation of a particular vehicle of retributive experience. For the "guest *jīva*," on the other hand, no karmic retribution is involved at this particular stage. The descent according to the "ways of the fathers" has its own order and regularity, with which karmic processes do not interfere; as far as this part of the journey is concerned, a *jīva* does not accumulate any new karma, nor does it experience the results of previous karma.[110] The juxtaposition and contrast of the two *jīvas* illustrate the interference of two different models of thought and, moreover, of different historical layers of the Indian tradition: a scheme which is, apart from certain crucial junctures, primarily left to "natural," seasonal, cosmic regularities interferes with the more comprehensive context of the universalized theory of karma and *saṃsāra.* Śaṅkara tries faithfully to preserve the peculiar teachings on the "five fires" and the "two ways." Yet, these ancient Upaniṣadic schemes appear as curious epiphenomena or as fossilized relics in a universe now thoroughly governed by karmic causality.

In the wider framework of Śaṅkara's thought, the explication of the peculiarities of karma and the exegesis of the sacred texts on this matter remain confined to the "lower level" of truth, to the realm of *vyavahāra.* Ultimately, the notions of karma and *saṃsāra* have only one meaning and function: to provide a counterpart and stepping-stone of liberating knowledge, to show us what ultimate reality is *not*, to expose the spatio-temporal universe in its ontological deficiency.

110. On BS 3.1.24 ff. The duplication of the *jīvas,* or rather the allocation of "guest *jīvas,*" is repeated when the vegetable is eaten and appropriated by a human being or an animal (on BS 3.1.26). Rāmānuja and other later commentators agree with Śaṅkara on the basic issues of this interpretation.

The whole world is only a stage for karmic processes,[111] or rather: it is itself nothing but a karmic play. It owes its very existence to karmic attachment and superimposition, to that ignorance *(avidyā)* which is the root-cause of our karmic involvement and in fact coextensive with it. To be in the world, to accept its reality as well as one's own worldly reality, means to *act* in the world, to accept it as a network of causal relations, of desires and results, as a context of practical, pragmatic truth and confirmation. Causality is in its very essence karmic causality; it constitutes the "reality" of the world, a reality which can be defined only in terms of means and ends, of practical consequences, of "reward" and "punishment," and which becomes transparent as soon as the practical involvement in the network of means and ends is terminated. To be in *saṃsāra* is not just the function of a particular demerit; it is the function of and coincides with the "involvement in causes and results" *(hetuphalāveśa)* as such.[112] The domains of karma and of cosmic ignorance and illusion *(avidyā, māyā)* are identical. Karma is thoroughly universalized and implemented in Śaṅkara's philosophy. Yet, this radical and uncompromising consummation of the principle of karma is at the same time a radical devaluation.[113] In a sense, the Lord *(īśvara)* is the only subject of transmigration *(saṃsārin)*, according to Śaṅkara;[114] in an even more radical sense, there is no *saṃsārin* at all.

111. Cf. Śaṅkara's commentary on *Aitareya Upaniṣad* 2.1: the world as providing manifold facilities ("seats") which are suitable for the manifold living beings to experience their karmic results (anekaprāṇikarmaphalopabhogayogyānekādhiṣṭhānavad).

112. Cf. Gauḍapāda, *Māṇḍūkyakārikā* 4.56: yavadd hetuphalāveśaḥ, saṃsāras tāvad āyataḥ/ kṣīṇe hetuphalāveśe saṃsāro na upapadyate//. Cf. also Sureśvara, *Naiṣkarmyasiddhi* 4.56. According to the tradition of Advaita Vedānta, Gauḍapāda was the teacher of Śaṅkara's teacher Govinda, while Sureśvara was Śaṅkara's direct disciple.

113. Universalizations which are at least equally radical and ambiguous are found in Buddhism. It is well known that Gauḍapāda is strongly influenced by the philosophy of Nāgārjuna.

114. Śaṅkara on BS 1.1.5.

12

Karma as a "Sociology of Knowledge" or "Social Psychology" of Process/Praxis

GERALD JAMES LARSON

Introduction

An interesting theoretical puzzle that has emerged from the series of conferences on the notion of karma in South Asian thought is the apparent anomaly between what might be called the "transference of karma interpretation" and the "non-transference of karma interpretation."[1] The former appears to correlate with McKim Marriott's and Ronald Inden's transactional analysis, involving giving and receiving (in the modalities of "optimal," "pessimal," "maximal," and "minimal") within the context of a unified coded substance and encompassing the entire range of *varṇāśramadharma* with all of its rules and principles regarding food, pollution, marriage, work, and kinship. Textual authority for such a transactional analysis (in addition to its

1. For Marriott's and Inden's "transactional" analysis, see the following: M. Marriott and R. B. Inden, "Caste Systems," *Encyclopaedia Britannica,* 15th edition (Chicago, 1974), *Macropaedia* III, pp. 982–991; Marriott and Inden, "Toward an Ethnosociology of South Asian Caste Systems," *The New Wind: Changing Identities in South Asia,* ed. K. A. David, World Anthropology Series (The Hague: Mouton, 1976); and Marriott, "Hindu Transactions: Diversity without Dualism," *Transactions and Meaning: Directions in the Anthropology of Exchange and Symbolic Behavior,* ed. B. Kapferer, ASA Essays in Social Anthropology, I (Philadelphia: ISHI Publications, 1976), pp. 109–142. See also the introduction to this volume.

contextual data) includes not only Manu and other traditions of *dharma-śāstra* but also Vedic traditions of transference (e.g., the *sapiṇḍīkaraṇa,* and so forth) and more popular notions of transference found, for example, in the epics, the *Purāṇas* and later *bhakti* traditions. The "non-transference of karma interpretation" appears to correlate with certain philosophical traditions (for example, Yoga and Vedānta), involving the notions of *liṅga, karmāśayas, vāsanās* and *saṁskāras,* in which a person's karmic heritage and karmic possibilities are construed individually with apparently no provision for transactional transference. Textual authority for such a "non-transference perspective" is, of course, the *darśana* literature or at least those portions of *darśana* literature concerned with *mokṣa.* Karl H. Potter has suggested that the "transference" orientation be designated the "*pravṛtti*-perspective" and the "non-transference" orientation the "*nivṛtti*-perspective." Potter has also suggested that these two perspectives may represent divergent historic traditions in South Asian thought that have coexisted with one another over many centuries and have generated various efforts at reconciliation—for example, the kind of reconciliation attempted in the *Gītā.*[2]

I wish to argue here that there are conceptual inadequacies both in the "transference of karma interpretation" (that is to say, in the transactional, *pravṛtti* orientation of Marriott and Inden) and in the "non-transference of karma interpretation" (that is to say, in the non-transactional, *nivṛtti* orientation of Potter), and that there is a larger conceptual framework within the South Asian tradition that encompasses both "transference" and "non-transference." Moreover, I also wish to suggest that this larger conceptual framework of karma serves as a rough equivalent in South Asia to what we would usually call a "sociology of knowledge" or an interactionist social psychology.

Before setting forth the larger conceptual framework, however, I want, first of all, to indicate why I find conceptual limitations in the "transference" and "non-transference" interpretations, for these limitations became the occasion for my attempting to devise a larger conceptual framework. The conceptual inadequacies or limitations to which I am referring emerge in the following way. The purpose of these conferences was to uncover and describe the system of karma in South Asia as an "indigenous conceptual system," and yet the two

2. See Karl H. Potter's contribution in this volume.

most cogent interpretations (namely, "transference" and "non-transference") appear to make that purpose unattainable. An impasse, indeed a kind of dilemma, shows itself which cannot be resolved without moving to a different level of interpretation. If, on the one hand, one accepts a "non-transference" interpretation, then it must be conceded that only a very few spiritual "virtuosos" (to use Weber's terminology) or "athletes of the spirit" (to use Zaehner's terminology) ever accepted such an "indigenous conceptual system," and that, in fact, we are not really talking about a pervasive or widespread "indigenous conceptual system" so much as we are talking about what is more adequately described as a minor elitist ideology. If, on the other hand, one accepts a "transference" interpretation, then it must be conceded that such an "indigenous conceptual system" was implicitly or explicitly accepted by everyone except those members of the culture who were primarily concerned with devising "indigenous conceptual systems."

At this point, of course, the obvious move is to argue that we have here a clear case of "divergent historic traditions" in need of cultural reconciliation, but methodologically this is an unwarranted move. Why? Because it introduces the interpretive notion of "history," a category which has no demonstrable place within any South Asian "indigenous conceptual system" (at least prior to the middle of the nineteenth century). Quite apart from the merit or lack of merit of an historical interpretation, it appears that South Asians themselves seldom if ever used such an explanation. In other words, however South Asians themselves dealt with the issues of "transference," "non-transference," and so forth, it certainly was not from the perspective of historical interpretation, and by providing historical interpretations of South Asian thought and culture modern interpreters are more or less talking to themselves. There is nothing wrong with the latter enterprise, for at some stage in our work we as modern interpreters of South Asian culture must "encompass" (in Dumont's sense) what South Asian culture represents in our experience. The crucial methodological issue, however, is that the "encompassed" can never pass itself off as an adequate characterization of an indigenous interpretation. In other words, to put it directly, historical interpretation is *ours,* not *theirs!* In a South Asian environment, historical interpretation is *no* interpretation. It is a zero-category.

Regarding karma as an "indigenous conceptual system" in South Asia, then, interpretive work thus far has reached an impasse, or indeed, as suggested above, a kind of dilemma. On the one hand, there is indisputable evidence for both a "transference" and a "non-transference" perspective (and various ambiguities in between), and it is not really possible to resolve the apparent anomaly by utilizing an historical interpretation, since that approach methodologically begs the question. On the other hand, McKim Marriott's transactional interpretation, which nicely avoids not only unwarranted historical interpretation but a number of other methodological biases as well, comes up against a remarkable piece of counterevidence. That is to say, Marriott's transactional interpretation, which is designed to be a theoretical clarification of indigenous South Asian social reality derived from within the theoretical categories of South Asian thought itself, nevertheless appears to be falsified by theoretical interpretations within the tradition which represent the tradition's own theoretical self-awareness, namely, the *darśanas.* The acid test of a theory like Marriott's must surely be the tradition's own theoretical reflection, and yet the theory appears *not* to pass the test. This impasse then leads to the following dilemma: either (a) karma as an "indigenous conceptual system" harbors an anomaly which cannot be resolved other than by going outside the indigenous tradition (in the direction of historical, structuralist, or some other non–South Asian interpretation) or (b) karma as an "indigenous conceptual system" was never recognized as such by those theoreticians within the tradition who were responsible for creating "indigenous conceptual systems." Moreover, if one is tempted to suggest a third alternative, namely, that we are talking about two or more "indigenous conceptual systems," that does not solve the anomaly, for such an alternative forces us either (a) to move back to the first part of the dilemma or (b) to argue that there is no "indigenous conceptual system" of karma that encompasses in any important theoretical way the plurality of systems that have been uncovered. All of the possibilities, in other words, lead to the remarkable conclusion that the original question for research cannot properly be asked—namely, what is the meaning of karma as an "indigenous conceptual system" in South Asia?

The only way out of this impasse, in my judgment, is to interrogate the South Asian tradition further in order to find a broader conceptual framework that overcomes the glaring anomaly of the "transference" and "non-transference" interpretations, and in the sequel I shall try to reconstruct such a broader conceptual framework. I shall utilize the Sāṅkhya philosophy as my primary body of evidence because (a) it is admitted by all researchers to be one of the oldest conceptual systems in South Asia; (b) it theoretically maintains, in my judgment, both a "transference" and a "non-transference" perspective; and (c) its influence within the tradition is evident in so-called transference environments (for example, the epics, the *Purāṇas,* and so forth) and in so-called non-transference environments (namely the technical *darśana* literature). (Moreover, I can claim a greater expertise in Sāṅkhya philosophy than in most other systems, and, hence, I feel more confident in reconstructing from it what I take to be a larger conceptual framework for an interpretation of karma as an "indigenous conceptual system" in South Asia.)

Toward a Larger (Encompassing) Conceptual Framework

I shall proceed, as it were, by moving sequentially from the "outside" to the "inside" (or, in other words, from more abstract general considerations to the specific issue at hand, namely karma as a conceptual system), utilizing, as was already indicated, a Sāṅkhya inflection of the indigenous conceptual system.[3]

AN ONTOLOGY AND EPISTEMOLOGY OF REDUCTIVE MATERIALISM APART FROM "CONSCIOUSNESS"

The notion of *prakṛti* in Sāṅkhya philosophy implies a closed causal system of reductive materialism—"reductive materialism" in the sense that all thinking, fantasizing, imagining, feeling, and willing can finally be reduced to a modality or function of sheer materiality. Sāṅkhya philosophy, to be sure, is not a crude materialism in the sense that awareness is simply an epiphenomenon of some kind of gross stuff. Indeed, it is the reverse of crude materialism in that Sāṅkhya argues that gross stuff is an epiphenomenon of subtle material energy. It is true, nevertheless, that Sāṅkhya refuses to make an ontological distinction between what Western thought would call

3. My treatment of the Sāṅkhya position is based largely on the *Sāṅkhyakārikā* and its important commentaries. For a study of the history and meaning of the Sāṅkhya (together with the Sanskrit text and English translation of the *Kārikā*), see my *Classical Sāṁkhya: An Interpretation of Its History and Meaning* (Delhi: Motilal Banarsidass, 1969; second revised edition, University of California Press and Motilal Banarsidass, 1979).

"mind" and "body" or "thought" and "extension," preferring, rather, to encompass all such distinctions within the closed causal system of emergent *prakṛti.* Ordinary "awareness" *(antaḥkaraṇa-vṛtti) (citta-vṛtti),* therefore, according to Sāṅkhya philosophy, is a manifestation of *prakṛti,* as are such residual constructs as intellect *(buddhi),* ego *(ahaṁkāra),* mind *(manas),* subtle body *(liṅga-śarīra),* gross body *(sthūla-śarīra)*—indeed, this entire manifest world *(vyakta, sarga, kṣetra,* and so forth). An obvious corollary of this reductive materialism is that *karman* is also a manifestation of subtle materiality and can only be construed within the closed causal system. "Action" in any of its modes is a manifestation *(vyakta)* of the continuous transformation *(pariṇāma)* and combination *(saṁghāta)* occurring within materiality *(prakṛti).* Similarly, the problem of bondage and release is to be construed solely within the closed causal system, and the experience of "release" in Sāṅkhya has no ontological implications whatever. That is to say, in Sāṅkhya the realization of discrimination *(viveka)* changes nothing ontologically. It only reveals what has always been the case, namely that there is a principle beyond the closed causal system that never, in fact, has been in bondage. Moreover, this realization itself (that is to say, the discrimination of *puruṣa*) occurs within the closed causal system on the level of the *buddhi* and, thus, has significance solely within the subtle material system. Hence, the assertion of the Sāṅkhya *ācārya:*

> Not any *(puruṣa),* therefore, is bound; nor released; nor does any *(puruṣa)* transmigrate. (Only) *prakṛti* in its various forms transmigrates, is bound and is released. *(Sāṅkhyakārikā* 62)

In addition, from the point of view of the analysis of experience, yet another corollary of this reductive materialism emerges, namely that in Sāṅkhya a definite distinction is made between "consciousness" *(puruṣa)* and "awareness" *(antaḥkaraṇa-vṛtti, citta-vṛtti).* Whereas "awareness" is active, intentional, engaged, and at every moment a reflection of subtle materiality, "consciousness" *(puruṣa)* cannot think, act, be ontologically involved or intentionally related in any sense whatever to *prakṛti.* "Consciousness" *(puruṣa),* in other words, is sheer contentless presence *(sākṣitva).* Because of its contentlessness, "consciousness" appears as what it is not, and "awareness" appears as if it were "consciousness," and it is this double negation occurring within *buddhi* that generates the epistemological confusion of bondage. When the fundamental epistemic distinction between "consciousness" and "awareness" is correctly apperceived, again on the level of the *buddhi, mokṣa* shows itself as being the case, and more than that, as having always been the case and forever to be the case subsequently. In other words, the final discrimination is that "bondage" and "release" as contraries or sub-contraries are both negated; and the *jīvan-mukta* has moved to a new meta-level of apperception referred to as *kaivalya.* Expressing these ontological and epistemological assertions in the more precise and technical Nyāya terminology, the Sāṅkhya perspective would appear to be the following: "bondage" is an example of *pradhvaṃsābhāva,* or "consequent non-existence," and "release" is an example of *prāgābhāva,* or "antecedent non-existence"; whereas the fundamental ontological difference between *puruṣa* and *prakṛti* is an example of *anyonyābhāva,* or "reciprocal non-existence" (or the logical absence of identity between *puruṣa* and *prakṛti* under all circumstances), and the lack of relation between *puruṣa* and *prakṛti* is an example of *atyantābhāva,* or "absolute non-existence" (or the material absence of relation between *puruṣa* and *prakṛti* under all circumstances).

To my knowledge there is no analogue in the history of Western thought to this eccentric form of Indian dualism (wherein *prakṛti* as a reductive materialism encompasses gross and subtle matter as well as "awareness," "egoity," "intellection," and all "strivings," and *puruṣa* as "consciousness" is simply contentless presence). The only possible exception could be certain traditions in phenomenology, although even in these traditions the non-intentionality of consciousness has never been seriously entertained. The issue, then, is that we are dealing here with a way of looking at the world that is remarkably different from our own. Put simply and in reference to these conferences on karma, our "awareness," our "identity," and all of our "intentional" acts have nothing whatever to do with our "consciousness," and more than that, the cycle of rebirth and the actions that determine our position in the cycle are functions of an "unconscious" (in the Indian sense) subtle materiality that is unfolding by means of continuous transformation *(pariṇāma)* and combination *(saṃghāta).*

In attempting to construct a larger conceptual framework, then, the first point to be stressed is the admittedly paradoxical one that "consciousness" and its freedom *(kaivalya)* must be, as it were, "bracketed" in any discussion of karma (either in terms of a "transference" interpretation or a "non-transference" interpretation). "Consciousness" is *not* a function of the closed causal system of reductive materialism, and *neither* bondage *nor* release pertains to it!

THE CONSTITUENT PROCESSES OF EXTERNALIZATION, OBJECTIVATION, AND INTERNALIZATION

Ordinary experience or apperception (as a mode of subtle materiality) presents itself as the awareness of "pain" *(duḥkha, aprīti),* the awareness of "alienation" *(moha, viṣāda),* and the awareness of "pleasure" *(sukha, prīti).* "Pain" as an awareness is a feeling of discomfort *(ghora)* arising out of the encounter with what appears to be outside of oneself (either from the outside world or from one's own mind/body insofar as it presents itself in awareness as "pain-ful"), and the awareness of "pain" always carries with it a desire to be free from it. "Alienation" as an awareness is a feeling of reification *(mūḍha),* of having been turned into an entity among entities, and the awareness of "alienation" carries with it a neutralization of motivation and affect. "Pleasure" as an awareness is a feeling of joyous and quiet fulfillment *(śānta),* of having appropriated (or interiorized) an object or an activity so that one is free from it, and the awareness of "pleasure" carries with it a reflective comprehension of what has been appropriated. According to Sāṅkhya philosophy, these primal feelings are taken to be manifestations of three procedural and structural tendencies that characterize the closed causal system of reductive materialism, namely, the constituent process of externalization (*pravṛtti* or *rajas*), the constituent process of objectivation (*sthiti* or *tamas*), and the constituent process of internalization (*prakhyā* or *sattva*). These constituent processes generate in turn a "constituted" world wherein the residual or "constituted" constructs are either (a) *sāttvika* (or *vaikṛta*)—that is to say, reflexive internalizations reified into ideas, verbal constructions, and so forth, or, in other words, what we usually mean by the term "subjective"—or (b) *tāmasa* (or *bhūtādi*), that is to say, intentional externalizations reified into subtle and gross objects (*tanmātras* and *mahābhūtas*), or, in other words, what we usually mean by the term "objective." This "constituted" world (made up of residual constructs that are *sāttvika* and *tāmasa*) is mediated by the constituent process of externalization. In other words, internalization and objectivation (both as constituent processes and as constituted constructs) cannot manifest themselves as what they are without the dialectically related process of externalization. Similarly, externalization cannot show itself as what it is without the dialectically implicit processes of internalization and objectivation. From the point of view of the "constituted" world, however, the constituent processes are to be construed not as *three* (namely, *sattva, rajas,* and *tamas*) but, rather, as *two* mediated by *one* (namely, *sattva* and *tamas* as mediated by *rajas*). Hence, the entire manifest world *(vyakta)* with all of its constructs *(buddhi, ahaṃkāra,* and so forth) shows itself as either (a) *sāttvika* or (b) *tāmasa* with *rajas (taijasa)* mediating throughout (*Sāṅkhyakārikā* 25, "*taijasād ubhayam*"). Because *rajas* or the constituent process of externalization is a fundamental mediation throughout the closed causal system, therefore, "suffering is of the nature of things" (*Sāṅkhyakārikā* 55, "*tasmād duḥkhaṃ svabhāvena*" or as the *Yuktidīpikā* puts it, "*duḥkhaṃ raja iti*"). The experience of suffering constitutes the basis for all reflection and all alienation as well as the desire to overcome suffering, for there can be neither internalization nor alienation without a prior *process* of externalization. The constituent process of externalization, then, is fundamental and basic in Sāṅkhya philosophy, and I would argue that it is the structural basis for the notion of karma in all of its modes. However, we have not yet reached the level of analysis in which it is appropriate to use the word "karma" in its ordinary Indian sense. We have only reached the level of fundamental "constituent process."

THE TWOFOLD CREATION *(dvividha-sarga): liṅga* and *bhāva*

According to Sāṅkhya philosophy, the "individual person" in our ordinary Western usage is construed to be "dividual" (in McKim Marriott's sense), or, perhaps better, a "residual construct" made up of what I shall call a "marked core" *(liṅga),* a "projecting set of predispositions" (*bhāvas, saṃskāras, vāsanās,* and so forth), a transmigrating "subtle body" *(liṅga-śarīra),* and a manifest "gross body" *(sthūla-śarīra),* and this "dividual" "residual construct" is located in a manifest world *(bhautika-sarga).*

The "marked core," or *liṅga,* is made up of *buddhi, ahaṃkāra, manas,* the five sense-capacities and the five action-capacities (and referred to as the "thirteenfold instrument," or *trayodaśa-karaṇa).* This "marked core," or *liṅga,* is devoid of ordinary experience *(nirupabhoga).* It can be predominantly *sāttvika* or *tāmasa,* as was indicated above, in its intentionality, and is mediated throughout by the constituent process of externalization *(rajas)*. (Cf. *Sāṅkhyakārikā* 23, 24, and 40.)

The "projecting set of predispositions" *(bhāvas)* are meritorious behavior *(dharma)*, unmeritorious behavior *(a-dharma)*, knowledge *(jñāna)*, non-knowledge *(a-jñāna)*, absence of passion *(vairāgya)*, passion *(rāga)*, power *(aiśvarya)*, and lack of power *(anaiśvarya)*. As is the case with the *liṅga*, so also with the "projecting set of predispositions," or *bhāvas*, they can be predominantly *sāttvika* or *tāmasa* with the constituent process of externalization mediating throughout. These *bhāvas* reside in the *buddhi* and generate or project the *pratyaya-sarga*, or "intellectual creation," of *viparyayas, aśaktis, tuṣṭis*, and *siddhis*—in other words, these *bhāvas* are the presuppositions or predispositions that render "ordinary awareness" or apperception possible.

The transmigrating "subtle body" *(liṅga-śarīra)* is made up of the five *tanmātras*, or subtle elements, and is the subtle *tāmasa*-vehicle that accompanies the *liṅga* in the process of transmigration.

The non-transmigrating "gross body" is the genetic *tāmasa*-form of body that is produced from the sexual relations of father and mother.

Finally, this manifest world *(bhautika-sarga)* functions as a kind of theatre, or to use a favorite Sāṅkhya analogy, a stage, on which these various constructs play their roles, and this manifest world is made up of a divine realm wherein the constituent process of internalization *(sattva)* is dominant; a human realm wherein the constituent process of externalization *(rajas)* is dominant; and an animal and vegetable world wherein the constituent process of alienation *(tamas)* is dominant.

Such, in brief, is the closed causal system of reductive materialism from "Brahmā down to a blade of grass" (*brahmādistambaparyantaḥ*," *Sāṅkhyakārikā* 54), or, again, as the frequently quoted refrain puts it, "*guṇā guṇeṣu vartanta iti.*"

The social extention of the system, though not directly stated in technical Sāṅkhya texts, can be easily reconstructed on the basis of references in the *Gītā*, Śaṅkara, and Rāmānuja (especially in the lengthy *guṇa*-passages of chapters 17 and 18 of the *Gītā* together with Śaṅkara's and Rāmānuja's comments). The reconstruction emerges in the following manner. The human realm is the realm in which *rajas* or externalization is dominant (*Sāṅkhyakārikā* 53–54). Since the whole system is a closed reductive materialism, on the highest human level there would naturally be a tendency to move into a purely internalized (divine) condition, and on the lowest human level there would naturally be a tendency to move into a purely alienated (animal or vegetable) condition. On every human level, however (following *kārikās* 53–54), externalization, or *rajas*, *must* be present. Thus,

	sattva (rajas/tamas)		"divine realm"
"human realm"	(1) *sattva/rajas (tamas)*	Brāhmaṇa	— "optimal"
	(2) *rajas/sattva (tamas)*	Kṣatriya	— "maximal"
	(3) *rajas/tamas (sattva)*	Vaiśya	— "minimal"
	(4) *tamas/rajas (sattva)*	Śūdra	— "pessimal"
	tamas (rajas/sattva)		"animal realm"

This is admittedly a very general and schematic reconstruction, and undoubtedly many other kinds of combinations and subcombinations could have been and probably were worked out (especially in juridical environments). This general presentation, however, is sufficient to show the basic thrust of an indigenous sociology.

The "dividual" residual construct—that is to say, the "individual person" in our ordinary Western sense—is, thus, a peculiar blending of *liṅga, bhāva, liṅga-śarīra, sthūla-śarīra,* and *bhautika-sarga,* all of which are manifestations of the closed causal system and its constituent processes *(guṇā guṇeṣu vartanta iti).* Ordinary awareness or experience within a hierarchical world arises when these subtle material components come together, and a kind of "feedback" continually operates on two distinct levels. On one level there is a *liṅga,* or "marked core," successively being correlated with a one-time-only genetically generated "gross body," and this *liṅga*-level is a sort of "deep-structural" predispositional set of possibilities. (I use the expression "deep-structural" to indicate that the *liṅga*-level, according to Sāṅkhya philosophy, is devoid of ordinary experience, or *nirupabhoga.*) On another level there is a *bhāva*-constellation, or a "projecting set of predispositions," characterized by ordinary awareness or experience in a hierarchical world, and this *bhāva*-level makes up the social reality of everyday life. Both levels reside in the *buddhi,* according to Sāṅkhya, a concept that also includes the crucial corollary that each level "feeds" the other. In any "dividual" life there is a deep-structural "marked core" *(liṅga)* which determines the place of the "dividual" life in the hierarchical scheme of things, and there is a surface-structural "projecting" or experiencing (a kind of usage, as it were) in the everyday social world which generates traces or further residues that will accrue to the "marked core" and in turn determine the future placement of the *liṅga.* Each level presupposes the other in a dialectical fashion. The very notion of a "marked core" *(liṅga)* being diachronically reborn presupposes a previous systemic "projecting" matrix in which the "core's markings" were synchronically derived. By the same token, the systemic matrix in which "markings" (that is to say, to use Marriott's idiom, substance-code transactions) can occur itself presupposes a sequence of "marked cores" *(liṅgas)* being diachronically reborn, for only a diachronically derived "marked core" could provide the constituents necessary for a (subjectively and objectively) meaningful set of synchronic transactions to occur in a given social reality. (An intriguing piece of evidence that is symptomatic of this point that a "marked core" is always presupposed even in the most thoroughly transactional set of matrices is the obsessive concern with astrology on all levels of Indian social reality.). At any given point-instant, therefore, there would appear to be operating an intersecting (in the *buddhi*) set of transactions, one diachronic (namely, a given *liṅga,* or "marked core," being re-embodied in a one-time-only genetically derived "gross body") and one synchronic (namely, the systemic substance-codes interacting vis-à-vis the living "entities" manifesting themselves in a given projective, contextual environment). The former (that is to say, the *liṅga*-level) at any given point-instant does not provide for "transference," since, of course, it is given at that instant. The latter (that is to say, the *bhāva*-level) at any given point-instant does provide for "transference," since it provides the futural projection for any subsequent point-instant. Putting the matter another way, the *liṅga*-level defines the appropriation of "pastness" in the present point-instant, whereas the *bhāva*-level defines the projective, futural possibilities for any subsequent point-instant in the present point-instant. (Such a temporal interpretation of these two levels finds some support in the Yoga discussions of the "moment," or *kṣaṇa,* and its modalities, *dharma-lakṣaṇa-avasthā.*) The *Sāṅkhyakārikā,* while remaining silent on the issue of temporality, does assert the dialectical significance of the two levels.

> The *liṅga* cannot function without the *bhāvas.* The *bhāvas* cannot function without the *liṅga.* Therefore, a twofold creation *(dvividhaḥ sargaḥ)* operates called *liṅga* and *bhāva.* (*Sāṅkhyakārikā* 52)

According to Sāṅkhya philosophy, therefore, it would appear to be the case that the term "karma" can be used appropriately both in the sense of determined "process" (namely, *liṅga*) and in the sense of determining "praxis," or purposeful human activity (namely, *bhāva*).

The dyad process/praxis (or, if one prefers, the dyad marked/marking, regressive/progressive, diachronic/synchronic, *avyakta/vyakta*, deep-structure/surface-structure, transferred/transferring, and so forth) manifests itself as the specifically human modality of the constituent process of externalization, or *rajas*, which in turn is the dialectically most significant constituent process of the entire closed causal system itself.

Conclusion

However one wishes to assess the significance of such an indigenous conceptual system, the least that can be said is that it invites us to look at the human condition in a way that is remarkably different from our usual perspectives. The system, to be sure, has interesting affinities with certain kinds of recent Western social-scientific theorizing, most notably, I would argue, with the school of "symbolic interactionism" in social psychology (in the work of George Herbert Mead, et al.), with the phenomenological sociology of everyday life (in the work of Alfred Schutz), and with the sociology of knowledge as set forth by Peter Berger and Thomas Luckmann in *The Social Construction of Reality.* The Sāṅkhya conceptual system as a whole, however, differs from such loose affinities in fundamental and striking ways, and let me conclude by briefly calling attention to the most striking differences in orientation.

The Sāṅkhya emphasis on karma as process/praxis avoids either "idealism" or "crude materialism" by encompassing both in a reductive materialism that transcends our usual polarities of "subjectivity" and "objectivity," "mind" and "body," "ideas" and "objects," and so forth. At the same time, of course, the system argues that there is a consciousness that is fundamentally "non-intentional" and that must be clearly distinguished from our "awareness." Whereas our "awareness" is derived from within the closed causal system and can be studied and measured and tested vis-à-vis the closed causal system, there is finally a radical principle of freedom apart from the system.

According to the Sāṅkhya, at any given point-instant, two kinds of perspective are always possible. From one point of view, the "distribution" of knowledge in a society is completely and utterly determined by the phylogenetic, socio-biological process occurring within the system as a whole. From another point of view, however, the system is completely open-ended ontogenetically in so far as my contextual praxis allows me to change my status either marginally (by becoming a "better" or "worse" Brāhmaṇa or Vaiśya) or radically (by becoming a *sādhu* and thereby opting out of the phylogenetic, socio-biological system altogether). Notions of the "individual," "ego," "society," "caste," are only apparent realities, and, finally, even my "marked core" *(liṅga),* though continuous over a potentially endless series of embodiments, is itself only a residual construct operating in the larger karmic environment. From one point of view the system is absolutely conservative and hierarchical (and was so developed in later Vedānta theorizing), and from another point of view the system is absolutely radical and revolutionary; and the Sāṅkhya would appear to be suggesting that *both* points of view are true. Vis-à-vis consciousness, or *puruṣa,* however, neither the one nor the other pertains, since "bondage" and "release" are both intrasystemic constructs that have no relevance outside the system.

The Sāṅkhya conceptual system of karma as process/praxis can, to be sure, be described as a "sociology of knowledge" in the sense that it accounts for the "distribution" of knowledge in a society by correlating "ideas" and "systems of thought" with certain distinct social realities and expectations *(varṇāśramadharma),* and as such it traces both "ideas" and "social reality" to a more fundamental level of process/praxis. Or, again, to be sure, one can describe the Sāṅkhya conceptual system of karma as a kind of interactionist social psychology in that it treats the "individual person" as "dividual," a product of the interacting of a "marked core," a gross genetically inherited physical body, and a social field *(varṇāśramadharma)* wherein a continuous process/praxis unfolds. What is so strikingly different, however, is the valuation which Sāṅkhya assigns to its sociology of knowledge and its social psychology. When one inquires into what Werner Stark has called the implicit "axiological grid" of a conceptual system, or what Max Weber has called variously the *Wertgesichtspunkt* (the "value view-point"), or the *Wertbeziehung* (the "value-relation") of a conceptual system, one encounters the remarkable conclusion that all of our "ideas" and all of our "social realities" are valuable only to the extent that they make us aware of that which is closest to us and yet irreducible to any intellectual or social formulation, namely, our simple presence to ourselves, our consciousness in and of itself.

Participants in the First Two American Council of Learned Societies-Social Science Research Council Karma Conferences

First Karma Conference (October 1976)

Ashok N. Aklujkar, University of British Columbia
Frank Conlon, University of Washington, Seattle
Edwin Gerow, University of Chicago
Wilhelm Halbfass, University of Pennsylvania
Paul Hiebert, Fuller Institute, Pasadena
Padmanabh S. Jaini, University of California, Berkeley
Charles Keyes, University of Washington, Seattle
J. Bruce Long, Cornell University
James P. McDermott, Canisius College
McKim Marriott, University of Chicago
Wendy Doniger O'Flaherty, University of Chicago
Karl H. Potter, University of Washington, Seattle (organizer)
Ludo Rocher, University of Pennsylvania
David L. Szanton, Social Science Research Council
Allen Thrasher, University of Washington, Seattle
A. Gabrielle Tyrner-Stastny

Second Karma Conference (January 1978)

Roy Amore, University of Windsor
Agehananda Bharati, Syracuse University
Daniel Bisgaard, University of Illinois
Kees W. Bolle, University of California, Los Angeles
S. M. S. Chari, University of California, San Diego
E. Valentine Daniel, University of Chicago

Joseph Elder, University of Wisconsin
Ram Chandra Gandhi, University of Delhi
Robert Gimello, University of California, Santa Barbara
Paul Hiebert, Fuller Institute, Pasadena
Padmanabh S. Jaini, University of California, Berkeley
Charles Keyes, University of Washington, Seattle
David M. Knipe, University of Wisconsin, Madison
Gerald J. Larson, University of California, Santa Barbara
McKim Marriott, University of Chicago
Gananath Obeyesekere, University of California, San Diego
Wendy Doniger O'Flaherty, University of Chicago
Karl H. Potter, University of Washington, Seattle (organizer)
A. K. Ramanujan, University of Chicago
K. Sivaraman, McMaster University
Allen Thrasher, University of Washington, Seattle
Guy Welbon, University of Pennsylvania

Bibliography

The Beginnings of a List of Publications Relating to Karma and Rebirth Compiled by Karl H. Potter, with Supplementary Material by James P. McDermott

Abhedanand. "Attainment of Mokṣa," *Darshana* 8, no. 2 (1968): 37–40.
Adams, H. J. "Karma." *Buddhist Review* 2 (1910): 124–143.
Amore, Roy Clayton. "The Concept and Practice of Doing Merit in Early Theravāda Buddhism." Ph.D. dissertation, Columbia University, 1971.
Aiyangar, K. V. Rangaswami. Introduction to vol. 14 of Bhatta Lakṣmīdhara's *Kṛtyakalpataru*, edited by K. V. Rangaswami Aiyangar *(Mokṣakāṇḍa)*. Baroda: Oriental Institute, 1945.
Arya, Usharbudh. "Hindu Contradictions of the Doctrine of Karma." *East and West* (Rome) 22 (1972): 93–100.
Arunachalam, M. "Prārabdha Karma and Grace." *Saiva Siddhanta* 3 (1968): 132–136.
Aseshananda. "Hindu View of Immortality." *Prabuddha Bharata* 62 (1956): 101–104.
Atisha (W. S. Bowes-Taylor). *Exposition of the Doctrine of Karma.* London: T. P. H., 1910. (120 pp.)
Barua, B. M. "Karma and Causation." *Buddhist Review* 9 (1917): 30–35.
Basham, Arthur L. *History and Doctrines of the Ājīvikas.* London, 1951.
Basu, Shobha Rani. "The Concepts of Bondage and Liberation in Ancient Hindu Thought." *Darshana* 10, no. 1 (1970): 59–66.
Baumann, Julius. *Unsterblichkeit und Seelenwanderung.* Leipzig: S. Hirzel, 1909.
Bedekar, V. M. "The Doctrine of the Colors of Souls in the Mahābhārata: Its Characteristics and Implications." *Annals of the Bhandarkar Oriental Research Institute* 49 (1968): 329–338.
Bertholet, Alfred. *Seelenwanderung.* Tubingen: J. C. B. Mohr, 1906.
Besant, Annie. *Karma.* London: Theosophical Publishing Society, 1895.
———. *Reincarnation.* London: Theosophical Publishing Society, 1905.
Bhattacharya, Haridass. "The Doctrine of Karma." *Visvabharati Quarterly* 3 (1925–26): 257–268. Also in *Philosophical Quarterly* (Amalner) 3 (1927): 226–257.
———. "The Brahmanical Concept of Karma." In *A. R. Wadia: Essays in Philosophy Presented in His Honor,* edited by S. Radhakrishnan and others. Madras: G. S. Press, 1954.
Bhattacharya, Harisatya. "Karma." *Mahabodhi* 33 (1925): 75–85.

Bhattacharya, Kalidas. "The Status of the Individual in Indian Philosophy." *Philosophy East and West* 14 (1964): 131–144. Reprinted in C. A. Moore (ed.), *The Indian Mind* (Honolulu: East-West Center Press, 1967), pp. 299–319, and in C. A. Moore (ed.), *The Status of the Individual: East and West* (Honolulu: East-West Center Press, 1968), pp. 47–64.

Bhattacharya, Siddheswara. "Eschatological Concepts in Indian Thought." *Visvabharati Quarterly* 17 (1952): 191–207.

Bhide, N. N. *The Karma Theory*. Mysore: University of Mysore, 1950.

Bohhili, Maharaja of. "There is No Modification in the Karma Doctrine." *Journal of the Royal Asiatic Society of Great Britain and Ireland*, N. S. 39 (1907): 397–401.

Carlos, Ernest R. "Transmigration in the East and West." *Buddhist Review* 2 (1910): 162–182.

Carus, Paul. "Karma and Nirvāṇa. Are the Buddhist Doctrines Nihilistic?" *Monist* 4 (1893–94): 417–439.

———. *Karma. A Story of Early Buddhism*. Chicago: Open Court, 1894, 1896.

———. "Karma. A Tale with a Moral." *Open Court* 8 (1894): 4217–4221.

———. "Immortality and the Buddhist Soul-conception." *Open Court* 8 (1894): 4259–4261.

———. "Pre-existence and Immortality." *Open Court* 8 (1894): 4315–4317.

Chakravarti, A. "Law of Karma in Jainism." *Aryan Path* 22 (1951): 315 ff.

Chakravarti, Budhindu Chandra. "The Doctrine of Karma and Fatalism." *Prabuddha Bharata* 72 (1967): 328–344.

Chatterjee, Satischandra. *Fundamentals of Hinduism*. Calcutta: University of Calcutta, n.d.

Chatterji, Sudhamoy. *Death and After*. Calcutta, 1968.

Chattopadhyaya, S. K. "Is Indian Philosophy Deterministic?" *Philosophical Quarterly* (Amalner) 34 (1961): 49–55.

Clark, Walter E. *Indian Conceptions of Immortality*. Harvard University Press, 1934.

Collins, Mabel. *Light on the Path and Karma*. New York: Lane, 1904. (103 pp.)

Constable, Adolph. "Karma." *Hawaiian Buddhist Annual*, 1930, pp. 55–58.

Dandoy, G. *Karma, Evil, and Punishment*. Ranchi: Catholic Press, 1940.

Dahlke, Paul. "Auch etwas über Wiedergeburt." *Der Buddhist* 2 (1906–1910): 7–12.

Das, A. C. "Advaita Vedanta and Liberation in Bodily Existence." *Philosophy East and West* 4 (1954): 113–124.

Das, Rasvihary, "The Theory of Karma and Its Difficulties." *Quest* 22 (1959): 15–18.

Das, Sarat Chandra. "The Doctrine of Transmigration." *Journal of the Buddhist Text Society of India* 1, no. 3 (1893): 1–5.

———. "On the Translation of the Soul from One Body to Another (The Story of Prince Blue-Neck)." *Journal of the Buddhist Text Society of India* 5, no. 3 (1897): 1–3.

Dasgupta, S. B. "Divine Grace and the Law of Karma." *Prabuddha Bharata* 66 (1961): 104–113.

Datta, S. "Personal Identity and the Law of Karma." *Allahabad University Studies* (Philosophy), 1955, pp. 1–8.

Demieville, Paul. "Sur la mémoire des existences antérieures." *Bulletin de l'École Français d'Extrême Orient* 27 (1927): 283–298.

de Silva, C. L. A. "Fourfold Kamma." *Mahabodhi* 49 (1941): 122–127, 382–386.

de Smet, R. V. "The Law of Karma: A Critical Examination." *Indian Philosophical Annual* 2 (1966): 328–335.

———. "Sin and Its Removal in India." *Indian Antiquary* (3rd series) 1 (1964): 163–173.

Devasenapathi, V. A. *Saiva Siddhanta as Expounded in the Sivajnanasiddiyar and Its Six Commentaries.* Madras Department of Indian Philosophy Publications 7, 1960.

———. "The Place of the Soul in Saiva Siddhanta." In *Essays in Philosophy Presented to Dr. T. M. P. Mahadevan.* Madras, 1962. Pp. 452–459.

Deutsch, Eliot. "Karma as a 'Convenient Fiction' in the Advaita Vedanta." *Philosophy East and West* 15 (1965): 3–12.

Deussen, Paul. *Philosophy of the Upanishads.* Translated by A. S. Geden. Edinburgh: T. & T. Clark, 1919.

———. *System of the Vedanta.* Translated by C. Johnston. Chicago: Open Court, 1912; New York: Dover, 1973.

Dhammaratna, U. "Kammic Ascent and Descent of Man." *Mahabodhi* 63 (1955): 44–46.

Dharmapala. "A Buddhist on the Law of Karma." *Open Court* 8 (1894): 4261 ff.

Diestel, Ernst. "Gedanken über das karma." *Sphinx* 21 (1896): 117–120.

Dilger, W. "Der Seelenwanderungsglaube und sein Einfluss auf das religiöse und sittliche Leben." *Allgemeine Missions-Zeitschrift* 35: 279–298.

———. *Der indischer Seelungswanderungsglaube.* Basler Missionsstudien 37. Basel, 1910.

Diwakar, S. C. "The Philosophy of Karma." *Jain Journal* 7 (1973): 133–141.

Dixit, K. K. "Problems of Ethics and Karma Doctrine as Treated in Bhagavatīsūtra." *Sambodhi* 2, no. 3 (1973): 1–14.

Edgerton, Franklin. "The Hour of Death: Its Importance for Man's Future Fate in Hindu and Western Religions." *Annals of the Bhandarkar Oriental Research Institute* 8 (1926): 219–249.

Edmunds, Albert J. "Dolden, or Pre-existence." *Buddhism* 1, no. 4 (1904): 636–638.

Falke, Robert. *Die Seelenwanderung.* Berlin-Lichterfelde: Erlange, 1913.

Farqhar, J. N. "Karma: Its Value as a Doctrine of Life." *Hibbert Journal* 20 (1921–22): 20–34.

Feer, Henri Léon. "Le séjour des morts selon les Indiens et selons les Grecs." *Revue d'Histoire des Religions* 18 (1888): 297–319.

———. "De l'importance des actes de la pensée dans le Bouddhisme." *Revue d'Histoire des religions* 13 (1886): 74–82.

Gandhi, Ramchandra. "The Theories of Karma and Maya and the Problem of Evil." *Radical Humanist* (Calcutta) 35, no. 25 (April 1972): 20–24.

Garbe, Richard. "Transmigration (Indian)." In *Encyclopedia of Religion and Ethics*, edited by James A. Hastings. Vol. 12, pp. 434–435.

Ghurye, G. S. *Religious Consciousness.* Bombay: Popular Prakashan, 1965.

Glasenapp, Helmuth von. *Die Lehre vom Karma in der Philosophie der Jainas.* Leipzig: Otto Harrassowitz, 1915.

———.*Unsterblichkeit und Erlösung in den Indischen Religionen.* Schriften der Königsberger Gelehrten Gesellschaft, Geistesgewissenschaftliche Klasse 14. Hall, 1938. Translated into English by E. J. F. Payne, as *Immortality and Freedom in Indian Religions.* Calcutta, 1963.

———. *The Doctrine of Karman in Jain Philosophy.* Bombay, 1942.

Gnaneswarananda. "Karma—Its Many Aspects." *Vedanta Kesari* 53 (1966–67): 398–403.

Gogerly, Daniel John. "On Transmigration." *The Friend* 2. Colombo, 1838.

Gombrich, Richard. "Merit Transference in Sinhalese Buddhism: A Case Study of the Interaction between Doctrine and Practice." *History of Religions* 11 (November 1971): 203–219.

Gomez, Luis O. "Some Aspects of the Free-will Question in the Nikāyas." *Philosophy East and West* 25 (1975): 81–90.

Gunaratna, Neville. "A Philosophical Approach to the Doctrine of Karma." *Mahabodhi* 79 (1971): 8–13.

Gunaratna, V. F. *Buddhist Reflections on Death.* Kandy: Buddhist Publication Society, 1966 (*The Wheel,* nos. 102–103).

———. *Rebirth Explained.* Kandy, 1971 (*The Wheel,* nos. 167–169).

Gupta, I. P. "Studies on Punarjanma or Rebirth." *Indian Philosophy and Culture* 19, no. 3 (1974): 209–228.

Hall, R. *Law of Karma.* Australian National University Press, 1968.

Hallen, G. C. "Karma and Crime." *Vedanta Kesari* 54 (1967–68): 24–29. Also *Journal of the Indian Academy of Philosophy* 7, no. 1 (1968): 54–60.

———. "Karma and Punishment." *Vedanta Kesari* 54 (1967): 220–227.

Hara, Minoru. "Transfer of Merit." *Adyar Library Bulletin* 31–32 (1967–68): 382–411.

Hartman, Franz. "Karma." *Lotus Bluthen,* 1897. Pp. 194–221, 277–296, 333–350, 440–464.

———. *Karma oder Wissen, Wirken und Werden.* Leipzig: Friedrich, 1897. (178 pp.)

Head, Joseph (ed.). *Reincarnation in World Thought.* New York: Julian Press, 1967.

Henseler, E. de. *L'âme et le dogme de la transmigration dans les livres sacrées de l'Inde.* Paris: E. de Boccard, 1928. (192 pp.)

Herman, Arthur L. *The Problem of Evil and Indian Thought.* New Delhi: Motilal Banarsidass, 1976.

Hick, John. "Reincarnation: A Critical Examination of One Form of Reincarnation Theory." *Journal of Religious Studies* 3, no. 1 (1971): 56–69.

Hiltebeitel, Alf. "The Mahābhārata and Hindu Eschatology." *History of Religions* 12 (1972): 95–135.

Hiriyanna, Mysore. "Reincarnation: Some Indian Views." *Aryan Path* 7 (1936): 350 ff. Reprinted in *Popular Essays in Indian Philosophy,* pp. 30–34 and 43–48.

Hodson, Col. T. C. "The Doctrine of Rebirth in Various Areas in India." *Man in India* 1, no. 2 (1921): 1–17.

Hogg, A. G. *Karma and Redemption.* Madras: Christian Literature Society, 1909.

Hopkins, E. W. "Modifications of the Karma Doctrine." *Journal of the Royal Asiatic Society,* 1906, pp. 581–594; 1907, pp. 665–672. See Bohhili above for a response.

Humphreys, Christmas. *Karma and Rebirth.* London: John Murray, 1959. 5th ed.

Hutton, J. H. "Metempsychosis." *Man in India* 12 (1932): 73–76.

Inada, K. K. "Some Basic Misconceptions of Buddhism." *International Philosophical Quarterly* 9 (1969): 101–119.

Isenberg, A. "Reflections on the Concepts of Karma and Dharma in Śankara's Advaita Vedanta." *Vedanta Kesari* 45 (1958): 145 ff.

Iswarananda. *Does the Soul Reincarnate?* Puranattukara, 1964.

Iyer, M. K. V. "The Finite Self: Its Nature and Destiny." *Prabuddha Bharata* 71 (1966): 140–147.

Jain, Champat Rai. "The Jaina Theory of Karma." *Indian Philosophy and Religion* 3 (1920): 149–164.

Jayatilleke, K. N. "The Buddhist Doctrine of Karma." *Mahabodhi* 76 (November–December 1968): 314–320.

———. "The Case for the Buddhist Theory of Survival and Kamma, V." *Mahabodhi* 78 (1970): 350–355.

———. *Survival and Karma in Buddhist Perspective.* Kandy, 1969 (*The Wheel* 8).

Jha, Ganganatha. *Pūrva Mīmāmsā in Its Sources.* Banaras, 1942, 1964.

Jinarajadasa, C. *How We Remember Our Past Lives, and Other Essays on Reincarnation.* Adyar: Theosophical Publishing House, 1915. (100 pp.)

Jnaneswarananda. "Reincarnation and Karma." *Vedanta and the West* 8 (1945): 78–88.

Joshi, K. S. "Liberation: The Avowed Goal of Indian Philosophy." *Philosophy East and West* 18 (1968): 77–81.

———. "The Concept of Liberation in Yoga Philosophy." *Madhya Bharati (Journal of the University of Saugar)* 16 (1965–67): 78–90.

Kaelber, Walter O. "Tapas, Birth, and Spiritual Rebirth in the Vedas." *History of Religions* 15 (1976): 343–386.

Kalghatgi, T. G. *Karma and Rebirth.* L. D. Series 38, Ahmedabad: L. D. Institute of Indology, 1972. (75 pp.)

——— ."Determinism and Karma Theory." *Indian Philosophical Annual* 4 (1968): 21–27.

———. "The Doctrine of Karma in Jaina Philosophy." *Philosophy East and West* 15 (1965): 229–242.

———. "In the Vestibules of Karma." *Sambodhi* 1, no. 1 (1972): 41–62.

———. "Karma—Its Operation and an Appraisal." *Sambodhi* 1, no. 2 (1972): 1–22.

———. "Rebirth—A Philosophical Study." *Sambodhi* 1, no. 3 (1972): 1–32.

Kalupahana, D. J. "The Problem of Psychological Causation and the Use of Terms for 'Chance' in the Early Buddhist Texts." *Vidyodaya* 2, no. 1 (1969): 37–41.

Kane, P. V. *History of Dharmaśāstra,* V, II. Government Oriental Series B.6. Poona, 1930–1962.

Karunaratne, W. S. "Concepts of Freedom and Responsibility in Theravāda Buddhism." *University of Ceylon Review* 17 (1959): 73–89.

Katre, S. M. "Some Fundamental Problems in the Upaniṣad and Pali Ballads." *Review of Philosophy and Religion* (Poona) 5 (1935).

Kaw, R. K. *The Doctrine of Recognition (Pratyabhijñā Philosophy).* Hoshiarpur, 1967.

Kolenda, Pauline. "Religious Anxiety and Hindu Fate." *Journal of Asian Studies* 23 (1964): 71–79.

Kunhan Raja, C. *Some Fundamental Problems in Indian Philosophy.* New Delhi, 1961.

———. "Where Ancient Thought and Modern Science Meet." *Adyar Library Bulletin* 16 (1952): 59–86.

Lamotte, Étienne. "Le traité de l'Acte de Vasubandhu Karmasiddhiprakaraṇa." *Melanges Chinois et Bouddhiques* IV (1935–1936): 151–288.

la Vallée Poussin, Louis de. "Dogmatique Bouddhique: La négation de l'âme et la doctrine de l'acte." *Journal Asiatique* 9, no. 19 (1902): 237–306.

———. "Dogmatique Bouddhique: Nouvelle recherches sur la doctrine de l'acte, etc." *Journal Asiatique* 10, no. 2 (1903): 357–450.

———. "Karma." In *Encyclopedia of Religion and Ethics,* edited by James A. Hastings. Vol. 7, pp. 673–676.

———. *The Way to Nirvāṇa.* Hibbert Lectures, 1916. Cambridge: Cambridge University Press, 1917. (Esp. pp. 30–106.)

Law, B. C. "Doctrine of Karma." *Professor M. Hiriyanna Commemoration Volume.* Mysore, 1952. Pp. 87–95.

———. "Buddhist View of Karma." *Aryan Path* 23 (1952): 124 ff.

———. "Karma." *The Cultural Heritage of India,* edited by S. Radhakrishnan and others. Calcutta: Ramakrishna Mission Institute of Culture, 1958. 2nd ed., I, 537–546.

———. "Jain View of Karma." *Bharatiya Vidya* 6 (1945): 145–147.

———. "Doctrine of Karma in Jainism." *Indian Culture* 13 (1946): 134–138.

Lewis, Oscar. *Village Life in Northern India.* Urbana: University of Illinois Press, 1958.

Ling, Trevor. "Re-Birth: The Need for Clarification." *World Buddhism Veesak Annual* 2 (Buddhist Annual 2511), 1967. Pp. 29–31.

McDermott, James P. "Developments in the Early Buddhist Concept of Kamma/Karma." Ph.D. Dissertation, Princeton University, 1971.

———. "Is There Group Karma in Theravāda Buddhism?" *Numen* 23 (1976): 67–80.

———. "Nibbana as a Reward for Kamma." *Journal of the American Oriental Society* 93 (1973): 344–347.

———. "Sadhina Jātaka: A Case against the Transfer of Merit." *Journal of the American Oriental Society* 94 (1974): 385–387.

———. "The Kathāvatthu Kamma Debates." *Journal of the American Oriental Society* 95 (1975): 424–433.

———. "Kamma in the Milindapañha." *Journal of the American Oriental Society* 97 (1977): 460–469.

McKenzie, John. *Hindu Ethics.* London, 1922.

Macnicol, Nicol. *Indian Theism.* Oxford, 1915.

Maheshwari, H. "Immortality: The Basic Inspiration of Hindu Philosophy." *Indian Philosophy and Culture* 15, no. 1 (1970): 26–37.

Maitra, S. K. *Main Problems of Philosophy: An Advaita Approach.* 2 vols. Calcutta, 1957, 1962.

Malalasekara, G. P. " 'Transference of Merit' in Ceylonese Buddhism." *Philosophy East and West* 17 (1967): 85–90.

Malkani, G. R. "The Rational of the Law of Karma." *Philosophical Quarterly* (Amalner) 37 (1964): 257–266.

———. "Some Criticism of the Karmic Law by Professor Warren E. Steinkraus Answered." *Philosophical Quarterly* (Amalner) 38 (1965): 55–162.

———. "A Note on Liberation in Bodily Existence." *Philosophy East and West* 5 (1955): 69–74.

Maloney, Clarence. "Religious Beliefs and Social Hierarchy in Tamil Nadu, India." *American Ethnologist* 2 (1975): 169–192.

Mehta, M. L. *Outlines of Jaina Philosophy.* Bangalore, 1954.

Misra, G. S. P. "The Buddhist Theory of Karman and Some Related Problems." *Visvabharati Journal of Philosophy* 8, no. 2 (1972): 34–44.

Mitchell, Donald W. "Analysis in Theravāda Buddhism." *Philosophy East and West* 21 (1971): 23–32.

———. "Buddhist Theories of Causation—Commentary." *Philosophy East and West* 25 (1975): 101–106.

Mitra, A. K. "Ponkavati, or the Girl Who Came to Life." *Man in India* 21 (1941): 46–54.

Mittal, Kewal Krishan. "The Jaina View of Karma." *Bulletin of the Institute of Post-Graduate (Evening) Studies.* Delhi, 1965. Pp. 102–106.

Mizuno, Kogen. *Primitive Buddhism.* Yamaguchi-ken: Karinbunko, 1969.

Mukherji, S. R. "Karma and Sannyāsa—a Linguist Analysis." *Philosophical Quarterly* (Amalner) 38 (1965): 37–40.

Nambudiripad, P. M. Bhaskaran. "The Destiny of the Human Soul." *Prabuddha Bharata* 71 (1966): 31–35.

Nandi, S. K. "Rebirth in Ancient Indian Thought." *Journal of Indian History* 43 (1964): 119–142.

Narada, Bhikkhu. "Kamma, or the Buddhist Law of Causation." B. C. Law Volume, 2, 158–175.

———. "Saṃsāra, or Buddhist Philosophy of Birth and Death." *Indian Historical Quarterly* 3 (1927): 561–570.

———. "Kammic Descent and Kammic Ascent." *Mahabodhi* 46 (1938): 291–295.

———. "What is Kamma?" *Mahabodhi* 45 (May 1937): 205–208.

Narada, Mahathera. "What Is It That Is Reborn?" *World Buddhism Vesak Annual* 2514 (1970): 24–26.

Narahari, H. G. "Śankara and Vyāsa on the Theory of Karma." *Bulletin of the Deccan College Research Institute* 17 (1955): 20–26.
———. "The Yogavasiṣṭha and the Doctrine of Free Will." *Adyar Library Bulletin* 10 (1946): 36–50.
———. "Karma and Reincarnation in the Mahābhārata." *Annals of the Bhandarkar Oriental Research Institute* 27 (1946): 102–113.
———. "The Doctrine of Karma in Popular Hinduism." *Aryan Path* 43 (1972): 53–58.
———. "The Doctrine of Karma in the Upanishads." *Aryan Path* 29 (1958): 15 ff.
———. *Atman in Pre-Upanishadic Vedic Literature.* Adyar, 1955.
———. "Karma and Reincarnation in Classical Sanskrit Literature." *Quarterly Journal of the Mythic Society* 37 (1946): 68–71.
———. "The Doctrine of Kamma in Popular Buddhism." *Adyar Library Bulletin* 25 (1961): 360–370.
Narain, Sheo. "Karmic Law." *Mahabodhi* 33. March 1925, 132–140; April 1925, 194–198.
Nayak, G. C. "The Doctrine of Karma and the Criterion of Falsifiability—a Critical Evaluation." *Calcutta Review* 180 (1966): 117–120.
Nikhilananda. "Rebirth and Liberation." *Vedanta Kesari* 52 (1965–66): 384–387.
Nyanatiloka, Thera. *Karma and Rebirth.* Kandy: Buddhist Publication Society, 1959, 1964.
Obeyesekere, Gananath. "Theodicy, Sin and Salvation in a Sociology of Buddhism." In E. R. Leach (ed.), *Practical Religion.* Cambridge: University Press, 1968.
Ozanne, C. H. "Karma." *Hibbert Journal* 20 (1921–22): 364–368.
Pandita, Samanera, "Kamma as the Primary, Basic Factor and Cause of the Variation in Life among Beings." *The Light of Buddha* 5, no. 12 (December 1960): 37–40; 6, no. 4 (April 1961): 91–94.
Panikkar, Raymond. "The Law of Karman and the Historical Dimension of Man." *Philosophy East and West* 22 (January 1972): 25–43.
Parrinder, Geoffrey. *Avatar and Incarnation.* London: Faber & Faber, 1970.
———. *The Indestructible Soul.* London: Allen & Unwin, 1973.
Parthasarathy, K. E. "The Law of Karma in Vedanta." *Aryan Path* 40 (1969): 160–164.
Pereira, A. C. "An Elucidation of Kamma." *Buddhist Review* 9 (1917): 54–72.
Phukan, Radhanath. *The Theory of Rebirth.* Calcutta, 1962.
Potter, Karl H. "The Naturalistic Principle of Karma." *Philosophy East and West* 14 (1964): 39–50.
———. "Naturalism and Karma: A Reply." *Philosophy East and West* 18 (1968): 82–84.
Puligandla, R. "Professor Deutsch on Karma." *Darshana* 38 (1970): 27–33; also in *Journal of Indian Academy of Philosophy* 10, no. 1 (1971): 42–49.

Punyanubhab, Sujib. *Some Prominent Characteristics of Buddhism.* Thailand: The Buddhist University, 1965.

Ramanathan, C. "Karma, Its Place in the Bhagavadgītā and Professor Hiryanna's Observations on It." *Mysore Orientalist* 5 (1972): 131–134.

Ramanujachari, R. "The Role of the Malas." *Saiva Siddhanta* 7 (1972): 135–140.

Ramasubramaniam, V. "Metempsychosis: A Study of Tamilian Traditions, Folk-lore and Philosophy." *Bulletin of the Institute of Traditional Cultures,* Jan.–June 1970, pp. 1–38.

Rajagopala Sastri, S. "Karma and Rebirth." *Indian Philosophical Annual* 2 (1966): 336–342.

Rao, P. Nagaraja. "The Doctrine of Karma." *Aryan Path* 30 (1959): 23 ff.

Ray, B. G. "The Law of Karma in Jainism, Buddhism and Sikhism." *Visvabharati Journal of Philosophy* 8, no. 1 (1971): 71–80.

Religious Hinduism. By Jesuit Scholars. Allahabad, Bombay: St. Paul Publications, 1964.

Rhys Davids, Mrs. C. A. F. *Indian Religions and Survival: A Study.* London, Allen & Unwin, 1934.

———. "The Scientific Conception of Karma Doctrine." *Mahabodhi* 41 (Jan.–Feb. 1933): 15–18.

———. "Ancient Conception of Life under the Figure of a Wheel." *Journal of the Royal Asiatic Society,* 1894, pp. 388–390.

———. "The Buddhist Doctrine of Rebirth." *The Quest* 13 (1921–22): 303–322.

Saddhatissa, H. "Process of Rebirth in Buddhism." *Mahabodhi* 79 (1971): 334–338.

———. "Conception of Buddhist Kamma." *World Buddhism Vesak Annual* 2513 (1969): 33–36.

Saksena, S. K. "Relation of Philosophical Theories to the Practical Affairs of Men." In C. A. Moore (ed.), *The Indian Mind* (Honolulu: East West Center Press, 1967), pp. 19–40.

Sasaki, Genun. "The Concept of Karma in Buddhist Philosophy." *Oriens Extremus* 3 (1956): 185–204.

Schrader, O. "Lingayats and Metempsychosis." *Wiener Zeitschrift für die Kunde des Morgenlandes* 31 (1924): 313–317.

Sharma, Om Prakash. "The Law of Karma and Rebirth." *Bulletin of the Mithila Institute* 3, no. 2 (1967): 15–27.

Sharma, Ursula. "Theodicy and the Doctrine of Karma." *Man* 8 (1973): 347–364.

Sikdar, J. C. "Fabric of Life as Conceived in Jaina Biology." *Sambodhi* 3, no. 1 (1974): 1–10.

Silacara, Bhikkhu. *Kamma (Karma).* Edited by Bhikkhu Kassappa. Colombo: Bauddha Sāhitya Sabhā, 1956.

Silburn, Lilian. *Instant et Cause: le discontinu dans la pensée philosophique de l'Inde.* Paris: Libr. Phil. J. Vrin, 1955.

Singh, J. "Karma in Yogasūtras of Patañjali." *Review of Philosophy and Religion* 8, no. 1 (1939): 27–34.

Singh, Balbir. *Foundations of Indian Philosophy.* New Delhi: Orient Longmans, 1971.

Singh, Hamam. *Sikh Religious Karma and Transmigration.* Ludhiana: Lahore Bookshop, n.d.

Smart, Ninian. *Doctrine and Argument in Indian Philosophy.* London, 1964.

Smith, Ronald M. "Birth of Thought: III. Transmigration and God." *Annals of the Bhandarkar Oriental Research Institute* 35 (1954): 176–193.

Srinivasiengar, K. R. "Fate or Free Will: The Indian Solution." *Philosophical Quarterly* (Amalner) 5 (1929–30): 106–125.

Steiner, Rudolf. *Destiny or Karma.* Translated by Harry Collison. London: H. Collison, 1931.

———. *The Manifestations of Karma.* London: Anthroposophical Society, 1925.

———. *Die Offenbarungen des Karma: Ein Zyklus von elf Vorträgen.* Dornach: Verlag des Rudolf Steiner, 1956.

Steinkraus, Warren E. "Some Problems in Karma." *Philosophical Quarterly* (Amalner) 38 (1965): 145–154.

Stevenson, Ian. *Twenty Cases Suggestive of Reincarnation.* 2nd ed. University Press of Virginia, 1974.

———. *Cases of the Reincarnation Type. I: 10 Cases in India.* University Press of Virginia, 1975. *II: 10 Cases in Sri Lanka,* 1976.

Story, Francis. *Rebirth as Doctrine and Experience.* Kandy: Buddhist Publication Society, 1975.

———. *The Case for Rebirth.* Kandy, 1959, 1964, 1973.

Strauss, Otto. "A Contribution to the Problem of the Relation between Karma, Jñāna, Mokṣa." *Kuppuswami Sastri Commemoration Volume.* Madras: G. S. Press, 1935.

Sudhi, Padma. "The Law of Karma and the Indian Ethical Outlook." *Indian Philosophy and Culture* 18, no. 3 (1973): 272–276.

Sundararanjan, K. R. "Karma and Avatāra—A New Direction to the Doctrine of Incarnation in Hinduism." *Saiva Siddhanta* 3 (1968): 146–148.

Suriyabongs, Luang. "Controversial Questions about Karma and Rebirth." *The Light of Buddha* 5, no. 4 (April 1960): 12–17.

———. "The Law of Karma and Rebirth." *The Light of Buddha* 2, no. 10 (October 1957): 5–8.

Suryanarayana Sastri, S. "Advaita, Causality and Human Freedom." *Indian Historical Quarterly* 16 (1940): 331–369.

———. "Karma and Fatalism." *Philosophical Quarterly* (Amalner) 16 (1940–41): 81–88. Also in *Collected Papers,* pp. 233–238.

Tatia, Nathmal. *Studies in Jain Philosophy.* Banaras, 1951.

Tattvabhushan, S. "The Vedantic Doctrine of Future Life." *Annals of the Vedanta,* pp. 83–107; *Indian Review* 4 (1903): 601–606.

Tucci, Giuseppe. *Theory and Practice of the Mandala.* Translated by A. H. Brodrick. London: Rider, 1961.

Upadhye, A. N. "Jainism and Karma Doctrine." *Jaina Antiquary* 2 (1936): 1–28.

Varadachari, K. C. "Karma and Rebirth." *Journal of the Ganganatha Jha Research Institute* 22 (1965–66): 1–12.

———. "Freedom and Karma." *Prabuddha Bharata* 42 (1952): 446–451.

Varma, Shrimati Krishna. "The Concept of Vikarma in Vinoba Bhave's Interpretation of the Bhagavadgītā." *Indian Philosophy and Culture* 15, no. 4 (1970): 17–24.

Varma, V. P. "The Origins and Sociology of the Early Buddhist Philosophy of Moral Determinism." *Philosophy East and West* 13 (1963): 25–47.

———. "Philosophy of Rebirth in Ancient Indian Thought." *Vedanta Kesari* 47 (1961): 462–466.

Veezhinathan, N. "The Nature and Destiny of the Individual Soul in Advaita." *Journal of the Madras University* 47, no. 2 (1975): 1–38.

Venkata Rao, M. A. "Doctrine of Karma and Kant's Postulate of Morality." *Aryan Path* 2 (1931): 315–320.

Wadia, A. R. "Philosophical Implications of the Doctrine of Karma." *Philosophy East and West* 15 (1965): 145–152.

Walhout, Donald. "A Critical Note on Potter's Interpretation of Karma." *Philosophy East and West* 16 (1966): 235–238.

Weeraratne, Amarasiri. "Nirvana, Karma and Rebirth." *World Buddhism* 19, no. 4 (1970): 97–98.

Welland, C. B. "Karma." *Hibbert Journal* 20 (1921–22): 362–364.

Woodward, Frank Lee. "The Buddhist Doctrine of Reversible Merit." *The Buddhist Review* (London) 6 (1914): 38–50.

Yevtic, Paul. *Karma and Reincarnation in Hindu Religion and Philosophy.* London: Luzac, 1927.

Index and Glossary

(Words that have been transliterated from Igbo, Pali, Sanskrit, Tamil, Tibetan, and Trobriand are placed in Roman alphabetical order.)

Designer: William Snyder
Compositor: Viking Typographics
Printer: Braun-Brumfield Inc.
Binder: Braun-Brumfield Inc.
Text: VIP Garamond
Display: VIP Garamond
Cloth: Holliston Roxite C 57533 Linen
Paper: 50 lb P&S Offset, B-32